Helena Gomm

Colin Benn
Simon Clarke
Gina Cuciniello
Paul Dummett
Paul Emmerson
Jon Hird
Mark Powell
Nicholas Sheard

in company

Intermediate
Teacher's Book

MACMILLAN

Contents

A Business English classroom

Madrid. 3pm. At 37° the city is starting to simmer. The teacher, Liz, arrives a couple of minutes early for her class with the bank on the thirteenth floor. The training room is tastefully ergonomic, if a little soulless. Liz plugs in her portable cassette player, cues the tape, flips through her handouts, decides there isn't time now for a quick coffee and waits.

There are normally five people in her group: three quiet types from the legal department, Pablo, a talkative mergers and acquisitions specialist, and Lourdes, a young trainee with rather better English than the others (sometimes a problem). They all get on well. But only three will turn up today – unfortunately, not exactly the same three who turned up last time, so there'll be some catching up to do. A chunk of the unit in the course book will probably have to be missed out and Liz will have to think of something else to do instead. The message is that Pablo may join them later if he gets out of his lunch meeting in time. But that's unlikely. He misses three lessons out of five. Busy guy.

Three months ago, when Liz's employer discussed the English course with the banks' training department, a formal needs analysis prioritised work on the language of meetings, telephoning and e-mail. Liz's students agreed that's what they need. But as the course went on, she noticed that they often didn't use the so-called useful expressions she was teaching them and they only really came to life when either talking about themselves or taking part in a light-hearted activity she'd originally planned as a filler. She's doing more of that kind of thing now, though, and it seems to be working.

This afternoon the students' heads are full of talk of the forthcoming merger. They're still arguing about it as they come in to the class. Gradually, animated Spanish dissolves into more hesitant English and the lesson begins. Today they're supposed to be doing 'fixing and changing appointments on the phone'. Present continuous. Here we go again. Grim prospect. But maybe Liz has a better idea …

In Company is Macmillan's skills-based Business English series, aimed at professional, adult learners seeking to realise their full potential as speakers of English at work – both in and out of the office – and in social settings.

In Company Intermediate takes students through twenty progressively more challenging units ranging from basic networking, information-sharing and small talk to higher order skills such as problem-solving, presenting and negotiating. The course reflects the need for students at this level to consolidate their grammatical awareness, increase their lexical range and, above all, boost their communicative power in both professional and social situations.

Ten key observations on the teaching of English to professional learners underpin the course:

1 Professionals like to be regularly reminded why they are studying and what's in it for them.

2 They are used to goal-setting and time constraints and tend to welcome a fairly fast pace.

3 They are motivated by topics which directly relate to their own personal experiences.

4 They expect to see an immediate, practical payoff of some kind at the end of each lesson.

5 It is English, not business, they have come to you for help with (but see 7).

6 They want to be able to actually *do* business with their English rather than just talk about it.

7 They appreciate texts and tasks which reflect what they have to do in their job.

8 They also appreciate texts and tasks which allow them to escape what they have to do in their job.

9 They don't regard having fun as incompatible with 'serious learning' (but see 1 and 4).

10 They like to see an overall plan and method behind the classes they attend.

Skills-based approach

In Company is a practical course in *how* to do business in English. With target language selectively introduced on a need-to-know basis, each unit is a fast track to competence in a particular business skill. Recognising that people need more than just phrase lists and useful language boxes to operate effectively in real-life business situations, each unit provides a substantial amount of guided skills work to give students the chance to fully assimilate the target language and 'make it their own', before going on to tackle fluency activities.

Target skills developed at this level include:

- keeping track in cross-cultural meetings
- creating a favourable impression in e-mails
- handling unexpected phone calls
- getting people to do things for you
- opening, closing and fuelling conversation
- querying and clarifying points under discussion
- making and reporting decisions
- applying and resisting pressure in negotiations
- exploiting the power of your voice in talks

Why are the units divided into categories?

In Company Intermediate contains four types of unit: *Talking points*, *Networking*, *Desk work* and *Meetings*. Categorising the units in this way means that you can teach the course in:

- *either* a **linear fashion**, starting at Unit 1 and finishing at Unit 20, selecting the most relevant material as you go, but knowing that you are varying your skills focus from lesson to lesson and covering the basic grammatical structures in a tried and tested order

- *or* a **modular way**, doing all the units in one category before moving on to the next, thereby ensuring that students see some real improvement in one area before going on to another.

The approach you choose will partly depend on your needs analysis with your class and partly on the importance you place on structural sequencing, bearing in mind that intermediate learners are likely to have met most of these structures before.

Within each category, you may want to consider the following:

Talking points

In these units, the emphasis is on using the English students already have to discuss a topic of general business interest. These units tend to rotate around a text or texts, usually with accompanying listening work. There is some lexical input but no grammar focus in *Talking points* units. Unit 1 assumes you are working with a new class and therefore acts in part as a kind of informal needs analysis.

Networking

Given the choice, most of us would prefer to do business with people we like. Networking and building business relationships are, therefore, important business skills and the focus of these units. Unless a strict structural syllabus is being followed, the units in this category can be taken in any order, with the exception of Unit 2, which is best done with a fairly new group.

Desk work

Business people now spend many hours on the phone and online, taking messages and sending e-mail. This places a new importance on listening acuity and writing skills. The units in this category can also be studied out of order. However, it is probably better to do Unit 3 before Unit 7, and to leave Unit 19 until last, since it brings together phone and e-mail skills.

Meetings

Meetings are endemic in business, but, of course, a lot will depend on the kind of meetings your students take part in. Unit 4 is the best one to start with as it provides communication techniques your students will certainly need later on in the course. Units 8 and 16 both address fairly common types of meeting. Unit 12 (Presenting) and Unit 20 (Negotiating) are more specialised, but nonetheless useful to anyone in business, not just presenters and negotiators.

Language input

At an intermediate level, students have typically met much more grammar than they have mastered, and recognise far more vocabulary than they are as yet able to produce. A certain amount of recycling is, therefore, essential, but the worst thing we, as teachers, can do is simply to go over old ground again. A better idea is to try to help students apply and begin to integrate their existing knowledge – 'noticing' grammatical patterns in lexis, lexical patterns in grammar and the underlying function in a business context of both.

For instance, in teaching the expression 'I'll get on to our suppliers right away', students' attention could usefully be drawn to any or all of the following:

- the phrasal verb *get on to* (*contact*) and its complement in a business context *get back to*
- the time expression *right away* and other time expressions (*later today, sometime this afternoon, when I've got a minute*) that could fill the same slot in the sentence
- the collocation *get on to our suppliers* and some collocates for *suppliers* (*negotiate with, check with, change*)
- the grammar of *will* as a modal verb and its use in the first person singular to respond to urgent requests (*I'll find out for you, I'll see what I can do, I'll get back to you on that*)

- the use of *get* as a generative verb in the context of communication (*get through on the phone, get your ideas across in a meeting*)

Lexical syllabus

In Company Intermediate devotes a lot of attention to lexis, showing students how to build words, many of which they may already know, into larger, multi-word items they do not know. For example:

- compounds – *search engine, help menu*
- collocations – *sharp rise, go out of production*
- noun phrases – *cost of living, rate of exchange*
- phrasal verbs – *sell out, buy up, cut back*
- discourse markers – *above all, by the way, to sum up*
- fixed expressions – *Leave it with me, I'll do my best, I'm afraid we'll have to break off here*
- partial frameworks or scripts – *[TIME] ago we were having difficulties with ..., which was also affecting ... and ..., not to mention ... . So, what was going wrong? Well, the problem we were facing was not ... but ... . Have a look at this ...*

Pre-constructed lexical chunks, like those above, are a crucial part of native-speaker interaction and, if judiciously selected, can significantly speed up the language processing time of non-native speakers too, allowing them to sound more fluent and confident in situations they can predict they are likely to encounter.

Lexis, therefore, is given a prominent place in the units themselves and, in addition, students are referred to optional Lexis links, which effectively double the lexical input in each unit and can either be set for homework or made the basis of vocabulary-building lessons.

Grammar syllabus

Of course, lexical chunks are only useful in so far as our students are able to produce them in real time, as and when they need them. When, for whatever reason, they are unable to do so, they will fall back on the generative power of grammar and the simplest words in their vocabulary to get the job done.

The approach in *In Company Intermediate* is to highlight target grammar as it naturally emerges in the activities, but there are no long detours in the units themselves into structural matters. The reasoning behind this is that, though some formal errors persist, when it comes to the basic grammar of English, intermediate students tend to have more problems with use than form – and such problems require more than a short exercise or two to put right. This is where the Grammar links come in. Fifteen Grammar links, cross-linked to the fifteen main skills-based units, systematically address the usual questions of time, tense, aspect, voice, modality and conditionality as well as broader areas such as reporting and diplomacy, where grammar becomes as much a matter of choice as of rules.

In the Grammar links, students are encouraged to explore grammatical use and, to some extent, fathom out the rules for themselves. Tenses are usually presented contrastively. Practice exercises are more commonly text- or dialogue-based (rather than simply sentence-based) to give a feel for the discoursal role of different structures.

Class Cassettes and CDs

Throughout the course, substantial use is made of audio recordings both to input business expressions and grammatical structures and to demonstrate subtler communication skills in action. Indeed, very little of the language work is not presented or recycled in a recording.

As well as the usual dialogues and narrative extracts, *vox pop* – ordinary people's views on a particular topic – is a characteristic feature of the recordings. These have been scripted for the sake of clarity, but they do help students in small classes and one-to-one – it's easier to articulate your views when there are other views to support or differ from.

The recordings feature both native and non-native speaker accents, providing the students with extensive exposure to real spoken English. There is frequently an element of humour in the recordings which, besides entertaining the students (and teacher!), motivates them to listen again for things they missed the first time round. The target language in the units is printed in bold in the recordings.

How can I exploit the dialogues further?

Play some of the dialogues a second time and:
- pause the cassette after questions for students to recall or predict the response (if they write these down as they go, you can ask them to recall the questions as well at the end)
- pause the cassette after responses to questions and ask students to think of other possible responses
- pause the cassette in the middle of lexical chunks (collocations, fixed expressions) for students to complete them either orally or by writing them down
- ask students to speculate about the personalities of the speakers in the dialogue
- ask students if they have ever met / done business with anyone like the speakers
- ask students if they would have reacted differently to the speakers in the dialogue

Reading texts

The reading texts in *In Company Intermediate* have been chosen to involve, entertain and provoke students into lively discussion, as well as to contextualise key target vocabulary. Squeezing a text completely dry of all useful language usually demotivates a class, but many of the longer texts in *In Company Intermediate* are informationally and lexically rich and can usefully be revisited.

How can I exploit the texts further?

Try some of the following:
- students set each other questions on a text
- students set you questions on a text, and vice versa
- give students several figures from a text and ask them to recall the context in which they were mentioned
- read the text aloud but slur certain words/phrases and students ask for repetition/clarification

- students read/listen to a text and complete sentences to reflect their own reaction to it, e.g. *I thought the point about ... was interesting; I'm surprised that ...; I'm not sure I agree with what it says about ...; I'm not convinced that ...; I completely disagree with the idea that ...*
- give students the first half of 8–16 collocations and a time limit in which to search for the collocates
- give students a set of miscollocates and ask them to correct them by referring to the text
- students find expressions which mean the same as, e.g. *incidentally = by the way; moreover = in addition; generally = by and large* or the opposite of, e.g. *in practice/in theory; in general/in particular*
- give students a set of prepositions and ask them to scan the text for noun phrases / phrasal verbs / idioms which include those prepositions
- read out the text pausing in the middle of collocations / fixed expressions / idioms for students to predict the completions either by shouting out or writing down the answer

Fluency work

Each unit culminates in at least one fluency activity which draws on both the specific language presented in the unit and the wider linguistic resources of the students. Activity types comprise:

1 skills workouts, where students practise a specific micro-skill (such as effective interruption or voice projection) in a semi-guided way
2 roleplays and simulations, where students are given a scenario and perhaps some kind of 'personal agenda'
3 case studies, where students are confronted with an authentic business problem and then compare their solution with that of the actual company concerned
4 'framework' activities, where the students decide on the content for a presentation, e-mail or phone call and the Student's Book provides them with a linguistic framework to help deliver that information

Preparation is essential for types 2–4 and it may sometimes be advisable to carry out the actual fluency activity in a subsequent lesson, allowing plenty of time for feedback.

Teacher's Book

In this book you'll find comprehensive teacher's notes that give an overview of each unit, detailed procedural instructions for all the exercises and an 'If you're short of time' section at the end of each unit. These are interleaved with the Student's Book pages and contain the recordings scripts that relate to the Student's Book page opposite. The Student's Book pages themselves are faded slightly so that the overprinted answer key stands out clearly, helping teachers to locate the answers more easily. Suggested answers for longer tasks are provided in the teacher's notes. The Grammar and Lexis links pages may be photocopied and given to students to check their answers.

The book also features a Resource materials section containing thirty photocopiable worksheets which extend and/or revise elements in the Student's Book. These were written by eight practising business English teachers and provide an extra twenty hours of material to supplement the Student's Book.

Helena Gomm

Colin Benn
Simon Clarke
Gina Cuciniello
Paul Dummett
Paul Emmerson
Jon Hird
Mark Powell
Nicholas Sheard

in company

Intermediate
Teacher's Book

MACMILLAN

1 International English

There has never been a language spoken by so many people in so many places.
Professor David Crystal, The Cambridge Encyclopedia of Language

Needs analysis

1 Complete the following sentence. Use the words in the box if you like. Then compare with other people in the class.

'For me, learning English is _____,'

a pleasure   a hobby   an opportunity
an investment   a necessity   an effort
a problem   a pain   a nightmare

2 Why are you learning English? Complete the sentences below and number them in order of importance for you. Compare with a partner.

In general, I want to:

learn   write   read   improve
feel   make

a <u>feel</u> more confident when I speak.

b <u>improve</u> my listening skills.

c <u>learn</u> lots of new vocabulary.

d <u>make</u> fewer grammar mistakes.

e <u>write</u> better, clearer English.

f <u>read</u> without using a dictionary so much.

In particular, I need English for:

taking   travelling   socialising
doing   giving   writing

g <u>travelling</u> on business.

h <u>doing</u> business on the phone.

i <u>writing</u> e-mails, faxes and letters.

j <u>socialising</u> with clients and colleagues.

k <u>taking</u> part in meetings.

l <u>giving</u> short presentations.

3 Are you learning English for any other reasons? Add them to the lists above.

Global communication

Quiz **1** How much do you know about the world's major languages? Try the quiz on the right. Then check your answers in the article opposite.

Test your knowledge ...

1 Approximately how many languages are there in the world?
a 650 (**b**) 6,500   **c** 65,000
d 650,000

2 Order the world's top ten languages according to the number of native speakers.

Portuguese	**6**	Arabic	**5**
Chinese	**1**	Japanese	**9**
Russian	**8**	German	**10**
English	**2**	Spanish	**3**
Hindi	**4**	Bengali	**7**

3 How many people speak English as a first, second or third language?
a 0.5 billion   **b** 1 billion
(**c**) 1.5 billion   **d** 2 billion

4 In a recent survey, how many Europeans said everyone should speak English?
a 49% (**b**) 69%   **c** 89%   **d** 99%

5 How much of the world's mail is written in English?
a 25%   **b** 50% (**c**) 75%   **d** 90%

6 How much of the world's e-mail is written in English?
a 50%   **b** 60%   **c** 70% (**d**) 80%

7 How many languages 'disappear' every year?
a 2   **b** 5   **c** 10 (**d**) 20

8 What is the world record for the most foreign languages spoken by one person?
a 14   **b** 24   **c** 44 (**d**) 64

9 Where is the record holder in 8 from?
(**a**) the USA   **b** Singapore
c Holland   **d** Nigeria

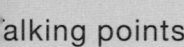 

1 International English

This unit is about both the role and importance of English in global communication, and its role and importance in the lives of the students. Students complete gapped sentences and phrases as they explore their need for English and their attitude to learning it.

They then try a quiz on the world's major languages and check their answers in a text on the predominance of English as the language of international business and communication.

They have the opportunity to discuss their own views and whether or not they agree with the article, before listening to six business people talking about their attitudes to learning English.

In this first section, students begin by exploring their own attitudes to learning the language, the specific areas they wish to concentrate on and their need for English in their everyday lives.

Warm-up

Particularly if this is a new class and the students are unknown to you and to each other, you might like to begin by asking them to share their experiences of learning English so far. Do not pre-empt the questions in the book, but try to establish what their history of learning English has been and whether or not it has been enjoyable.

Needs analysis

1   Allow students to discuss their sentence completions in pairs or small groups before they report back to the class. Encourage them to give reasons why they chose the words they did by asking follow-up questions such as: *What kind of opportunity? Why is it a necessity for you? In what way is it a problem? What would turn it from a nightmare into a dream?*

2   Students should work individually at first and then compare their lists in pairs. You might like to point out the grammatical structures of the two sentences: *want to* + infinitive and *for* (preposition) + -*ing* form. Then ask for further examples.

3   Make it clear that students are never limited to the choices given in the book and encourage them to tell the class if they have any other ideas.

Global communication

In this section, the focus changes to the place of English in the world, particularly in the business arena. Students are encouraged to react to and discuss information in an article and listen to business people talking about their attitudes to learning English.

Quiz

1   Encourage students to try to answer all the quiz questions and discuss their answers in pairs or groups before turning to the article on page 5 to see if they were right. You may need to point out that the answers are not in order in the text and that the answers to question 2 are in the panel to the right of Exercise 2 on page 5, rather than in the article itself. Give students time to read the article, find the answers and give their reactions. Ask them if they found any of the answers surprising.

Discussion

2 Students should discuss the questions in pairs or small groups and report back to the class. Before they begin, you might like to put some expressions for commenting, agreeing and disagreeing on the board or OHP. For example:

I thought the point about ... was interesting.
I'm surprised that ...
I'm not sure I agree that ...
I'm (not) convinced that ...
I totally (dis)agree that ...

When they report back to the class, encourage them to use some of these expressions.

Attitudes to English

3 🔲 **1.1** Suggest that students write the numbers 1 to 6 on a piece of paper and make notes as they listen to the six speakers. They can then compare notes with a partner. Encourage them to use the expressions for agreeing and disagreeing that they studied in the previous exercise.

4 Ask individual students to read out the sentences, completing the gaps.

To add a little movement and make this more fun, as each sentence is completed, ask the rest of the class to stand up if they think the answer is correct and to remain seated if they think it is wrong. Play the recording again for a final check.

If you're short of time

Do the quiz orally with the whole class, reading out the questions and possible answers and asking students to raise their hands to indicate which answer they would choose. Then move straight on to the article.

🔲 **1.1**

Speaker 1
Well, to be honest, **learning English isn't my idea of fun**. I mean, rock concerts are fun. Motorbikes are fun. Snowboarding is fun. Learning English isn't fun. It's hard work. But it's worth it. I don't need English every day in my job right now. But if **I want to get on in my career**, I know I'm going to need it more and more. English is where the money is, so I just think of it as an investment in my future. We Swiss are very practical like that.

Speaker 2
Hm, well, I accept that **English is the language of the media**, but I'm not so sure about business. Personally, I know a lot of business people who speak almost no English at all. Twenty-five per cent of the world speaks English. OK, but that means 75% don't. The way I see it, if I'm trying to sell you something, I should speak your language. But if you come to Ecuador to sell me something, then you should speak Spanish.

Speaker 3
Coming from a tiny country like the Netherlands means we've always had to speak foreign languages. So it's nothing new for us. The same goes for people from Luxembourg, Belgium, Scandinavia. Eighty per cent of Dutch people speak English. Most of us speak some German too, or French. We certainly don't expect anybody to speak Dutch! In fact, the firm I work for recently introduced English as the official company language. So now I speak English all day – to other Dutch people!

Speaker 4
I'm afraid I really don't like English that much. I find the pronunciation very difficult. **It's certainly not as beautiful a language as my language, which is Italian.** And, anyway, **I think it's more difficult as you get older** to learn foreign languages. But my company wants me to learn English, so I don't really have much choice. If a quarter of the world speaks it, I suppose I must too. But **I'll always think in Italian**. My brain works in Italian.

Speaker 5
I don't know why people who speak European languages complain about learning English. Try learning it when your native language is Korean! Actually, I find I can speak English OK, if I'm doing business with other non-native speakers, like Argentinians or Japanese. But **with native English speakers, I do feel at a disadvantage**. I've heard that 66% of British people don't speak a foreign language at all. Hardly surprising when so many of us have to learn English.

Speaker 6
Well, actually, I love English. It's true the pronunciation is quite hard to get right, but the grammar is much simpler than my language, Hungarian – at least at the beginning. **That's the thing about English – it's easy to speak a little quite quickly.** It gets harder later, of course. Frankly, I don't know why some French and Germans are against using English words. It seems to me that English is full of foreign words – especially French and German!

English Inc.

English is to international communication what VHS is to video, Microsoft to software and Pentium to the microchip. It is, for better or worse, the 'industry standard'. And those who don't speak at least a little risk
5 losing business to the increasing number who do. A quarter of the planet currently speaks English. That's one and a half billion people, two-thirds of whom speak it as a foreign language.

In a recent survey*, 69% of Europeans said they thought
10 everyone should speak English. More than half of them already do. For most, it's not a question of choice but of necessity, as English has rapidly become the first language of business, science and popular culture. Three-quarters of the world's mail is in English. So are four out of five e-mails and
15 most of what you find on the Internet.

However, not everyone welcomes this linguistic monopoly. The French Ministry of Finance, for instance, recently surprised the international business community by banning English terms like *e-mail* and *Internet*. In fact, seven
20 teams of language experts have been employed to come up with French alternatives. *Le Web* is not acceptable. *La toile* is. And when the French President himself referred to start-up companies as *les start-upistes* in a televised speech,

*by Eurobarometer

he was strongly criticised for failing to defend France against
25 the advance of the English language.

The French have a point. Twenty languages disappear every year because nobody speaks them anymore. At that rate, by the end of the 21st century almost a third of the world's six and a half thousand languages will be dead. Even
30 in Germany, where *Denglish* is fashionable, and phrases like *Jointventure*, *Powerpartner* and *Fitness-Training* are common, the leader of the Free Democrats has expressed concern about the 'flood of anglicisms descending on us from the media, advertising, product descriptions and technology'.
35 Some go so far as to call it 'a form of violence'.

Maybe it is, and big business certainly accelerates the process. As Professor David Crystal, author of *The Cambridge Encyclopedia of Language*, puts it, 'wave dollar bills in front of someone, and they will learn complicated
40 spellings and grammar.'

But what about people who learn foreign languages just for fun? A 37-year-old American, Gregg Cox, has taken this simple pleasure to extremes. He holds the world record for speaking the most foreign languages – sixty-four at the last
45 count! He would undoubtedly be an asset to any company doing international business. But for those of us who are less gifted linguistically, the power of the American dollar means there may soon be only one foreign language we need to learn, and that language will be English.

The Cambridge Encyclopedia of Language

The number of native speakers of the world's top ten languages

1	Chinese	726m
2	English	427m
3	Spanish	266m
4	Hindi	182m
5	Arabic	181m
6	Portuguese	165m
7	Bengali	162m
8	Russian	158m
9	Japanese	124m
10	German	121m

Discussion 2 Discuss the following questions.

a Do you think the article overstates the importance of English?

b What other languages might eventually take over from English as the international language of business?

c Do you agree that big business accelerates the advance of the English language?

Attitudes to English 3 ▭ **1.1** Listen to six business people talking about their attitudes to learning English. Take notes. Whose opinion is closest to your own?

4 Complete the following expressions. They were used by the people you just listened to.

a Learning English isn't my idea _of_ fun.

b I want to get _on_ in my career.

c English is the language _of_ the media.

d It's certainly not _as_ beautiful a language as ... Italian.

e I think it's more difficult _as_ you get older.

f I'll always think _in_ Italian.

g With native English speakers, I do feel _at_ a disadvantage.

h That's the thing _about_ English – it's easy to speak a little quite quickly.

2 Making contacts

A conference is a gathering of important people who singly can do nothing, but together decide that nothing can be done. *Fred Allen, US comedian*

1   Which of the following cities would you most like to visit for a conference or on holiday? Discuss with a partner.

> Barcelona   London   Rio de Janeiro   Hong Kong   Paris   Prague
> Sydney   Venice   New York   Buenos Aires   Tokyo

2   Some business people were asked for their opinions about conferences. Complete what they said using the words in the box:

> days + year   excuse + gossip   videoconferencing + bar
> cards + intention   time + ideas   audience + stomach

   a   Frankly, they're a complete waste of <u>time</u> – same old faces, same old <u>ideas</u>.

   b   I can often learn more in three <u>days</u> than I do in the rest of the <u>year</u>.

   c   The worst thing is having to get up in front of an <u>audience</u> with that sick feeling in your <u>stomach</u>.

   d   I usually end up with a million business <u>cards</u> from people I've absolutely no <u>intention</u> of contacting.

   e   They're really just an <u>excuse</u> to have fun on expenses and catch up on all the <u>gossip</u>.

   f   We do a lot of <u>videoconferencing</u> these days. The trouble with that is you can't meet in the <u>bar</u> afterwards.

3   Which opinions in 2 do you agree with?

Conference venues

1   ▭ 2.1 Listen to three extracts from a business travel programme. Which venues below do you think the extracts refer to?

   Venue 1 = Extract <u>3</u>   Venue 2 = Extract <u>2</u>   Venue 3 = Extract <u>1</u>

2 Making contacts

Most business people attend a conference at some point in their careers and this unit is about making business contacts and socialising at conferences.

Students begin by talking about their attitudes to conferences and discussing conference venues. They learn language for engaging in small talk and keeping the conversation going and they listen to people chatting at a conference. They will also practise doing it themselves.

The grammatical focus is on the Present Simple and Present Continuous tenses and the lexical focus is on collocations relating to conferences.

This first section is about attitudes to conferences. It gives students an opportunity to talk about their own experiences and opinions.

Warm-up

Read the quotation by Fred Allen at the beginning of the unit to the class and ask for reactions. Find out how many of your students have attended a conference, where it was and whether they enjoyed it. If they have wide experience of attending conferences, ask them to tell the class which was the best conference they have attended and why.

1 As students discuss the cities in pairs, go round listening to their conversations and make a note of any interesting points. At the end, ask for any interesting information to be reported back to the whole class.

2 When students have finished completing the sentences, ask them to say whether each of the speakers has a positive or a negative attitude towards conferences. Encourage them to read the sentences aloud, reflecting that attitude in their intonation.

3 Do this either as a class discussion or ask students to discuss in pairs which statements they agree with.

Conference venues

In this section, students meet some common collocations associated with conference venues. Recorded extracts from a business travel programme are used to show these collocations in action and also to train students to listen for detail, in this case picking out numbers and saying what they refer to.

1 **2.1** Focus attention on the three photos and ask students to say which of the conference venues they would be most interested in going to.

As you play the recording, students match the extracts with the venues.

2.1

Extract 1

Half an hour from the world's most romantic city and rated by conference organisers the 'hottest' venue in Europe, Disneyland Paris's corporate clients include American Express, Unilever and MCI WorldCom. If you think business and the Lion King don't mix, the Disney magic will soon change your mind. With its **unique atmosphere** and superb fully equipped **convention centre** for 2,300 people, its 95 meeting rooms and 3,000 square metres of **exhibition space**, Disney's theme park is sure to be a huge success with both you and your family. As well as fabulous **banqueting facilities** for over a thousand people, Disney is able to arrange special private events, such as the amazing 'Journey through Time' and the 'Cape Caribbean' adventure or, if you prefer, **golf tournaments** and **team-building activities**. Walt Disney's aim was always 'to make people happy' and that aim now extends to corporate hospitality in the cultural heart of Europe.

Extract 2

Two thousand years ago it was the home of the ancient Mayan civilisation. Today, Cancun is the most popular resort in Mexico, its unspoilt coastline a watersports paradise. With its 426 rooms overlooking the Caribbean, **24-hour room service**, **express checkout**, **outdoor pools**, residents-only **health club** and 200 metres of **exclusive private beach**, the Hilton Cancun is rated among the three best hotels in Latin America. Whether swimming with the dolphins or playing roulette in its own offshore casino, you can be sure of an experience to remember. Or why not take advantage of the Hilton's **car-rental service** and explore the nearby ruins of Chichen Itza? Whatever your company's needs, send them your requirements and they will plan the logistics for you. What's more, if you book on special value dates, you'll get a generous 10–30% discount. This year, why not let your annual conference be part of Cancun's 2,000-year-old tradition?

Extract 3

At 321 metres high, higher than the Eiffel Tower and only 60 metres shorter than the Empire State Building, the magnificent Burj Al Arab is the world's tallest and most luxurious hotel. Diamond white by day and a rainbow of colours at night, occupying a **central location** in Dubai with **flight connections** to all the major cities of the world, the Burj Al Arab combines the latest technology with the finest traditions of the past. **Spacious deluxe suites** from 170 to 780 square metres, in-room laptops with **Internet access**, full conference facilities on the 27th floor, a VIP helipad on the 28th, a golden domed ballroom and a **world-class restaurant** with **spectacular views** across the Arabian Gulf all go to make this the ultimate business venue. As they say in the Emirates, 'Welcome honoured guest'.

2 Before playing the recording, read all the figures aloud, or ask students to read them, ensuring that everyone is clear how each is pronounced.

You may need to play the recording several times and pause it between extracts for students to match the figures to the venue and note down what the figures refer to.

3 See if students can complete the collocations from memory before playing the recording again for them to check.

To make the activity more interactive, you could divide the class into two teams. In turn, one member of each team calls out the first word in a collocation and the corresponding member of the other team replies with the second word.

For homework, you could ask students to use all or some of the collocations in sentences.

Direct the students' attention to the Lexis link on page 89 where they will find more on conference vocabulary.

4 Students can discuss the question in pairs or groups and report back to the class.

Who's who?

This section begins by introducing students to the kinds of things they will need to say at conferences, beginning by identifying specific people by appearance, manner, location, etc. and saying something about them.

Describing people

1 This exercise equips students to identify people they want to talk about. When students have completed the questions and answers individually, ask them, in pairs, to act out the dialogue with one student choosing a question and the other giving an appropriate response. Do not let this go on for too long as they will be doing a similar thing in the next activity, but with a freer choice of words.

2 Put students in pairs to make new sentences following the structures practised in Exercise 1.

Make sure students can pronounce some of the trickier items such as *pharmaceuticals, buffet* and *moustache* before they start.

Invite some pairs to perform short dialogues for the class.

2 Listen again and match the figures to each venue. What do the figures refer to?

321 Venue **1** <u>height of the building in metres</u>

426 Venue **2** <u>number of rooms</u>

27th Venue **1** <u>floor with conference facilities</u>

2,300 Venue **3** <u>number of people the convention centre can house</u>

10–30% Venue **2** <u>discount available on special value dates</u>

3,000 Venue **3** <u>size of exhibition space in square metres</u>

170–780 Venue **1** <u>size of deluxe suites in square metres</u>

95 Venue **3** <u>number of meeting rooms</u>

200 Venue **2** <u>length of private beach in metres</u>

3 What other facilities does each venue have? Complete the collocations below. They were all in the extracts you just listened to.

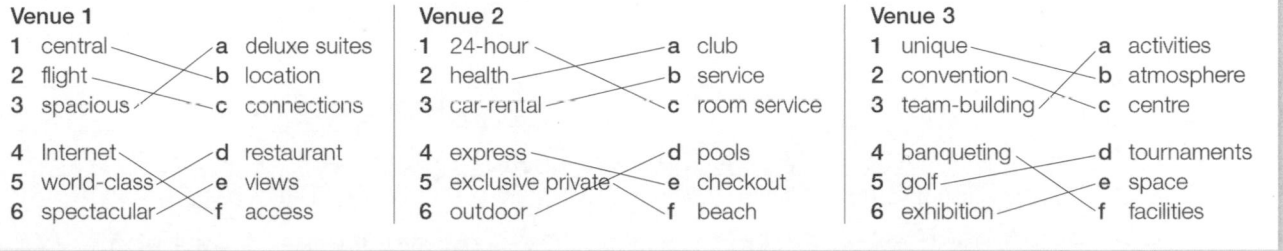

Venue 1
1 central — a deluxe suites
2 flight — b location
3 spacious — c connections

4 Internet — d restaurant
5 world-class — e views
6 spectacular — f access

Venue 2
1 24-hour — a club
2 health — b service
3 car-rental — c room service

4 express — d pools
5 exclusive private — e checkout
6 outdoor — f beach

Venue 3
1 unique — a activities
2 convention — b atmosphere
3 team-building — c centre

4 banqueting — d tournaments
5 golf — e space
6 exhibition — f facilities

Lexis link

for more on conference
vocabulary see page 89

4 Your company agrees to send you to an international conference at one of the venues above, provided that you give a presentation in English. Which would you choose and why?

Who's who?

Describing people

1 One of the main reasons for going to conferences is to meet the right people. Complete the following questions and answers using the prepositions in the box.

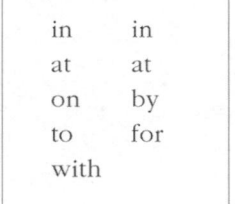

in	in
at	at
on	by
to	for
with	

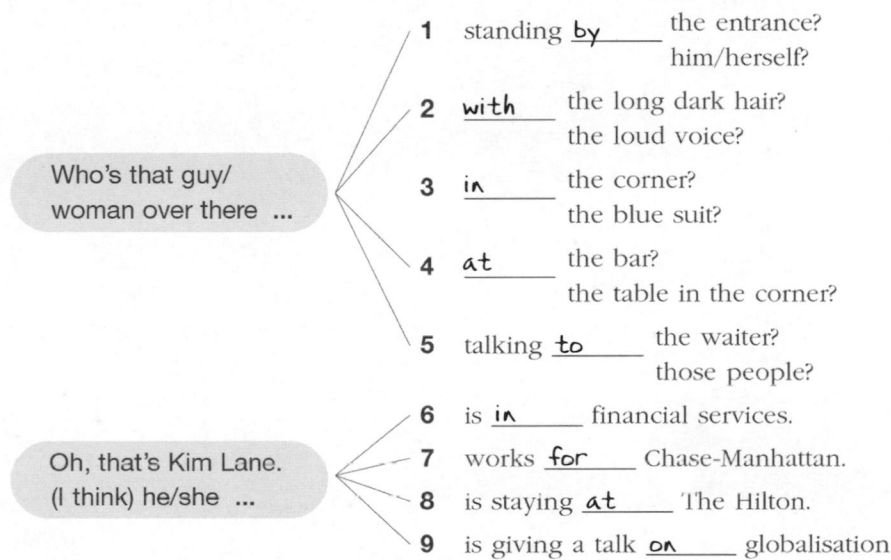

Who's that guy/
woman over there ...

1 standing **by** the entrance?
   him/herself?

2 **with** the long dark hair?
   the loud voice?

3 **in** the corner?
   the blue suit?

4 **at** the bar?
   the table in the corner?

5 talking **to** the waiter?
   those people?

Oh, that's Kim Lane.
(I think) he/she ...

6 is **in** financial services.

7 works **for** Chase-Manhattan.

8 is staying **at** The Hilton.

9 is giving a talk **on** globalisation.

2 Use the model above to make new sentences with the following.

the Hyatt   pharmaceuticals   the buffet   the glasses   the pony-tail
Renault   negotiating skills   the long dress   the conference organiser
the moustache   the awful tie   the Italian accent   her back to us

Grammar link

for more on the Present
Simple and Continuous
see page 88

3   ▭ 2.2 Listen to some conference delegates gossiping during a coffee break.
Decide which four people in the photo they are talking about and complete the
information below.

1

Name _Klaus Müller_

Job/Line of business _e-business_

Based in _Stuttgart or Hamburg_

Hotel _Hyatt_

Subject of talk _online banking_

Gossip _had an argument with speaker_

2

Name _Hannah James_

Job/Line of business _stress management_

Based in _Oxford_

Hotel _Sheraton_

Subject of talk _executive burnout_

Gossip _Course in Copenhagen was a disaster_

3

Name _Pietro Bianco_

Job/Line of business _human resources_

Based in _Rome_

Hotel _Hilton_

Subject of talk _interviewing skills_

Gossip _extremely difficult to work with_

4

Name _Carla Hall_

Job/Line of business _sales manager_

Based in _Edinburgh_

Hotel _Hyatt_

Subject of talk _customer relations_

Gossip _having problems at work with
ex-husband; new job a demotion_

3 ▭ **2.2** Focus students' attention on the photograph and ask them to use some of the language they have been practising to identify the people. For example, *the woman in the pink sweater with the short blonde hair.*

For fun, you might like to invite students to see who can put together the longest description of one of the people in the photograph. For example, *the young woman with short blonde hair in the pink sweater with the patterned skirt and the silver bracelet, holding a glass of orange juice, standing next to the woman in the blue blouse and grey skirt and talking to the man in the white shirt.*

Before playing the recording, establish the meaning of *gossiping*. Either here or at the end of the activity you might like to invite students to suggest some potential gossip about the people in the photograph.

Play the recording and ask students first to decide which of the people in the photograph the speakers are discussing.

Play the recording again for students to complete the information. You may need to play the recording several times and pause it between extracts to give students time to write their answers.

Draw students' attention to the Grammar link on page 88 where they will find more information about the uses of the Present Simple and Present Continuous.

▭ **2.2**

Conversation 1

A: ... So, that's why it took us five hours to get from the airport to the hotel. Who's that guy over there, by the way?

B: Hm?

A: The one at the table in the corner in the dark tie. Over there, talking to those people.

B: Oh, him. That's Klaus Müller. I think he works at the Stuttgart office. Or is it Hamburg now? He's in the e-business division, anyway. Why?

A: He's giving a talk, isn't he?

B: Um, I think so. Yeah, something about online banking. Hi-tech stuff.

A: Hm. I'd quite like to talk to him if I get the chance. Is he staying here, do you know?

B: Erm, no, he's probably at the Hyatt. That's where most of the Germans are staying.

A: You couldn't introduce us, could you?

B: Well, to tell you the truth, we don't really get on. I had a rather nasty argument with him once. So maybe I'm not the best person to ask ...

A: Oh, right. Never mind. Perhaps I'll catch him later.

Conversation 2

C: Hi, Max. How are things? We were just talking about that woman over there.

D: Who?

C: The woman in the pink top – with the blonde hair.

D: Oh, yes.

C: You know her?

D: Er, yes. That's Hannah James.

C: Hannah who?

D: James. She works for some weird stress management organisation in Oxford. You know, meditation, put a crystal on your desk, find your inner child. All that kind of rubbish.

C: What on earth is she doing here?

D: No idea. Trying to get us to buy another course on stress management, I imagine.

C: You mean we use her company?

D: Yes. Apparently she did something at our Copenhagen office. I heard it was a total disaster ...

C: Really?

D: Mm. It's a long story. She's giving a talk on executive burnout on Thursday. I'd give it a miss if I were you.

C: Right. Actually, she's staying at my hotel, the Sheraton. I saw her last night.

D: Oh, you're at the Sheraton, are you? What's it like?

C: Very comfortable. Bit big and impersonal, though. You know what these places are like.

Conversation 3

E: Tom, you know nearly everybody here. Who's that guy by the door – with the brown sweater and the Italian accent?

F: Oh, you mean Pietro Bianco?

E: Is that his name? Who is he?

F: He's in human resources, based in Rome – does all our recruiting in Southern Europe. Amazing speaker. I think he's doing a session this year on interviewing skills. Should be good.

E: Really? I must go to that. Rome, you say? You know, I've been trying to get a transfer to the Rome office for years.

F: Well, Pietro's the person you want to talk to. I think he's staying at your hotel. The Hilton, right? I should warn you, though ...

E: What?

F: Well, from what I hear, he's extremely difficult to work with. Big ego. A friend of mine applied for a job with him last year.

E: Did they get it?

F: I'm afraid not. Actually, they were quite pleased. They said he'd make a terrible boss.

E: Oh, well, maybe I should go to his talk first.

Conversation 4

G: Chris, who's that woman over there by the table – with the short dark hair?

H: Oh, yes. That's, er, what's-her-name? Carla Hill? Hall. Carla Hall, that's it. I saw her coming out of the Hyatt this morning. She's a sales manager at the Edinburgh office. Giving a talk on customer relations tomorrow. I saw it on the programme.

G: Oh, yeah, that's right. Isn't she supposed to be joining the Bucharest office soon?

H: Yes, well, don't tell anyone, but, apparently, it's a demotion.

G: A demotion – no! How did that happen?

H: It's all a big secret. But you see that guy over there in the corner by the entrance? The tall one in the grey shirt talking to Pietro? That's her ex-husband. They put him in charge of Edinburgh three months ago, the two of them had problems and now Carla's leaving to take up a more junior position in Romania.

G: How awful! Perhaps I'll go over and cheer her up. She looks a bit lonely over there all by herself.

Taboo or not taboo?

In this section, students discuss the issue of what is and is not a suitable subject for conversation with people you meet at a conference for the first time.

1 Establish the meaning of *taboo*. Ask students whether taboo subjects in their culture differ according to how well you know the people you are talking to and the circumstances of the conversation. Invite them to suggest topics which they think would be taboo when meeting someone at a conference for the first time and which would be safe.

Point out the other categories given in this exercise: *conversation killers* and *a bit risky*. Ask for examples, e.g. subjects that are not exactly taboo but wouldn't encourage people to continue a conversation, and subjects that are risky because they may cause offence.

Ask students to share with the class any amusing or embarrassing moments they've actually experienced in conversation. If your students are from different cultures, ask them to work individually at first to group the items in the box under the headings. They can then compare their answers in pairs or small groups. If students share a culture, encourage them to discuss and do the grouping in pairs.

2 ▣ **2.3** Students may be able to decide whether the speakers get on or not before they identify the specific details of the topics of conversation. Ask only for this the first time you play the recording to encourage students to realise that it isn't always necessary to understand every word of a listening in order to pick up the gist of what is said or the attitude of the speakers.

Play the recording again for them to note down the topics of conversation that they hear and allow them to compare answers in pairs before checking with the class.

Keeping the conversation going

This section gives students some of the tools for keeping a conversation going once it has started.

1 Write the expressions on the board as the students complete them. Then wipe off some of the words and see if the students can still remember the expressions. Gradually wipe off more words so that fewer and fewer remain, each time checking if the students can still remember.

Play the recording as a final check.

2 Ask students to discuss the questions in pairs or small groups. Then have a class discussion on what they would do in their own language(s) to open, continue or end a conversation.

▣ **2.3**

Conversation 1
A: **Is this your first visit to Russia?**
B: Er, yes it is, actually. Fascinating place.
A: Yes, isn't it? I come here quite a lot. **What do you do, by the way?** I see you work for Glaxo.
B: How did you know? ... Oh, yeah, my badge. Yeah, I'm in R&D. Molecular modelling to be precise.
A: Really? We should talk. **Can I get you a drink?**
B: Er, no thanks. I'm fine.
A: Sure?
B: Well, just a top-up, then. Thanks.
A: What are you drinking? The Chardonnay, isn't it?
B: Erm, yeah. So, **what line of business are you** in?

Conversation 2
C: Hi, Fiona Hunt. SunMicrosystems. Mind if I join you?
D: Erm, no. Er, Michael Steele.
C: Pleased to meet you, Mike. **Try one of these – they're delicious.**
D: Er, thanks, but seafood doesn't agree with me.
C: Oh, then try the cheese dips instead. They're good, too. **Have we met somewhere before?** Oslo, perhaps?
D: I don't think so.
C: Mm. I was sure I recognised you ... You're an Aquarius, aren't you? I can tell.
D: Well, I don't know. I'm not really into horoscopes, I'm afraid.
C: When's your birthday?

D: Oh, er, February the 2nd.
C: I knew it! A typical Aquarius.
D: Er, yes. Geez, is that the time? **If you'll excuse me, I have to make a phone call. It's been nice talking to you.**

Conversation 3
E: **I really enjoyed your talk this morning.**
F: Oh, thanks. Yeah, it went quite well, I think.
E: You had some very interesting things to say. I'm Amy Cooper, by the way. Yes, I'd like to talk to you about some of your ideas. My company may be interested in your product. Where are you staying?
F: At the Regency.
E: I'm at the Hyatt. Why don't we fix up a time to chat over a drink? Here's my card.
F: Oh, thanks. I've got mine here ... somewhere.
E: Don't worry. I know who you are. So, **how are you enjoying the conference?**
F: Well, it's been good so far. More people than ever this year. But, er, **isn't this weather awful? Half a metre of snow this morning**, I heard.
E: Yeah, it gets pretty cold here in Moscow, that's for sure.
F: Erm, **would you excuse me a moment? I'll be right back.**

Conversation 4
G: So, how's business?
H: Fine. This merger's meant quite a lot of work for us, but, fine.
G: Hm. Well, mergers are often difficult. So, er, what do you think about the Middle-East situation?

H: I'm sorry?
G: The crisis in the Middle East. It was in the news again this morning.
H: Er, well, I, er ...
G: I mean, it must affect a company like yours – you being in oil.
H: Er, no, I think you've made a mistake. I'm not in oil. I work for Audi.
G: Audi? Oh, sorry. Thought you were someone else.
H: That's OK. Er, if you'll excuse me, **I must just go and say hello to someone**.

Conversation 5
J: I like your watch. An Omega, isn't it?
K: Er, well, to be honest, don't tell anyone, but it's a fake.
J: No! Well it looks real to me. Where did you get it?
K: Turkey. It cost me twenty-five dollars.
J: Amazing! So, **do you know many people here?**
K: No, not really. It's the first time I've been to one of these conferences.
J: Me too. So, what's your hotel like?
K: Hm, pretty comfortable. Nothing special, but it's OK, I suppose.
J: Yeah, you're at the Sheraton, aren't you? Last year they held this thing in Mexico. The Hilton Cancun. Fabulous hotel, they say.
K: Cancun! A bit warmer than here, then!
J: Oh, yeah. I went there on holiday once. Beautiful place. **Can I get you anything from the buffet?**
K: Oh, that's all right. I'll come with you. I'd like some more of that Beluga caviar before it all goes!

Taboo or not taboo?

1 Work with a partner. Imagine you meet some business people at a conference for the first time. Which of the following topics are

- interesting? • safe? • conversation killers? • a bit risky? • taboo?

family	the news	your country	religion	clothes	your health
politics	sex	sport	the weather	food & drink	
people you both know		how work's going		the city you're in	
the hotel you're staying at		your holiday plans			

2 🔲 **2.3** Listen to some people socialising at a conference. What are they talking about? Do they get on with each other?

Topics of conversation	Do the speakers get on?
1 Russia, work, drink	yes
2 food, astrology	no
3 conference, weather	yes
4 work (the merger), politics	no
5 watch, hotel, Mexico, food	yes

Keeping the conversation going

1 The expressions below were in the conversations you just listened to. Can you remember the first three words of each expression? Contractions (*it's, you'll, I'm* etc.) count as **one** word. If necessary, listen again and check.

a	Is	this	your	first visit to Russia?
b	What	do	you	do, by the way?
c	Can	I	get	you a drink?
d	What	line	of	business are you in?
e	Try	one	of	these – they're delicious.
f	Have	we	met	somewhere before?
g	If	you'll	excuse	me, I have to make a phone call.
h	It's	been	nice	talking to you.
i	I	really	enjoyed	your talk this morning.
j	How	are	you	enjoying the conference?
k	Isn't	this	weather	awful? Half a meter of snow this morning!
l	Would	you	excuse	me a moment? I'll be right back.
m	I	must	just	go and say hello to someone.
n	Do	you	know	many people here?
o	Can	I	get	you anything from the buffet?

2 Look at the expressions in 1.

a, c, e, f, i, j, k, n, o   **a** Which would be good ways of opening a conversation?

b, c, d, e, j, k, n, o   **b** Which would help you to keep a conversation going?

g, h, l, m   **c** Which could you use to politely end a conversation?

At a conference drinks party

Work as a class to keep the conversation going at a conference drinks party at Disneyland, Paris. It's a warm summer evening and the place is full of delegates. The conference theme is *Business in the Twenty-first Century*.

1 Invent a name and nationality for yourself.

Name: _____ Nationality: _____

2 Then, complete the questions below. Think of possible answers for each and make notes in the space provided.

Q So, who / work for? *So, who do you work for?* _____
A _____

Q And what / do there? *And what do you do there?* _____
A _____

Q Where / based? *Where are you based?* _____
A _____

Q How / business? *How's business?* _____
A _____

Q Can / get / drink? *Can I get you a drink?* _____
A _____

Q Where / from originally? *Where are you from originally?* _____
A _____

Q first time / Paris? *Is this your first time in Paris?* _____
A _____

Q How / enjoying / conference? *How are you enjoying the conference?* __
A _____

Q giving / presentation? *Are you giving a presentation?* _____
A _____

Q know many people here? *Do you know many people here?* _____
A _____

Q So, where / staying? *So, where are you staying?* _____
A _____

Q Can / get / anything / buffet? *Can I get you anything from the buffet?*
A _____

3 When everyone is ready,
   • mingle with other people in the class.
   • introduce yourself to as many people as possible and show interest in what they tell you.
   • use the questions above to try to keep the conversation going. Remember that you can talk about other people in the room as well as yourself.
   • exchange business cards or fix an appointment with anyone you could do business with.

At a conference drinks party

In this section, students put into practice what they have learnt about starting and maintaining a conversation at a conference by roleplaying a conference drinks party. Students work together as a class to do this and they are given plenty of support by preparing questions and answers in advance.

1 Students could use their real names and nationalities here, but some may find it easier and less embarrassing to assume a fictitious identity when taking part in a roleplay. The fantasy role approach may also work better with in-company groups and those who already know each other well; it certainly allows more room for gossip.

2 Ask students to complete the questions first and check the answers with the whole class before getting them to fill in the answers. Students should work individually to devise answers for their character, and you will need to go round offering help and advice where needed.

3 If you have the time and the facilities to do so, you might like to add to the reality of this by having some refreshments available and by encouraging students to bring to class business cards (real or imaginary) and name badges.

Draw students' attention to the fact that they are not limited to the questions and answers they have just prepared. They have already practised other techniques in this unit for talking about other people in the room and keeping the conversation going. They could even engage in a little (fictitious) gossip about the other people they have met at the conference.

Conduct a feedback session at the end in which students report back to the class on the fascinating people they met, the interesting gossip they heard and the appointments they have made.

If you're short of time

Set *Conference venues* Exercise 3 for homework and have a quick class vote rather than a discussion in Exercise 4.

Restrict the length of time students are given to mingle in *At a conference drinks party* Exercise 3 and set a target, for example, introduce yourself to three people and ask each of them a different question.

Set the Grammar and Lexis links exercises for homework and check the answers at the beginning of the next class.

Desk work

3 Making calls

Making and receiving telephone calls in English is perhaps one of the most difficult skills which business students need to acquire, and certainly one which can cause a lot of stress.

This unit provides strategies to make telephoning in English less stressful and gives some useful formulaic expressions which will facilitate dealing with calls. Students practise listening to and dealing with voice mail messages and returning calls. Finally, students do a guided roleplay, initiating a phone call in order to find out certain information.

The grammatical focus is on the Past Simple and time adverbs, and the lexical focus is on telephone expressions.

This first section provides an opportunity for students to explore their attitudes and worries about speaking English on the phone. The aim here is to demonstrate to students that many people have difficulty with telephone calls and it is nothing to be ashamed of. Several techniques will be given in this unit which should help.

Warm-up

Find out how often students have to make or receive phone calls in English and what problems they have experienced.

Read the quotation at the beginning of the unit to the class and ask for reactions. How do the students feel when they encounter a telephone answering system that requires them to make endless choices, pressing different keys on their phone and they never get to speak to a real person?

Questionnaire

1 Give pairs time to think about and discuss the questions, encouraging them to give details of the incident when their answer is yes. Ask them to report back to the class on any interesting anecdotes they shared.

Planning your calls

Planning calls in a foreign language is vitally important. If you prepare what you are going to say when you make a call, the conversation is likely to progress much more smoothly and with less chance of misunderstanding. If you are aware of what you should say when you receive a call, then you will sound more confident, and you are less likely to cause offence by not using the established formulae, which the caller will expect.

2 **3.1** Play the recording and elicit answers to the question around the class. Encourage students to suggest the kinds of things the person answering the phone could have said instead of his abrupt one-word responses (*Hello. Yes. Yes*) which would have been more helpful.

3 **3.2** Play the recording for students to listen and complete the gaps. When you have checked the answers, ask them to say what would be an appropriate way of answering the phone in their own situations.

4 **3.3** Play the recording and elicit answers to the question. Again, you could ask students to say how the caller's utterances could be improved before you play the better version.

5 **3.4** Play the recording for students to listen and complete the gaps. In pairs, ask students briefly to roleplay the first part of a telephone call, with one answering the phone properly and the other saying who they are, where they are calling from, who they want to speak to and what it is about. They can then swap roles.

3.1

A: Hello?
B: Hello.
A: Hello. Is that Dutch Hydro?
B: That's right.
A: Can I have the accounts department, please?
B: Yes.
A: Sorry?
B: This is the accounts department.
A: Oh, right. Erm, I'd like to speak to Marius Pot, please.
B: Yes.
A: Sorry?
B: That's me.
A: Well, why didn't you say so?
B: Can I help you?
A: I hope so! I'm calling about an invoice I received.

3.2

B: **Hello**, accounts **department**. Marius Pot **speaking**.
A: Ah, Mr Pot. Just the person I wanted to speak to. I'm calling about an invoice I received.

3.3

A: Good morning, Cheney & Broome. Can I help you?
B: Yes, please ... er, ... Just a moment ...
A: Hello? Are you still there?
B: Yes, sorry ... erm ...
A: How can I help you?
B: Oh, yes, can I speak to, er, to, er ... just a minute ... yes, to, er, Catherine Mellor, please?
A: Certainly. Who's calling, please?
B: Sorry?

A: Can I have your name, please?
B: Oh, yes, it's Ramon Berenguer ... from Genex Pharmaceuticals.
A: Thank you. Can I ask the purpose of your call, Mr Berenguer?
B: Oh, yes. It's about, er ... an invoice.
A: Thank you, Mr Berenguer. Putting you through now.

3.4

A: Good morning, Cheney & Broome. Can I help you?
B: Er, yes. **This is** Ramon Berenguer **from** Genex Pharmaceuticals. **Can I speak to** Catherine Mellor, **please**?
A: Certainly, Mr Berenguer. Can I ask the purpose of your call?
B: **It's about** an invoice.
A: Putting you through now.

3 Making calls

Our telephone answering system has broken down. This is a human being. How can I help you? *Anonymous customer service representative*

Questionnaire

1 How comfortable are you speaking English on the phone? Work with a partner. Complete and discuss the questionnaire below using the correct form of the following verbs:

> have   lose   shout   wish   keep   try   want
> sound   misunderstand

Be honest! Can you remember a time when you ...

1 totally **misunderstood** what someone said on the phone?	Oh, yes ☐	No ☐
2 really **sounded** rude and unhelpful because you were busy?	Oh, yes ☐	No ☐
3 constantly **had** to ask the other person to repeat what they said?	Oh, yes ☐	No ☐
4 just **kept** putting off a call because you didn't want to speak English?	Oh, yes ☐	No ☐
5 actually **shouted** at someone on the phone?	Oh, yes ☐	No ☐
6 completely **lost** track of the conversation?	Oh, yes ☐	No ☐
7 just **wished** you could talk to the other person face to face?	Oh, yes ☐	No ☐
8 even **tried** pretending you were out to avoid taking a call?	Oh, yes ☐	No ☐
9 really **wanted** to kill the person on the other end of the phone?	Oh, yes ☐	No ☐

Planning your calls

Making phone calls in a foreign language requires planning. It's especially important to know what to say right at the beginning of the call.

2 ▭ 3.1 Listen to the phone call. Why does the caller get angry?
<u>The person who answers is abrupt and unhelpful.</u>

3 ▭ 3.2 Listen to a better version of the same phone call and complete the following: Hello <u>   </u>, accounts <u>department</u>. Marius Pot <u>speaking</u>.

4 ▭ 3.3 Now listen to another phone call. Why does the caller sound so unprofessional? <u>He hesitates a lot and has not prepared what to say.</u>

5 ▭ 3.4 Again, listen to a better version of the same phone call and complete the following:
<u>This</u> <u>is</u> Ramon Berenguer <u>from</u> Genex Pharmaceuticals.
<u>Can</u> <u>I</u> <u>speak</u> <u>to</u> Catherine Mellor, <u>please</u> ?
<u>It's</u> <u>about</u> an invoice.

6 A lot of the English you need on the phone is just a small number of key words used in different combinations. Work with a partner. How many telephone expressions can you make in **2 minutes** using **one** word or phrase from **two or more** sections below (eg. *Can I have your name, please?*). Write them down.

| can | I you | ask
check
speak to
take
see if
help
have
give
speak up
hold on
get
tell
leave
say
spell
read
get back to | who's
me
you
he/she
him/her
your name
a message
someone
something
a moment
it
that | please
about it
again
with me
with you
back to me
I called
within the hour
to call me back
a few details
on that
is there
for me
later today
calling
when he/she'll be back |

Lexis link

for more on telephone expressions see page 91

7 You overhear a colleague say the following things on the phone. What questions do you think she was asked? Use some of the telephone expressions you made in 6.

a Can I help you ?

Yes, I'd like to speak to Ifakat Karsli, please.

b Can I have your name please? / Can I ask who's calling ?

Yes, it's Ivana Medvedeva.

c Can you spell that, please ?

M-E-D-V-E-D-E-V-A, Medvedeva.

d Can I give her a message ?

Yes. Can you just tell her Ivana called?

e Can you tell him I called ?

Yes, I'll tell him as soon as he gets in.

f Can you read it back to me ?

Of course. Your reference number is 45-81099-KM. OK?

g Can you speak up, please ?

Sorry, is that better?

h Can you tell me when he/she'll be back ?

Around three, I should think.

i Can you get back to me within the hour ?

Can we make that *two* hours?

j Can you ask him/her to call me back ?

Certainly. Can you give me your number?

k Can I get back to you on that ?

Sure. When can I expect to hear from you?

l Can I leave a message with you ?

Sure. Just a minute. Where's my pen? OK, go ahead.

Telephone phrases

6 Students will find the phrases given here useful in a wide variety of phone calls. When they have found as many expressions as possible, divide the class into two teams. Each team takes a turn to call out the first part of an expression and the other team has to complete it.

Point out to students that the key to successful telephoning in English is confidence. If they have a range of expressions at their fingertips to cope with all the practical aspects and eventualities of telephoning (the person being out, on another line, offering to take a message, etc.), then they will sound more confident and will have more time to concentrate on the more important parts of the call (imparting information, finding something out, etc.).

7 In this exercise, students predict what the person at the other end of the phone must have said to cause the responses given. Give students time to complete the questions individually.

For a more interactive way of checking answers, select a pair of students and ask one of them to read out the question they have written. If the question is correct, the other student should give the response from the book. If the question is not correct, he/she should either say nothing or give a response which is appropriate to the question that has actually been asked. Establish what the correct question should be before moving on. Do this for all the questions, selecting a different pair of students each time.

Direct students' attention to the Lexis link on page 91 where they will find more useful telephone expressions for dealing with difficulties and distractions.

Voice mail

In this section, students practise listening to voice mail messages and identifying the important information in them. The messages are then used for grammar work on the Past Simple and pronunciation of Past Simple regular verb endings.

1 ▣ **3.5** Encourage students to take meaningful notes when they listen to the messages. Elicit that these notes should contain the important information from the messages, which is likely to include the name of the caller, what the message is about and any action that the receiver of the call is required to take.

2 Make sure students have read the questions before you play the recording so that they know exactly what information they are listening for.

Past Simple endings

3 You might like to ask the students to try to put the words into the correct columns before you play the recording, and just use the recording for them to check their answers. When students have to categorise things by pronunciation, always encourage them to say the words aloud to see what sounds right. Developing an instinct for what sounds right will help them throughout their language learning careers.

Elicit that the verbs in the /id/ column all have infinitives ending in *t* or *d*.

Students will find more information on the form of the Past Simple in the Grammar link on page 90.

Focus attention on the cartoon. Ask students whether they sympathise with the woman's frustration. Do they find that increased technology in the office gets in the way of communication rather than facilitating it?

▣ **3.5**

Message 1
Hello. This is Cheryl. I **phoned** you about five times yesterday, but you weren't in. Anyway, I **corrected** those figures you **faxed** me. OK, speak to you later.

Message 2
Hi, Peter. Anne here. I **wanted** to talk to you about the project meeting tomorrow, but you're obviously not there. The good news is we **finished** Phase One on time. As I **explained**, I may be a little late for the meeting. So just go ahead and start without me. I'll join you about 10.

Message 3
Er, this is Zoltán. Just to let you know, I **started** the report this morning and just **e-mailed** you the first part. Oh, I **included** the quarterly accounts in the report, too. Let me know what you think.

Message 4
Mr Carter. It's Philip Heath. I **talked** to our stock control manager about the Venezuelan consignment and he says we **despatched** the goods a week ago. The shipping agent says they **delivered** them this morning. So, problem solved!

Message 5
Hello, Mr Carter. This is Ryan Hope from SilverStar. I **called** you a couple of weeks ago about an estimate for a contract in Malaysia. Erm, we **discussed** my client's requirements and, well, I **expected** to hear from you last week. Could you give me a call on 01865 555959 as soon as possible, please?

Message 6
Pete. It's me. Sorry, mate, I **tried** everything, but head office say we can't have any more time. They say they **waited** six months for the preliminary report, another six months for the feasibility study and now they want to see some results. Anyway, I **booked** the conference room for three tomorrow. Give me a call when you get in. We need to talk.

Voice mail

1 🔊 3.5 Listen to six voice mail messages. Take notes. Which message is about

a an order? $\boxed{4}$ **d** a deadline? $\boxed{6}$

b some figures? $\boxed{1}$ **e** a report? $\boxed{3}$

c a meeting? $\boxed{2}$ **f** a reminder? $\boxed{5}$

2 Listen again and answer the questions.

Message 1 How many times did Cheryl phone yesterday? _about five_

Message 2 What's the good news about Phase One? _it was finished on time_

Message 3 What did Zoltán include in his report? _the quarterly accounts_

Message 4 When was the delivery? _this morning_

Message 5 How late is the estimate? _a week_

Message 6 What do you think is happening at 3 tomorrow? _(students' own ideas)_

Past Simple endings

3 The messages above contain the following verbs.

1 phoned, corrected, faxed
2 wanted, finished, explained
3 started, e-mailed, included
4 talked, despatched, delivered
5 called, discussed, expected
6 tried, waited, booked

The '-ed' endings of regular verbs in the Past Simple can be pronounced in three different ways: /d/, /t/ or /ɪd/. Listen to the messages again. Which verbs take the /ɪd/ ending? Why? Put them in the third column below.

/d/	/t/	/ɪd/
phoned	faxed	corrected
explained	finished	wanted
e-mailed	talked	started
delivered	despatched	included
called	discussed	expected
tried	booked	waited

Now put the other verbs in the correct column.

ALICE, I JUST SENT YOU AN E-MAIL.

HERE'S A COPY OF MY MESSAGE BUT I'LL JUST TELL YOU WHAT IT SAYS.

IT SAYS I SENT YOU A VOICE MAIL TELLING YOU TO LOOK FOR A FAX THAT SAYS I WANT TO TALK TO YOU.

Returning a call

1    3.6 Listen to two telephone calls and answer the questions.

Call 1

1   **a**   Whose answerphone are we listening to? _Sylvia Wright's_

  b   What does the caller want? _to know how the meeting with Tesco went_

2   Put the recorded message into the right order. The first and last parts are in the right place.

☐1 Hello. This is Patterson Meats,	☐9 after the tone, and I'll get back
☐6 but if you'd like to leave	☐2 Sylvia Wright's office. Thank you
☐3 for calling. I'm afraid	☐4 I'm not able to take
☐8 a fax, please do so	☐7 a message or send
☐5 your call right now,	☐10 to you as soon as I can.

Call 2

1   Who didn't come to the meeting?

  a Bill Andrews   **(b)** Stephanie Hughes   **c** Jonathan Powell   **d** Melanie Burns

2   Who does Tim already know?

  (a) Bill Andrews   **b** Stephanie Hughes   **c** Jonathan Powell   **d** Melanie Burns

3   What didn't the visitors from the UK see?

  a   the processing plant   **c**   the packing department   **e**   a presentation
  (b)   the factory   **d**   the freezer units

4   Tim was interrupted during the phone call. Complete what he said to Sylvia.

Sorry _about that_ . I just _had to sign something_ .

Where _were we_ ?

5   What were the British visitors worried about?

UK customers accepting kangaroo meat

6   Would the product they came to see be popular in your country? Would you try it?

Talking about the past

2   Put these irregular verbs from Call 2 into the Past Simple. You have 45 seconds!

get _got_	meet _met_	take _took_
do _did_	speak _spoke_	say _said_
go _went_	think _thought_	have _had_
send _sent_	come _came_	tell _told_
be _was/were_	give _gave_	

3   One of the following extracts is from the phone call. The other is incorrect. Which is incorrect and why?

  a   So who else did come?
      Came Stephanie Hughes?

  b   So who else came?
      Did Stephanie Hughes come?

  'a' is incorrect because

  the word order is wrong.

Grammar link

for more on the Past Simple see page 90

Returning a call

In this section, the work on telephoning is expanded to responding to a voice mail message.

1 ▣ **3.6** Play Call 1 and do the questions relating to it before you play Call 2.

Call 1

1 Make sure students have read the questions in 1 before they listen to the recording so that they know exactly what information they are listening for. Reassure them that this is all they are listening for at this stage and they shouldn't worry if they don't understand everything that is said.

2 Allow students to work in pairs to number the message in the correct order and to compare their answers with other pairs before you play the recording again for them to check their answers.

Call 2

Again, make sure students have read the questions before they listen so that they concentrate on listening only for the information they need. Encourage discussion in pairs or small groups for the questions in 6.

Talking about the past

2 Students should not have much difficulty in putting these verbs into the Past Simple, so the time element has been introduced to encourage them to work quickly and to give an element of fun. You could structure the activity as a race, with the first student to write all 14 verbs in the Past Simple and raise their hand being declared the winner.

When checking the answers, you could write the irregular Past Simple forms on the board as students call them out. As they listen to the recording again, ask them to raise their hands every time they hear one of these forms.

3 Students should be able to identify fairly readily that extract a is incorrect because the word order is wrong in both questions.

Direct students' attention to the Grammar link on page 90 which has more information about the formation of the Past Simple.

▣ **3.6**

Call 1

B: Hello. This is Patterson Meats, Sylvia Wright's office. Thank you for calling. I'm afraid I'm not able to take your call right now, but if you'd like to leave a message or send a fax, please do so after the tone, and I'll get back to you as soon as I can.

A: Hello, Sylvia. It's Tim Curtis from the Sydney office. I just wanted to know how the meeting with the people from Tesco Supermarkets went. This is a really good chance for us to start exporting to Britain. I hope their visit was a success. Er, give me a ring when you get in, would you? Bye now.

Call 2

A: Hello. Tim Curtis.

B: Hi, Tim. It's Sylvia here. I got your message.

A: Sylvia, hi. So, how did it go?

B: It went pretty well, I think. They sent three people in the end.

A: Three? Well, that's a good sign.

B: Yeah, there was Bill Andrews, head of meat purchasing. I think you met him when you went to the UK last month.

A: That's right. He seemed pretty interested when I spoke to him then.

B: Yeah, he asked me a lot of questions about our quality control.

A: Uh-huh. I thought he might. I hope you told him he's got no worries there.

B: I certainly did.

A: Good. So who else came? Er, did Stephanie Hughes come?

B: Er, they sent Jonathan Powell from their marketing department instead, and Melanie Burns, who's in charge of imported produce.

A: Oh, right. I didn't meet them in London. So, did you show them the processing plant?

B: I did. There wasn't time to do a tour of the factory, but I showed them the packing department and the freezer units. Then we gave the presentation – me and Ian – and took them out to dinner afterwards.

A: Great. Did they say when they'd let us know? I mean do you think they'll place an order or not?

B: Well, it's too early to say. But I think they were quite impressed.

A: Hm.

B: They said they'd be in touch in the next couple of days or so. They were a bit worried at first about British customers accepting our product. Although they do sell other exotic meats already. Ostrich, for example, and that's quite popular.

A: Erm, excuse me for a moment, Sylvia ... Sorry about that. I just had to sign something. Where were we? Oh, yes, they were worried about UK customers accepting our product, you say?

B: Well, I don't think it's a problem. Er, you know what the Brits are like – animal lovers and all that. They weren't sure if people would accept kangaroo meat as an alternative to beef.

A: Kangaroos are too cute and lovable to eat, huh?

B: Well, something like that. But I told them they're not exactly endangered. There are twice as many kangaroos in Australia as there are Australians. Kangaroo's been on the menu here for years. They agreed it tastes good and, as I said to them, it's a really healthy option – ten times less fat than a beef steak and no chance of getting mad cow disease!

Finding out

Fluency

The aim here is to get students to put into practice all the skills they have learned in the unit so far. They have a choice of subjects on which to base their roleplay and there is plenty of preparation work and guidance before they embark on their calls.

Make sure they don't just rattle off a string of questions when it is their turn to initiate the call. They have a lot of information to find out, but they must listen and react to their partner's answers to one question before they proceed to the next. It might also be useful to go over some of the language they could use to introduce each new question so that the impression of a list is reduced. For example:

By the way, which ...
Oh, and I've been meaning to ask, what ...
And I was wondering how long ...

Draw students' attention to the useful expressions for showing interest in the box at the side. If necessary, practise a few of these around the class by telling individual students some information and getting them to react appropriately. For example:

You: *I've just won a lot of money.*
Student 1: *Great!*
You: *I've just bought a new car.*
Student 2: *Really?*
You: *Someone I haven't seen for twenty years is coming to dinner on Sunday.*
Student 3: *Oh, that's interesting.*

When students have done their roleplays, encourage some of them to perform them for the rest of the class.

If you're short of time

Set *Telephone phrases* Exercises 6 and 7 and *Voice mail* Exercise 3 for homework.

Ask students to do the preparation stage of their roleplays (*Finding out*) at home.

Set the Grammar and Lexis links exercises for homework and check the answers at the beginning of the next class.

Finding out

Fluency Work with a partner. Phone each other in order to find out some information to help you

    1   do business in a foreign city
or **2**   give a presentation
or **3**   attend a job interview

Talk to your partner before you begin and decide on the subject of your phone calls. Think of the language you will need.

Begin your phone call in this way:

Hi, _____ (your partner's name). It's _____ (your name) here. How are things? ... And how's business?

Then use the notes below to help you ask your questions. Ask other questions if you like.

> Remember to show interest in what your partner tells you.
> *Really?*
> *I see.*
> *Right.*
> *Uhuh.*
> *Good.*
> *Great.*
> *Oh, that's interesting.*
>
> Finish your call like this:
> *Anyway, look, I must let you go. Thanks a lot for your help. Speak to you soon. Bye now.*

I A business trip

Listen, I'm going to _____ (city?) on business in a couple of weeks. I know you did some business there a while ago and I just wanted to ask you how it went.

I	Which airline / fly with?	7	meetings go OK?
2	business class?	8	language problems?
3	Where / stay?	9	chance / see much / city?
4	What / food like?	10	What / do / evenings?
5	What / people like?	11	invite / their home?
6	easy to work with?	12	take a present?

2 A presentation

Listen, I'm giving a presentation at _____ (a meeting? a conference?) in a couple of weeks. I know you had to give a presentation a while ago and I just wanted to ask you how it went.

I	Do / talk / your own?	7	How many / visuals?
2	How long / take / prepare?	8	tell jokes?
3	How big / audience?	9	give / handouts?
4	How long / speak for?	10	take questions / the end?
5	nervous?	11	any difficult ones?
6	use PowerPoint?	12	How / deal with them?

3 A job interview

Listen, I'm going for an interview at _____ (company?) in a couple of weeks. I know you had an interview with them a while ago and I just wanted to ask you how it went.

I	How long / interview / last?	7	trickiest question?
2	How many interviewers?	8	ask / personal questions?
3	How friendly?	9	Have / do / a test?
4	say what / looking for?	10	ask them / questions?
5	refer / your CV?	11	What / salary / like?
6	How interested / qualifications?	12	offer you / job?

4 Keeping track

When the result of a meeting is to schedule more meetings it usually signals trouble.
Mike Murphy, business writer

Checking understanding

1 When you take part in meetings in English, it is easy to lose track of what people are saying. Who do you generally find the hardest to understand?

> native speakers   other non-native speakers   people who speak too fast
> people with strong accents

2 Here are six simple ways of checking what someone has just said. Write in the missing pairs of words.

> see + be   catch + slow   missed + say   follow + run
> 'm + go   understand + explain

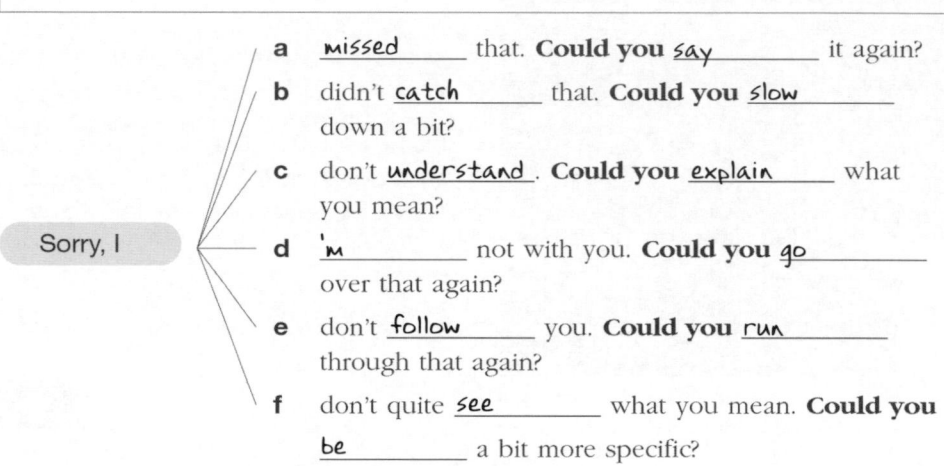

Sorry, I

a _missed_ that. **Could you _say_** it again?

b didn't **catch** that. **Could you slow** down a bit?

c don't **understand**. **Could you explain** what you mean?

d **'m** not with you. **Could you go** over that again?

e don't **follow** you. **Could you run** through that again?

f don't quite **see** what you mean. **Could you be** a bit more specific?

3 Which of the above do you use when you

a didn't hear? [a] [b]   **b** didn't understand? [c] [d] [e] [f]

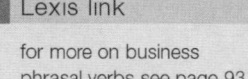
Lexis link

for more on business phrasal verbs see page 93

4 Match the phrasal verbs from 2 to the meanings on the right.

a slow down   **1** mention quickly
b go over   **2** speak more slowly
c run through   **3** examine, discuss

5 Can you remember the phrases in 2 when you need them? Work with a partner. Take it in turns to throw dice and try to produce the exact expressions using the words below to help you.

missed –	not with you –	didn't catch –	don't follow you –	don't understand –	don't quite see –
say –	go over –	slow –	run through –	explain –	mean –
again?	again?	bit?	again?	what you mean?	bit more specific?

4 Keeping track

Preparation:

Bring to class enough dice for pairs to have one die each for activity 5.

Meetings in a foreign language pose a problem for many business students. Loss of concentration when meetings drag on is one issue, and inability to obtain clarification on points that have been missed or misunderstood can be a tremendous obstacle to business success.

This unit provides some simple techniques which students can use to keep themselves abreast of what is being said. Then they learn some formulae for asking for clarification, checking what people have said, and asking them to repeat or slow down. These can go a long way towards making students more adept at dealing with meetings in English.

The grammatical focus is on comparatives and superlatives, and the lexical focus is on phrasal verbs.

This first section begins with an examination of the problem of conducting meetings in a foreign language.

Warm-up

Read the quotation by Mike Murphy at the beginning of the unit to the class and ask for reactions. How often have they attended meetings which they felt were a complete waste of time? How do they avoid this happening?

Checking understanding

1 The aim is for students to identify what they personally find the hardest in meetings and who they find the hardest to understand. Have a class discussion on this question and encourage students to be honest about what they find most difficult. If anyone has an interesting story about a time they misunderstood something in a meeting, they should be encouraged to tell the class about it.

2, 3 Once they have completed the gaps and identified which expressions you can use when you didn't hear and which when you didn't understand, give students practice in actually using these expressions by saying something to them in a way that will make it very hard for them to understand, for example, mumbling, speaking too fast or too softly, being too general, using too much technical jargon, etc. Select individual students and elicit an appropriate response from them.

4 Direct students' attention to the Lexis link on page 93 which introduces some more common phrasal verbs which are frequently used in business.

5 This game helps students to remember the key expressions by giving them only a few prompt words to use to reproduce them. They roll the die and recreate the sentence for that number. Make sure that students have covered Exercise 2 before they play so that they have to reproduce the expressions from memory.

Sorry?

In this section, students practise pinpointing the exact information that they have missed.

Clarifying specific points

1, 2 🔲 **4.1** Once students have completed the gaps and have checked the answers by listening to the recording, you could give them more practice by devising some more prompt sentences to feed to individual students who then have to come up with appropriate clarification questions. Respond to their questions and encourage them to end the exchange with one of the expressions used in the exercise.

Some extra prompts you might use:

Our main difficulty is the timing of the project.
We have to deliver these units by February 25th.
New equipment will cost us at least $25,000.
Yolanda Squatbush told me about the problem.
The components are sent from the warehouse in Pocatello.
It will take at least six months to get the project started.

Alternatively, you could ask the students to prepare some suitable prompts themselves and have conversations in pairs.

Fluency

3 Students turn to their respective pages and read out the Budweiser texts, asking for clarification where necessary. Make sure that as they do this they are genuinely making the words in bold difficult to hear or understand and that their clarification questions are appropriate.

4 Students work in pairs to put the summary in order.

5 Elicit examples of comparatives and superlatives. Ask students to underline them in the summary. When checking the answers, write the word on the board and elicit the superlative form of each comparative, and vice versa.

Direct students' attention to the Grammar link on page 92 where there is more work on comparatives and superlatives. If your students need more work on this point, you could do the exercises in class.

🔲 **4.1**

Extract 1
A: The problem is money.
B: Sorry, **what** did you say?
A: The problem is money.
B: Oh, as usual.

Extract 2
A: We have to reach a decision by next week.
B: Sorry, **when** did you say?
A: Next week.
B: Oh, I see.

Extract 3
A: An upgrade will cost $3,000.
B: Sorry, **how much** did you say?
A: $3,000, at least.
B: Oh, as much as that?

Extract 4
A: Ildikó Dudás spoke to me about it yesterday.
B: Sorry, **who** did you say?
A: Ildikó Dudás – from the Budapest office.
B: Oh, yes, of course.

Extract 5
A: The company is based in Taipei.
B: Sorry, **where** did you say?
A: In Taipei.
B: Oh, really?

Extract 6
A: The whole project might take eighteen months.
B: Sorry, **how long** did you say?
A: Eighteen months.
B: Oh, as long as that?

Sorry?

Clarifying specific points

1 In meetings where you are discussing facts and figures, saying *Sorry?* or *I don't understand* is not always enough. Sometimes you need to be more precise. Look at the following short extracts from meetings. Complete the second speaker's responses with the correct question words.

who	where	when	what	how long	how much

1 **A** The problem is money.
   B Sorry, **what** did you say?
   A The problem is money.
   B Oh, as usual.

2 **A** We have to reach a decision by next week.
   B Sorry, **when** did you say?
   A Next week.
   B Oh, I see.

3 **A** An upgrade will cost $3,000.
   B Sorry, **how much** did you say?
   A $3,000, at least.
   B Oh, as much as that?

4 **A** Ildikó Dudás spoke to me about it yesterday.
   B Sorry, **who** did you say?
   A Ildikó Dudás – from the Budapest office.
   B Oh, yes, of course.

5 **A** The company is based in Taipei.
   B Sorry, **where** did you say?
   A In Taipei.
   B Oh, really?

6 **A** The whole project might take eighteen months.
   B Sorry, **how long** did you say?
   A Eighteen months.
   B Oh, as long as that?

2 ▭ **4.1** Listen to the conversations in 1 and check your answers.

Fluency

3 Work with a partner to practise clarifying specific points. You are going to read about two different companies, both called Budweiser. Speaker A see page 118. Speaker B see page 122.

4 Work with a partner to put this summary of the texts you read in 3 in the correct order. The first and last parts are in the right place.

☐ **1** American Budweiser is the world's bestselling
☐ **11** than forty different countries. Its slogan is
☐ **7** other hand, is one
☐ **10** fewer resources than US Budweiser, it markets its product in more
☐ **4** output than its nearest
☐ **8** of the world's oldest and most
☐ **2** brand of beer. The company that makes it is the biggest in
☐ **6** slogan was 'Budweiser: the King of Beers'. Czech Budweiser, on the
☐ **9** famous beers. With far
☐ **5** competitor, Heineken. By far its most successful advertising
☐ **3** the world with 50% greater
☐ **12** simply: 'Budweiser: the Beer of Kings'.

Grammar link

for more on comparatives and superlatives see page 92

5 How many comparatives and superlatives can you find in the summary?

2   5

Didn't I say that?

A So that's $13 million.

B 13 million? Isn't it 30?

A Oh, yes, sorry. 30 million.

A These are the figures for 2001.

B 2001? Don't you mean 2002?

A No, I mean 2001.

A This represents 8.6% of total sales.

B 8.6? Shouldn't that be 6.8?

A Yes, 6.8. Didn't I say that?

1 People sometimes disagree about facts in meetings. One way of politely querying something is simply to repeat the part you think is wrong and ask a question. Look at the examples on the left.

2 Work with a partner. Take it in turns to read out the following false information. Query each other using the correct information from the box. The first one has been done for you as an example.

> Finland   music   1997   Ford   Korean   software   ~~the Netherlands~~

a The biggest Benelux country is Belgium.
Belgium? Don't you mean the Netherlands?

b Daewoo is a well-known Japanese car manufacturer.
Japanese? Don't you mean Korean?

c China regained control of Hong Kong in 1998.
1998? Don't you mean 1997?

d Microsoft is the world's leading computer hardware manufacturer.
Hardware? Don't you mean software?

e Rolls-Royce was eventually taken over by General Motors.
General Motors? Don't you mean Ford?

f America has more mobile phones per household than any other country.
America? Don't you mean Finland?

g MTV is the biggest news channel in the world.
News? Don't you mean music?

3 Write down a few false business facts of your own. Read them out to the rest of the class. Can they correct you?

4 4.2 Listen to an extract from a meeting and tick the sentences which are correct.

a The meeting is being held to discuss last month's sales figures. ✓
b Overall, sales are up by 2.6%. **6.2%**
c The best results are in Denmark and Norway. ✓
d 30,000 units have been sold in Scandinavia. ✓
e Last month was June. July
f John Munroe is head of Northern Europe. Jim
g Munroe is in Scotland at the moment. He is not in Scotland. He is playing golf.

5 Listen again and correct the mistakes in 4.

6 The following expressions are used to query information you are less sure about. They were all in the conversation you just listened to. Complete them.

sound	mistake
right	sure

a Are you _sure_ ?   **c** That can't be _right_ .
b There must be some _mistake_ .   **d** That doesn't _sound_ right to me.

Didn't I say that?

In this section, students practise techniques for dealing politely and appropriately with situations where they disagree about facts in meetings.

Querying information

Warm-up

Ask students if they have had any experience of having to correct inaccuracies in what someone has said. Encourage them to tell the class of any incidents they can remember and what strategies they used for correcting the person.

1   Read the explanation with the class and then ask them to look at the dialogues in the side panel.

    Point out that in each case B is politely correcting a factual mistake that A has made and that B is sure that his or her information is correct. By doing this indirectly, asking a question rather than simply stating what is wrong, the correction is softened. Intonation is also important here. A tone of mild puzzlement is polite in these situations, intonation suggesting astonishment would not be polite. Read one of B's lines first with intonation suggesting astonishment and then with intonation suggesting slight puzzlement so that students can hear the difference.

    Then ask students to practise the dialogues in pairs.

2   Students take turns to read and respond to the statements. Go round making sure that their intonation is appropriate. Encourage students to also use *Isn't it ...?* and *Shouldn't that be ...?* where appropriate.

3   Students work individually to invent their own false statements for the rest of the class to correct. This could be done in the form of a team game with teams writing a series of false statements and taking turns to call out each one. The opposing team has to come up with an appropriate correction in order to win a point.

4   ▭ **4.2** Give students time to read the sentences before you play the recording so they can identify exactly what information they are listening for. Check the answers before going on to Exercise 5.

5   Play the recording again and then ask individual students to correct sentences b, e, f and g.

6   The expressions given here are useful when something does not sound quite right, but you are less sure about what is wrong.

    Students should be able to complete the expressions without listening to the recording again, but be prepared to play it if necessary. Note that these expressions don't represent the total response to a mistake. The person using them is likely to go on to say what they think the real facts are, as in the dialogues in the box at the top of the page:
    Isn't it ...? Don't you mean ...? Shouldn't that be ...?

    You could invite students to make up some more false statements, perhaps with mistakes not quite as obvious as the ones they wrote before, and practise using the expressions to respond to each other's statements. Make sure they use follow-up questions to establish what they think the facts are.

▭ **4.2**

A: OK, so, just to give you a summary of the sales figures for last month.
B: Last month? **Don't you mean** this month?
A: No, I mean last month. This month's figures aren't ready yet, are they?
B: Oh, no, of course not. Sorry.
A: So, overall, sales for *last* month are up again – by 2.6%, in fact, which is pretty good.
C: Er, 2.6%? **Shouldn't that be** 6.2?
A: Yeah, up by 6.2%. Didn't I say that?
C: No, you said 2.6.
A: Oh, ... right. Well, you know what I mean. So, anyway, the thing is, we're getting the best results in Denmark and Norway – 30,000 units.

C: 30,000? **That doesn't sound right to me**. 13,000, **surely**?
A: No, the figures are here – Denmark and Norway: 30,000 units.
B: Denmark and Norway? **Are you sure? That can't be right**. Sales have never been good in Scandinavia.
A: That's just the point. Sales in Scandinavia are usually terrible, but they were excellent in June.
C: June? **Isn't it** July we're talking about?
A: July! Yes, of course, July! If you'd just let me finish! What I want to know is if we could sell product in Scandinavia in June, ...
C: July.
A: ... in July, then why can't we sell it there every month?

B: Good point. Have you spoken to John about it?
A: John? **You mean** Jim.
B: Jim, yes. Whoever's in charge of Northern Europe these days.
A: Jim Munroe. I couldn't. He's had to fly to Scotland. His mother's ill apparently.
C: **There must be some mistake**.
A: Hm?
C: Well, I saw Jim this morning as I was coming in – on his way to play golf, by the look of it.
A: What? **Are you sure?** Wait till I see him!

7 It doesn't matter how many of these the students actually get right, as disagreement over the facts will lead to more language practice. Students can find the correct answers on page 124 of their books.

Pointing out discrepancies

8 Discrepancies are mismatches with information that someone has given earlier. Ask a pair of students to demonstrate the example dialogue.

Fluency

9 Students turn to their respective pages and practise the dialogues. The discrepancies are fairly obvious, but you might like to check in a feedback session that everyone has understood them. You could ask students to explain the discrepancies for homework.

Speaker A
a Dublin is in Ireland, not Scotland.
b Bordeaux is a French wine, not a German wine.
c Ulrike can't be one of the speaker's closest friends if he or she only met her yesterday.
d Someone who smokes as many as 30 a day cannot be said to have nearly given up smoking.
e If the woman is the speaker's wife, he cannot introduce someone to her husband as that is himself.

Speaker B
a One of each means one of each sex. There are only two sexes, male and female, so if the speaker has three children they can't be one of each sex. Two of them must be the same sex.
b Lisbon is the capital of Portugal, so the French negotiating team would not have their headquarters there.
c Dutch is the language of the Netherlands, not Denmark.
d If the managing director is 70, then his grandfather is unlikely still to be alive, let alone running the company.
e A company called Network Software is more likely to make computer software than domestic appliances.

The briefing meeting

🔲 **4.3** Go through the instructions carefully and allow students time to read the notes so they know exactly what information they are listening for.

The briefing meeting is quite complicated, so you may need to play it in sections and repeat parts of it.

When you have checked the answers, ask the students if they have ever experienced a situation where they were expecting to do one job and suddenly found that things had changed and they had to do something completely different.

If you're short of time

Omit *Checking understanding* Exercise 5 or ask students to complete the sentences for homework.

Set *Sorry?* Exercise 5 for homework.

Set *Didn't I say that?* Exercise 3 for homework and ask students to read out their sentences in the next class for other students to correct. Omit Exercise 7.

Set the Grammar and Lexis links exercises for homework and check the answers at the beginning of the next class.

🔲 **4.3**

A: So, welcome to Tokyo, Matt. It's good to have you on the team.
B: Thanks, Sally. It's good to be here.
A: I think you're going to enjoy your three months here, Matt. Now, this is Sharon Hall. She's the person you'll mostly be working with on the project.
C: Hi, Matt.
B: Hi ... **Sorry, I didn't catch your name**.
C: Sharon. Sharon Hall.
B: Hi, Sharon.
A: Sharon's in charge of our corporate loan department. She's sorting out an office for you at the moment. You'll probably be working over at Empire House.
B: **Sorry, where did you say?**
C: Empire House. It's our office building on the other side of town.
B: Oh, OK.
A: Don't worry, I'll take you over there later. Now, you and Sharon will be reporting directly to Daniel Cash, our VP for corporate finance.
B: **Sorry, who?**

C: Daniel Cash.
B: Oh, right. **And he's the vice-president for ...?**
A: Corporate finance. I thought you two had met? Anyway, Daniel's had to rush off to a meeting, but he told me to say he'd meet you both at two tomorrow.
B: **Sorry, I don't understand**. I thought the whole team was meeting tomorrow at nine?
A: We were. But, er, something came up. Anyway, Sharon can fill you in on most of it. Sharon?
C: Yes, you'll have two assistants working with you, Matt. Janet White and Robin Sellers.
B: OK, (writing it down) Janet White and **Robin ...?**
C: Sellers. Janet's our top mergers and acquisitions specialist. I think you two will get on well. She'll be helping you with your research. And Robin's your interpreter. He's very familiar with business procedures here – as well as being fluent in Japanese, of course.

B: **Sorry, I'm not with you. Interpreter?** What do I need an interpreter for? **I thought I was just here as an advisor**.
A: Erm ... The situation's changed a little since we last spoke, Matt. We'd now like you to lead the negotiations with the Sapporo Bank. In fact, that will be your main responsibility.
B: **I don't quite see what you mean, Sally**. Erm, I'm no negotiator, especially not for a takeover as big as this. I'm the guy with the pocket calculator. I just make sure the figures add up.
C: Oh, come on, Matt. You're too modest. We know your track record. Janet can take care of the figures. We want you to lead the first round of negotiations on the 13th.
B: **You mean the 30th, right?** The 13th is next week.
A: That's right. We've scheduled the first meeting for next Wednesday. Janet will be able to brief you before then. This is your big chance. I'm counting on you, Matt. I know you won't let me down.

7   How good is your business general knowledge? <u>Underline</u> the correct information below.

World business records

1 The number of Cokes consumed in the world per day exceeds
ten million / a hundred million / <u>a billion</u>

2 The highest paid employee of the 20th century on a salary of $200 million was
Jack Welch of General Electric / <u>Michael Eisner of Disney</u> / Steve Jobs of Apple

3 The world's bestselling car ever was
the Mini / the Citroen CV / <u>the VW Beetle</u>

4 The world's oldest airline is
<u>KLM</u> / British Airways / Singapore Airlines

5 The world's bestselling business paper is
The Wall Street Journal / The Financial Times / <u>The Yomiuri Shimbun</u>

6 The world's second most powerful brand name after Coca-Cola is
<u>Microsoft</u> / Sony / Mercedes

7 The world's most popular toy is
<u>Barbie</u> / Lego / PlayStation

8 The single invention with the highest global turnover is
the personal computer / <u>the electric light</u> / the automobile

9 The world's biggest exporter of computer software is
the USA / <u>Ireland</u> / India

Answers on page 124

Now work with a partner to practise querying information. Take it in turns to read out your answers to the quiz. Query anything you think is wrong.

Pointing out discrepancies

8   Sometimes what people say in meetings conflicts with what they said earlier:

A   Eight out of ten members of staff liked the proposal. So, 90% is a good result.
B   **Wait a minute**. 90%? **I thought you said** eight out of ten ...
A   Oh, yeah. Sorry, 80%, of course.

Fluency

9   Work in pairs to practise pointing out discrepancies. Speaker A see page 118. Speaker B see page 122.

The briefing meeting

🔊 4.3 A mergers and acquisitions specialist has been transferred to the Tokyo office of his bank to work as part of a project team during a takeover bid. He is attending his first briefing meeting, but things don't go quite as he expected. Listen and complete his notes.

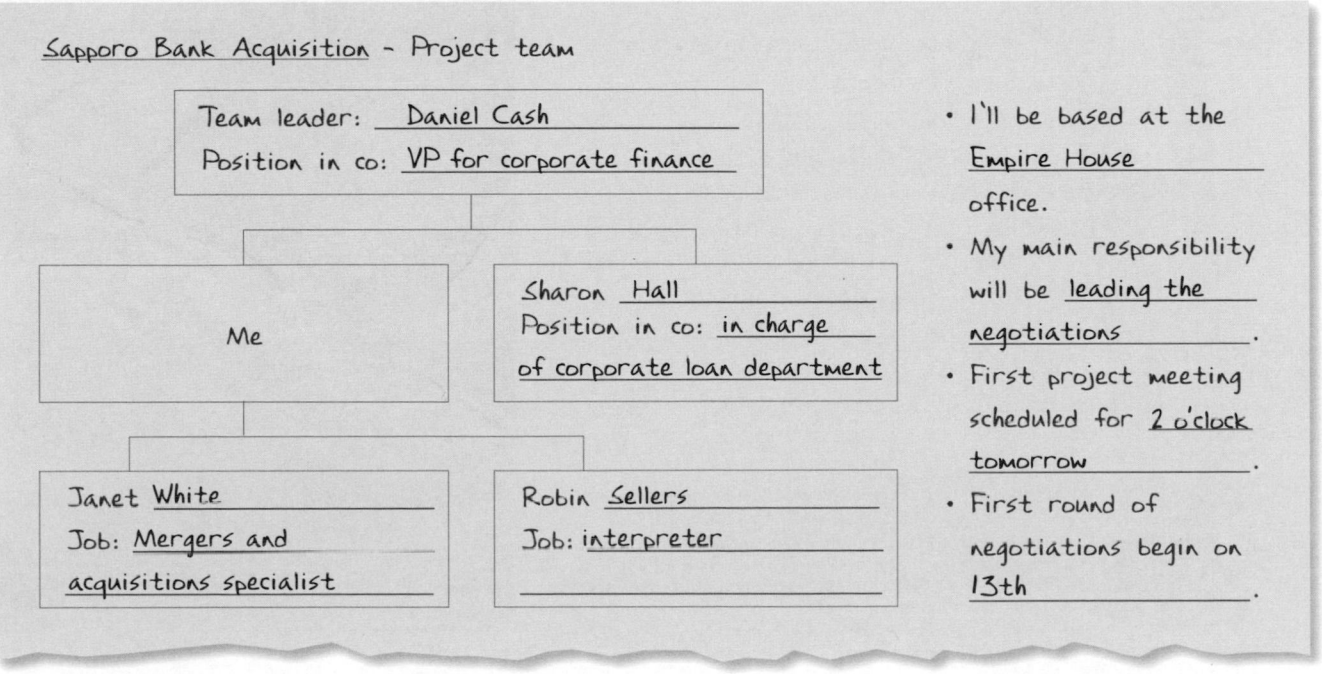

<u>Sapporo Bank Acquisition</u> – Project team

Team leader: ___Daniel Cash___
Position in co: ___VP for corporate finance___

Me

Sharon ___Hall___
Position in co: ___in charge of corporate loan department___

Janet ___White___
Job: ___Mergers and acquisitions specialist___

Robin ___Sellers___
Job: ___interpreter___

• I'll be based at the ___Empire House___ office.
• My main responsibility will be ___leading the negotiations___.
• First project meeting scheduled for ___2 o'clock tomorrow___.
• First round of negotiations begin on ___13th___.

5 Speed of life

If everything seems under control, you're just not going fast enough.

Mario Andretti, Formula One racing driver

1   Are we all working harder than we used to? Does it seem like your working week is getting longer and longer? Read the texts below. Which statistics surprise you most?

Thinking space

When Dr Rosemary Stewart asked 160 British managers to keep a diary of their activities for a month, she discovered the average manager had only nine 30-minute periods without interruption. Those she interviewed complained that 'there is just no time to think' and that 'it's one damn thing after another'.

Multi-tasking

Canadian professor, Dr Henry Mintzberg found that half the tasks managers perform take only nine minutes or less. Only 10% last more than an hour. Typically, executives work very fast on several things at once, and welcome any interruption to their schedule to stop and take a break.

Land of the free?

According to a survey published in *Wired* magazine, US executives work 25% longer hours than they did in the 1970s. Market researchers at Kellogg's discovered that 13% of them eat breakfast in the car. The most shocking study shows that the average American father spends just six minutes a day talking to his kids.

Tough at the top

In a recent interview for a profile of global business leaders, famous workaholic Bill Gates revealed that he can at last afford to slow down. 'There are days that I work 14 hours,' he admits, 'but most days I don't work more than 12 hours. On weekends I rarely work more than 8 hours.'

2   How pressured do you feel at work? Indicate your level of pressure on the thermometer on the left. Then compare with other people in the class.

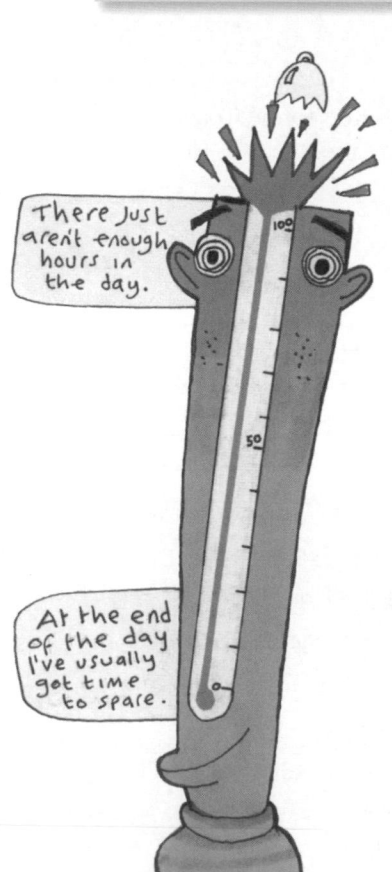

There just aren't enough hours in the day.

At the end of the day I've usually got time to spare.

Time management

1   Look at these strategies for managing your time.

- say 'no' more often
- make lists of things to do
- throw things away
- keep a record of how long each task takes you
- hold fewer meetings
- screen phone calls
- check e-mail at specific times of the day
- delegate more
- plan ahead
- maximise your 'uptime'
- do 'nasty' jobs first

Do you do any of these things? Add your own ideas to the list.

5 Speed of life

This unit is about pressure at work, the pace of business life, time management and relaxation.

Students start by reading some statistics about working hours and working practices. They are invited to comment on what surprises them most about these statistics, and then talk about how much pressure they feel they are under at work.

The next section investigates some strategies for managing time better and students are invited to add their own ideas to the list. A reading text, written by a management training specialist, then offers advice on a technique for finding a magic hour in which to catch up with everything you've been too busy to do.

Students then listen to four speakers talking about how the need to be faster than the competition affects their work. They match statements to speakers and then relate the information to their own industries.

The final section looks at ways in which people unwind at the end of the day. Students listen to a recording and identify the things that each speaker does to relax.

In this first section, students read and talk about working hours and pressure at work.

Warm-up

Ask students how far they agree with the quotation from Mario Andretti at the beginning of this unit. How far is it the ethos of their company or industry? What problems does the pace of modern business have for them? What, if anything, do they think should be done about it?

1 Ask students to read the text individually. Test comprehension by asking each student to write two or three questions on the text for other students to answer. Students take turns to choose another student and ask one of their questions. That student then chooses another student, and so on.

Alternatively, you could have two teams and score points for correct answers.

Ask students if any of them regard themselves as workaholics. It is unlikely that any of them can match Bill Gates, but it might be interesting to see how many hours a day or week they work. To make this more interactive, you could ask them to stand in line with the person who works the longest hours at one end, and the person who works the shortest hours at the other.

2 Each student should decide where on the stress thermometer they should appear and then compare notes with others. Ask them to comment on what they think the causes of their stress levels are. Is it just a matter of long working hours or are there other factors?

Time management

This section investigates some techniques for time management and focuses on a strategy recommended by a management training specialist for finding a magic hour in which to do all the things you want to do but never seem to have time for.

1 Encourage students to discuss the list in pairs or small groups and to come up with some ideas of their own. In a class feedback session, write the new ideas on the board and ask students to say which strategies they find most successful.

You could also establish with a show of hands who uses which of the strategies and which strategies are the most popular.

2 Focus students' attention on the photograph and ask questions such as *What is the man doing? Where is he? Does he look relaxed or stressed? Is this something you would like to do in the middle of the working day? If not, is there anything you would like to do as a break from work?*

Ask students to read the text individually. Make sure they follow the instructions and write down the things the text tells them to write, so that they have something to discuss in the next exercise.

3 Allow students to compare what they have written in pairs or small groups, then conduct a class feedback session.

Ask students if they have read any 'self-help' books on avoiding stress. What do they themselves do to relax? What works and what doesn't work? Compile a list of *dos* and *don't*s for the classroom wall.

2 In *Getting Things Done*, management training specialist Roger Black talks about 'the magic hour', an extra hour to catch up with everything you've been too busy to do. Read the text and do what he suggests.

3 Compare what you wrote with other people in the class. Is there anything everybody wanted to use the extra hour for?

The Magic Hour

Imagine you have one extra hour every week: your 169th hour. It occurs whenever you want it to, and you can do whatever you want with it. You don't have to see anyone that you don't want to see, or write letters to them,
5 or do anything that you're currently feeling guilty about.

- Write down five things that would make you happy in that hour (don't give yourself any restrictions or nagging guilt feelings about other jobs to be done).
- Write down five things that would give pleasure to
10 someone else in that hour.
- Finally, write down five important things that you have been putting off, that you could at least start in the hour.

Then consider: If you could have last week all over again, where could you fit in the magic hour? Resolve to fit it into
15 this week at that same point. If you find that simply the process of deciding to do this makes you feel good, you probably are not making enough decisions of this nature. Make the magic hour a weekly habit.

Stepping up the pace

1 **5.1** Listen to four business people talking about how being faster than the competition affects their work. Which industry does each speaker belong to?

Speaker 1 <u>car</u>   Speaker 3 <u>computer</u>

Speaker 2 <u>electronics</u>   Speaker 4 <u>finance</u>

2 Each speaker makes three main points from the list below. Write the number of the speaker in each box.

  a The industry is more and more research-led. ☐ 2

  b You can't stop competitors copying your ideas. ☐ 2

  c You need to move inventory very rapidly. ☐ 3

  d It's the little details that add value to your product or service. ☐ 1

  e There's no customer loyalty anymore. ☐ 4

  f It's very difficult to differentiate your product from the competition. ☐ 1

  g As much effort goes into branding as into technology. ☐ 2

  h Customers are better informed about the services you offer. ☐ 4

  i Product lead times are getting shorter and shorter. ☐ 1

  j Technology is advancing almost daily. ☐ 3

  k Costs are steadily falling. ☐ 3

  l You're open for business all the time. ☐ 4

3 <u>Underline</u> the points in 2 which are also true for your industry. Discuss them with other people in the class.

4 Speed is important at every stage of the development of a product or service. Do you agree? Discuss with a partner.

Take it easy!

 5.2 We asked ten people how they unwind at the end of the day. Listen and write down the main thing(s) they do. Do you do any of the same things?

1 <u>have a drink</u>   6 <u>chat on the phone</u>

2 <u>go for a run</u>   7 <u>read</u>

3 <u>read kids a story</u>   8 <u>watch TV or a video</u>

4 <u>drink, music, foot massage</u>   9 <u>go out with friends</u>

5 <u>cook a good dinner</u>   10 <u>have a bath</u>

Stepping up the pace

In this section, students listen to four business people in competitive industries for whom being faster than the competition is vital. They discuss the implications of speed in their own line of work.

1 ▣ **5.1** Play the recording. Students identify and make notes on the industries involved. Check answers with the class before moving on to Exercise 2.

2 Allow students to read through the statements and discuss in pairs before playing the recording again. Students might like to see how much they can remember of what was said.

3 Students work individually to decide which of the statements are true for their industries and then discuss this in groups. If you have a large class and students are from several different industries, you might like to get a representative from each industry to give a mini-presentation to the class on the points which are true for them. These could be prepared for homework, if necessary.

4 Students discuss the statement in pairs and then report back to the class on their discussions. Encourage them to back up their arguments with examples.

Take it easy!

▣ **5.2** After all the work on stress and fast-paced business life, this section on unwinding and relaxing should come as something of a relief.

Ask students to tell the class what they do to relax after a hard day at work and to share any successful relaxation techniques that they employ.

Play the recording for students to identify and note down what each of the ten speakers does to unwind. Then continue the class discussion by finding out if any of them do the same things.

If you're short of time

Have students write comprehension questions on the texts on page 20 at home to exchange with other students in the next lesson.

Set *Time management* Exercise 2 for homework and have the discussion in the next lesson.

▣ **5.1**
Speaker 1
I am an engineer for a car company in Detroit. These days we all have access to the same technology, which means that we're really competing with other car makers on how fast we can develop, manufacture and launch new models. Ten years ago, it took maybe six years to develop a new car. Today, we take two years. One day it may be six months. I hope I'm not working here by then! If I'm honest, I'd have to say the cars we build are basically the same as what our competitors build. Frankly, you pay $20,000, you get pretty much the same family car, whether it's a Ford or a Renault. Two things you *can* beat the competition on are little extras like electric mirrors on an economy model and delivery times. I mean, at Toyota, you can order your car on Monday, have it customised to your requirements and drive it away on Friday. That's what I call added value!

Speaker 2
Erm, I work for a consumer electronics company in the Netherlands. We make DVD players, digital video cameras, that kind of thing. I can tell you being a major player in this business simply depends on how fast you can innovate. Of course, if your researchers come up with a new idea, you know your competitors are going to steal it within two to three weeks. So you need a constant supply of new ideas. I've heard at Sony they develop two new products per working hour, which is just amazing. Obviously, Sony is a household name. And that's the other thing you can trade on in this business – your name. You'd be surprised how much more people will pay just to have the right name on their Walkman, which, of course, is Sony, although I'm not supposed to say that!

Speaker 3
OK, well, I work in the computer industry

and, believe me, in this business, if you slow down for a instant, you die. Take component costs. The price of those is coming down about 1% a week. At the same time, the amount of information you can get on a microchip is going to double about every 18 months. So, whatever you manufacture this week, someone will be able to do it better for less money next week! So you don't want product piling up in your warehouses. Take a company like Dell. Apparently, they completely turn around their entire stock every five days. Amazing! But that's what you have to do when you're selling products that are still developing to a market that's still developing using technology that's still developing day by day.

Speaker 4
Erm, I work in fund management, which is now a 24-hour, seven-days-a-week business. Your local branch of Barclays may close at four in the afternoon, and the manager goes home to her husband and kids, but we never stop! The stock markets trade around the clock. And so do we. The thing these days is that people have constant and instant access to information via the Internet, so they're all amateur fund managers! If they spot an investment you missed, they want to know why. Being quick to see opportunities is essential. If you fail, the client will just take their business somewhere else. Sometimes I feel like I'm playing a never-ending game of roulette with other people's money. I usually only sleep about five or six hours a night. And I generally get up to check the markets at least once. I mean, if you were in a casino, you wouldn't walk away and leave your chips at the table, now would you?

▣ **5.2**
1
The first thing I do is make myself a nice gin and tonic. The second thing I do is make myself another!

2
If it's a warm evening, I usually go for a run after work. Otherwise, I'll go to the gym and work out for an hour or so. It helps me clear my mind and keeps me fit.

3
I always try to be home in time to tell my kids a bedtime story. I've got really good at it. I don't think there's a single storybook they haven't got. The funny thing is, they always want the same story.

4
Drink. Music. Foot massage – if my husband's in the mood.

5
I live alone, but I love cooking, so I make sure I have a really good dinner every evening – two courses and a decent bottle of wine.

6
I chat on the phone for hours. My phone bills are enormous!

7
Erm, read mostly. Non-fiction. I'm just finishing a history of Japan at the moment. A thousand pages, but absolutely brilliant!

8
Television or a video usually. It's all rubbish, I know, but I can just let my mind switch off.

9
Go home, freshen up and go out on the town. Not every night, obviously, but quite often. After a day of insanity, it's great just to relax with friends.

10
Never mind candle-lit dinners. Try candle-lit baths. Lots of bath oils. And maybe a bit of classical music. Much more fun. Especially if you have company.

6 Business travel

Aspects of business travel covered in this unit include attitudes to travel, requests that business travellers might make, and methods of coping with nightmare journeys involving a succession of problems. Students read about the modern phenomenon of living simultaneously in London and New York and commuting between the two. This stimulates an activity on differences between English in the USA and Britain. The unit closes with some practice of things people say when they meet business colleagues at the airport.

This unit teaches some useful expressions for talking about opinions on business travel, making requests, dealing with problems and greeting people at the airport, and making polite conversation.

The grammatical focus is on polite question forms and the lexical focus is on collocations relating to travel.

In this first section, students have an opportunity to explore their attitudes to business travel and talk about what they like and dislike about it. They are introduced to some ways of emphasising opinions and some words other than *like* which they can use to make their conversations about likes and dislikes more varied and interesting.

Warm-up

Ask your students to complete the sentence *Business travel is ...* in any way they like and then share their sentences with the class.

1   Find out how often your students travel on business, where they generally go and whether or not they enjoy it. Put a list of their ideas for the worst things about business travel on the board and encourage them to negotiate with each other to number these in order, starting with 1 as the very worst thing.

Sentence-building

2   To make this more interactive, or to check the answers, you could get individual students to pick another student and then read out words from the first three sections for the other student to finish. That student then chooses another student and reads another set of words for completion by their chosen student, and so on.

3   Direct students' attention to the Lexis link on page 95 where they will find some useful vocabulary for talking about business trips. If you have time, you might like to start with the first two exercises on page 95, calling out the first part of the collocation for the students to complete. They could do Exercise 3 for homework.

Go through the expressions for adding emphasis to opinions and then put students into groups to practise using them. Encourage them from now on to use these expressions when they want to give a strong opinion.

6 Business travel

There is not much to say about most airplane journeys. Anything remarkable must be disastrous, so you define a good flight by negatives: you didn't get hijacked, you didn't crash, you didn't throw up, you weren't late, you weren't nauseated by the food. *Paul Theroux, travel writer*

1 Do you ever travel on business? If not, would you like to? What do you think are the worst things about business travel?

Sentence-building

2 Combine one word from each section to make at least ten sentences. Start by making collocations from columns 3 and 4. Add your own ideas, if you like.

		late	interesting people
		getting	problems
		losing	jams
		the endless	lag
		flight	my luggage
don't like		meeting	food
can't stand		tight	queues
hate		missing	schedules
dread		finding out	nights
like		strange	lost
look forward to		language	my family
enjoy		jet	the office
love		getting away from	about different cultures
		traffic	foreign places
		having	new experiences
		being away from	delays
		visiting	

Lexis link

for more on the vocabulary of business trips see page 95

3 Look at these ways of emphasising your opinions:

What I really like is *finding out about different cultures.*
What I hate most is *being away from my family.*
The thing I love most is *visiting foreign places.*
The best thing for me is *getting out of the office for a few days.*
The worst thing for me is *flight delays.*

Work in groups. Tell other people in the group what you like and dislike most about travelling.

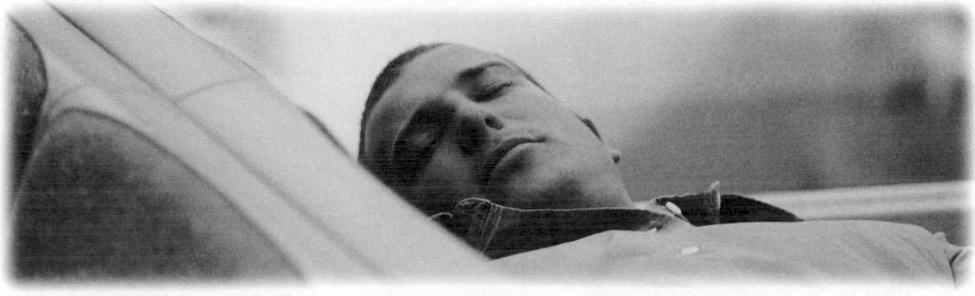

On the move

1 **▭ 6.1** Listen to eighteen short conversations involving people travelling on business. Where are the speakers? Write the numbers of the conversations under the correct location below.

In the taxi

| 7 | 12 | 16 |

On the plane

| 5 | 9 | 15 |

At check-in

| 2 | 4 | 10 |

At customs

| 3 | 11 | 14 |

In departures

| 8 | 13 | 18 |

At the hotel

| 1 | 6 | 17 |

Polite requests and enquiries

2 Now match the halves of the following questions. They were all in the conversations you just listened to.

1 Could I   **a** what time you stop serving dinner?

2 Could you   **b** have your room number, please?

3 Would you mind   **c** switch off your laptop now, please, sir?

4 Can you tell me   **d** not smoking, please?

5 Would you please   **e** to open your luggage, please, madam?

6 Could I ask you   **f** make sure your seatbelt is fastened?

7 Do you think I could **g** send a fax from?

8 Is there somewhere I could **h** have an alarm call at half past six tomorrow morning?

Grammar link

for more on polite question forms see page 94

3 Which first halves of the questions above could go before:

... borrow your mobile? **1, 7**

... buy some stamps? **1, 7, 8**

... hurry or I'll miss my plane? **2, 5**

... which terminal I need? **4, 6**

... lending me some money until I find a cashpoint? **3**

... to wait outside for five minutes? **6**

The nightmare journey

Fluency

How well do you cope on business trips? Work with a partner to sort out a series of problems. Speaker A see page 118. Speaker B see page 122.

On the move

This section provides more useful structures relating to business travel. Students first listen to some conversations involving business travellers and identify where the speakers are. They then examine some of the language used, notably structures for making polite requests and enquiries. They then practise using them in new requests.

1 📼 **6.1** Reassure students that although there are eighteen conversations, they are very short, and all they have to do initially is to identify where the speakers are and write the correct numbers in the boxes.

When you are checking the answers, you could ask students to tell you what clues they used to deduce where the people were.

Polite requests and enquiries

2 Ask students to do this individually or in pairs and then check answers. Help them to practise using the language by getting one student to read out the first part of a question and another student to finish it.

3 Direct students' attention to the Grammar link on page 94 where they will find more help with and opportunities to practise polite question forms.

Ask students to match the first halves of the questions in Exercise 2 with the new endings. Check the answers by having one student ask a question and another give a suitable response.

The nightmare journey

Fluency

In this section, one student takes the role of a harassed business traveller for whom nothing seems to be going right, whilst the other takes a variety of roles representing the people the traveller encounters on the journey. They practise asking and responding to polite questions.

Less confident students may need some time to prepare what they are going to say, but discourage them from simply writing out their parts and reading them. Confident students could perform their nightmare journeys for the class, perhaps with mimed gestures and/or props.

In a feedback session, encourage students to tell the class of any nightmare journeys they have experienced.

📼 **6.1**

1
A: Excuse me. **Is there somewhere I could send a fax from?**
B: Certainly, sir. There's a business centre on the third floor.

2
A: Did you pack your bags yourself, sir?
B: Well, no, my wife ... Oh, er, I mean, yes. Yes, of course.

3
A: **Could I ask you to open your luggage, please, madam?**
B: Oh, ... all right. Will this take long? Only someone's meeting me.

4
A: Window or aisle?
B: Er, window, please. But not near an emergency exit, if possible. You can't put the seats back.

5
A: This is your captain speaking. We're now at our cruising altitude of 11,000 metres, making good time and just passing over the Costa Brava.
B: Oh, look. There it is. Full of British tourists.

6
A: **Can you tell me what time you stop serving dinner?**
B: Half past ten, madam. Are you a resident? I can reserve you a table if you like.

7
A: Er, Heathrow airport, please. Terminal 1. I'm in a bit of a hurry.

B: Well, I'll do what I can, sir. But the traffic's terrible this morning. Some sort of accident it said on the radio. Might be quicker taking the Tube.

8
A: British Airways regrets to announce the late departure of flight BA761 to Buenos Aires. This is due to the late arrival of the plane from Argentina. Estimated departure time is now 15.10.
B: Oh, here we go again!

9
A: This is your captain speaking again. We're in for some turbulence, I'm afraid. So, for your own safety **would you please return to your seats and make sure your seatbelt is fastened** while the 'fasten seatbelt' sign remains on? Thank you.
B: Erm, excuse me. You're sitting on my seatbelt. Thanks.

10
A: I'm sorry but this bag is too heavy to take on as hand luggage. You're only allowed six kilos. You'll have to check it in, I'm afraid, sir.
B: But I've got my computer and everything in there. And gifts for my family.

11
A: I'm afraid I'll have to check your hand luggage too, madam. Could you open this side pocket? And, er, **would you mind not smoking, please**?
B: Oh, I'm sorry. I didn't realise.

12
A: Have you got anything smaller, sir? Don't think I can change a twenty.

B: Uh? Oh, just a minute. I'll see.

13
A: There has been a change to the schedule for flight BA761 to Buenos Aires. This flight will now depart from Gate 59. Would all passengers travelling to Buenos Aires please go to gate 59?
B: Gate fifty-what?

14
A: Right. That's fine, thank you, madam. You can go through now.
B: What! You've just unpacked everything in my suitcase! How am I supposed to go through like this?

15
A: **Could you switch off your laptop now, please, sir?** We're about to land.
B: Uh? Oh, yes, of course.

16
A: Here you are. Keep the change.
B: Oh, thank you very much, madam. Have a good flight.

17
A: Excuse me. Erm, **do you think I could have an alarm call at half past six tomorrow morning?**
B: Certainly, madam. **Could I have your room number, please?**

18
A: Good afternoon, ladies and gentlemen. Flight BA761 to Buenos Aires is now ready for boarding. Would you please have your passports and boarding cards ready for inspection?
B: And about time too!

Transatlantic crossing

The text in this section presents an unusual situation, but one which may become increasingly common: living in two countries simultaneously and commuting between the two. Students are invited to talk about whether they would prefer to relocate to Britain or the States and to discuss questions on the text with a partner.

1 Ask students to give reasons for their answers and find out if any of them have spent a prolonged period of time in either Britain or the States as part of their work.

2 Ask students to speculate on the title before they read the first paragraph. Check that students understand that *NY-Lon* here refers to New York and London, but that *nylon* is a man-made fabric.

3 Students read the text and discuss the comprehension questions in pairs. Get feedback on students' answers to question 4 as the difference between the English spoken in New York and that in London will be the focus of the next section, and it will be useful to establish what students already know on the subject.

4 Guessing the meaning of new words from context is an extremely important skill. Point out that sometimes there are clues in the surrounding words, for example, *trendy* and *modern, drawn together* and *shared*. Sometimes we can infer from the context, for example, a *penthouse* must be a very desirable property because Joel Kissin dreamed of living in New York and this represented the fulfilment of his dream.

Start of Recordings for page T26

▣ 6.2

1
A: Excuse me, could you tell me where the rest room is?
B: Certainly, sir. There's one just across the lobby, by the elevators.
A: Thank you.
B: You're welcome.

2
A: That's five quid, please, mate.
B: Erm, I've only got a ten, I'm afraid.
A: That's fine. So that's five pounds I owe you. Just a minute.
B: By the way, could you tell me which way's the nearest Underground?

3
A: Excuse me, am I going the right way for the shopping mall?
B: Er, no. Erm, you need to go back the way you came till you come to a big drugstore.
A: Uh-uh.
B: Turn left, then take a right at the parking lot and the mall's right in front of you.
A: Thanks.
B: Have a nice day!

4
A: Day return, please.
B: To the City?
A: Yes, please ... Oh, my god!
B: Is there a problem?
A: I've just realised I left my briefcase with my wallet in the boot of that taxi!

5
A: Your bill, madam.
B: Oh, thank you. Er, who do I make the cheque out to?
A: Er, just Webster's will be fine. Did you enjoy your meal?
B: Er, yes ... Everything was ... fine. Er, is there a chemist's nearby, do you happen to know?

6
A: Which way you headed, ma'am?
B: Er, Liberty Street.
A: That's quite a few blocks from here. Can I call you a cab?
B: Won't that be expensive? Maybe I should take the subway.
A: I wouldn't at this time of night. Cab'll probably only cost you five or six bucks.

Transatlantic crossing

1 If your company asked you to relocate to Britain or the States, which would you choose?

2 Look at the article below. What do you think the title means? Quickly read the first paragraph to find out.

3 Now read the article and think about the questions on the right. Then discuss them with a partner.

Adapted from *Newsweek* magazine

The NY-Lon Life

Ron Kastner is a classic New Yorker: first off the plane, first out of the airport. Carrying a single small bag, he walks straight through immigration and customs. He doesn't look like he's spent six hours in the air
5 (business class will do that to you). He owns an apartment in the East Village in Manhattan, but tonight London is home: a flat in Belgravia, London's **wealthiest neighbourhood**. Kastner is a resident of a place called NY-LON, a single city inconveniently separated by
10 an ocean. He flies between the two cities up to five times a month. David Eastman lives there too. A Londoner who is a VP at Agency.com in New York, he travels the JFK–Heathrow route so often he's **on a first-name basis** with the Virgin Atlantic business class cabin crew.

As different as New York and London are, a growing number of people are
15 living, working and playing in the two cities as if they were one. The cities **are drawn together by** a shared language and culture, but mostly by money – more of which **flows** through Wall Street and the City each day than all the rest of the world's financial centers combined. The **boom** in financial services attracted advertising agencies, accounting firms and
20 management consultancies to both cities. Then came hotel and restaurant businesses, architecture and design, **real estate** and construction, air travel, tourism and other service industries.

Trevor Beattie, the London-based creative director of ad agency TBWA says 'New York and London are both so **trendy** and so modern now in terms of
25 fashion, art, photography, music.' 'We dream about each other's cities,' says Joel Kissin, a New Zealander who after 25 years in London bought a **penthouse** on New York's Fifth Avenue. 'If you're in New York your dream is London, and if you're in London your dream is New York.'

1 Is business class really that much better than economy?

2 Would you like Ron Kastner's life?

3 Do you have a favourite airline?

4 Do New York and London share a culture? Or even a language?

5 What other financial centres could eventually overtake London and New York?

6 What are the other boom industries these days?

7 How would you describe the city where you live?

8 Which two cities would you like to have homes in?

4 Try to guess the meanings of the words and expressions in **bold** from their context.

Where in the world?

1 Where would a business traveller see the following? Half of them are in New York and half in London. Write NY or L next to each.

a Walk/Don't walk __NY__   j Open Mon thru Fri __NY__

b Freeway 2m __NY__   k Parking lot __NY__

c City center __NY__   l Taxis: queue here __L__

d Rest rooms __NY__   m Car park full __L__

e Underground __L__   n Chemists __L__

f Lift out of order __L__   o Truck stop __NY__

g Gas station __NY__   p Colour copies 10p __L__

h Motorway services 15m __L__   q Subway __NY__

i Roundabout ahead __L__   r Trolleys __L__

2 6.2 Listen to the cassette. Where do the conversations take place? Write the numbers in the boxes.

London 2 4 5 8   New York 1 3 6 7

In arrivals

1 6.3 Listen to four conversations in which people meet at the airport and answer the questions.

	Conversation 1	Conversation 2	Conversation 3	Conversation 4
Have the speakers met before?	No	Yes	No	No
What topics do they discuss?	flight, weather	family, promotion	business, flight	business colleagues, tiredness
What plans do they make?	go to hotel; meet Mr Hill in two hours	have lunch; go to office; Greg is staying with Caroline	meet team this afternoon; relax in evening	go to hotel, meet in 45 minutes

Where in the world?

This section gives practice in differentiating between American and British English. It is fairly light-hearted as it really doesn't matter which form students choose to use. It will, however, be useful for them to be able to recognise and understand the differences.

1 You could do this as a quiz with students working individually and score points for correct answers.

It might be interesting to see if students can suggest what the equivalents in the opposite city might be for some of the words in the signs. Many of the signs themselves, such as Walk/Don't walk don't have a direct verbal equivalent (crossings in Britain have a picture of a man which flashes green when it is safe to cross and is red when it is unsafe) but there are many words which have UK or US equivalents.

b US freeway = UK motorway
c US center = UK centre
d US rest rooms = UK toilets (sometimes lavatories)
e US subway = UK underground (in Britain a subway is a passage under a road for pedestrians)
f UK lift = US elevator
g US gas station = UK petrol station
h see b
i UK roundabout = US traffic circle
j US Monday thru (through) Friday = UK Monday to Friday
k US parking lot = UK car park
l UK taxi = US cab; UK queue = US line
m see k
n UK chemists = US drugstore or pharmacy
o US truck = UK lorry
p UK colour = US color
q see e
r UK trolleys = US luggage carts

2 ▬▬ **6.2** Ask students to identify the locations as they listen and afterwards to say what clues helped them to decide.

In arrivals

Meeting or being met by business colleagues at an airport is a common experience for business travellers. Students here practise greetings, offers and ways of making polite conversation in such situations. They begin by listening to some people being met at the airport and answer questions about them. They then go on to complete expressions used in the listening and practise using them in an airport roleplay.

1 ▬▬ **6.3** Play the recording. You may need to pause between each conversation to give students time to make notes on what they discuss and what plans they make. Check the answers with the class and play the recording again to confirm these.

Recordings continued from previous page

7
A: One way or round trip?
B: Er, one way, please. Is there a cart I could use for my baggage?
A: Sure. They're over by the phone booths. You'll need two quarters.
B: Oh, then could you change this for me?

8
A: Erm, excuse me. I'm looking for a gas station.
B: Oh, right. A petrol station. I think there's one at the next roundabout.
A: Pardon me? ... Oh, you mean a traffic circle. Great. Thanks a lot.
B: No problem.

▬▬ **6.3**
Conversation 1
A: Hello. **You must be waiting for me.**
B: Mr de Jong?
A: That's right.
B: How do you do, sir. **Let me take those for you.** Did you have a good flight?
A: Not bad, not bad. It's even colder here than Cape Town, though. And we're having our winter.
B: Oh, yes. It's rained all week, I'm afraid. Always does for Wimbledon.
A: Hm? Oh, the tennis. Actually, **I was expecting to meet Mr Hill.**
B: Yes, sir. I'm afraid Mr Hill had to go to a meeting. **He sends his apologies.** He said to take you straight to your hotel, give you a chance to freshen up and he'll meet you in a couple of hours or so.
A: Oh, right. Fine.
B: **You must be tired after your long flight.**
A: Oh, not too bad. **Luckily, I managed to get some sleep on the plane.**

Conversation 2
C: Greg! I'm over here ...
D: Caroline! Good to see you again! God, it's crowded here. I nearly missed you.
C: I know. Didn't you see me waving? **So, how are things?**
D: Fine, fine. **Susan sends her love.**
C: How is she?
D: Very well. Congratulations, by the way.
C: Hm?
D: On your promotion.
C: Oh, that. Yeah, well, if you work for the same company long enough ... Now, my car's just five minutes away. **Let me help you with your bags.**
D: Oh, that's all right. Well, maybe the really heavy one.
C: Now, **I thought we could get some lunch** first and then go back to the office and do some work. Oh, you're staying with us, by the way. David's dying to meet you.
D: Sounds good to me. David, yes. A new job and a new husband. **So, how's married life?**

Conversation 3
E: Miss Sheridan?
F: Yes, **you must be Alan Hayes.**
E: That's right.
F: Hello. **Thanks for coming to meet me.**
E: Not at all. We thought it would be quicker. This way you can meet the whole team this afternoon. We thought you might just want to relax this evening.
F: Oh, yes. Probably.
E: **So, how's business?**
F: Couldn't be better. So we're all set for the meeting tomorrow?
E: We certainly are. **Martin sends his regards**, by the way.
F: How is he?
E: He's fine. **So, how was your flight?**
F: Oh, pretty good. **I got upgraded.**
E: Lucky you! That never seems to happen to me.
F: Mm. It certainly makes a difference. I could get used to it.

E: Well, now, we'll go straight to the office **if that's OK with you. I'd like you to meet Graham Banks**. He's the head of our legal department.
F: Yes, I think I spoke to him on the phone.
E: Oh, yes, of course. **Now, let's see if we can get a taxi ...**

Conversation 4
G: Mr Okada?
H: Er, yes.
G: Hello. Welcome to London. I'm Sharon Miller.
H: Er, from Sabre Holdings?
G: That's right. I'm the head of the M&A department – Mergers and Acquisitions.
H: I see. I was expecting ... Never mind. So, Miss Miller. **Pleased to meet you.**
G: Pleased to meet *you*, Mr Okada. Now, **I've got a taxi waiting outside.** So why don't we let the driver take those bags of yours?
H: Oh, thank you very much.
G: We'll drop your things off at the hotel. **We booked you into the Savoy. I hope that's OK.** I think you'll be comfortable there.
H: Yes, that will be fine.
G: Great. Then **I thought we could** meet up with my assistant Geri King and **get some lunch**.
H: Geri King? I don't think I know him.
G: Her, actually. No, she's just joined us. She's got a lot of questions she'd like to ask you.
H: Yes, of course. I wonder ... It was a very long flight ... Do you think I could go to my hotel first?
G: Yeah, sure. **We booked a table for 1.30**, but that's OK.
H: I am a little tired and I need to freshen up.
G: Of course. We'll check you into your hotel and then meet in, say, three quarters of an hour?

Greeting visitors

2 Before looking at the chart of expressions, ask students if they can remember any of the things that the speakers on the recording said when they greeted each other. It might be helpful to have students close their books at this point and write anything they can remember on the board.

Students then complete the boxes with the missing words. When they have done this, they will have a bank of useful expressions for greeting people. Encourage them to use these when they do the roleplay in the next exercise.

Fluency

3 Give students plenty of time to turn to their respective pages and read the situations outlined there. Working individually, give students time also to think about what they are going to say and decide on expressions from Exercise 2 that they can use, but discourage them from writing anything down and then reading it out. Ask confident students to perform their roleplays for the class.

If you're short of time

Set *On the move* Exercises 2 and 3, reading the text in *Transatlantic crossing*, *Where in the world?* Exercise 1 and *In arrivals* Exercise 2 for homework.

Set the Grammar and Lexis links exercises for homework and check the answers at the beginning of the next class.

Greeting visitors   **2**   Complete the following by putting one word in each box. All the expressions were in the conversations you just listened to.

You [ ] be waiting for me.
You **must** be tired after your long flight.
You [ ] be Alan Hayes.

Let me take those for you.
me help you with your bags.

We **booked** you into the Savoy.
We [ ] a table for 1.30.

So, [ ] are things?
So, **how** is married life?
So, is business?
So, was your flight?

I **got** upgraded.
I've a taxi waiting outside.

... if that's **ok** with you.
I hope that's

He [ ] his apologies.
Susan **sends** her love.
Martin [ ] his regards.

Luckily, I managed to [ ] some sleep on the plane.
I thought we could **get** some lunch.
Now, let's see if we can a taxi.

I was expecting to [ ] Mr Hill.
Thanks for coming to **meet** me.
I'd like you to Graham Banks.
Pleased to you.

Fluency   **3**   The red-eye is a longhaul night flight. Work with a partner to practise meeting a colleague off the red-eye in New York. Speaker A see page 119. Speaker B see page 123.

7 Handling calls

The reason computers can do more work than people is that computers never have to answer the phone. *Anonymous*

Discussion

1 Work in groups and discuss the questions.

 a What percentage of your time at work do you spend on the phone?

 b How many of the calls you make and receive are essential?

 c Can you **not** answer the phone? When you answer, is it:
 • out of curiosity – it might be some good news for a change?
 • with a sigh of relief – it must be less boring than whatever you're doing?
 • because you're so indispensable, no one else is capable of dealing with it?
 • force of habit – the phone rings, you pick it up?
 • because if you don't, no one else will?
 • for fear of what might happen to you if you don't?

2 Read the statistics below. What points are they making about phone calls at work?

When the Northwestern Mutual Life Assurance Company decided to block all incoming calls for just one hour a week, productivity rose by an amazing 23%.

Time-management consultancy Priority Management found that 55% of all calls received by executives are less important than the work they interrupt. 21% are a complete waste of time.

Research shows that managers underestimate the time they spend on the telephone by up to 50%. Perhaps that's how over two trillion dollars get spent annually on phone calls!

7 Handling calls

In Unit 3, students learnt some strategies for making and receiving telephone calls in English. This unit continues this topic, first by giving students the opportunity to discuss how important phone calls are in their work and how they handle calls when they are busy.

They then learn and practise useful expressions for making polite requests. The next section gives them strategies and language for dealing with unexpected phone calls.

They practise dealing with incoming phone calls in a roleplay and use some of the expressions they have learnt to make excuses to end a call and get the other person off the phone.

The grammatical focus is on *will* and the lexical focus is on collocations relating to work routines.

In this first section, students begin by discussing the amount of time they spend on the phone and the importance of this. They discuss attitudes to answering or not answering the phone and look at some statistics which suggest that answering the phone may not be the best use of a business person's time.

Warm-up

Read the quotation at the beginning of the unit to the class and ask for reactions. Ask students whether they use an answerphone or some other device to find out who is calling them before they answer the phone. Brainstorm other ways you can avoid receiving phone calls and on what occasions people are likely to try to avoid them.

Discussion

1 Students discuss the questions in groups and report back to the class.

2 Instead of just getting the students to read the texts, you might like to use them to revise some of the telephone techniques the students have already learnt: asking for repetition or clarification, getting the speaker to slow down, etc.

Ask students to close their books and tell them that you are going to make a phone call to them. Then, holding a mobile phone or other prop to your ear, read the first text but slur some of the words, speak too quickly or too softly for the students to hear or mispronounce some words.

Encourage students to use the skills they have learnt to ask you to repeat, slow down, spell out a word, etc. You could then ask two students to do the same with the other two texts, with the rest of the class interrupting and asking for clarification. Students should politely keep asking the speaker to repeat and clarify until they have understood the whole of each text.

You can then ask them what points each text is making about phone calls at work.

Suggested answers:

Business phone calls can reduce productivity because of the time they take up. Even a modest reduction in calls can increase productivity.

Most business calls are not important enough to justify executives stopping what they are doing to answer them.

Business phone calls cost companies a lot of money, possibly because people are very bad at judging how long they spend on the phone.

3 Students work individually to complete the sentences. Check the answers with the class.

4 Students decide individually which of the sentences in Exercise 3 are true for them and then compare with a partner. If they disagree with any of the sentences, ask them to explain what they would do in a similar situation.

Asking politely

This next section gives students training in making polite requests. It also provides a lot of vocabulary which they will find useful when talking about office procedures or asking people to do things around the office.

Expressions with *if ...*

1 Once students have completed the expressions, ask them to read them out aloud to the class, giving each one an ending, e.g. *If possible, I'd prefer to meet on Friday. If you would send me confirmation of the order, I'd be very grateful*, etc. See how many alternatives students can come up with for each one.

Requests

2 Students will find all this vocabulary useful for talking about office life.

Direct students' attention to the Lexis link on page 97 where they will find more vocabulary on office life which is presented in the form of an amusing poem. You could ask students to complete the poem for homework.

3 In pairs, students roleplay making and answering polite telephone requests. To make this a little more realistic, it is often useful to have pairs of students sit back to back when they do phone call roleplays. This removes the visual clues that we tend to rely on when speaking face to face with someone, and which tell us when something we have said has not been understood. Without visual clues, students have to rely on voice alone and ask for repetition or clarification when they need it. Encourage students to use as much of the language from the previous exercises as they can. The phone calls do not have to be long and complicated. Once the request has been made and agreed or refused, pairs should swap roles and start a new call.

3 Use the pairs of words in the box to complete the sentences.

> disturbed + hold   expecting + pick up   real + unplug
> possible + answer   busy + ring   important + switch on

a If I'm _busy_ , I just let the phone _ring_ .

b If I don't want to be _disturbed_ , I tell my secretary to _hold_ all my calls.

c If _possible_ , I try to _answer_ the phone before the fourth ring.

d If I'm _expecting_ a call from the boss, I _pick up_ the phone immediately.

e If I'm in the middle of something _important_ , I _switch on_ the answerphone.

f If I'm having a _real_ crisis, I _unplug_ the damn thing!

4 How many of the statements in 3 are true for you? Compare with a partner.

Asking politely

Expressions with if ...

1 Use the words and phrases in the box to make seven useful expressions which start with *if*.

> got a minute   not too much trouble   got time   possible   would
> not too busy   can

if ...   _possible_

you _would_

you _can_

you're _not too busy_

you've _got a minute_

you've _got time_

it's _not too much trouble_

Requests

2 Divide the text into twelve things someone might phone to ask you to do. All the requests start with *Could you ...?*

Lexis link

for more on the vocabulary of office life see page 97

> **Could you ...?** emailmemyflightdetails|letmehaveacopyofthe
> report|getontooursupplier|getbacktomewithinthe
> hour|takeaquicklookattheproposal|arrangefor
> somebodytomeetthematthestation|setupameeting
> withtheheadsofdepartment|sendtheiraccounts
> departmentareminder|fixmeanappointment|book
> theconferenceroomforthree|faxthefiguresthrough
> tome|organiseatouroftheplantforsomevisitors

3 Work with a partner. Take it in turns to make and answer polite telephone requests. Use the language from 1 and 2 above.

For example:

A *If you've got a minute, could you get on to our suppliers?*

B *Sure. I'll do it now.*

A *Thanks.*

A *Could you book the conference room for three if you can?*

B *Well ... I'm a bit busy.*

A *OK, I'll do it myself.*

Unexpected phone calls

1    7.1 Listen to four telephone calls and match them to their description.

Call 1   **a**   The caller is kept waiting.

Call 2   **b**   A business contact calls to ask a favour.

Call 3   **c**   A sales executive calls with a quote.

Call 4   **d**   There is a communication breakdown.

2   Listen again and answer the following questions.

Call 1

a   What's the misunderstanding? _The receiver doesn't speak English well._

b   How does the man receiving the call deal with the problem?
He fetches someone who speaks better English.

c   Do you ever have difficulties answering calls in English?

Call 2

a   How does the person receiving the call avoid another call?
He says he's in a meeting and asks the caller to e-mail the figures.

b   Do you think he is really in a meeting? _(students' own answers)_

c   Do you ever pretend you're busy just to get someone off the phone?

Call 3

a   How would you describe the telephone manner of the person
receiving the call? _unprofessional, informal, casual_

b   What is the caller calling about? _a pension fund_

c   Have you ever been treated unprofessionally on the phone?

Call 4

a   Where did the speakers meet? _at the Expo in São Paolo_

b   What does the caller want? _an introduction to the boss_

c   Have you ever received a phone call from someone you have met but
can't remember?

3   All the expressions below were in the telephone conversations you just listened
to. Can you remember the first three words of each expression? *It's* and *I'm*
count as **one** word.

Call 1   **a**   _Can_   _you_   _put_   me through to Yves Dupont?

        b   _I'm_   _afraid_   _I_   don't understand.

        c   _Can_   _you_   _speak_   more slowly, please?

Call 2   **a**   _I'm_   _calling_   _about_   those prices you wanted.

        b   _I'm_   _afraid_   _I_   can't talk right now.

        c   _Can_   _I_   _call_   you back – say, in an hour?

Call 3   **a**   _What_   _can_   _I_   do for you?

        b   _Do_   _you_   _know_   when he'll be back?

        c   _Who_   _am_   _I_   speaking to?

Call 4   **a**   _I'm_   _sorry_   _to_   bother you.

        b   _Can_   _I_   _ask_   who's calling?

        c   _Can_   _you_   _give_   me a contact number?

Unexpected phone calls

This section, as the title implies, is all about dealing with phone calls which occur unexpectedly. These are probably the most difficult to deal with, particularly when they come in a foreign language. The aim is to prepare students for these eventualities and give them some strategies to deal with calls which come as a complete surprise, so that they can appear confident and professional on the phone at all times.

Warm-up

Have the students close their books. Tell them that the next section is called *Unexpected phone calls*. Ask them to brainstorm ideas for what unexpected calls they might receive in a day at the office. Try to find out what is the most unexpected phone call anyone in the class has received. Why was it such a surprise and how did the student deal with it?

1 ▭ **7.1** Go through the descriptions with the class before you play the recording so they know exactly what they are listening for. Allow students to compare their answers in pairs before checking with the class.

2 If your students are confident, you might like to see how many of these questions they can answer before you play the recording again. Even if they can't answer every one, going through the questions and thinking about the answers will be good preparation for the second listening.

Play the recording again and check the answers with the class. See how much agreement there is over question c for each call; these questions ask about the students' own experience and opinions.

3 When students have completed the expressions, checking the answers might be more fun if you ask individual students to read out at random the beginning of an expression for the rest of the class to finish.

▭ **7.1**

Call 1
A: Allo!
B: Oh, hello. Do you speak English?
A: Er, ... yes, a little. **Can I help you?**
B: This is Anne Cook from *What Car?* magazine.
A: I'm sorry?
B: Anne Cook. *What Car?*
A: What car?
B: Yes, that's right.
A: You want a car?
B: No, no, sorry. I work for *What Car?* I'm a journalist. Er, **can you put me through to** Yves Dupont?
A: **I'm afraid I don't understand. Can you speak more slowly, please?**
B: Yes, I'd like to speak to Yves Dupont, if he's available.
A: Ah ... One moment, please. **I'll get someone who speaks better English**.
B: Thank you!

Call 2
A: Hola ...
B: Hello. **Is that Joaquín Fuentes?**
A: Er ... **Yes, speaking.**
B: Joaquín. It's Geoff White.
A: Geoff White?
B: NetWorth Systems? We spoke last week.
A: Oh, yes. I'm sorry. Geoff, of course.
B: Er, yes. Anyway, **I'm calling about those prices you wanted, ...**
A: Oh, yes ... Listen, Geoff, **I'm afraid I can't talk right now**. I'm in a meeting.
B: Oh, I see.
A: Yeah. **Can I call you back – say, in an hour?**

B: Erm, yeah, sure ... No problem.
A: OK, **I'll speak to you later** ... Or better still, could you e-mail me the figures?
B: Erm, yeah, yeah, sure.
A: Thanks a lot.
B: **I'll do that right away.**
A: Great. Thanks for calling.
B: Yeah, bye.
A: Bye.

Call 3
C: Jim, can you get that?
A: Uh? Oh, OK. ... Yeah?
B: Hello? Is that Western Securities?
A: Uh-huh. **What can I do for you?**
B: This is Laura Como from Tricolor. I'd like to speak to Karl Lesonsky, please. It's about a pension fund.
A: Just a minute. Anybody seen Karl? ... He's not here.
B: **Do you know when he'll be back?**
A: No idea. He's usually in by now. Probably taken a long lunch.
B: Oh, I see. Well, perhaps you can help. **Who am I speaking to?**
A: Er, Jim Savage. But, er, ., Oh, just a minute ... (puts her on hold)
B: Oh, come on!
A: Er, hello Ms Como?
B: Yes!
A: Look, I don't normally deal with pensions. I think you'd better wait till Karl gets back.
B: Well, when will that be?
A: I really don't know.
B: Well, that's helpful.
A: OK. Look, give me ten minutes. **I'll see if I can reach him on his cellphone**.
B: No, don't bother. **I'll call back later**.

Call 4
A: José Senna.
B: Ah, Mr Senna. Hello. **I'm sorry to bother you**. Your secretary gave me your mobile number.
A: Er, that's OK. ... **Can I ask who's calling?**
B: Oh, I'm sorry. This is Nigel Waters. We met at the Expo in São Paolo last year.
A: Oh, yes, Mr Waters. How are you?
B: Fine, fine. You said if I was ever in Rio you'd introduce me to your boss? Remember?
A: Oh, ... Yes. Um, so you're here in Rio?
B: That's right.
A: Erm, well, it's a bit difficult right now. I'm on my way to a meeting. But ... er, leave it with me. **I'll see what I can do**.
B: Right.
A: **Can you give me a contact number?**
B: Oh, yes, I'm staying ...
A: Just a minute, where's my organiser? ... OK.
B: Yes, I'm staying at the Mirador in Copacabana. It's 548 8950, er, room 314.
A: 3-1-4. ... OK. I'll try to make the arrangements. Don't worry, **I'll sort something out**.
B: Great.
A: And, er ... Oh, the traffic's moving. Look, **I'll get back to you tomorrow**. OK?
B: I can't hear you very well.
A: No, **the signal's breaking up**. Speak to you tomorrow.
B: OK, fine. **I'll wait to hear from you then**. Bye.

Expressions with *I'll ...*

4   Once students have completed the expressions, read out the statements and ask individual students to give the correct response. Alternatively, get students to practise the statements and responses in pairs.

Direct students' attention to the Grammar link on page 96 where they will find more on *will*.

Fluency

5   Again, sitting back to back will make these roleplays more realistic for the students. Give students time to read the instructions on their respective pages and to think about what they are going to say, but discourage them from writing down their lines and reading them out. As you go around the class listening to the roleplays, make a note of any particularly good or amusing ones and ask those students to perform their roleplays for the class.

Fluency

6   This exercise leads up to another phone roleplay, but the aim here is to personalise it so that students are dealing with calls from people that they know and about things which they actually have to deal with in their daily lives. Students can have great fun thinking up imaginative ways of putting an end to a call.

See if you can establish a class champion for getting people off the phone as quickly as possible (whilst still remaining polite). Ask a volunteer who believes they are good at this skill to take the role of the receiver. Using a stopwatch to time the calls, invite other students to challenge the receiver by attempting to keep him or her on the line as long as possible.

If you're short of time

Reduce the amount of time for discussion in the first section on page 28 or go through the questions with the whole class.

Set all the fill in the gaps exercises in this unit for homework and concentrate on the roleplays.

Set the Grammar and Lexis links exercises for homework and check the answers at the beginning of the next class.

Expressions with *I'll* ...

Grammar link

for more on *will* see page 96

4 Use the phrases in the box to make nine responses to the statements on the left. All the responses were in the telephone conversations you just listened to.

back to you tomorrow	what I can do	to hear from you then
if I can reach him on his cellphone	to you later	something out
someone who speaks better English	back later	that right away

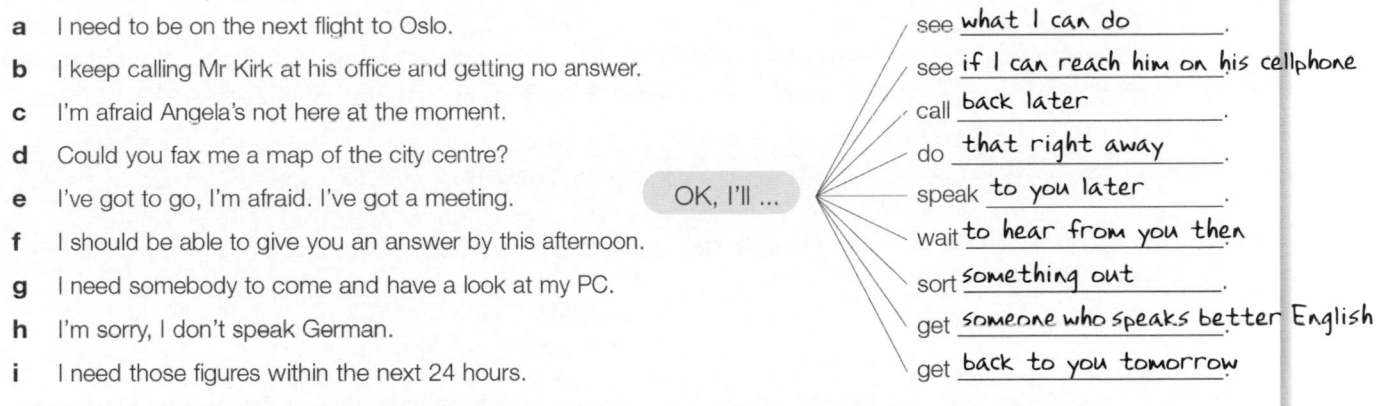

a I need to be on the next flight to Oslo.

b I keep calling Mr Kirk at his office and getting no answer.

c I'm afraid Angela's not here at the moment.

d Could you fax me a map of the city centre?

e I've got to go, I'm afraid. I've got a meeting.

f I should be able to give you an answer by this afternoon.

g I need somebody to come and have a look at my PC.

h I'm sorry, I don't speak German.

i I need those figures within the next 24 hours.

OK, I'll ...

see **what I can do** .

see **if I can reach him on his cellphone**

call **back later** .

do **that right away** .

speak **to you later** .

wait **to hear from you then** .

sort **something out** .

get **someone who speaks better English** .

get **back to you tomorrow** .

Fluency **5** Work in pairs to deal with incoming phone calls. Speaker A see page 119. Speaker B see page 123.

Fluency **6 a** Complete the diagram below with the names of four to six people who typically phone you at work to ask you to do things. Write down what they usually ask you to do. Include private calls if you like.

b Categorise each call: *urgent* (must be done now), *important* (but can wait), *social* (just keeping in touch), *a nuisance* (time-wasting).

c Swap diagrams with a partner and practise phoning each other. What excuses can you give to avoid doing what they ask? Try to get them off the phone.

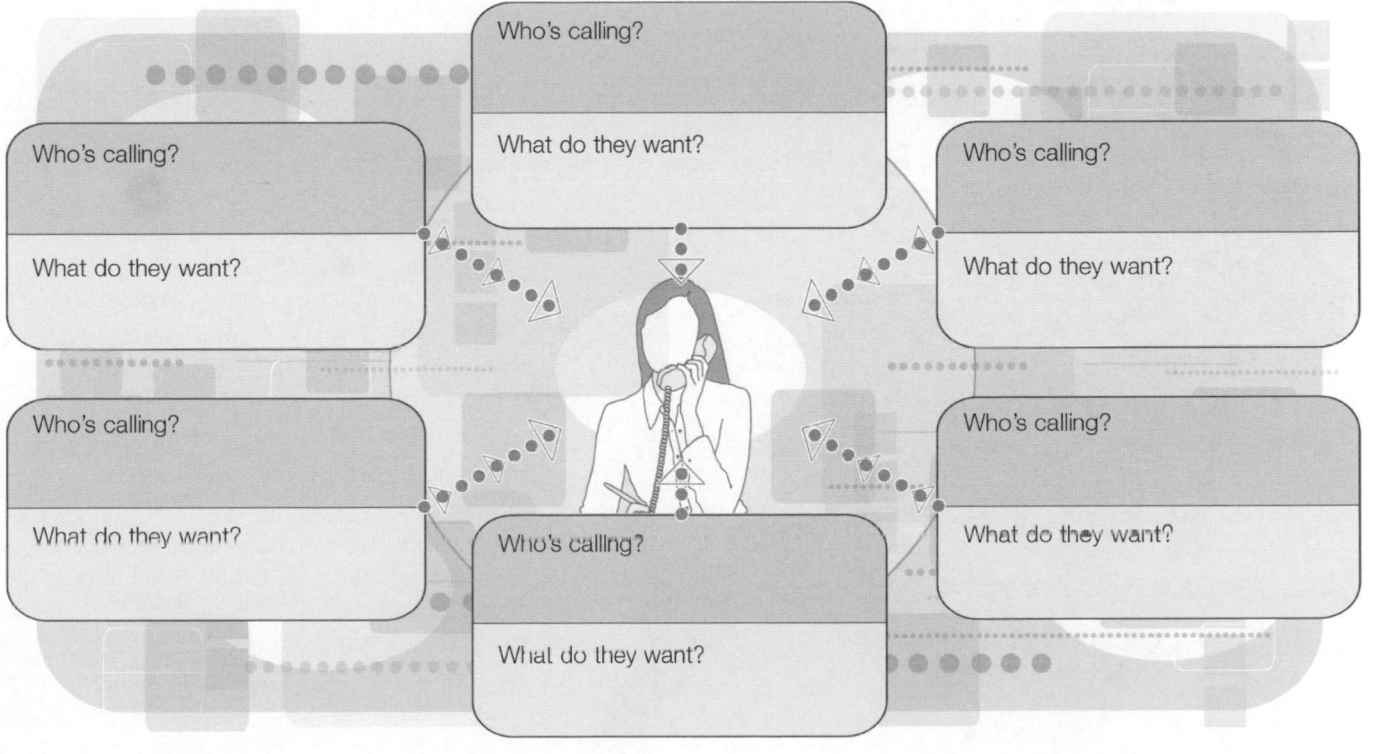

Who's calling?

What do they want?

Who's calling?

What do they want?

Who's calling?

What do they want?

Who's calling?

What do they want?

Who's calling?

What do they want?

Who's calling?

What do they want?

8 Making decisions

Nothing is more difficult, and therefore more precious, than to be able to decide.
Napoleon Bonaparte

Questionnaire

1 Are you good at making quick decisions or are you a more methodical thinker? Answer *yes, no* or *it depends* to the following in under 90 seconds.

How decisive are you?

a You're writing a report. The deadline's tomorrow, but it's your partner's birthday. **Do you work late to finish it?**

b You're with a major client who wants to stay out clubbing all night. You don't want to. **Do you politely say good night?**

c You're shopping for a suit, but the only one you like costs twice what you want to pay. **Do you buy it anyway?**

d A friend in banking gives you an investment tip. You could make or lose a lot of money. **Do you take the risk?**

e You're beating your boss at golf and he's a really bad loser. You could drop a shot or two. **Do you?**

f A good friend is starting her own business. She asks you if she can borrow $10,000. You can afford it. **Do you lend it to her?**

g You're offered twice your current salary to take a boring job in a beautiful city. **Do you take it?**

For an analysis of your answers see page 124.

2 What kind of decisions do you have to make at work? What's the hardest decision you've ever had to make?

The best and worst business decisions ever made

1 You are going to listen to eight extracts from a radio documentary about the best and worst business decisions ever made. First, check the meaning of the following words and phrases in a dictionary.

strategy   fortune   royalties   output
supply   manufacturer   brandstretching
conglomerate   outsell the competition
collaborate with another company
license products   retain ownership
buy the rights to a product

8 Making decisions

In this unit students look at decision making, beginning by answering a questionnaire on how good they are at making quick decisions. They then listen to extracts from a radio documentary on the best and worst business decisions ever made, identify the relevance of some figures they have heard and talk about the best or worst decisions they, personally, have ever made.

The next two sections look at the decision-making process and how it affects the language of meetings.

Students then practise taking part in a decision-making meeting to decide who should play James Bond in the next Bond film.

The grammatical focus is on conditionals and the lexical focus is on collocations relating to the market place.

This first section is about making a quick decision. Students answer a questionnaire and then read an analysis of their answers. They then personalise the subject further by talking about the kind of decisions they have to make at work and the hardest decision they have ever had to make.

Warm-up

Write the word *decision* in a circle in the centre of the board and brainstorm all the words that the students know that are derived from it, e.g. *decide, decisive, indecisive, deciding (factor), indecision, undecided, decided(ly)*. Write these at the ends of spokes radiating out from the circle. Ask students to explain the meanings of the words or to use them in sentences which demonstrate their meaning.

Quiz

1   Make sure students realise that they have only 90 seconds to answer the questionnaire and that they can write *yes, no* or *it depends* to each question. Then get them started, so that they don't have time to realise that any yes or no answers are irrelevant to the purpose of the questionnaire, which is to determine how many of the questions they would answer with *it depends*.

The analysis of the answers is on page 124. See how many students fall into each of the three categories and ask if anyone is surprised at their analysis.

2   This could be a class discussion. Particularly if students are from different industries, encourage listening students to respond to what they are told by their classmates by saying if they too have to make the same kinds of decisions and if they would find a particular decision very hard to make.

The best and worst business decisions ever made

This section examines some famously good and bad business decisions. Two exercises practise listening for specific information, the second one requiring students to identify what figures in the listening refer to.

Warm-up

Start by looking at the title. Ask students if they can imagine what any of these best and worst decisions might be. Discourage them from talking about personal experience at this stage as they will be asked about their own best and worst decisions later.

1   Go through the words and phrases in the box and find out how many of them the students already know. If some are known to some students, encourage them to explain them to the rest of the class before they turn to their dictionaries. If you ask students to look the words up for homework, start the next class by asking them to put each word into a sentence.

2 📼 **8.1** Tell students that the first time they listen, all they have to do is note down the name of the company or product referred to. Play the recording, then allow students to compare their answers in pairs before checking with the class.

3 Allow students to read through the figures carefully before playing the recording again. Ask individuals to read out the figures so you can check pronunciation. You might like to pause between each section to allow students to make notes of their answers. Check the answers with the class.

4 Encourage students to talk about the consequences of the decisions they made. If they are happy to talk about their personal lives, you could extend this to include the best and worst decisions they have ever made in their business and personal lives.

The decision-making process

Students begin by putting the stages of decision making into the most likely order. They then match the items on a meeting agenda to the things that were said at that meeting.

1 The order given in the answers matches that demonstrated in the meeting in Exercise 2, but students may argue that they would consider the options before collecting information.

2 When students have matched the agenda items with the things that were said, invite one or two of them to read out the things said at the meeting in the correct order.

📼 **8.1**

1
Asa Candler's best business decision was definitely deciding to **buy the rights to** Coca-Cola from its inventor, Dr John Styth Pemberton. Unfortunately, in one of the worst business decisions ever, Mr Candler went on to sell Coke's bottling rights for just **$1**. Coca-Cola's daily **output** is **one billion** bottles.

2
Between the mid-70s and the early 80s Swiss watchmaking companies saw their world market share fall from 30 to just **9%**. Then, in response to strong Japanese competition, came the decision to **collaborate**. The result was the Swatch, and market share shot up to **50%**.

3
In **1991** Dell Computers almost made its biggest mistake when it decided to expand and start selling through high street stores. Boss, Michael Dell, quickly changed his mind and returned to selling PCs direct to consumers, a **strategy** which has put Dell, a company that now employs **21,000** people, consistently amongst the top three PC manufacturers in the world.

4
In **1955**, small record producer, Sam Phillips sold the exclusive contract he had with a young unknown singer to RCA for the grand sum of **$35,000**. Unfortunately for Phillips, the singer was Elvis Presley and he lost the **royalties** to over a billion record sales.

5
The world's bestselling toy, Barbie, is over forty years old. The decision in **1961** to give her a boyfriend, Ken, was the first step in a successful **brandstretching** exercise, which now includes Barbie CD-ROMs and Barbie digital cameras. As a result, the toy continues to **outsell** even Nintendo and Lego. Somewhere in the world a Barbie is bought every **two seconds**.

6
In **1938** two talented artists, Joe Shuster and Jerry Siegel, sold the rights to the comic-book character they designed to their publisher for **$130**. The decision cost them a **fortune** – the millions they would have made by **retaining ownership** of Superman.

7
In **1977** Steve Jobs invented what many consider to be the first personal computer – the Apple 1. Xerox, in *their* worst decision ever, missed a similar opportunity. Unfortunately, Apple refused to **license its products** to other **manufacturers**. By trying to keep control, Jobs lost out to Microsoft. And it was Bill Gates, not Steve Jobs, whose personal worth first broke the **$100 billion** barrier.

8
And finally, in what is perhaps the most tragic business decision ever, in 1886, gold prospector, Sors Hariezon, decided to stop digging for gold and sell his land to a South African mining **conglomerate** for $20. Over the next ninety years that land produced over **a million kilos** of gold a year – **70%** of the gold **supply** to the Western world!

2 🎞 **8.1** Listen and write down the name of the company or product referred to:

1 Coca-Cola   **3** Dell Computers   **5** Barbie   **7** Apple

2 Swatch   **4** RCA (Elvis)   **6** Superman   **8** gold

3 Listen again. What do these figures refer to?

1 $1 price paid for Coke's bottling rights

    1 bn daily output of Coca-Cola in bottles

2 9% Swiss watchmaking companies' world market share in early 80s

    50% percentage their market share rose by when Swatch invented

3 1991 year when Dell decided to sell through high street stores

    21,000 number of Dell employees now

4 1955 year Sam Phillips sold Elvis Presley's contract to RCA

    $35,000 price RCA paid for Elvis Presley's contract

5 1961 year Barbie's boyfriend Ken was launched

    2 secs rate at which Barbie is bought

6 1938 year the rights to Superman were sold

    $130 price paid for Superman rights

7 1977 year Apple I computer invented

    $100bn Bill Gates' personal worth

8 1m kg amount of gold Hariezon's land produced every year for 90 years

    70% percentage of gold supply to Western world from this field

4 What are the best and the worst decisions you've ever made at work?

The decision-making process

1 Put the following stages in the decision-making process into the most likely order.

- consider the options
- collect information
- implement your decision
- define your objectives
- monitor the effects
- choose the best course of action

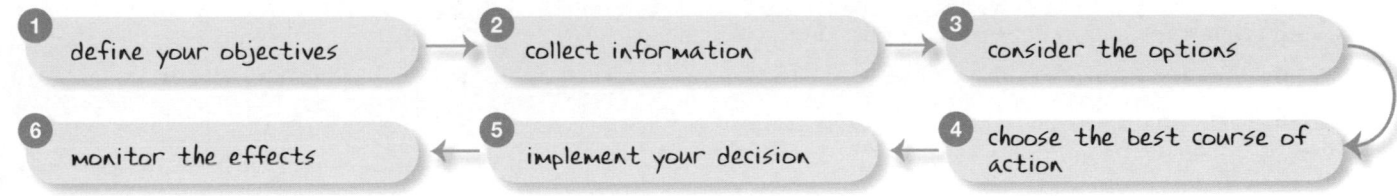

1 define your objectives → **2** collect information → **3** consider the options → **4** choose the best course of action → **5** implement your decision ← **6** monitor the effects

2 Look at the agenda for a decision-making meeting on the left. Decide which two statements below were made at each stage in the meeting.

AGENDA

1 Objectives [a] [j]
2 Priorities [c] [f]
3 Data analysis [e] [k]
4 Alternatives [b] [h]
5 Pros & cons [d] [i]
6 Final decision [g] [l]

a **We're here to decide** whether to go ahead with the project.
b **One option would be to** do detailed market research.
c **The most important thing is:** can we make this profitable?
d **The advantage of** doing market research is we reduce risk.
e **Have a look at** these figures.
f **Above all, we must** be sure there's a market for our service.
g **What we've agreed, then, is to** start marketing this service now.
h **Another alternative is to** offer the service on a trial basis.
i **On the other hand**, market research takes time.
j **Our aim is to** find out if there's a good chance of success.
k **As you can see**, client feedback is very positive.
l **So, that's it – we're going ahead with** the project.

The language of meetings

1 The following expressions are useful in meetings, but some letters are missing from the final words. When you have completed them, the letters in the box spell out a good piece of advice for the chairperson!

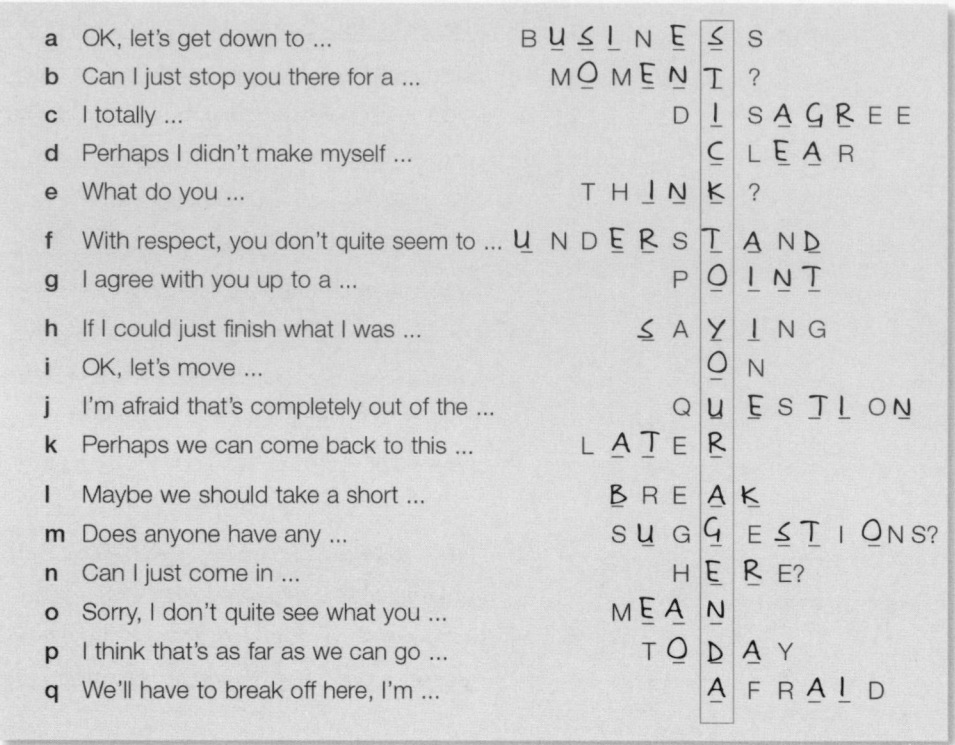

a	OK, let's get down to ...	B U S I N E S S
b	Can I just stop you there for a ...	M O M E N T ?
c	I totally ...	D I S A G R E E
d	Perhaps I didn't make myself ...	C L E A R
e	What do you ...	T H I N K ?
f	With respect, you don't quite seem to ...	U N D E R S T A N D
g	I agree with you up to a ...	P O I N T
h	If I could just finish what I was ...	S A Y I N G
i	OK, let's move ...	O N
j	I'm afraid that's completely out of the ...	Q U E S T I O N
k	Perhaps we can come back to this ...	L A T E R
l	Maybe we should take a short ...	B R E A K
m	Does anyone have any ...	S U G G E S T I O N S ?
n	Can I just come in ...	H E R E ?
o	Sorry, I don't quite see what you ...	M E A N
p	I think that's as far as we can go ...	T O D A Y
q	We'll have to break off here, I'm ...	A F R A I D

2 8.2 Listen to an extract from a meeting about a company relocating to the UK and tick the expressions in 1 as you hear them. Which one is not used? P

3 Which expressions are used to:

1	open a meeting a	6	speed things up i	11	delay k
2	ask for an opinion e	7	ask for clarification o	12	ask for ideas m
3	interrupt b n	8	disagree c	13	reject a proposal j
4	prevent interruption h	9	half-agree g	14	close a meeting p q
5	get some fresh air l	10	explain d f		

Expressions with *if ...,* *unless ..., provided/ providing (that) ...*

4 Some managers are facing a cashflow crisis. Match the halves of the statements in the conversation below.

1 I just don't see how we can go on
2 No, I think we'll be OK,
3 Maybe, but unless we do,
4 In my opinion, we'd save a lot of money,
5 Look, we're in a hi-tech industry. If we cut wages,
6 No, wait. If we gave them a stake in the company,
7 No, no, no. How is that going to work,
8 OK. Look, if we can't reach agreement on this,

a I suggest we break off here.
b they might stay on. Or how about profit share?
c our people will simply go and work for the competition.
d if we keep overspending like this.
e if we aren't making any profit?
f we're going to be in serious financial trouble.
g if we just reduced wages. Our wages bills are enormous!
h providing we get this Russian contract.

Grammar link

for more on conditionals (future reference) see page 98

The language of meetings

This section looks at the sorts of things people actually say in meetings.

These are presented in a crossword, and then students listen to an extract from a meeting in which all but one of the expressions are used. They then examine the function of each of these expressions. Next they match statement halves with *if ..., unless ..., provided /providing (that) ...*

1 You could make this a race with the first student to fill in all the clues and shout out the advice spelled out in the box as the winner.

2 🔲 **8.2** Students tick the expressions as they listen and should, at the end, be able to identify expression p as the only one not used.

3 Identifying the function of each of the expressions should help students to make them their own and to use them in their own speaking practice.

Expressions with *if ..., unless ..., provided/providing (that) ...*

4 Allow students to work in pairs to match the statements before checking the answers with the class.

Direct students' attention to the Grammar link on page 98 for more information and practice exercises on conditionals with future reference. You might like to point out that in the *if*-clause, both present and past tenses can be used to refer to the future. When we use a past tense to refer to the future, it makes the statement more tentative, hypothetical or off the record. For example:

If we laid off half the staff, we might just be able to save the company. (I know this is extreme, but it's an idea.)

If we didn't have a stand at the Fair, it would be a disaster. (We must have a stand!)

When we use a past tense to refer to the present, we are imagining a totally unreal situation. For example:

If we were already based in Europe, it would be a lot easier to sell in Italy. (But we aren't.)

You wouldn't say that if you had to deal with the marketing department. (But you don't.)

🔲 **8.2**

A: Thanks for coming everybody. **OK, let's get down to business**. As you know, we're here to talk about the relocation to the UK and I'd like to hear what you have to say. Now, the plan is to make the final move in January, but that's a busy month for us. So, **what do you think?**

B: **Can I just stop you there for a moment**, Elke? This relocation idea – I mean, it's ridiculous. I don't think anyone here actually wants to go and live in Britain.

A: **With respect, you don't quite seem to understand**, Erich. The decision has already been taken.

B: **Sorry, I don't quite see what you mean**. I thought we were here to discuss it.

A: No, **perhaps I didn't make myself clear**. We *are* relocating to Cambridge in November. That's been decided ... .

B: So why are we having this meeting?

A: **If I could just finish what I was saying.** What we are discussing today is how to implement the decision. This affects our Scandinavian office, too, you know. There's a lot to talk about. Now ...

C: **Can I just come in here?**

A: Yes, what is it Axel?

C: Well, I can see why we should have a branch in the UK, instead of Scandinavia. We do most of our business there. But we're a German company. Head office should be here in Germany, surely.

A: **I'm afraid that's completely out of the question.** The decision to relocate makes good logistic and economic sense. We're still a fairly small business. Having branches in different countries is just not an option.

B: **I totally disagree.** Our market is Northern Europe and Germany is at the heart of Northern Europe.

A: Yes, but 70% of our market is in the UK. Look, **perhaps we can come back to this later**. I can see some of you are not happy about it, and **I agree with you up to a point**, but I am not in a position to change company policy. **OK, let's move on**. How are we going to handle administration during the relocation? **Does anyone have any suggestions?** How about using the Stockholm office while we move from Bremen to Cambridge? Kjell?

D: Well, to be honest, Elke, we feel very much the same as our German colleagues here. We think the decision to close down the Bremen and Stockholm offices is a mistake.

A: I see ...

C: Look, **maybe we should take a short break**, Elke. I think one or two of us would like to have a word with you – in private if that's OK.

A: Right. Well, sorry everybody. **We'll have to break off here, I'm afraid**. Axel, Kjell, Erich, I'll see you in my office ...

The decision-making meeting

This section gives students the opportunity to use the language and skills they have learnt in this unit in a simulated decision-making meeting.

Warm-up

Explain to students that they are going to make a decision regarding the actor who will play James Bond in the next Bond film. Find out how many of them have seen a Bond film, whether they have a favourite one and which of the actors who have already played Bond (Sean Connery, Roger Moore, Timothy Dalton, Pierce Brosnan) they liked best in the role.

1 Students work in pairs. When they have finished, get one pair to read out the first part of a collocation and another pair to supply the second part.

Then ask them to read the text.

Alternatively, once they have matched the collocations, ask the students to close their books and read the text aloud yourself, pausing every time you read the first part of each of the collocations for the students to call out the second part. Award points to students who complete the collocations correctly. Then ask them to open their books and read the text again to themselves.

This text could also be used for a homework activity in which students write six comprehension questions. They bring these to class and exchange them with other students who have to answer the questions they are given.

2 You might like to ask students to say whether or not they agree with the analysis in the text of the success of the Bond films.

3 Give the students plenty of time to list the qualities they think an ideal Bond actor should have.

Help them prepare for the meeting by reminding them of useful language patterns to express their list of ideas such as *The role requires someone who …; An actor who plays Bond should be able to … .* Then point out to them the meeting agenda and the actor profiles on page 36. When the students start their meetings, go round offering help and encouragement where necessary.

Encourage the students to evaluate how each candidate rates against their ideal qualities. For example:
If he can … then he can …
He won't be suitable if he can't …
The disadvantage with X is that he …
X is the sort of person who could …
Even though X can … he can't;
Despite his lack of experience in acting, X can …

For contrasts of the four candidates, encourage the use of patterns such as *Although X is … Y is …; X has …, whereas Y has …; X is not as good as Y in that … .*

When they come to item 4 of the agenda and need to listen to the interview extracts (8.3), either take the cassette player round to individual groups or stop the activity and get all groups to listen together.

Direct students' attention to the Lexis link on page 99 where they will find more vocabulary about money and markets.

The decision-making meeting

1 One of the toughest businesses is the film business, with millions of dollars made or lost on a single decision: who to cast as the star. First, work with a partner to match up and check the meaning of the collocations below in a dictionary. Then read the article.

a current ——— brand
b profit ——— turnover
c bestselling ——— margins

d combined ——— earnings
e key ——— awareness
f brand ——— factor

g commercial ——— news
h front-page ——— series
i film ——— success

NOBODY does it better

THE JAMES BOND movies are the longest-running, highest grossing film series in history. Current turnover stands at over $6 billion. In fact, the
5 combined earnings of the *Star Wars* and *Star Trek* series and the most successful single film ever, *Gone with the Wind*, still fall $750 million short of Bond at the box office.
10 Bond is also the most profitable film series ever. The special effects may cost much more these days, but the films still enjoy 30% profit margins, not including merchandising. Even Stephen Spielberg's
15 blockbusters *ET*, *Jurassic Park* and the *Indiana Jones* trilogy can't compete.
Bond appeals to men and women, adults and children alike. *From Russia with Love* was one of President
20 Kennedy's top ten favourite books. But James Bond is no longer just a Hollywood hero; he's a bestselling brand. Although the actor playing Bond has changed several times over the last
25 forty years, and although there are no more Ian Fleming novels on which to

base the films, the series goes on and on.
The film business is risky –
30 seven out of ten movies lose money. But brand awareness of Bond is so strong that even people who don't like the films instantly recognise the Bond music, fast cars
35 and glamorous women. They know that James takes his vodka Martini 'shaken not stirred'.
And then there is Bond himself – certainly
40 the key factor in 007's commercial success. With so much money at stake, the choice of a new Bond always makes front-page news. Not
45 everyone agreed in 1962 with the decision to choose a virtually unknown Sean Connery as the first James Bond, and Connery was only paid £7,000 for *Dr No*, but it
50 was perhaps one of the best recruitment decisions ever made. And the rest, as they say, is history.

2 According to the article, what are the main reasons for the success of the Bond films? Tick the correct answers.

the special effects ☐

the sex and violence ☐

the 007 brand name ☑

the actors playing Bond ☑

the novels the films are based on ☐

the Bond character ☑

3 Now work in small groups to decide who's going to be the next Bond! First, make a list of the qualities you think an ideal Bond actor should have. Then look at the actor profiles on the next page and read the agenda of the casting meeting. You may find the expressions on pages 33 and 34 useful in your decision-making meeting.

Lexis link

for more on the vocabulary of money and markets see page 99

CASTING MEETING

1 Appoint a chairperson

2 Review actor profiles

3 Discuss alternatives

4 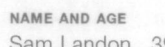 8.3 Listen to interview extracts

5 Make final decision

NAME AND AGE
Peter Aston-Sharpe   43

NATIONALITY
English

MARITAL STATUS
divorced

HEIGHT AND BUILD
1.83m   slim

PHYSICAL PURSUITS
scuba-diving, pilot's licence

EXPERIENCE
Leading actor for the last 8 years with the Royal Shakespeare Company, Stratford. Has also done a lot of TV work, playing mostly romantic leads in costume dramas. Has starred in two fairly low-budget, but successful, British films.

ACHIEVEMENTS
Won an Oscar nomination for his part in *Shadows*, a psychological thriller.

USUAL FEE
Doesn't earn much in the theatre, but was paid $750,000 for his last TV series.

COMMENTS
Some say he can be moody and difficult to work with. Ex-wife says 'he's just the sort of male chauvinist pig you need to play Bond.'

NAME AND AGE
Sam Landon   39

NATIONALITY
American

MARITAL STATUS
single

HEIGHT AND BUILD
1.90m   muscular

PHYSICAL PURSUITS
body-building, kick-boxing

EXPERIENCE
Discovered by Hollywood while working as a cocktail waiter in LA. Has starred in several high-action blockbusters, although his last film, a comedy, lost money. Best-known for his cop movie character, Detective Eddie Stone, in the late 90s.

ACHIEVEMENTS
Surprise winner of an Oscar for Best Supporting Actor for his role as a disabled war veteran.

USUAL FEE
A run of box-office hits behind him, he is now firmly established as a $20 million-a-film actor.

COMMENTS
Seems easy-going, with none of the ego problems big stars usually have. Has calmed down a lot since his early 'hell-raising' days.

NAME AND AGE
Jon McCabe   31

NATIONALITY
Scottish

MARITAL STATUS
single

HEIGHT AND BUILD
1.83m   athletic

PHYSICAL PURSUITS
shooting, climbing, hang-gliding

EXPERIENCE
Ex-European light-heavyweight boxing champion turned male model. Very little acting, but his recent supporting role in a London gangster movie won praise on both sides of the Atlantic. Soon to star in the new Jaguar commercials.

ACHIEVEMENTS
Voted 'World's Sexiest Man' two years running by *She* magazine.

USUAL FEE
As a model, he earns $15,000 a day, but is prepared to do his first Bond film for just $200,000.

COMMENTS
A charismatic and intelligent man, who knows what he wants and usually gets it. His failure to win a world boxing title is something he still refuses to talk about.

NAME AND AGE
Charles Fox   35

NATIONALITY
English

MARITAL STATUS
married

HEIGHT AND BUILD
1.88m   muscular

PHYSICAL PURSUITS
canoeing, passion for motorbikes

EXPERIENCE
Big British star who has never quite lived up to his potential. Lost out to Val Kilmer for the lead in *The Saint*, but made a successful comedy with Julia Roberts last year. 'Britain's favourite sex symbol.'

ACHIEVEMENTS
Won a television award for his role in a long-running hospital drama.

USUAL FEE
Makes $3–5 million per film.

COMMENTS
Apparently desperate to get the Bond part. He wanted it last time it was on offer, but was unable to break his contract with another studio. According to his agent, 'Charles is obsessed with Bond.'

4   If you are unable to reach a decision, see page 120 for Plan B.

4 📼 **8.4** Students should try to reach a decision before they turn to Plan B on page 120, which offers a radical alternative – a female Bond. The recording script for this activity is at the bottom of this page.

before they turn to Plan B on page 120

If you're short of time

Set the whole of *The decision-making process* for homework.

Set *The language of meetings* Exercise 1 for homework.

In *The decision-making meeting*, have the students read the profiles of the potential male Bond actors at home and be ready to come to the meeting in the next class with an opinion on which one they would choose.

Set the Grammar and Lexis links exercises for homework and check the answers at the beginning of the next class.

📼 **8.3**

Interview 1

A: So, Peter, how do you see the Bond role?
B: Well, Richard, I see Bond as essentially a very private man. He travels the world, meets beautiful women, finds himself in dangerous situations, but we never really know him. I think too many actors want to make Bond ... erm ... an obvious superhero, a lover, even a comedian. Of course, he's all those things, but above all he's ... erm ... a man of mystery, a spy, someone outside the ordinary world. Bond is his own man. A loner. Quite cold. On one level, Bond is about simple, basic ideas like love, humour and death. He's also a fantasy, completely unreal. I think Bond himself knows he's unreal. I want to play him as a man ... erm ... living up to his legend.

Interview 2

A: Well, Sam, you're an American. Is that going to be a problem for you playing Bond?
C: No, I've played Brits before and my English accent's OK. How's this? 'The name's Bond. James Bond.' But actually, Richard, ... er ... I don't see why Bond can't be an American, or at least a Canadian. I mean, Bond's just whatever you want him to be. The music, the cars, the bad guys, ... they're what make the film. Humour is the important thing. If Bond isn't funny, then it's just a silly film with lots of explosions and fast cars and women who get killed just after they sleep with Bond. Er, but Bond has a certain style ... stylish, funny, but not too sexist – that's how I'd play Bond. Bond for the 21st century.

Interview 3

A: Now, Jon, how do you see yourself playing the part of Bond?
D: Well, firstly, I think over the years Bond has lost some of his danger. And I'd like to change that. Maybe people are worried about too much violence in films, but let's face it, Bond kills people, lots of them – for a living. He has a licence to kill. He's not just a pretty face. He's a dangerous man. A man who knows he could die at any moment – although we know he won't! I think people need to believe in the actor playing Bond, believe that he's capable of violence, even does his own stunts. Of course, people expect the special effects and the glamour, but that's no good unless Bond looks like he really means business. So I'd just play Bond as me, Richard. That's all I ever do anyway!

Interview 4

A: Charles, you've wanted the Bond part for a long time. How would you play him?
E: I'd like to see Bond return to the old style of those early films, Richard. I think Bond has become too techno these days. And it's difficult to compete with films like *Star Wars* and *The Matrix* on special effects. Bond shouldn't take himself too seriously, but he shouldn't be a joke either. That's difficult to get right, but a good story helps. Bond – the real Bond – belongs to the 1960s, a more optimistic, less cynical age. My Bond would be ... er ... traditional, intelligent, charming. He'd drive his old Aston Martin, not a BMW! He'd keep his old-fashioned values, but in a modern world of real dangers. Bond is something unique. A British institution. He shouldn't be modernised.

📼 **8.4**

A: Diane, this would be quite a professional challenge for you, taking over as Bond. Would people accept a woman in the part, do you think?
F: Well, frankly, no, I don't think they would, Richard. It'd be like having a woman play *Superman* or *Indiana Jones*. And what are you going to call her? Jane Bond? It would be ridiculous. But ... erm ... I don't really see myself *becoming* Bond ... so much as *replacing* him. I think you've got to begin again really. Maybe have James finally killed off in one of those spectacular opening sequences before you introduce the new female character. Now, Bond is a pretty hard act to follow after forty years, so, obviously, my character has to be larger than life and twice as dangerous! The great thing would be you could do all the old sexist jokes in reverse and nobody would complain. But ... erm ... I think the secret of a female Bond is, she's got to have style and a wicked sense of humour or everyone will just hate her for getting James's job. What I want to know is: James always had his Bond girls; will I be getting any Bond boys?

 # 9 Big business

This unit looks at the advantages and disadvantages of large companies, both from the perspective of the employees and out in the global marketplace. This is a subject that most business students are likely to have an opinion on and a provocative article is provided to prompt them into expressing their views.

There are several opportunities throughout the unit for class or group discussion and useful language and structures are provided to facilitate this.

This first section concentrates on the impact of a company's size on its employees. Students talk about their own companies, their preferences and then listen to eight speakers giving their views on the advantages and disadvantages of working for big and small companies. The discussion is then widened to examine the students' views on the future of big companies.

A text then asserts that big business is more important than politics in the world today and will become increasingly so in the future, contradicting recent thinking that small entrepreneurial companies would kill off corporate dinosaurs. Students are invited to discuss this article and express their own opinions on the subject.

Warm-up

Look at the quotation from Bill Gates at the beginning of the unit and ask students to say whether or not they agree or disagree. Ask if they can give any examples to support their opinions.

1 If your students are from different companies, invite each of them to explain the situation for their company to the rest of the class and to express their own preference.

2 🔊 **9.1** Students simply have to listen to the speakers and note down whether they are talking about a big or a small company. However, after checking the answers, you might like to ask students to talk about anything they remember hearing that they found interesting or surprising.

Discussion

3 Students work in pairs to discuss the two questions. Then invite them to compare their results with other pairs before a feedback session with the whole class. Encourage students to give reasons for their decisions and for the order in which they have placed the people in b.

Collocations

4 Students match up the collocations and then in the next exercise match these with their definitions. If students want a further explanation of the term *corporate dinosaurs*, there is one in the notes for Exercise 6, but you might like to wait until then to see if you can elicit an explanation from the students themselves.

5 For homework, students could write sentences using each of the collocations.

🔊 **9.1**

Speaker 1
Sometimes you feel like a very small part of an enormous machine. But, at least there's a career structure. You may get promoted – eventually!

Speaker 2
I think there's greater job satisfaction, more variety. You certainly get to do a lot of different things. But there are no real fringe benefits – pensions, health insurance or anything like that.

Speaker 3
Well, it's easier to actually get to speak to the boss, that's for sure. But it's much more difficult to take time off. You're always needed. And if the boss gets sick, so does the company.

Speaker 4
People don't always notice if you're not actually working very hard, which is a good thing if you're lazy, but a bad thing if you're ambitious, because good work goes unnoticed too sometimes.

Speaker 5
There's obviously more security. Companies like mine don't just go out of business overnight. On the other hand, if there's a takeover or a merger, you may lose your job.

Speaker 6
I sometimes get sick of just seeing the same old faces every day. A firm like this is a lot like a family. That can be an advantage, of course. But, let's face it, some people hate their family!

Speaker 7
Well, it looks good on your CV, having worked for a company everybody's heard of. So there's more status, I think. But you can stay in the same job for years before anyone notices you!

Speaker 8
I like the amount of autonomy I get. I mean I'm pretty much left to do things the way I want to. In many ways, it's like being my own boss. And the decision-making process is so much faster!

9 Big business

Size works against excellence. *Bill Gates*

1   How big is the company you work for? Given the choice, would you prefer to work for a big or a small firm?

2    **9.1** Listen to people talking about the companies they work for and take notes. Do you think they are talking about a big corporation or small enterprise? Write 'big' or 'small'.

Speaker 1 big   Speaker 3 small   Speaker 5 big   Speaker 7 big

Speaker 2 small   Speaker 4 big   Speaker 6 small   Speaker 8 small

Discussion 3   Work with a partner and discuss the following:

a   What kind of companies do you think will be the most successful in the future? Hi-tech companies like Glaxo Smithkline, dotcoms like Amazon, multinationals like Ford? Something else?

b   Put the following in order of how powerful you think they are:
   • the President of General Motors   • the Secretary-General of the UN
   • the President of the USA   • New Zealand

Collocations 4   You are going to read an article about large companies. First, match up the collocations below.

national   trade
mass   frontiers
cross-border   production

marketing   election
substantial   resources
general   strategy

annual   assets
productive   dinosaurs
corporate   turnover

run   the competition
beat   currency
issue   a company

5   Which of the above mean:

a   buying and selling between countries? cross-border trade

b   big, old-fashioned companies? corporate dinosaurs

c   lots of money, materials and manpower? substantial resources

d   the process of choosing a political leader? general election

e   the money a company makes in a year? annual turnover

f   print money? issue currency

g   producing large quantities of the same product? mass production

h   everything a firm owns which makes money? productive assets

LAND OF THE
GIANTS

IGNORE the politicians. Big business is now the most powerful force on Earth. Countries don't matter any more. Companies do. Don't worry about who wins the next general election. Worry about who's running General Electric. Company
5 presidents, not White House presidents, are finally in charge.

Nearly as many people work for General Motors as live in Wales. Fewer than four hundred billionaires control as much capital as half the global population. Bill Gates alone is worth more than a hundred and thirty-five countries. If we compare the biggest companies'
10 annual turnover with national GDP, Philip Morris makes more money than New Zealand, Ford makes more than Thailand, and Exxon Mobil as much as South Africa and Nigeria put together.

Just three hundred corporations control 25% of all the productive assets on earth. Within the next ten years, many
15 multinationals could open their own embassies and even start issuing their own currency! Impossible? Not according to futurists, Jim Taylor and Watts Wacker. They argue that as cross-border trade increases, national frontiers become increasingly unimportant and global business begins to take over from government. Goodbye United
20 Nations. Hello United Corporations.

A few years ago, it was fashionable to disregard the 'Old Economy', as we welcomed in the Digital Age. Small entrepreneurial companies were going to kill off 'corporate dinosaurs' like Ford and Levi's. It never happened. Billions were wasted on dotcom disasters
25 run by kids with no business brains, while the big companies, slow at first, simply took the technology and used it more intelligently.

Size alone may not guarantee competitiveness, but to go from innovation to mass production quickly and efficiently takes a big company with substantial resources and an aggressive marketing
30 strategy. In the words of Andrew Grove, head of Intel: 'We don't beat the competition, we crush it.' Now, more than ever, big is beautiful.

a   What attitude does the writer have towards politicians?

b   Who *is* running GE these days?

c   Roughly what *is* the global economy currently worth? 100 trillion dollars? 200 trillion? More?

d   Do you know what *your* company's annual turnover is?

e   According to Taylor and Wacker, why will companies become more like governments?

f   Do you think a United Corporations could work?

g   Are dotcoms really dead?

h   Is it true what the article says about technology?

i   What view of competition does the article take? Do you agree?

Warm-up

As an introduction to the text, write up on the board in random order: *Bill Gates, General Electric, the White House, Wales, Philip Morris, Exxon Mobile, Ford, United Nations, Levis, Intel, New Zealand, South Africa, Nigeria*. Invite students to categorise these into, e.g. small countries, companies, centres of influence, etc. Ask them to specify the influence (or lack of it) that these items exert on the world economy. In the light of their answers to 3b, can the students predict what the text might say?

Alternatively, write on the board *Big is Beautiful* and ask students for their reaction. This is the opposite of the popular dictum *Small is Beautiful*. Discuss to what extent either extreme is a useful business concept.

6 Allow students to discuss the title and the first paragraph in pairs. Ask them also what the significance of the illustration is. (Large old-fashioned companies are often referred to as *corporate dinosaurs*, the analogy being that they have become too big and unwieldy to compete successfully against smaller more streamlined companies, and just as the dinosaurs died out, giving way to the smaller, more efficient mammals, so large corporations will be superseded by smaller operations that can manoeuvre more effectively in the modern marketplace.)

7 Give students plenty of time to read the article and to think about what it says. The questions to the right of it are there to encourage discussion between pairs of students and to draw out their own opinions. Allow plenty of time for this and ask them to report back to the class on their discussions.

8 Make this a whole-class discussion activity, inviting individual students to give their reactions, using the expressions given.

For homework, you might like to ask students to read through the article again, underlining all the collocations from Exercise 4 that they can find in it.

Points of view

This section also exploits the text on page 38. Students listen to some business people giving their reactions to the article and they have to determine the degree to which they agree or disagree with it. They then have to focus on more specific information from the recording and give a personal response to what is said.

1 ▭ **9.2** In this first exercise, students simply have to determine who agrees with the article, who disagrees and who agrees up to a point (but has some reservations about it).

Allow students to compare and discuss their answers in pairs before checking the answers with the class. Encourage them to cite the parts of what the speakers said that helped them make up their minds whether or not they were agreeing. You could play the recording again, pausing after each section, to jog their memories.

2 Go through the questions before playing the recording again so that students know exactly what they are listening for. Point out that each question has a second part, inviting a personal reaction. Stop the recording after the first speaker and ask a student to answer the first question. Then elicit various responses from around the class, encouraging students to use the expressions they have learnt for agreeing and disagreeing where appropriate. Do the same with each section of the recording.

Make a choice

This section invites students to make a choice between two offers (with the option also of neither of them) and give a small presentation explaining their preference.

1 Give students a few minutes to look at the choices and allow them to discuss with a partner if they wish.

2 Go through the expressions in the box with the class and then give students time to prepare their explanations individually. This could be done for homework with time being allotted in the next lesson for some students to give their explanations orally to the class.

If you're short of time

Students could read the article *Land of the giants* at home and come to the next class prepared to discuss it.

▭ **9.2**

Speaker 1
Hm. Basically, I think it's right. A few years ago everyone was saying all these small dynamic companies were going to take over the world, but, um, the problem with small companies is, erm, well, in a word – capital. They usually run out of money before they can establish themselves. I've heard that about half of new companies go out of business in the first two years. Unless they get taken over, of course, by a big company. And those which do succeed, well, they just become big companies, too.

Speaker 2
Well, I'm quite shocked that 400 people are as rich as half the world. In fact, I can hardly believe it, but, oh, I suppose it must be right. I do think national governments are less powerful than they were. But that's because of globalisation and organisations like NAFTA, and the ASEAN league and the EU, not just because companies are getting bigger and bigger. And I really can't see companies being allowed to print their own money! But, well, who knows?

Speaker 3
I think it misses the point. Two things. First of all, whoever said that successful dotcoms were small? If you want to succeed on the Internet, you have to get big fast. Look at companies like Amazon and Yahoo and eBay. So that's wrong for a start. On the other hand, these days, you don't necessarily have to be big to be a multinational. It depends what business you're in. If you're in a specialist business, you can sell your products or services all over the world and have just twenty or thirty people working for you. That's e-commerce for you!

Speaker 4
Well, I agree with what it says about politicians, but it's nothing new. Politicians were never as important as they thought they were. And to be honest, I'd rather have the CEO of a big successful company running the country than most of the prime ministers we've had over the last few years. But I wouldn't put a prime minister in charge of my company, thank you very much!

Speaker 5
I agree with most of what it says. The firm I work for tried to break up into smaller separate companies, er, oh, about eight years ago. A lot of people lost their jobs. There was quite a bit of bad feeling, I can tell you. The idea was to make ourselves more competitive. Re-engineering, they called it. Huh! It was a disaster. Small is good for new ideas, but it doesn't last. Big is best.

Speaker 6
It's total rubbish. I mean, OK, so some of the biggest companies in the world are enormously powerful. Obviously. That's rather worrying, actually. I don't like the idea that Nokia can be making more money than Norway or whatever it is. But there's no security in size nowadays. I read somewhere that half the Fortune 500 companies weren't even in business twenty years ago. So, what does that tell you? Change – that's what modern business is about. And the bigger you are, the slower you react to change. Smaller companies are the future.

6 Look at the article on page 38. What do you think the title means? Read the first paragraph to check your answer.

7 Read the article and think about the questions on the right. Then discuss each question with a partner.

8 What's your overall reaction to the article? Use the expressions below to help you.

> Basically, I think it's right.   I agree up to a point.   On the other hand, ...
> I agree with what it says about ...   It's a bit one-sided.
> It's total rubbish!   I'm quite shocked that ...   To be honest, I think ...
> I'm not really surprised about ...   I think it misses the point.

Points of view

1 ▭ 9.2 Listen to some business people talking about their reactions to the article on page 38. Who **a** agrees with what it says, **b** disagrees and **c** agrees up to a point? Write **a**, **b** or **c**.

Speaker 1 ⟦a⟧   Speaker 3 ⟦b⟧   Speaker 5 ⟦a⟧
Speaker 2 ⟦c⟧   Speaker 4 ⟦c⟧   Speaker 6 ⟦b⟧

2 Listen again and answer the following questions:

  a What has Speaker 1 heard? <u>about half of new companies go out of</u>
    Have you heard the same? <u>business in the first two years.</u>

  b What is Speaker 2 shocked about? <u>400 people are as rich as half the world.</u>
    Does it shock you?

  c What two points does Speaker 3 make about e-commerce?
    <u>Successful dot.com companies aren't small.</u>
    <u>Specialist e-commerce businesses don't have to be big to be mulitnational.</u>
    Do you agree with her?

  d What are Speaker 4's views on politicians? <u>They aren't important and aren't</u>
    Do you agree with him?   <u>good at running things.</u>

  e What happened to Speaker 5's company? <u>It tried to break up into several</u>
    Has your company been involved in anything similar? <u>smaller, separate companies.</u>

  f What did Speaker 6 read? <u>Half the Fortune 500 companies weren't in</u>
    Do you think it's right?   <u>business 20 years ago.</u>

Make a choice

1 Which would excite you more?

    a the offer of enough venture capital to start your own business
  or **b** the job of chief executive for a large multinational
  or **c** neither of the above

2 Take a few minutes to prepare a one-minute explanation of your preference.

> I've always wanted ..., so that's what I'd do.
> I'd prefer ..., because I'd be able to ...   That's easy. I'd definitely ...
> To be honest, both offers would frighten the life out of me!
> I'm not sure. I think, on balance, I'd probably ...   Why not do both?

10 Small talk

A friendship founded on business is better than a business founded on friendship.
John D Rockefeller, American industrialist

1 What exactly is small talk? How important do you think it is in business?

Questionnaire **2** How culturally aware are you? Try the following short questionnaire:

QUESTIONNAIRE

a You meet a Spanish business contact you haven't seen for ages who wants to stop and chat, but you're running late for an appointment. **Do you stay or do you make your excuses and go?**

b A British salesman is giving you a demonstration of a new office product. He seems to like telling a lot of jokes. **Do you join in the joke-telling or wait until he gets to the point?**

c You are having a pre-negotiation coffee at a potential client's headquarters in Bonn. **Do you mingle with the opposing team or stick with your own people?**

d Your new American boss organises a weekend barbecue. You find yourself amongst a lot of people you've never met. **Do you join in the fun or slip away quietly?**

e A Finnish colleague invites you to conduct the final stages of an important meeting in the sauna. **Do you accept or politely decline?**

For comments on your answers see page 124.

Getting down to business

1 In *When Cultures Collide* cross-cultural consultant Richard D Lewis talks about the role of small talk in international business. The diagram below shows how long it takes different nationalities to get down to business. Try to complete the chart with the names of the countries in the box.

| USA | Japan | Germany | UK | Finland | France | Spain & Italy |

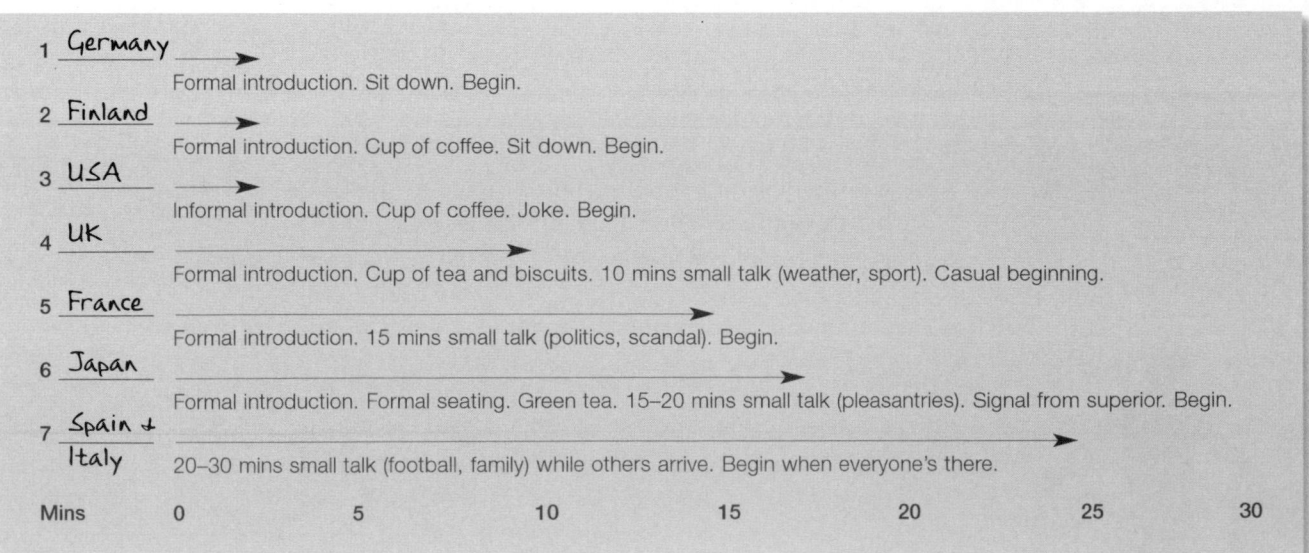

1 _Germany_ →
Formal introduction. Sit down. Begin.

2 _Finland_ →
Formal introduction. Cup of coffee. Sit down. Begin.

3 _USA_ →
Informal introduction. Cup of coffee. Joke. Begin.

4 _UK_ →
Formal introduction. Cup of tea and biscuits. 10 mins small talk (weather, sport). Casual beginning.

5 _France_ →
Formal introduction. 15 mins small talk (politics, scandal). Begin.

6 _Japan_ →
Formal introduction. Formal seating. Green tea. 15–20 mins small talk (pleasantries). Signal from superior. Begin.

7 _Spain & Italy_ →
20–30 mins small talk (football, family) while others arrive. Begin when everyone's there.

| Mins | 0 | 5 | 10 | 15 | 20 | 25 | 30 |

10 Small talk

Small talk can be a minefield when engaging in international business, because both cultural and personal factors come into play as well as any language difficulties. This unit addresses the issues of what is normal or acceptable in different cultural contexts and looks at some techniques for making successful small talk before getting down to business.

A listening activity gives students the chance to eavesdrop on some business small talk and try to determine what the speakers are talking about – a useful skill, as topics of conversation are often assumed to be understood and not made explicit.

Students are then given guided practice in making conversation themselves and finally have the chance to try out their skills in a conference dinner roleplay.

The grammatical focus is on the Past Simple and the Present Perfect, and the lexical focus is on common adjectival collocations and exaggeration and understatement.

You might like to refer students back to the work they did in Unit 2 on taboo subjects and techniques for keeping the conversation going.

This first section starts with a quiz about cultural differences when it comes to small talk.

Warm-up

Direct students' attention to the quotation from John D. Rockefeller and ask them for their opinions on whether, and if so how far, friendship and business can be mixed. How many of their closest friends are business colleagues or associates, and does this link affect either the friendship or the business in any way?

1 Do this as a whole-class discussion and encourage students to relate their own personal experiences of business small talk.

Quiz

2 Note that it is dangerous to make any sweeping generalisations about cultures, so be prepared for students to disagree with the analysis of the quiz or the diagram from *When Cultures Collide* in the next section, particularly when it comes to their own nationalities. Encourage open discussion, with provision of examples to back up viewpoints, but be very careful not to encourage comments on particular nationalities that may cause offence to other students in the class.

Getting down to business

This section takes the discussion of the implications for business small talk of the cultural context further with a diagram showing how much small talk different nationalities are likely to engage in before they get down to business.

Students then listen to extracts from several meetings and match each to one of the countries in the diagram. They then listen again for specific information to answer questons and do some grammar work on some of the things that are said.

1 Students will be guessing or giving a personal opinion when they fill the chart in for the first time. Allow them to discuss their answers in pairs or small groups if they wish. Then find out what everyone thinks in a class feedback session.

2 🔲 **10.1** The recording should give students the answers that Richard D Lewis believes to be correct. Note that the names of the countries are not always given in the extracts. The students must work them out from clues.

Extract 1 Japan (Clues: Sakamoto, Mizoguchi Bank, Usami-san, green tea)
Extract 2 Germany (Clues: Berlin, Wolfgang)
Extract 3 Italy (Clues: Juventus, Lazio, Italian football, Luigi)
Extract 4 UK (Clue: cricket)
Extract 5 Finland (Clue: Finland)
Extract 6 USA (Clue: New York)
Extract 7 France (Clue: president of France)

3 Go through the questions with the class before you play the recording again so that they know what information they are listening for. Can anyone answer any of the questions without listening to the recording again?

4 With multinational groups, encourage students to explain why they have put their nationality in a particular place on the chart and to give the class a brief explanation. With single nationality groups, find out how much agreement there is within the class on the position in the chart their nationality should occupy.

Past Simple or Present Perfect

5 This exercise involves closer study of the language used in listening 10.1. i.e. the choice of Past Simple or Present Perfect tenses.

When students have underlined their chosen forms, instead of playing the recording again, ask pairs to stand up and read out their dialogues. The rest of the class should stand up too if they believe the dialogues to be correct and remain seated if they believe there is a mistake. The students who have read the dialogues can amend them if they wish until they can persuade the whole class to stand up. Students who believe that they are correct (or when the class is divided) can appeal to you to indicate whether there is a mistake or not.

Play the recording again as a final check at the end.

Direct students' attention to the Grammar link on page 100 where they will find more on these tenses.

🔲 **10.1**

Extract 1
A: Er, how do you do. I'm Tom Pearson, Export Manager, Falcon Petroleum.
B: How do you do, Mr Pearson. I am Sakamoto, Assistant Director of International Investments, Mizoguchi Bank. Please sit here opposite the door. You'll be next to Usami-san.
A: Oh, OK. I sit here, right?
B: That's right. **Have you tried** green tea before, Mr Pearson?
A: Er, yes I **have**. I **had** it last time I **was** here. I like it very much.

Extract 2
A: Good morning, everyone. I'd like to introduce you all to Dr Alan Winter, who**'s come** over from the Atlanta office to spend a few days at our research centre. Welcome to Berlin, Dr Winter.
B: Thank you very much, Wolfgang. It **was** kind of you to invite me.
A: OK, let's get down to business, shall we?

Extract 3
A: ... And then Juventus **scored** the winner. It **was** an incredible goal! **Did you see** the Lazio game last night, Miss Sterling?
B: Yes, I **did. Wasn't** it a great match? One of the best **I've ever seen**. But then there's nothing like Italian football.
A: So, you like football then?
B: Oh, yeah. I love it. In fact, my father was a professional footballer.
A: Really?
B: Yes. He wasn't a superstar or anything, but he, er, played for Leeds.
A: Leeds United?
B: Yes, that's right.
A: They were a great team in the 70s, weren't they?

B: Yeah, that's when he played for them.
A: Amazing. Wait till I tell Luigi. Our new partner's father played for Leeds United, ha!
B: Where is Luigi, by the way?
A: Oh, he'll be here soon. He's never the first to arrive, not Luigi ...

Extract 4
A: Rain **stopped** play again yesterday, I see.
B: Sorry?
A: The cricket. They **cancelled** the match.
B: Oh, they **didn't**! Well, we certainly **haven't seen** much cricket this summer.
A: No. Chocolate biscuit?
B: Oh, have we got chocolate ones? Business must be good.
C: Right, everyone. Er, I suppose we'd better get started ...

Extract 5
A: Right, shall we start? First of all, this is Catherine Anderson from London. I think this is your first time in Finland, isn't it Catherine? Or **have you been** here before?
B: Actually, I **came** here on holiday once, but that **was** a long time ago.
A: Well, we hope you enjoy your stay with us. Now there's fresh coffee if you'd like some before we begin ...

Extract 6
A: OK, you guys. Thanks for coming. Now, to business ... Oh, did you all get coffee?
B: Hey, wait up. I got a great one here.
C: Oh no, it's one of Marty's jokes.
B: See, there's this guy George goes for a job, right? And it's a really cool job. Right here in New York. Big money. So, anyway, he takes a test, like an aptitude test, you know, him and this woman. There's two of them. And they have to

take a test to get the job.
C: Yeah, yeah, so ...?
B: So they both get exactly the same score on the test, George and the woman – ninety-nine per cent.
C: Uh-huh.
B: So George goes into the interviewer's office. And the interviewer says 'Well, you both got one question wrong on the test, but, I'm sorry, we're giving the job to the other candidate.' So George says 'Hey, that's not fair! How come she gets the job?' And the interviewer says 'Well, on question 27, the question you both got wrong, she wrote "I don't know" and you wrote "Neither do I".'
C: That's a terrible joke, Marty.
B: No, you see, he **copied** her test, right?
A: Marty, we**'ve heard** the joke before. It's ancient. OK, everybody, time to work.
B: I **thought** it **was** funny.

Extract 7
A: As you know, Albert, I'm the last person to talk about other people's private lives. If the president of France himself wants to have an affair, I don't care. I mean, this is not the United States.
B: Yes, quite.
A: What I do worry about is what's going on between our vice-president and our head of finance.
B: They're having an affair?
A: **Haven't you heard? I thought** everybody **knew**.
B: God, no! No one ever tells me anything.
A: I mean, it's not the affair I care about. It's how it affects our meetings. Haven't you noticed?
B: Noticed what?
A: How they always agree on everything.
B: Well, now you mention it ...

2 🔊 **10.1** Listen to extracts from seven meetings. Check your answers in 1 by matching each extract to the correct country.

3 Listen again and answer the questions. There is one question for each extract.

1 Where exactly is Tom Pearson asked to sit? _opposite door, next to Usami-san_

2 How long is Dr Alan Winter going to spend in Berlin? _a few days_

3 What was Miss Sterling's father's job? _professional footballer_

4 What kind of snack is served at the meeting? _chocolate biscuits_

5 Why was Catherine in Finland before? _she was on holiday_

6 In the joke, what score do both the man and the woman get in the test? _99%_

7 What commonly happens in their meetings these days? _the vice-president and the head of finance agree on everything_

4 Place your own nationality on the chart, if it's not there already. If it is there, do you agree with where it's placed?

Past Simple or Present Perfect

5 Look at these excerpts from the conversations you just listened to and <u>underline</u> the best grammatical choice. Then listen again and check.

1 A **Did you try** / **Have you tried** green tea before, Mr Pearson?

B Er, yes I **did** / **have**. I **had** / **have had** it last time I **was** / **have been** here. I like it very much.

2 A I'd like to introduce you all to Dr Alan Winter, who **came** / **has come** over from the Atlanta office to spend a few days at our research centre. Welcome to Berlin, Dr Winter.

B Thank you very much, Wolfgang. It **was** / **has been** kind of you to invite me.

3 A ... And then Juventus **scored** / **has scored** the winner. It **was** / **has been** an incredible goal! **Did you see** / **Have you seen** the Lazio game last night, Miss Sterling?

B Yes, I **did** / **have**. **Wasn't it** / **Hasn't it been** a great match? One of the best I **ever saw** / **have ever seen**.

4 A Rain **stopped** / **has stopped** play again yesterday, I see.

B Sorry?

A The cricket. They **cancelled** / **have cancelled** the match.

B Oh, they **didn't** / **haven't**! Well, we certainly **didn't see** / **haven't seen** much cricket this summer.

5 A I think this is your first time in Finland, isn't it Catherine? Or **were you** / **have you been** here before?

B Actually, I **came** / **have come** here on holiday once, but that **was** / **has been** a long time ago.

6 A That's a terrible joke, Marty.

B No, you see, he **copied** / **has copied** her test, right?

A Marty, we **heard** / **have heard** the joke before. It's ancient. OK, everybody, time to work.

B I **thought** / **have thought** it **was** / **has been** funny.

7 A What I do worry about is what's going on between our vice-president and our head of finance.

B They're having an affair?

A **Didn't you hear** / **Haven't you heard?** I **thought** / **have thought** everybody **knew** / **has known**.

B God, no! No one ever tells me anything.

Grammar link

for more on the Past Simple and Present Perfect see page 100

What are they talking about?

1 ▣ 10.2 Listen to different people chatting in an office. How quickly can you guess what they are talking about? Five of the following topics are mentioned.

> sport   news   books ✓   music   the economic situation ✓   films ✓   holidays ✓
> weather   clothes ✓   people

2 Which words helped you guess?

Talking about experiences

1 Complete at least six of the following sentences with information which is true for you. Use the verbs and adjectives in the boxes below to help you, if necessary. You will need to change their grammatical form.

> be   have   do   go   see   hear   meet   stay   buy

> fabulous   stupid   marvellous   ridiculous   exciting   wonderful   silly
> great   boring   violent   amazing   hard   disgusting   strange   nice
> lousy   attractive   delicious   brilliant   fascinating   frightening   dull
> luxurious   wild   beautiful   pathetic   funny   interesting   terrible
> nasty   relaxing   stressful   entertaining

1 I've _____ in some _____ hotels, but the one I _____ in in _____ (*where?*) must be the _____ I've ever _____ in.

2 The _____ city I've ever _____ to must be _____. I _____ there _____ (*when?*).

3 I've _____ some _____ people, but the guy/woman I _____ in _____ (*where?*) must be the _____ I've ever _____.

4 The _____ job I've ever _____ must be when I was a _____ (*what?*) for _____ (*who?*). I _____ that job for _____ (*how long?*).

5 I've _____ to some _____ parties, but the one I _____ to in _____ (*where?*) must be the _____ I've ever _____ to.

6 The _____ holiday I've ever _____ was when I _____ to _____ (*where?*). I _____ there for _____ (*how long?*).

7 I've _____ some _____ meals, but the _____ (*what?*) I _____ in _____ (*where?*) must be the _____ I've ever _____.

8 The _____ game of _____ (*what?*) I've ever _____ was _____ (*what?*). The _____ thing was _____ (*what?*).

9 I've _____ some _____ films, but _____ (*what?*), which I _____ _____ (*when?*), must be the _____ I've ever _____.

10 The _____ joke I've ever _____ was probably the one about _____ (*what?*). Don't ask me to tell you it!

Lexis link

for more on the vocabulary of conversation see page 101

2 Walk around the class and read out some of your experiences to different people. Try to say a little more about each one. Ask questions to find out more about their experiences.

What are they talking about?

This short section gives students the chance to listen in on some conversations. The topics are not immediately obvious so they must listen hard to work out what is being talked about.

1 ▭ 10.2 Again, you could make this more lively by having students stand up (or raise their hands) as soon as they think they know what is being talked about. As soon as a student stands up, stop the recording and ask for the answer. Tell the class simply whether this answer is correct or not. If it is not correct, the game goes on when you play the rest of the recording. The first student to correctly identify the topic wins a point.

2 Ask the students who won points to tell the others what clues helped them to guess. Ask others to contribute further clues that they spotted.

Strong students might like to make up their own short dialogues in which clues to the topic are given, but the topic itself is not revealed until the end. They can then perform these and challenge the rest of the class to identify what they are talking about.

Talking about experiences

In this section, students prepare some sentences about their own experiences which will be useful when making small talk. They then try them out on other students and take turns asking questions to find out more.

1 Give students time to complete the sentences. Be prepared to help with any unknown vocabulary in the boxes. Alternatively, you could ask students to do this preparation at home and bring their sentences to the next lesson to use in Exercise 2.

It is always helpful and encouraging to the students if you can join in with activities such as these, so complete the sentences for yourself and be prepared to mingle with the students in Exercise 2 and talk about your experiences. The students will appreciate it and you will get a good idea of how well they are coping with the task.

2 Allow plenty of time for this because it is useful language practice in talking about experiences, responding to what is said, asking questions and keeping a conversation going (if necessary, remind students of the techniques they learnt in Unit 2).

Direct students' attention to the Lexis link on page 101 which has some useful language and strategies for making conversation more interesting, using exaggeration and understatement.

▭ **10.2**

Conversation 1
A: Hello, you look tanned.
B: Oh, thanks. I'm afraid it's started to fade already.
A: When did you get back, then?
B: A couple of days ago. I still haven't got used to being back at work.
A: No, I bet you haven't. Tobago, wasn't it?
B: Yeah. It was the best holiday we've ever had.

Conversation 2
C: Did you go, then?
D: Yeah, I went last week. I've wanted to see it for ages.
C: And?
D: Mm, it was OK, I suppose. I was a bit disappointed, actually.

C: I thought it was great. Because I didn't like him at all in *Titanic*.
D: No, that was a terrible film, wasn't it?

Conversation 3
E: Could I have it back when you've finished?
F: Yes, of course. Sorry I forgot I still had it.
E: It's all right. Only I promised I'd lend it to someone else.
F: Don't worry, I've nearly finished it. I'm on chapter fifty.
E: It's OK. There's no rush.
F: Thanks. It's a brilliant book, isn't it?

Conversation 4
G: Where did you get that?
H: What? Oh, this. Well, you know that shop we went into a few months ago?
G: No.

H: Yes, you do. The one you didn't want to go into.
G: Oh, that one! You didn't buy it there?
H: Yeah.
G: Well, you always did have a funny taste in clothes. It suits you, though.

Conversation 5
J: Have you read this?
K: No, what does it say?
J: It's about all these job losses in e-commerce.
K: Oh, that. Yeah, well, I knew that was going to happen.
J: So much for the age of the Internet!
K: Hm. It's certainly bad news for the stock markets.

At a conference dinner

This section provides students with a roleplay in which they practise small talk at a conference dinner. They can put into practice all the language and strategies they have learnt in this unit.

Fluency

This roleplay is guided so students don't have to use their imaginations too much to think up what to say. This will ensure they can concentrate on fluency and using the language they have been studying to keep the conversation flowing.

However, although it is nice to keep an element of spontaneity in this activity, students should prepare the information they'll need before they start. For example:

Which city are they in? (They should make it one they both know quite well.)

Has it been a good or bad conference in general? What talks did they go to?

What did they eat? Did they enjoy it?

Where are they staying? What's it like?

What's the weather been like? How has that affected what they've done?

Go through the introduction with the class and then give them plenty of time to read through their roles and think about what they are going to say. Discourage them from writing their lines down and simply reading them out. Point out that they should respond to what they hear, rather than ignoring it and just going on to the next item on their role card. Remind them to listen carefully to what their partner says so that they can respond appropriately.

A good way of encouraging this is to make them swap partners immediately after the roleplay and do it again with someone new. If you do this, they won't be able to plan together how the roleplay will work and will have to listen carefully to what their new partner says.

If you're short of time

Set *Getting down to business* Exercises 1, 4 and 5 and *Talking about experiences* Exercise 1 for homework.

If you don't have time for two roleplays, keep *Talking about experiences* Exercise 2 short and instead of having all the students mingling around the class, choose pairs of students to have a brief conversation about each statement in front of the class.

Set the Grammar and Lexis links exercises for homework and check the answers at the beginning of the next class.

At a conference dinner

Fluency Work with a partner to practise small talk at a conference dinner.

You are sitting next to each other at a conference dinner in a city you both know well, and have just sat through an incredibly long and boring opening speech. You have not been properly introduced.

Speaker A

Start the conversation:

'I think that must be the longest opening speech I've ever heard! I'm _____ (name), by the way. I don't think we've met.'

Speaker B

'Pleased to meet you. I'm _____ (name).'
Continue the conversation by asking about **one or more** of the following:

- what your partner thought of the conference (fun? dull?)
- talks your partner's been to (any interesting ones?)
- the dinner you've just eaten (local dishes, wine)

Speaker A

Continue the conversation by asking about **one or more** of the following:

- your partner's company (location, main activities)
- your partner's job (how long he/she's had it)
- where your partner's staying (service, comfort, convenience)

Speaker B

Continue the conversation by talking about **one or more** of the following:

- the city (architecture, people, prices, local economy)
- the weather (typical for the time of year?)
- shopping (the best places you've found to buy presents)

Speaker A

Continue the conversation by talking about **one or more** of the following:

- sightseeing (a place of interest you've visited)
- the nightlife (a restaurant, bar or club you've been to)
- a recent item of news (politics, sport, scandal)

Speaker B

Break off the conversation:

'Oh, wait a minute, it looks like the next speaker is going to begin. Let's hope this one's better than the last.'

11 E-mail

When you write a letter, you take some care over your words. Why is ti that when we send an e-mail we jutst wirte down anyold nonselnce? and press send and thetn hoep for the best ½. *Lucy Kellaway, Financial Times*

1 Do you prefer e-mailing to picking up the phone? Do you set aside a particular time to check your e-mail? Discuss with a partner.

2 ▣ **11.1** Listen to four business people talking about their attitudes to e-mail. Do they mention any of the points you discussed in 1?

3 Listen again. Tick which statements best summarise what each speaker says.

Speaker 1	**Speaker 2**	**Speaker 3**	**Speaker 4**
✓ **a** E-mail is immediate and efficient. The downside is that you are always available.	**a** E-mail is great but it always gets lost, unlike telephone messages.	**a** If people forget to complete the subject line, it means the e-mail isn't important.	✓ **a** Everyone does their own secretarial work because the secretaries were sacked.
b You waste a lot of time e-mailing people, especially if you are writing in English.	✓ **b** E-mail is great but people are often slow to reply to their messages.	✓ **b** If there's no subject line, you have to read the e-mail in case it's important.	**b** Everyone does their own secretarial work because the secretaries left.

4 Work with a partner. Complete the texts below with the numbers in the box.

> 70   2½   115   ~~30~~   ⅓   15–20   ¼   326   ¾   5

According to the Institute of Directors, the majority of business people receive around __30__ e-mails a day. As it takes about __5__ minutes to read and reply to (or ignore) each, that means __2½__ hours' work or __¼__ of the working day.

According to Ferros Research, the average executive spends __326__ hours a year dealing with e-mail, and this actually increases productivity by __15–20__ %. Unfortunately, another __115__ hours are wasted deleting 'spam' (unwanted publicity material) from their inboxes.

According to a recent Internet survey, nearly __¾__ of business people have sent an e-mail and then regretted it. Hastily written messages can easily sound too direct or even rude, and upsetting a colleague with an angry e-mail (or 'flame') can seriously damage your professional relationship.

According to the Society for Human Resource Management, roughly __⅓__ of employers look at their employees' e-mail, and over __70__ % believe they have a right to read virtually anything written on the company's electronic communications system.

Answers on page 125

5 Work with a partner. Decide how the information you just read could affect:
- the way you manage your time
- who you give your e-mail address to
- the content of your e-mails
- your writing style

6 The statistics in 4 contain several examples of approximation. Find words meaning:

a approximately __around__   __about__   __roughly__   d more than __over__

b almost __nearly__   __virtually__   e typical __average__

c most __majority__

11 E-mail

Students begin by talking about attitudes to e-mail. They look at some statistics about its use and how much of people's time it takes up. They learn some useful language for talking about approximations and then look at the style of English used for writing e-mails. An extract from *The Bluffer's Guide to the Internet* gives some amusing advice for would-be e-mailers and students discuss how much truth there is in it. They then look at some rules for e-mail and complete and improve some examples. Finally, they work in groups to exchange e-mails.

The grammatical focus is on future forms and the lexical focus is on collocations relating to computers.

In this first section, students begin by exploring attitudes to e-mail and how it affects time management.

Warm-up

Find out how much your students use e-mail and whether they consider it to be a blessing or a curse. Put two columns on the board to list the good and bad points of e-mail, e.g.

Good points
- E-mail is fast.
- It is cheaper than a telephone call.

Bad points
- It takes a long time to download and respond to messages, particularly if you've been away for a couple of days.
- People expect an immediate reply and you spend your whole day answering e-mails.

Focus attention on the quotation from Lucy Kellaway and ask for comments.

How does carelessness in composing e-mails affect the impression the receiver gets of the sender? What extra problems does it pose if the e-mail is in a foreign language?

1 Students discuss the questions in pairs. Encourage them to give reasons for their decisions. They should note down the points they make to refer to in the next exercise.

2 ▸ **11.1** Tell students to listen to the four speakers to see if they mention any of the points they discussed in Exercise 1. They will have the opportunity to listen again for detail in the next exercise. Play the recording and get feedback from the class.

3 Go through the statements with the students before you play the recording again so that they know exactly what they are listening for. In a class feedback session, find out how many people agree with each speaker.

4 Students work in pairs to read the texts and complete them with the numbers. Ask them to read the numbers aloud first to ensure that they can pronounce them correctly. See how much agreement there is on the correct positions of each of the numbers before you give students the answers. Ask them to note down the correct answers as they will need the corrected texts for the next exercise.

5 Students discuss in pairs how far the information they have read could affect them. Have a class feedback session to find out what everyone thinks.

6 Encourage students to produce sentences of their own using these expressions.

▸ **11.1**

Speaker 1
Well, e-mail has several obvious advantages over the phone. I mean, for me, the main one is that it's instantaneous. You can get straight down to business, without wasting time on getting through to the person you want and then having to ask them how they are, about their family and so on and so on. So it's more efficient. Also, it's a lot easier if I'm using English – gives me time to think about what I want to say. Of course, the downside to e-mail is that you can't stop people you don't want to talk to from sending you endless messages!

Speaker 2
Oh, e-mail's great. All you have to do is key in your message, click send and it's all done.

Moments later your message will arrive at its destination – if it doesn't get lost on the way, that is. Of course, it doesn't usually get lost. It usually just sits there for weeks waiting for an answer! You wouldn't dream of just letting the phone ring and ring without answering it. So why do some people never answer their e-mail?

Speaker 3
Someone told me that at Sun Microsystems one and a half million e-mails are sent and received each day. That's about 120 per employee! It's not quite as bad as that here, but it's bad enough. The worst thing is when people forget to complete the subject line. Then you've no idea what the message is about, so you have to read it just in case it's important, which it usually isn't. But if it's really urgent, people phone.

Speaker 4
A few years ago, our company did the same thing as SEI Investments in California. It gave everyone a PC, a laptop and a mobile and sacked all the secretaries. Well, some of them got other jobs, but most of them just went. So overnight we had to do all our own secretarial work. But I'm not so sure it's a good idea. A friend of mine works for Labconco – they make laboratory equipment – and what happens there is they don't let their customers into their e-mail or voice mail systems at all! They say they like to keep the client relationship personal. 'People buy from people,' their CEO says. I think a lot of our secretaries went to work there!

Writing e-mail

In this section, students look at the style of e-mails and some suggested rules for writing them. They read an extract from a humorous book on the subject and practise changing formal letters into a style more suitable for e-mails. They then work on making e-mails clearer and better organised.

Warm-up

If students have little experience of e-mails in English, start by giving them some examples to look at. There are various sites on the Internet which offer collections of authentic e-mails which you can take to class. Type *e-mail* into any search engine to get a list of these.

1   Students could answer these questions with reference to their own languages first and then exchange views on their experience of the style of e-mails in English.

2   *Bluffer's Guides* are a series of humorous books on various subjects. Their function is partly to inform, but mostly to entertain. A bluffer is someone who doesn't actually know very much about a subject but is able to convince other people that he or she does. Bluffers usually achieve this by peppering their conversations with technical terms relevant to the subject concerned. Have a class discussion on how much truth there is in the extract given here.

E-mail guidelines

3   Check the answers by having one student read out the rule and another provide the reason.

4   The three types of grammar words are pronouns, verbs and articles.

Sample answer:

> Hi Rosa I've been in meetings all day, so I just got your message plus the attachment. It sounds great. I particularly like your suggestion about (the) discount rates. One or two points are a bit unclear perhaps, but basically it's good stuff. You could add something about packaging. You've done a nice job, anyway. I'll see you on Friday. Leo

Writing e-mail

1 Do you use a different style for writing e-mails, compared to letters and faxes? Are there any 'rules' for writing e-mails?

2 Read this extract from the book *The Bluffer's Guide® to the Internet*. Is there any truth in it?

Adapted from *The Bluffer's Guide® to the Internet*

e-mail style

Because e-mail makes people write to each other rather than phone, the art of writing – which was being undermined by the telephone – is no longer dying. It has been killed off completely.

The reason lies in the usually sketchy typing skills of most computer users. To test these skills as little as possible, e-mails are generally brief. Often they consist merely of the previously received message sent back with a 'Yes' or 'OK, ten tomorrow' or 'Rubbish!' or similar tag appended.

Many verbless sentences too.

Short paragraphs.

Lots.

Strange word order often there is also.

Sometimes e-mails are typed entirely in upper case with the 'shift' key down, WHICH YOU COULD SAY IS THE EQUIVALENT OF SHOUTING.

Glossary
- **undermined =** weakened
- **sketchy =** inadequate
- **tag appended =** short additional message
- **upper case =** capital letters

E-mail guidelines

3 There are no universally accepted rules for writing e-mail, but here are some useful guidelines. Match each rule (a–g) to the reason why it is useful.

a Create a subject line with impact.
b Write short sentences.
c Keep paragraphs short.
d Don't always trust your spell check.
e Put your signature on the message.
f Proofread the message before sending it.
g Use headings, bullets and numbering.

[e] It saves people scrolling down to see if there's more text.

[g] These will guide the reader and make the message easier to grasp.

[d] It can't tell the difference between *your* and *you're*, or *theirs* and *there's*!

[a] It is more likely that someone will read your e-mail.

[c] There's less chance the reader will miss anything.

[f] It creates a more professional image if there are no silly errors.

[b] You don't need complex grammar or punctuation.

4 People you know well may send you e-mails with certain grammar words missing. What three types of grammar word are missing in these examples?

~~It's a~~ great idea.   ~~I'm~~ presenting it to ~~the~~ board today.   ~~I'll~~ speak to you later.

Now put the missing words back into the e-mail below.

Sanyo proposal – I like it!

Subject: Sanyo proposal – I like it!

▷ Attachments: *none*

| Geneva | Medium | **B** *I* U T |

Hi Rosa – been in meetings all day, so just got your message plus attachment.

Sounds great – particularly like your suggestion about discount rates. One or two

points a bit unclear perhaps, but basically good stuff. Could add something about

packaging. Nice job, anyway.

See you Friday. Leo

---

5 E-mails generally contain fewer fixed expressions and are less formal than business letters. Rewrite the following extracts from business letters as e-mails using the expressions in the boxes.

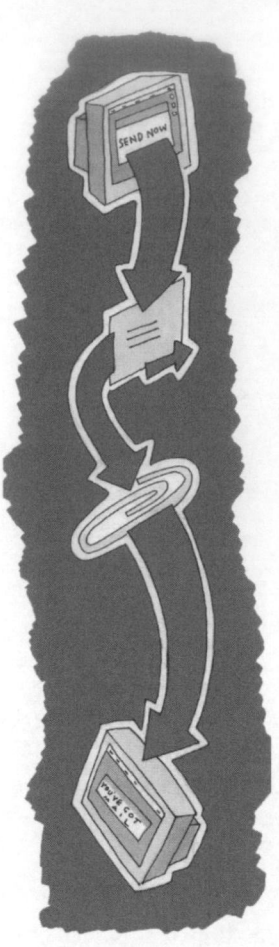

Sorry about ...	Bad news: ...	Could you do me a favour and ...?
Got your message on ...	Cheers.	Sorry, but I can't make ...
Hi ...	Good news: from ...	Shall I ...?

Dear Louisa,
Thank you for your letter of September 12th. **Unfortunately, I shall be unable to attend** the meeting on the 21st. **I would appreciate it if you could** send me a copy of the minutes.

Best wishes,
Tom Hunt

I'm delighted to tell you that as of Jan 2 we are offering substantial discounts on all orders over 1000. **If you wish, I would be happy to** send you further details and a copy of our new catalogue.

I regret to inform you that the board turned down your proposal. **I would like to apologise for** not getting back to you sooner on this, but I've been in Montreal all week.

If you have any questions, let me know.	Following ...
Are we still OK for ...?	About ...	I'm sending you ... as an attachment.
Speak to you soon.	Please ...	Thanks.	See you ...

I am writing to confirm our appointment on May 3rd. My flight gets in about 11am. **With regard to** my presentation on the 4th, could you make the necessary arrangements? **I enclose** a list of the equipment I'll need.

I look forward to meeting you next week.

Charlotte De Vere

Further to our telephone conversation this morning, **I'd be grateful if you could** send me a full description of the problem and I'll pass it on to our technical department.

Thank you for taking the time to do this. If I can be of any further assistance, please do contact me again.

I look forward to hearing from you.

5 Elicit or explain that fixed expressions are sequences of words which often occur together, and that they are particularly common in formal letters. For example, *Thank you for your letter of ..., I regret to inform you that ..., I look forward to hearing from you.* Although the language of e-mails is in many ways simpler than that of formal letters, the lack of formulaic expressions like these which can be memorised and used for a variety of situations may make e-mail writing more challenging for some students.

Answers

Hi Louisa

Got your message on September 12th. **Sorry, but I can't make** the meeting on the 21st. **Could you do me a favour and** send me a copy of the minutes?

Cheers

Tom Hunt

Good news: from Jan 2 we are offering substantial discounts on all orders over 1000. **Shall I** send you further details and a copy of our new catalogue?

Bad news: the board turned down your proposal. **Sorry about** not getting back to you sooner on this, but I've been in Montreal all week.

Are we still OK for May 3rd? My flight gets in about 11am. **About** my presentation on the 4th, could you make the necessary arrangements? **I'm sending you** a list of the equipment I'll need **as an attachment.**

See you next week.

Charlotte De Vere

Following our telephone conversation this morning, **please** send me a full description of the problem and I'll pass it on to our technical department.

Thanks. If you have any questions, let me know.

Speak to you soon.

6 Elicit or explain that a new paragraph begins where there is a change of idea. Although e-mails are less formal than letters, it is still very helpful for clarity if they are divided into paragraphs. Discuss with students what makes a good subject line for an e-mail: a good subject line is short, creates a context and gives clues about what is in the message.

Sample answer

> Subject: Quarterly figures
>
> Otto
>
> How are you doing? Got the joke you sent me. Very funny. Spoke to Cheryl in accounts today. She sends her regards. On the subject of accounts, I don't seem to have your quarterly figures. Did you send them in? I've faxed you those statistics you wanted, by the way. Hope they come in useful for your presentation. Let me know how the presentation goes. And don't forget those figures.

To practise writing good subject lines, give each student two pieces of paper. On one they write a short message of one or two lines. On the other, they write the subject line for that message. They then exchange the message only with a partner. They then each read the message they have received, write a subject line for it at the top and return it to the sender, who compares it with the original subject line. Pairs can discuss the reasons for any similarities or differences between the two.

[With thanks to John Hughes for this idea.]

7   Sample answer

> Mr Nordqvist,
>
> Thank you for your hospitality during our stay. Karen and I felt that the meeting was a great success and we look forward to discussing our ideas in more detail.
>
> I passed on your comments to Diane Lee and she assures me she will contact you over the next couple of weeks.
>
> It was a pleasure meeting you and exploring the possibilities of a joint venture between us.
>
> Best wishes
>
> Sam White

6 Rearrange the information in the e-mail below and rewrite it to make it clearer. Give it paragraphs and a suitable subject line.

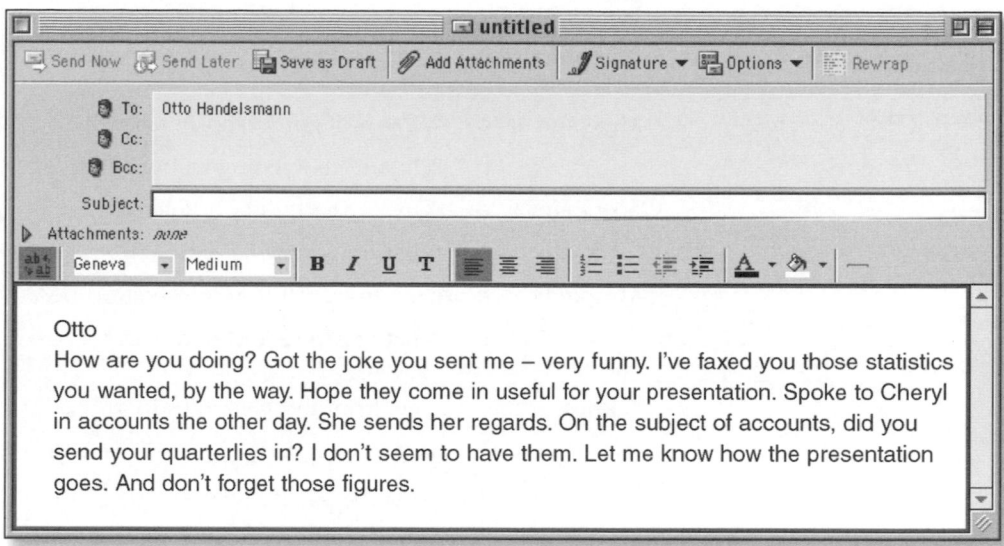

Otto

How are you doing? Got the joke you sent me – very funny. I've faxed you those statistics you wanted, by the way. Hope they come in useful for your presentation. Spoke to Cheryl in accounts the other day. She sends her regards. On the subject of accounts, did you send your quarterlies in? I don't seem to have them. Let me know how the presentation goes. And don't forget those figures.

7 Make the message below simpler and clearer by deleting as many unnecessary words as possible without changing the meaning.

Fact finding trip to B&C (Sweden)

To: nielsnordqvist@bergman.com
Cc: Jonas Kamprad
Bcc: Diane Lee, Karen Sharpe
Subject: Fact finding trip to B&C (Sweden)
Attachments: *none*

Dear Mr Nordqvist,
On behalf of myself and my colleague, Karen Sharpe, may I take this opportunity to thank you and your team once again for your kind hospitality during our brief stay in Malmö. Karen and I both felt that the two-hour meeting we had with you at your headquarters last week was, without doubt, a great success, and we very much look forward to discussing our ideas with you in much more detail than we were able to in that extremely short but highly productive meeting.

I am sure you will be pleased to know that I passed on your valuable comments to our Managing Director, Diane Lee, and she assures me that she will certainly be in contact with you over the next couple of weeks or so. In the meantime, let me just say that it was a very great pleasure meeting you, your managers and enthusiastic staff and exploring the possibilities of some kind of a joint venture between us in the not too distant future.
With my very best wishes,
Sam White, Senior Product Manager, Thermoflex (UK)

Changing arrangements

Lexis link

for more on the vocabulary of computers see page 103

1 [cassette icon] 11.2 Sarah is organising a business trip to Japan for herself and her colleague Peter. She has left three voice mail messages for Koichi, her contact in Nagoya. Listen and answer the questions.

Message 1   **a**   When will Sarah and Peter arrive in Nagoya? <u>Wednesday</u>

            b   Why are they going to be 2 days late? <u>Sarah has to be in Edinburgh on Monday.</u>

Message 2   **a**   Why can't Sarah and Peter stay at the Radisson? <u>it's full</u>

            b   What does Sarah ask Koichi to do? <u>find another hotel for them</u>

Message 3   **a**   How long will the presentation be? <u>about 45 minutes</u>

            b   What software and hardware do they need? <u>PowerPoint, projector, screen</u>

2 Complete the extracts from the messages in 1.

  a   Peter and I <u>were hoping to</u> arrive in Nagoya on Monday ...

  b   That <u>'s not going to be</u> possible now, I'm afraid ...

  c   So, we <u>'re aiming to</u> get there by Wednesday ...

  d   Peter and I <u>were planning to</u> stay at the Radisson ...

  e   ... I <u>was going to</u> e-mail you about this yesterday.

  f   We <u>'re intending</u> to keep the presentation itself quite short ...

  g   ... we <u>'re going to</u> use PowerPoint ...

  h   ... we <u>'re going to</u> need a projector and screen ...

Grammar link

for more on future forms see page 102

3 Which of the above

  1   are predictions? [b] [h]

  2   refer to current plans or intentions? [c] [f] [g]

  3   refer to past plans or intentions? [a] [d] [e]

4 Write the e-mail that Koichi might write in response to Sarah's messages.

You've got mail

Work in groups of three or four to exchange e-mails.

- Change of plan. I was going to ..., but ...
- Have you heard ...?
- Don't want to be a pain, but ...
- I was thinking of ...
- I want to go on a training course to ...
- I've just heard ...
- I'm giving a presentation about ...
- A few of us are planning to ...

1 Write a short e-mail message (no more than 60 words) to each member of your group, starting with one of the introductory expressions on the left. Make sure the information in your e-mail is connected to your own job or experience. Include your e-mail address, that of the person you are e-mailing and a suitable subject line.

2 After five minutes place your message in the 'inbox' at the front of the class and take out any messages addressed to you.

3 Write a reply to each message you receive directly below the original message. Invent any information you have to.

4 After another five minutes, put your replies back in the 'inbox' and take out any addressed to you.

5 Repeat the above procedure until you have dealt with at least five different topics.

6 In your group, compare the sequences of e-mails you have produced.

Changing arrangements

1 🔲 **11.2** Go through the questions with the class before you play the recording so that they have some idea what they are about to hear and know what they are listening for.

Direct students' attention to the Lexis link on page 103 for more vocabulary of computers.

2 Encourage students to try to remember what Sarah said, but play the recording again for them if necessary. Check the answers before going on to Exercise 3.

3 Direct students' attention to the Grammar link on page 102 where they will find more information and practice of future forms.

4 This could be set for homework. Start students off by brainstorming suggestions for Koichi's subject line. Display the completed e-mails in the classroom for everyone to read and enjoy.

Suggested e-mail:

> Subject line: Arrangements for Nagoya trip
>
> Hi Sarah
>
> Thanks for letting me know about the change of plan. Have booked rooms for you and Peter at Nagoya Holiday Inn. No problem with equipment – have already arranged projector and screen. Have a good time in Edinburgh. Looking forward to seeing you on Wednesday. Let me know flight details and I'll meet you at the airport.
>
> Koichi

You've got mail

To make this more authentic and fun, prepare a box to put at the front of the class in which completed e-mails can be posted and from which they can be collected. Making an electronic bleeping noise and reading out the names of students who have incoming mail will add to the fun and keep the activity moving briskly. Separate boxes for the different groups might help avoid too much confusion at the front.

Go through the introductory expressions with the class and make sure everyone understands them. You might like to ask for a few suggestions for situations in which they might be used.

Students start writing their e-mails. Ensure that there is enough space on each piece of paper for subsequent responses. To avoid a crush at the front of the class, encourage students to post each e-mail as it is written and then return to their seats to prepare the next one.

The sequences of e-mails would make an interesting display for the classroom walls.

If you're short of time

Set *Writing e-mail* Exercises 5 and 6 for homework.

Set the Grammar and Lexis links exercises for homework and check the answers at the beginning of the next class.

🔲 **11.2**

Message 1

Hi Koichi, it's Sarah Greenwood here. There's been a change of plan. **Peter and I were hoping to arrive in Nagoya on Monday. That's not going to be possible now, I'm afraid**, because I have to be in Edinburgh that day. **So, we're aiming to get there by Wednesday**, but that should still give us plenty of time to get organised before the presentation.

Message 2

Hi Koichi, it's Sarah again. **Peter and I were planning to stay at the Radisson**, because it's near, but apparently there's a conference next week and it's already fully booked. Sorry, **I was going to e-mail you about this yesterday**. Could you find us somewhere else? Thanks very much.

Message 3

Hi Koichi, it's me again. Just one more thing, sorry. **We're intending to keep the presentation itself quite short** – about 45 minutes – to allow plenty of time for questions, and **we're going to use PowerPoint**, so **we're going to need a projector and screen**, if you can organise that. Thanks, See you on Wednesday.

12 Presenting

This unit is about presenting successfully. Students begin by identifying the elements that make a good presentation and ranking them in order of importance.

The next section emphasises the importance of delivery and teaches students to distinguish between the delivery required for a presentation and that employed in normal conversation. They practise making a short toast to a great contemporary, using correct pausing and emphasis.

The focus on delivery continues in the next section and students are introduced to devices such as repetition and rhetorical questions which will enhance their presentation style. The emphasis then moves on to the best way to structure a presentation using discourse markers to help listeners recognise in which direction it is going.

The use of visuals is examined next. Students then listen to a presentation involving visuals and analyse what the speaker says and how he presents his material.

Finally, they practise making their own presentations with a framework to guide them.

The grammatical focus is on past forms and the lexical focus is on expressions and collocations relating to presentations.

This first section focuses on what makes a good presentation. Students identify and rank qualities in order of importance and discuss good presentations they have been to.

Warm-up

Ask students to identify the photograph on page 49 (Dr Martin Luther King giving his famous *I have a dream* speech at the Lincoln Memorial, Washington DC in August 1963) and find out if anyone has ever heard a recording of the speech. Ask why Martin Luther King was such a powerful speaker and if they can name any other public speakers that they have found impressive.

Draw students attention to the quotation from film star John Wayne at the top of the page and ask whether they think this is good advice for people speaking in public.

1 Students choose the words to complete the list. Encourage them to talk about successful talks they have been to, where these elements were particularly noticeable.

Discussion

2 Students work in pairs to number the elements in the order they think is most important. Let them compare and discuss their results with other pairs before a class feedback session.

3 Elicit suggestions for other elements that make a good presentation. Write them on the board and discuss their ranking in the overall list.

12 Presenting

Talk low, talk slow and don't say too much. *John Wayne, Hollywood film star*

1 Think of successful talks you've been to in the past. What made them so successful? Complete the following list of elements that make a good presentation using the words in the boxes.

a – e	humour	talk	contact	appearance	knowledge
f – j	preparation	language	attitude	voice	visuals

To be a good presenter you need ...

a a well-structured *talk*

b thorough subject *knowledge*

c a smart and professional *appearance*

d a good sense of *humour*

e good eye *contact*

f an enthusiastic *attitude*

g a strong *voice*

h a creative use of *visuals*

i expressive body *language*

j careful *preparation*

Discussion **2** With a partner, discuss the elements in 1 and number them in order of importance. Use the phrases below in your discussion.

What you need most of all is ...	... can make a real difference
Another important thing is ...	It helps if ..., but it's not essential
I think ... is pretty important too	You don't need ..., as long as ...

3 Add your own ideas to the list in 1.

Delivery

1   Read the text below. Is it good advice?

Did you know ... that almost thirty million business presentations are given every day? And yet, in surveys, most managers say they are more afraid of public speaking than anything else – even death! To overcome nerves, a lot of presentation trainers advise you to 'just be yourself'.

2   **12.1** Listen to three people speaking. Concentrate on the way they *sound*. Are they having a conversation or giving a presentation? How do you know?

	Conversation	Presentation			Conversation	Presentation
1	✓	☐		4	✓	☐
2	☐	✓		5	✓	☐
3	☐	✓		6	☐	✓

3   Discuss with a partner. How is speaking to an audience – even a small one – different from speaking to a group of friends? Think about the following:

- how clearly you speak
- how often you pause
- how quickly you speak
- how emphatic you are

4   **12.2** Look at this famous toast to Albert Einstein by writer, George Bernard Shaw. The extract is unpunctuated. Mark (|) where you think the speaker paused. Then listen and check.

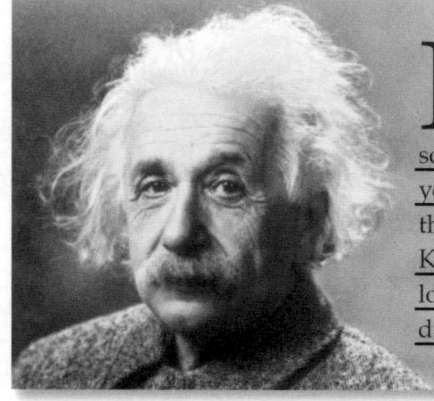

The British Library CD, *The Century in Sound*

I have <u>said</u> that <u>great men</u> are a mixed <u>lot</u>|but there are <u>orders</u> of <u>great men</u>|there are <u>great men</u>|who are <u>great men</u>|amongst <u>all</u> men|but there are also <u>great men</u>|who are <u>great</u>|amongst <u>great</u> men|and <u>that</u> is the <u>sort</u> of <u>great man</u>|whom you have <u>amongst</u> you <u>tonight</u>|I <u>go</u> back 2,500 <u>years</u>|and how <u>many</u> of <u>them</u> can I <u>count</u> in that <u>period</u>|I can <u>count</u> them|on the <u>fingers</u> of my <u>two hands</u>|<u>Pythagoras</u>|<u>Ptolemy</u>|<u>Aristotle</u>|<u>Copernicus</u>|<u>Kepler</u>|<u>Galileo</u>|<u>Newton</u>|<u>Einstein</u>|and I <u>still</u> have <u>two fingers</u> left <u>vacant</u>|my <u>lords</u>|<u>ladies</u>|and <u>gentlemen</u>|are you <u>ready</u> for the <u>toast</u>|<u>health</u>|and <u>length</u> of <u>days</u>|to the <u>greatest</u> of our <u>contemporaries</u>|<u>Einstein</u>.

5   **a**   Listen again and <u>underline</u> the stressed words.

    b   Is there a connection between what we stress and where we pause? <u>We tend to pause after stressed words, usually the main 'content words' such as nouns and verbs.</u>

    c   What's the effect of pausing

       less often? <u>It sounds more fluent (but not enough pausing can become monotonous and difficult to follow).</u>

       more often? <u>It can sound powerful and dramatic (but too much pausing can sound pretentious or aggressive).</u>

6   Write a toast to your greatest contemporary but don't mention his or her name until the end. Then present it to the class. Can anyone guess who it is?

A team presentation

1   Look at the following information from First Direct. You are going to use this information to practise delivering a presentation. Mark the pauses and stressed words. With a partner, first 'present' the information clearly and professionally. Then 'present' the information enthusiastically and dramatically. Which sounds better?

Delivery

The focus in this section is on how the way we sound differs when we are giving a presentation as compared with normal conversation. Students learn to distinguish between the two and focus on those aspects of delivery that mark out a presentation. They read and listen to a toast to Albert Einstein and focus on where the speaker uses stress and pauses for effect. They then practise making their own toasts.

Warm-up

Ask students to talk about times when they have had to give presentations. How do they feel about presenting? Are they nervous beforehand? Do they look forward to it or do they dread it? What are the best and worst aspects of giving presentations?

1   You might like to ask several students to read the text in different ways: one to a neighbour as if it is an interesting piece of gossip they have just heard; one as if they are a spy passing on secret information to a contact in a bar; one as if they are selling a course on presentation to the class, etc. Then have a class discussion on how useful the advice is.

2   **12.1** Go through the instructions and make sure students know that all they have to do is to identify whether each extract is a conversation or a presentation from the way they sound. Tell them in advance that the six extracts are in pairs and that extracts in each pair are delivered by the same speaker, but in two different ways.

3   Allow pairs to compare their ideas with other pairs before you have a class feedback session.

4   **12.2** Check that students understand *toast* (a short speech in praise of someone, given before everyone drinks to that person's good health). With multinational groups, it might be a good idea at this point to go round the class and find out what people say in their country just before they take a drink. In English, *Cheers* is common.

Students will almost certainly have heard of Albert Einstein and if you have time, you might like to divide the class into two teams and see which team can come up with the longest list of facts about him within a two-minute time limit.

Students may like to know that George Bernard Shaw was a famous Irish playwright. *Pygmalion*, the play on which the musical *My Fair Lady* is based, is one of his best-known works.

Elicit from the class the reasons why we pause when we speak (to take a breath, to allow listeners to digest what has been said, to allow thinking time, for dramatic effect, etc.). Encourage students to read the toast aloud in order to get a feel for what sounds right as they mark in the pauses.

Allow them to work in pairs or small groups if they wish. Then play the recording for them to check.

5   Play the recording again for students to underline the stressed words. Ask them to discuss the questions in pairs or small groups, then have a class feedback session.

6   The preparation for this could be done for homework if you have limited time in class. Make sure students don't discuss with each other who they are writing about or include the person's name in the toast. Allow time in class for everyone to make their toast and for the others to guess who is being toasted. If practicable, you might allow them to have glasses to drink from as each toast is delivered. Note that it is customary for everyone to stand as they drink the toast.

12.1

1
They tried it. They liked it. So they bought it.

2
They tried it. They liked it. So they bought it.

3
We can never be the biggest, but we can be the best.

4
We can never be the biggest, but we can be the best.

5
Did you know that the whole thing was absolutely free?

6
Did you know that the whole thing was absolutely free?

12.2
I have said that great men are a mixed lot, but there are orders of great men. There are great men who are great men amongst all men but there are also great men who are great amongst great men. And that is the sort of great man whom you have amongst you tonight. I go back 2,500 years, and how many of them can I count in that period? I can count them on the fingers of my two hands: Pythagoras, Ptolemy, Aristotle, Copernicus, Kepler, Galileo, Newton, Einstein. And I still have two fingers left vacant.
My lords, ladies and gentlemen, are you ready for the toast? Health and length of days, to the greatest of our contemporaries, Einstein.

A team presentation

The focus in this section remains on the delivery of a presentation. Students are given material to present and have to decide where to pause and which words should be stressed. They are invited to make the presentation in two different ways and decide which way sounds best.

1   The aim of having the students present the material together is to give them the confidence and security of a joint presentation before they have to do any public speaking on their own.

Before they start, elicit from the class the difference between presenting clearly and professionally and presenting enthusiastically and dramatically. You might like to write a sentence or two on the board and either demonstrate the difference yourself or ask a confident student to do it.

With a small class, you could ask each pair to do their presentation in front of the class, perhaps with the others deciding which presentation style they are using each time and commenting on how successful they think it is.

With larger classes, go round giving help and encouragement as students practise giving the presentations together.

2   You may need to explain that rhetorical questions are those which are asked purely for effect; the speaker does not expect or require an answer.

3   Students should have little trouble matching the techniques to the reasons why they are effective. Ask if such techniques are common in the students' own languages.

Structuring a presentation

The focus of the work now changes from style of delivery to the best way to organise material for a presentation. The aim is to teach students techniques for making their presentations clearer and easier for the audience to follow.

1   When the students have completed the expressions with the correct prepositions, you might like to ask them to read each one and complete the sentence in an appropriate way. By doing this, they hear the expressions in action. This could be done after the matching activity in Exercise 2.

2   Students identify the functions of the expressions they have just completed.

First Direct, a member of HSBC Group

Presenter 1

When you join First Direct you experience something unbelievable. A bank designed around you, which doesn't expect you to fit round it. **d**

Presenter 2

A bank which recruits people who like to talk. A bank which gives its people all the information they need to enable them to help you. A bank which believes in sorting your money out for you without you having to ask. **a**

Presenter 1

b Funny kind of bank? Unbelievable? Even a little magical? Yes, but also efficient, safe and secure. **c**

Presenter 2

You can, naturally, choose when, where and how to deal with your money. We're open 24 hours a day. Our people are ready to talk to you, whenever you call. **c**

Presenter 1

a And wherever you might be in the world, you can bank online. Receive information online. Buy online. We can even send banking messages to your mobile phone.

Presenter 2

Join First Direct and feel good about your bank; it's your money after all.

2 In the extract above find examples of

a repetition   **c** grouping points in threes

b rhetorical questions   **d** pairs of contrasting points

3 Match the items in 2 to why they are effective:

1 you invite your audience to try to anticipate your answer `b`

2 you create a satisfying sense of completeness `c`

3 you make sure your audience doesn't miss your main points `a`

4 you emphasise what you're saying by using the power of opposites `d`

Structuring a presentation

1 The following expressions help you to give a clear structure to a presentation. Complete them using the correct preposition.

to	on	of	off	for	back	about	up

1 To start _off_, then, ...

2 To move _on_ to my next point, ...

3 To go _back_ to what I was saying, ...

4 To turn now _to_ a different matter, ...

5 To say a bit more _about_ that, ...

6 To give you an example _of_ what I mean, ...

7 To digress _for_ a moment, ...

8 To sum _up_, then, ...

2 Which of the expressions above are used to

a return to an important point? `3`

b repeat the main points? `8`

c talk about something unconnected? `7`

d begin the presentation? `1`

e expand a point? `5` `6`

f change the subject? `2` `4`

Using visuals

Lexis link

for more on the vocabulary
of presentations see
page 105

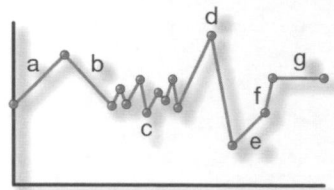

1 You can draw attention to your visuals by using the phrases below. Complete them using the words in the box.

give	see	point	have	show

1 _Have_ a look at this.

2 As you can _see_, ...

3 I'd like to _point_ out ...

4 Let me _show_ you something.

5 To _give_ you the background to this.

2 Which parts of the graph on the left do the following verbs refer to?

rise ⊡a level off ⊡g fluctuate ⊡c peak ⊡d recover ⊡f bottom out ⊡e fall ⊡b

A technical problem

1 ▭ 12.3 Listen to a stock trading company manager describe how his team solved a problem with the company's website.

Part A

1 Underline the two things the manager does to open his presentation.
ask a question / tell a joke / tell a story / quote some figures

2 What's the significance of the following facts and figures?

9 _number of months since they went online_

250,000 _number of hits a day nine months ago_

3 _number of months Gary Cale has been with the company_

60,000 _number of hits a day three months ago_

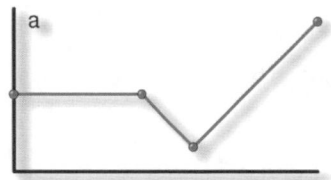

Part B

3 What three problems was the company having with its website?
a _slow access speed_   b _too complicated_   c _poor search engines_

4 Having improved the website, what are E-Stock's two current objectives?
a _to win back customer confidence_
b _to make a profit_

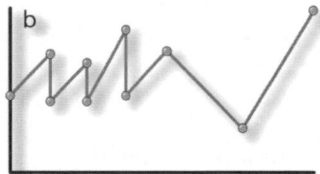

Part C

5 Which graph on the left does the speaker refer to? ⊡b

6 What three things does the manager do to close his presentation?

a he sums up his talk ✓   c he refers people to his report
b he quotes a well-known person ✓ d he invites questions ✓

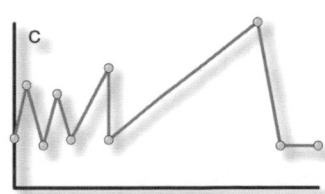

2 Read the following sentences from the presentation in 1.

a When we first **went** online, we **were getting** over 250,000 hits a day.

b The problem **was** not the service we **were offering**, but the website itself.

c A fault **we hadn't noticed** in the programming **caused** 1,500 people to invest in a company that didn't even exist.

d The next thing **was** Internet advertising, winning back the customer confidence **we'd lost**.

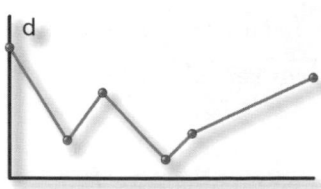

In which of the sentences above do the **highlighted** verbs refer to things

happening at the same time? ⊡a ⊡b

happening one after the other? ⊡c ⊡d

Grammar link

for more on the Past
Continuous and Past
Perfect see page 104

Using visuals

Many successful presentations involve the use of visuals. Correct use of these will enhance a presentation and make the information more accessible to the audience. Here, students learn techniques for referring to their visuals.

1 Direct students' attention to the Lexis link on page 105 which gives them more expressions which they will find useful when making a presentation. The expressions they complete in this exercise are good ways of drawing the audience's attention to a visual.

2 Graphs are common in business presentations and students will find it useful to learn these basic ways of referring to movements on a graph.

A technical problem

In this section, students listen to and analyse a presentation given by a stock trading company manager.

1 **12.3** Play the whole recording first for the students merely to listen and gain a general understanding of the content of the presentation, its structure and how successful it is. Then go through the instructions in Parts A–C so that students know what information they are listening for. Then play the individual sections, pausing the recording for students to discuss and decide their answers to each set of questions.

2 This exercise focuses more closely on the choice of tenses used by the presenter. Direct students' attention to the Grammar link on page 104 where they will find more information and exercises on the form and use of the Past Continuous and the Past Perfect.

12.3

Part A

A: OK, this brings us on to the next item on our agenda this morning, which is online business. Now, I know some of you are concerned about the recent performance of E-Stock, our online subsidiary. So I've asked Gary Cale, our new head of e-business, to bring us up to date. Over to you, Gary.

B: Thanks, Michelle. To start off, then, I know you have all seen the figures up to the last quarter – disappointing to say the least. **Nine** months ago, when we first **went** online, we **were getting** over **250,000** hits a day. **Three** months ago, when I joined this company, we were getting just **60,000** and it was obvious we were failing to attract sufficient customers to our website. So, what was going wrong? In a word, technology. The problem **was** not the service we **were offering**, but the website itself.

Part B

B: Now, three things make a good website. First, access to the website must be fast. The slow access speed of our website meant people were getting bored waiting for pages to load and simply going somewhere else. Second, a good website must be easy to use. Ours was so complicated, customers sometimes didn't know if they were buying or selling! And third, a good website must have excellent search engines. Ours didn't. To give you an example of what I mean, a fault **we hadn't noticed** in the programming **caused** fifteen hundred people to invest in a company that didn't even exist. Yes, embarrassing. I'm glad I wasn't here to take the blame for that one!

OK, to move on. Greenbaum-Danson is unquestionably one of the world's leading financial services companies. We're the biggest, oldest and most respected firm in the business. But to succeed in online stock trading, to succeed in any area of e-business, you need a first-class website. So, creating a first-class website was our first priority. The next thing **was** Internet advertising, winning back the customer confidence **we'd lost**. That's a longer job, but we're making progress. The final thing, and this always takes time in e-business, will be to actually make a profit. Well, we can dream!

Part C

B: Have a look at this. It's a graph showing the number of trades our customers make per day on our website. As you can see, the figure was fluctuating for the first three months and then fell sharply to bottom out at just 10,000 trades a day. For a company of our size, that wasn't too impressive. But look. We're up to nearly 40,000 trades now, our highest ever, and still rising.

OK, I'm going to break off in a minute and take questions. So, to sum up. One, improvements in our website have led to more hits and increased trading. Two, advertising on the Internet will help us win back customers. Three, profits will follow. E-trading in stocks *is* the future. In the US alone it's the way a quarter of the public choose to buy their shares. This is the information age and the Internet is the ultimate information provider. I'm reminded of what banker Walter Wriston once said: 'Information about money is becoming more valuable than money itself.' Thank you.

Presenting a solution

In this section, students are given the opportunity to use the skills they have been learning to give their own presentations.

Fluency

Students will need plenty of time to prepare their presentations and you will need to allot class time to hearing each of them. Encourage students where possible to use their own experience as the basis of their presentations, but allow them to invent the details if they wish. Reassure them that the language in the boxes on the left is there to help them, but they can make changes to it if they wish.

The boxes on the right are for them to make brief notes. You will probably have established in earlier discussions that the worst presentations are those in which speakers bury their heads in written speeches which they simply read out. Remind students that they should not read their presentations but can refer to brief notes from time to time if they find this helpful.

Remind them too of the skills they have discussed and practised in earlier sections of this unit: eye contact and body language, good delivery with correct stress and pauses, a clear structure so the audience can follow what is being said, effective use of visuals where appropriate.

Encourage listening students to ask questions when invited to do so at the end. As each student has to take a turn to be the presenter, they should realise that it is not in their own interests to make the questions they ask too tricky to answer.

Public speaking can be an ordeal for many people, so ensure that other students are quiet and pay polite attention to each speaker, and that the response to each presentation is positive and encouraging.

If you're short of time

Have students prepare their toasts in *Delivery* Exercise 6 at home to bring to the next lesson.

In *A team presentation* Exercise 1, have pairs perform their presentations simultaneously and go round listening to them and giving feedback.

Ask students to do the preparation for their final presentations for homework.

Set the Grammar and Lexis links exercises for homework and check the answers at the beginning of the next class.

Presenting a solution

Fluency Using the framework below, prepare a short presentation of a problem you solved at work. It can be any kind of problem, big or small.

Complete the boxes on the right with brief notes. If you like, prepare simple visual aids based on the information you put in these boxes. Use the language on the left to help you structure your talk, but change it if you need to.

A ten-point PRESENTATION PLAN

1 Impact opening (choose one)
(Ask a question) Have you ever ...? How would you ...?
(Quote some surprising figures) Did you know ...?
(Quote someone well-known) (*Name*) once said ...
(Use a newspaper headline) Have a look at this.

Title

2 Give the background to the problem
OK. (*Time*) ago we were having difficulties with ...
We couldn't ...
And we weren't ...

Background
1
2
3

3 Ask a rhetorical question
So, what was going wrong?

4 Describe the problem
Well, the problem we were facing
was not ...,
but ...

Problem

5 Describe its effects
Now, obviously, this was having an effect on ...
as well as ...
and ...

Effects
1
2
3

6 Ask another rhetorical question
So, how did we deal with the problem?

7 Describe the action you took
Well, basically, there were three things we had to do.
Our first priority was to ...
The next thing was to ...
And, finally, we ...

Action
1
2
3

8 Ask a third rhetorical question
The question is, did it work?

9 Describe the results (perhaps a graph)
Have a look at this.
Here are the results.
As you can see ...

Results

10 Close
OK, I'm going to break off in a second and take questions.
To sum up, ...
Thank you.

Summary

13 Technological world

Ninety per cent of all scientists who have ever
5 lived are alive now. There is more microchip technology in the average car than there was in the first Apollo
10 spacecraft to take men to the moon. The electronic singing birthday card you can buy at any newsagent's is
15 technically superior to all the computers on earth in 1950 put together. Global computing power is now greater than the
20 combined intelligence of every human being on the planet. At least, that's the opinion of some of the world's leading
25 scientists. Perhaps we should be asking the computers what *they* think. But that's just the point. Computers can't
30 think. Artificial intelligence is a contradiction in terms. In the words of Pablo Picasso, 'Computers are useless.
35 They can only give you answers.'

In the world of high technology it's not what you've got, it's when you've got it.
Jonathan Waldern, CEO of Virtuality

1 Technology – you either love it or hate it. Read the article on the left. Is the author a technophobe or a technophile? Which are you? **a technophobe**

Points of view

2 Look at the following points of view. Complete them using the words in the box.

> mobile + do   technology + programme   screen + work   fan + watch
> gadgets + spend   toy + preview   nerd + write   organiser + use

a Don't talk to me about **technology**! I can't even **programme** the video.

b I'm never off my **mobile**. I couldn't **do** without it.

c My favourite **toy** is my digital camera. It's just great being able to **preview** what you print.

d I bought an electronic **organiser** the other day. It took me a week to work out how to **use** it!

e I'm a bit of a **nerd**. I actually **write** my own programs.

f I've got a thing about **gadgets**: Camcorders, Palmtops, anything small, quirky and mechanical that makes my life more fun. I **spend** a fortune on them!

g I'm a big **fan** of DVD. It's the only way to **watch** films.

h I hate all this electronic stuff: tiny keys, tiny **screen**. And half the time it doesn't **work** properly.

3 Do you share any of the views above? Tell the class about one of your favourite or least favourite gadgets.

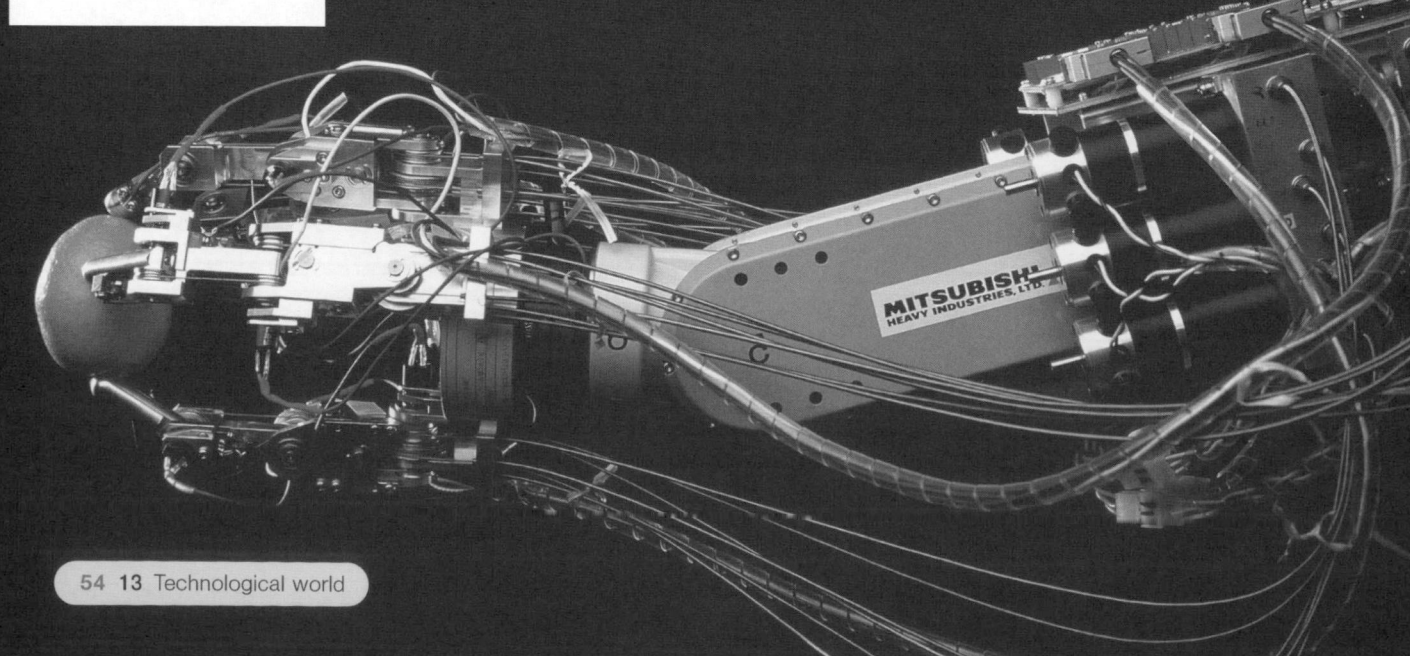

This is a discussion unit on technology. It begins by looking at attitudes to technology and finding out if students are technophiles (love technology) or technophobes (hate it).

There is a short text which gives some surprising information about how technology has advanced in recent years and students also read some different points of view about gadgets and give their own opinions.

The focus then changes to talking about likely future developments in technology. Students make some predictions of their own and then listen to some people talking about technological advances, some of which have already been developed and some of which are predicted for the future.

In this first section, the aim is to get students talking about attitudes to technology and to teach some useful language for expressing points of view.

Warm-up

Ask one of the students to read out the quotation from Jonathan Waldern at the top of the page. Ask the class if this is true for their own industries and if they can give any examples of where possessing the latest technology ahead of your competitors has been a crucial factor in business success.

1   Students work individually to read the article. Elicit from the class whether the author is a technophobe or a technophile. (The author is technophobic. All the statistics he quotes are objective. His own view seems to be sarcastic – for all the amazing power of computers, they still can't think.) Ask them which piece of information in the text they found most surprising, and put them in pairs to discuss whether they, themselves, are technophobes or technophiles.

Points of view

2   Ask students to complete the sentences. To check the answers, ask individual students to read out the completed sentences and the rest of the class to make a thumbs up sign if the speaker is a technophile and a thumbs down sign if they are a technophobe.

Go through any difficult vocabulary. *Nerd* is a slightly derogatory term for someone who spends a lot of time talking about and working with computers (American equivalent, *geek*). Draw students' attention to the useful language given here for expressing points of view. Write these expressions up in two columns on the board:

Negative	*Positive*
Don't talk to me about …	*I've got a thing about …*
I hate all this …	*I'm a big fan of …*
Half the time …	*I couldn't do without …*

Ask students to use them to express their own points of view about downloading, backing up files, updating software, viruses, etc.

3   Read the sentences again and ask students to put up their hands if they share the view expressed in each one. Then ask them to talk about their favourite and least favourite gadgets.

To get them started, you might like use one of yours as an example, perhaps bring it to class and give the class a brief talk on what it is and why you like or dislike it so much.

Start of Recordings for page T55

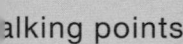 **13.1**

1
A: ... Oh, yeah. I've heard about this. It's sometimes called 'free energy'.
B: Free energy?
A: Yeah, it's this guy, what's his name? Nikola Tesla, that's it. He believes that there's all this electricity just floating about in the environment. And once we know how to use it, we won't need coal or gas or oil or anything ever again. We'll be able to power all our machines with natural electricity.
B: But that's rubbish! ... Isn't it?
A: Well, a lot of scientists say so. But some of them agree with Tesla. He's started a whole new branch of physics. There's a lot of research into it going on.
B: Hm. Still sounds like science-fiction to me ...

2
B: Isn't this something to do with putting tiny computers into your clothes?
A: I think so.
B: Yeah, they sew computers into your clothes – don't ask me how – and they do stuff like check air temperature, switch lights on and off, take phone calls for you.
A: You can take phone calls?
B: Apparently.
A: What, through your shirt? You're joking! What's the point of that?
B: Don't know. Saves you carrying a mobile, I suppose ...

3
A: Eh, this is looking at people's genes and seeing if they're likely to get certain diseases like cancer or Alzheimer's, isn't it?
B: Yeah, it sounds like a bad idea to me.
A: Oh, why? Maybe it could help prevent those conditions before they happen.
B: Yeah, but I've heard that they can give that kind of information to insurance companies and even your employer. Or maybe you apply for a job and you have to send them your genetic profile as well as your CV. So they can reject you just because you might get ill sometime in the future.
A: Can they do that?
B: Oh, yeah.
A: But that's terrible ...

Future developments

The focus in this section is on making predictions about likely developments in technology.

Warm-up

Ask students to say what they think the man in the photograph is doing (looking into a crystal ball, to see the future). What does his expression suggest that he can see?

1 Read the question and the quotation from Scott Adams. Ask for comments.

2 Students work individually to make their predictions. Tell them that in the next exercise they will have to support their views so they should think carefully about their reasons for making each prediction.

3 Students read out their sentences. Encourage students who disagree to say so and to ask questions so that each speaker has to support his or her opinions.

4 Go through the language in the box first, then put students in pairs or small groups to discuss the items in the list. Go round making sure they are using the language correctly. In a class feedback session; get students who know something about the more obscure items in the list to share with the rest of the class what they know. Make sure that the eight topics discussed in the recording in Exercise 2 have been covered in these discussions.

5 ▭ **13.1** Make sure students realise that only eight of the topics will be discussed. Warn them that the speakers will not name the topics, but will simply talk about them. They should put the number against the topic.

6 Play the recording again. Students make notes of anything they don't understand. They then use these notes to form questions and ask other students in the class to answer them if they can.

If you're short of time

Omit the second part of *Points of view* Exercise 3.

Limit the discussion in *Future developments* Exercise 4 to a couple of minutes only.

Recordings continued from previous page

4
B: Well, this is that sheep, isn't it?
A: Sheep?
B: You know, the one those Scottish biologists made an exact copy of. Wasn't it called Dolly? Dolly the sheep. All the newspapers went mad about it.
A: Oh, yeah, of course. But now everybody's worried about the ethics of it, aren't they?
B: Well, I don't think they're so worried about sheep. It's if they do it on humans.
A: You think they haven't already? We don't know what goes on in those laboratories.
B: True. It's a bit like Frankenstein, isn't it? Playing God ...

5
A: Eh, um, I've forgotten what this is. Oh, yeah. It's freezing people who've died. So they can be brought back to life sometime in the future, if we have the technology by then.
B: That's right. Didn't Walt Disney have it done?
A: Did he? Walt Disney's in a fridge somewhere? Could they do it in those days?
B: I think so.
A: Actually, I heard they just freeze the heads now, not the whole body.
B: Oh! That's horrible! Why do they do that?
A: I suppose it's cheaper ...

6
B: This is quite interesting. This is making computers the size of molecules so they can put them into your body to repair injuries and fight viruses and so on.
A: Yes, I read somewhere the Pentagon is funding research into this. These nanobots measure about a billionth of a metre across or something.

B: That's right. And it's not just medicine. Apparently, these molecular machines will be able to build other machines as well.
A: Eh, you've lost me.
B: Well, the idea is that as well as downloading software off the Internet, for example, you'll actually be able to download hardware, too.
A: No way! I'm going to be able to download a whole computer complete with mouse and printer? Ta-da! Straight into my office?
B: Well maybe not a whole computer, but certainly a new hard disk. It's just rearranging molecules ...

7
A: Now, this, in my opinion, is going to be *the* big thing in the next fifty years or so.
B: What, more than IT?
A: Oh, yeah. I mean you can only make computers so fast and mobiles so small. After that, it's just a waste of time. This is where the really exciting work is going to be done.
B: Well, they've already done it, haven't they?
A: What?
B: Mapped human genes.
A: Well, yes and no. Actually, they can't even agree on how many genes we have. Some people say 90,000. Some say only 35,000.
B: 35,000? Doesn't sound like a lot. I thought there'd be millions!
A: Well, no, you see only about 3% of our DNA is actually genes. The rest is just junk.
B: Really?
A: Yeah. And 70% of our DNA is the same as a worm's! And so some scientists are saying it's going to take years just to separate out the important stuff. Of

course, there's this guy, Bill Haseltine – he runs some big bio-tech company – who says we should stop trying to map every gene and get on with designing genetic medicines from the ones we already know about. They reckon he'll be genomics' first billionaire.
B: A sort of Bill Gates of biology.
A: Exactly.

8
B: I haven't got a clue what this is. Have you?
A: Erm, yeah. I saw an advert for one the other day, actually.
B: Yeah?
A: Yeah. It's like a machine that gives you energy, I think. You know, 'chi'. That's Chinese for energy, isn't it?
B: Like in 'Tai chi'?
A: Yeah. It's supposed to give you the energy you get from doing yoga or something like that.
B: All the 'chi' without the yoga?
A: Right.
B: Sounds like a crazy Californian idea to me. How much do they cost, then?
A: About $500, I think.
B: $500! Well, No 'chi' for me, thanks!

Future developments

1 In a time of rapid change, is there any point in trying to predict the future or do you agree with Scott Adams?

'There are many methods for predicting the future. For example, you can read horoscopes, tea leaves, tarot cards or crystal balls. Collectively, these methods are known as *nutty methods*. Or you can put well-researched facts into sophisticated computer models, more commonly referred to as *a complete waste of time*.'

Scott Adams, creator of the Dilbert cartoon

2 What developments do you expect to see over the next ten to twenty years in computers, communications, energy, medicine? Complete **at least three** of the following statements.

    a I think the biggest changes will be in _____.

    b I think the most exciting developments will be in _____.

    c I think the predictions about _____ will turn out to be exaggerated.

    d I think the effects of _____ will be _____.

    e I think the main thing we have to worry about is _____.

3 Read your sentences to the class. Be prepared to support your views.

4 Look at the list of technological developments below. Discuss what you know about them.

> Isn't this something to do with ... ?   I've heard about this – I think it's ...
> I haven't got a clue what ... is.

- video-on-demand
- robotic surgeons
- cloning 4
- automated habitat systems
- smart clothing 2
- microchip implants
- genome project 7
- bio-electric limb regeneration
- cryogenics 5
- human-computer interface

- nuclear fusion
- zero point energy 1
- organic computers
- virtual retinal display
- ion propulsion
- genetic profiling 3
- voice recognition
- nanotechnology 6
- chi kung machine 8

5 🔊 13.1 Listen to people discussing eight of the technological developments in 4. Number the topics in the order they mention them.

6 Listen again. Write questions about anything you don't understand. Ask other people in the class if they can explain.

14 Being heard

Why is there no conflict at this meeting? Something's wrong where there's no conflict. *Michael Eisner, head of Disney*

1 Work with a partner. Complete and discuss the statements below.

> make   find   waste   discuss   exchange   criticise   chat

Meetings are ...

a an ideal opportunity to __exchange__ points of view.

b the best place to __make__ key decisions.

c a safe environment in which to __discuss__ important issues.

d a rare chance to __chat__ with people from other departments.

e the only way to __find__ out what's really going on.

f an open invitation to __criticise__ each other.

g the perfect excuse to __waste__ an entire morning!

Which is closest to the kind of meetings you have?

2 🔊 **14.1** Listen to ten business people from different countries complaining about meetings. Match each extract with the correct topic below.

a there's no fixed agenda ⬜ 5   **f** the follow-up is never clear ⬜ 2

b meetings are boring ⬜ 8   **g** the venues are inappropriate ⬜ 10

c preparation is lacking ⬜ 3   **h** meetings go on too long ⬜ 7

d only the boss' opinions count ⬜ 1   **i** no decisions are made ⬜ 9

e it's all about status ⬜ 6   **j** interruption is a problem ⬜ 4

3 Read the statements in 1 again. Do you agree or disagree with them?

14 Being heard

This unit is about meetings, with particular emphasis on cultural differences in discussion styles and ways of making your voice heard.

Students look first at opinions on the function of meetings and explore differences between different cultures, moving on to an exploration of the acceptability of assertiveness in meetings. This provides an opportunity for practising modal verbs, which indicate a speaker's attitude to what is being said.

Cultural aspects are then explored further with information from a communications expert on the different discussion styles that prevail in different cultures. Students listen to some extracts from business meetings and identify the cultural types they represent.

The next section provides students with some useful strategies for interrupting, so that they can make their views felt in meetings. They practise using these techniques by taking turns to read a text and interrupt the speaker. The unit ends with three case studies of a British salesman's experiences in different cultures.

Students identify and discuss the different attitudes displayed to such things as relationship-building, time, interruption and delegation.

The grammatical focus is on modal verbs and the lexical focus is on collocations relating to meetings and expressions for stating opinions.

In this first section, students look at different attitudes to why we hold meetings. They complete sentences giving different points of view and talk about their own opinions. They then listen to some business people from different countries complaining about meetings and discuss what they say. Students then examine the question of how assertive they are in meetings and practise using modal verbs to complete a questionnaire on assertiveness in meetings.

Warm-up

Ask for reactions to the quotation from Michael Eisner at the top of the page. In a multinational class, ask different nationalities to say whether conflict is an acceptable or even desirable element of business meetings for them.

1 Students complete the sentences with the words from the box. Check the answers and ask students to choose which sentence most closely describes the type of meetings they normally have.

2 [cassette] **14.1** Reassure students that the ten extracts are quite short. All they have to do is to match them with the correct topics. Go through the topics with them first so that they know what they are listening for. Pause the recording after each extract to give them time to scan the list and identify the correct topic.

Though the comments in the extracts are likely to be based on personal opinion rather than cultural preference, ask students to speculate on what nationality each of the speakers might be.

3 Go through the statements again and ask for a show of hands on who agrees and disagrees with them.

[cassette] **14.1**

Extract 1
It's a joke, really, this idea that everyone's opinion is valued. I mean, how much can you disagree with the boss? After all, she's the boss!

Extract 2
You often leave a meeting not really knowing what you're supposed to do next, what the action plan is. I usually end up phoning people afterwards to find out what we actually agreed.

Extract 3
Nobody seems to come to the meeting properly prepared. If you want a copy of the report, they don't have it with them. Need to see the figures? They'll get back to you. It's hopeless!

Extract 4
You often get several people all talking at the same time. So no one's really listening to anyone else. They're just planning what they're going to say next. It's survival of the loudest!

Extract 5
They're usually badly organised. Nobody sticks to the point. People get sidetracked all the time. It takes ages to get down to business. As they say: 'If you fail to plan, you plan to fail.'

Extract 6
You know even before you begin who's going to argue with who. The facts don't seem to matter. It's all about scoring points, looking better than your colleagues and impressing the boss.

Extract 7
I try to stop them over-running. We sometimes hold meetings without chairs. That speeds things up a lot! I've even tried showing the red card to people who won't shut up, like in football. Not popular.

Extract 8
The same two or three people always seem to dominate. The rest of us just switch off – doodle, daydream, count the minutes. I sometimes play Tomb Raider on my laptop with the sound off.

Extract 9
Well, to be honest, everybody knows we don't actually decide anything in meetings. The boss already knows what he wants to do anyway!

Extract 10
Well, nothing interesting was ever discussed in a boardroom. That's why it's called a boardroom – people go there to be bored. Most offices are unsuitable for long meetings. And as for breakfast meetings, no way! My idea of a breakfast meeting is breakfast in bed with my wife.

4 Establish the meaning of *assertive*. Someone who is assertive is confident and good at making their views known and often good at getting their own way. Assertiveness is different from rudeness, though in some cultures it may be interpreted as such. Employees in British and American companies where assertiveness is, on the whole, valued, may even be offered assertiveness training if it is felt that they are weak at putting across their point of view.

Where assertiveness ends and rudeness and bullying begin is something you could discuss with the students. Ask them to tell the class if they have had any experience of being in a meeting in which they were made uncomfortable by someone's assertive behaviour.

5 Allow students to work in pairs to complete the questionnaire. Check answers to make sure each pair has a correctly completed questionnaire. They should then discuss each point and decide whether they agree or disagree.

Refer them to page 125 for comments on their answers, which divide them into the types of animals they are in meetings: mice, foxes, horses or bulldogs.

Ask students for their reactions to the comments. If they like the animal idea, you could use this as a way of dividing them into groups for later exercises.

Direct students' attention to the Lexis link on page 107 where they will find more vocabulary for talking about the sorts of things that happen in meetings and some useful language that students can use to introduce their own comments and opinions.

6 Direct students' attention to the Grammar link on page 106 where they will find more information on the form of modal verbs and some exercises to practise using them. Modal verbs are auxiliary verbs that show the speaker's attitude and express such things as obligation, necessity, permission, probability, ability, etc.

When students have matched the sentences in 5 to their functions, ask them to make their own sentences using each of the modal verbs.

Cultural differences

In this section, students look at three different discussion styles, identified by Fons Trompenaars, a communications expert. They say which group they would place different nationalities in, based on their own experience. They then listen to extracts from three business meetings and match them to the three styles.

1 In all questions of cultural differences, it is important to point out that identifying differences between cultures does not imply that one is better than another. Celebration, rather than criticism, of the differences between cultures should be the aim. It is also very hard to generalise about cultures, and students' experiences may be very different from what is put forward by culture gurus as facts. Those experiences should be valued and students should be encouraged to express them.

2 There are no fixed answers here. Students should decide where to place the different nationalities according to their own experience.

4 Are you assertive in meetings? What if the meeting is held in English?

Lexis link

for more on the
vocabulary of meetings
see page 107

5 Complete the questionnaire using the words below. Then discuss each point.

> things   conversation   silences   room   rubbish   conflict
> people   time

QUESTIONNAIRE

a	You shouldn't interrupt too much – it just creates **conflict**.	agree ☐ disagree ☐
b	If someone's talking **rubbish**, I'm afraid you just have to stop them.	agree ☐ disagree ☐
c	You should always try to avoid embarrassing **silences** in meetings.	agree ☐ disagree ☐
d	You must always think before you speak – take your **time**.	agree ☐ disagree ☐
e	You can't expect everybody to see **things** your way all the time.	agree ☐ disagree ☐
f	You mustn't let other **people** push you around.	agree ☐ disagree ☐
g	You don't have to wait until the **conversation** stops before you speak.	agree ☐ disagree ☐
h	If people refuse to listen, you can just walk out of the **room**.	agree ☐ disagree ☐

For comments on your answers see page 125.

Grammar link

for more on modal verbs
see page 106

6 Each sentence in 5 contains a modal verb. Match each modal verb to its meaning below.

1 it's a good idea ☐c☐   **4** it's not necessary ☐g☐

2 it's a bad idea ☐a☐   **5** it's acceptable ☐h☐

3 it's necessary ☐b☐ ☐d☐   **6** it's not acceptable ☐e☐ ☐f☐

Cultural differences

1 In *Riding the Waves of Culture*, communications expert Fons Trompenaars shows how different cultures have different discussion styles. The diagram below illustrates his results. The lines represent the two speakers and the spaces represent the silences. When lines and spaces overlap, this shows that people are speaking at the same time.

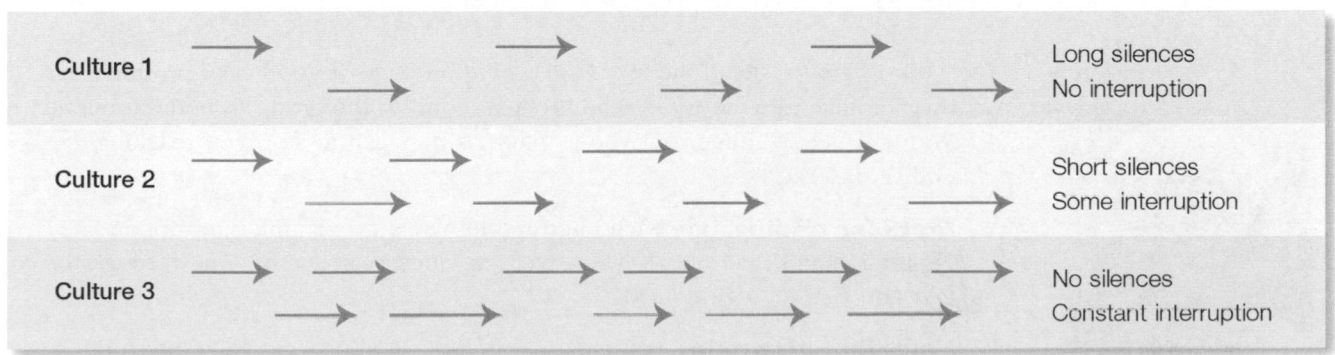

Culture 1	Long silences No interruption
Culture 2	Short silences Some interruption
Culture 3	No silences Constant interruption

2 Work with a partner. On the diagram above, where would you typically place

a Asians?   **d** Middle Easterners?   **g** Africans?

b Northern Europeans?   **e** North Americans?   **h** Australasians?

c Southern Europeans?   **f** Latin Americans?   **i** your own nationality?

3 📻 14.2 Listen to extracts from three business meetings. Which of the cultural types are you listening to?

	Culture 1	Culture 2	Culture 3
Extract 1		✓	
Extract 2	✓		
Extract 3			✓

Interruption strategies

1 What do you think is the most effective way to do the following? Circle your answers.

Interrupt in meetings	**Prevent interruption**
I raise my hand.	I gesture that I haven't finished.
I cough.	I raise my VOICE!
I say *Errrrrm ...*	I avoid eye contact with the other person.
I say the speaker's name.	I just keep talking!
I just start speaking!	I glare at the person interrupting.

2 Rearrange the words to make complete expressions. They were all in the conversations you just listened to.

a a just minute _just a minute_

b me let finish _let me finish_

c no me out hear _no, hear me out_

d on hang second a _hang on a second_

e again to sorry interrupt _sorry to interrupt again_

f could if finish I just ... _if I could just finish ..._

g here can just I in come? _Can I just come in here?_

h just I something say can? _Can I just say something?_

i what I finish could just saying was I? _Could I just finish what I was saying?_

3 Label the expressions in 2 'interrupting' or 'preventing interruption'. Which two can be both?

a, d   a, d, e, g, h   a, b, c, d, f, i

Hang on a minute!

Fluency

1 Work in groups. Read the text *Fast talking* on page 59 to check you understand it. Then take turns to try to read the text aloud to the group in under a minute. Your partners will interrupt you as often as they can to stop you reaching the end of the text.

Notes for reading After each interruption, use a preventing interruption expression and read on. Don't answer any questions. See how far through the text you can get. Good luck!

Notes for interrupting You may find it easier if you begin each interruption with *Errrrm ...* . To be even more effective, use the reader's name as well: *Errrrm, Maria. Can I just come in here?*

This is a test of your assertiveness and determination. Remember the famous words of film mogul, Sam Goldwyn: *Don't talk to me when I'm interrupting!*

Sam Goldwyn: *Don't talk to me when I'm interrupting!*

3 ▭ **14.2** Remind students of the three cultural types identified in Exercise 1. Play each extract on the recording more than once if necessary so that students can identify the cultural type.

Interruption strategies

Interrupting someone, and dealing with interruptions, especially in a foreign language, can be rather intimidating for students. This section will give them some useful techniques.

1 Establish the meaning of *interrupt* (to stop someone speaking in order to make a point yourself). Go through all the strategies in the list for interrupting and preventing interruption, making sure everyone understands them and ask students to circle the ones they think are the most effective.

Allow them to compare answers in pairs before checking with the class. If anyone chooses gesturing or glaring as effective techniques for preventing interruption, ask them to demonstrate the gesture or look they would use.

2 Point out that students heard all these expressions in the last listening exercise. They should be able to unjumble them fairly easily, but allow them to work in pairs or small groups if they wish.

3 Students divide the expressions into the two categories and identify the two that can go in both.

Get students to practise the expressions in Exercise 2 by having them prepare a few sentences on how they feel about being interrupted. They then start saying these to a partner who has to interrupt, using one of the expressions from Exercise 2. The first student should try to prevent the interruption. Do not let this go on for too long as there is extended practice of these techniques in the next section.

Hang on a minute!

This section gives students practice in groups of using the interrupting techniques they have just learnt.

Fluency

1 Make sure that the text on fast talking is fully understood before students start practising interruptions. You might like to get them to write comprehension questions on it to exchange and answer.

Students then take turns to try to read the text aloud in under a minute.

Other members of the group attempt to interrupt as often as they can to stop them achieving this. One member should be the time keeper and needs a watch with a second hand. This person could also award each reader with a grade from the Interruptometer on page 59, according to the length of time it takes them to complete the text. Go through the notes giving advice for reading and interrupting. Just ignoring each interruption is not acceptable; the speaker should deal with it by using an expression for preventing interruption and then continue.

Each group could put forward a champion reader for a play-off with other groups to find the person in the class who displays the most determination and assertiveness in getting to the end of the text within the time limit.

▭ **14.2**

Extract 1

A: OK. You've all had a chance to look at the quarterly sales figures.

B: Yes. They're terrible.

A: Agreed, but **if I could just finish**. We're 30% down on projections. The question is why?

C: **Can I just come in here?** It seems to me that our marketing strategy is all wrong.

B: Now, **just a minute**. Are you trying to say this is our fault?

C: Well, what else can it be? We're offering generous discounts ...

B: Look, **sorry to interrupt again**, but ...

C: **No, hear me out**. We're offering very generous discounts to our biggest customers as part of our introductory offer. And sales are still slow. Something's going wrong, and I say it's the marketing.

B: Well, if you ask me, the problem is the product itself.

C: And what is wrong with the product? BabySlim is an innovative addition to our product line.

B: Innovative, yes. But there is no market for diet baby food. I said so at the very beginning. Who's going to admit they've got a fat baby?

A: You know, maybe he has a point ...

Extract 2

A: So, that's the position. The company has been officially declared bankrupt.

B: Yes.

A: And our chief executive officer has been arrested on charges of corruption.

B: Yes.

A: Of course, our company president has been on television to make a public apology.

B: Of course.

A: But there was nothing he could do.

B: Of course not. Gentlemen, it is a black day in our company's proud history.

A: Yes. A very black day. Very, very black.

C: **Can I just come in here?**

B: Please, do.

C: Well, it's just a suggestion, but shouldn't we all be looking for new jobs?

Extract 3

A: Now, **just a minute, just a minute!**

B: There's no way we're going to accept this!

A: Could I just ...?

B: They can't make English the official company language!

A: Could I just ...?

B: If head office thinks we're all going to speak English from now on ...

A: **Could I just finish what I was saying?**

B: Frankly, it's bad enough that we have to speak English in these meetings.

A: Please! **Let me finish**. ... No one is suggesting we can't speak our own language.

B: But that is exactly what they *are* suggesting!

C: **Can I just say something?**

B: Go ahead.

C: Well, as I understand it, this is only a proposal at this stage.

A: That's precisely what I was trying to say – before I was interrupted.

B: Now, **hang on a second ...**

C: **If I could just finish ...** . The idea is to introduce English gradually over the next two years ...

B: Oh, no! Not while I'm in charge of Human Resources.

A: Yes, well, that brings us on to item two on the agenda: restructuring the Human Resources department.

2 This activity extends the practice to dealing with interruptions by answering questions before moving on. In practice, this is what most good speakers do. Constantly refusing any interruptions could appear impolite. Students may need time to prepare their interrupting questions in advance.

Meeting across culture

In this section, students each read one of three case studies about the experience of a British businessman doing business abroad. They answer questions on their cases and then discuss the different attitudes displayed in each with students who have read a different case.

1 Divide the class into three groups. Each group should read a different case study and answer the questions on it. You could go round and check the groups' answers individually or bring the class together at the end to go over the questions.

Fast talking

'The most important thing in communication is to hear what isn't being said.' That, at least, is the opinion of management guru, Peter Drucker. But, for most of us, hearing what **is** being said is quite difficult enough! Part of the problem is that languages are spoken at very different speeds. Polynesians, for example, some of the world's slowest speakers, converse at a leisurely 100 syllables a minute. The English too take their time at 150 to 200. Germans, on the other hand, can often manage a swift 250. But it is the French and Spanish who are the true Olympic champions, racing along at 350 syllables a minute. If they were driving, they would be stopped for speeding! Surprisingly, the Japanese speak at an 'almost Spanish' 300 syllables a minute. But that doesn't take account of the long periods of silence they are also famous for. Some of these can last nearly a minute themselves, for in Japan silence is just another form of communication. That's why you should never interrupt it.

Interruptometer

↑ You're hopeless!

Learn to be more assertive.

OK, but avoid doing business in Latin America.

Pretty good.
You could be a politician.

↓ Excellent! Nobody else can get a word in.

2 Try the activity again, this time without the time limit. The people interrupting should not only interrupt, but also ask questions. The reader should try to deal with each question before moving on.

Meeting across culture

1 Work in three groups. Choose one of the following three case studies about a British salesman's experience in one of three different countries. Read the text and do the vocabulary exercises in your group. Then look at question 2.

Case study 1

Sao Paolo. 2am. A jet-lagged British salesman and his better-dressed Brazilian client wait outside the elegant restaurant in which they've hardly talked business all night. Their car is driven right up to the door. This is a good part of town, but you don't want
5 to be walking to the parking lot in a smart suit and expensive watch. The Brazilian suggests a night-club, but tomorrow's meeting is scheduled for 9am, and maybe the salesman's already had one *caipirinha too many.

By 9.35 the following morning the meeting's about to begin. The salesman is introduced to everyone round the table in turn. A large number of them
10 seem to be related. The conversation ranges from football to families to traffic problems and back to football. The atmosphere's relaxed, but the salesman's barely started his technical presentation before someone cuts in. Soon everybody's joining in the discussion with wildly creative ideas of their own. If this is a negotiation, it's hard to see how the Brazilians are working as a team.
15 The salesman is surprised to find his hosts so enthusiastic about his product. Did he really win them over that easily – or will there be problems later on? The meeting has overrun. He decides to press them for a decision. All eyes turn to the boss. 'We needn't worry about the contractual details at this stage,' says the senior Brazilian manager, smiling, his hand on the
20 Briton's shoulder. 'I'm sure we can work something out. Let's think about the future.'

*a Brazilian drink made from sugar cane alcohol, crushed limes, ice and sugar

a Match the following to make collocations from the text.

talk ⟍⟋ a decision
schedule ⟍⟋ a team
work as ⟍⟋ business
press for ⟍ a meeting

b Find the words or phrases which mean:

interrupt (para 2)
cut in

persuade (para 3)
win over

continue for too long (para 3)
overrun

find a solution (para 3)
work something out

Case study 2

Rain beats against the mirror-glass windows of a Frankfurt office block. The British salesman's appointment was fixed for 9.30. At 9.29 he's shaking the hand of his prospective client and stepping into the spot-lit orderliness of the German's office. Technical
5 diagrams and flowcharts cover the magnetic whiteboard. A secretary brings machine coffee in styrofoam cups and it's straight to business.

The salesman starts to set up his PowerPoint presentation, but there's a problem loading the disc and he ends up borrowing the German's top-of-the-range Fujitsu. He tries to make a joke of the problem – rather unsuccessfully.
10 When he finally gets going, objections seem to be raised to nearly everything in his proposal. 'Are you sure this is a more efficient system?' 'Do you have figures to back that up?' 'Ah, we tried that before and it didn't work.'

Sixty minutes have been allocated to the meeting. An electronic alarm on the German's watch marks the hour. Two minutes later there's a call from
15 reception to say the salesman's taxi has just arrived. He is accompanied to the lift staggering under the weight of six technical manuals, a 200-page printout of production quotas and a promotional video.

Over the next eighteen months the Germans have an endless supply of questions. Dozens of e-mails are exchanged and diagrams faxed before any
20 agreement is reached. After the deal goes through, the salesman is surprised to be invited to dinner at the German manager's family home. But he never gets to meet 'the big boss'.

Case study 3

Brilliant white walls, luxurious carpets and the soft hum of air conditioning. A British salesman sits a little uncomfortably in the office of a Saudi manager. An hour passes in little more than small talk – recent news, horse-racing, the Royal Family. The salesman
5 casually compliments his host on his taste in art and, after several futile attempts to refuse, ends up accepting a valuable-looking vase as a gift.

When the meeting finally gets underway there are almost constant interruptions and it is difficult to stick to any kind of agenda. People drift into the office unannounced, talk loudly and excitedly and leave. Several subjects
10 seem to be under discussion at once. It is sometimes difficult to be heard above the noise. The salesman smiles uncertainly as he accepts a third cup of hot sweet tea.

Five days later a second meeting is in progress. This time the questions are more direct. A senior Arab manager is present on this occasion, but says
15 very little. The arrival of yet another visitor holds up the conversation by a further 40 minutes. The salesman tries hard to hide his frustration.

Meeting three. Terms are negotiated in a lively haggling session. The salesman finds the Saudis more easily persuaded by rhetoric than hard facts. They clearly want to do business. The question is whether they want to do
20 business with *him*. Their initial demands seem unrealistic, but slowly they begin to make concessions. As the Arabs say, 'When God made time, he made plenty of it!'

c Match the following to make collocations from the text.

raise — agreement
allocate — objections
exchange — time
reach — e-mails

d Find the words or phrases which mean:

get something ready (para 2)
set up

start (para 2)
get going

support a fact (para 2)
back up

be completed (para 4)
go through

e Match the following to make collocations from the text.

stick to — the conversation
hold up — concessions
negotiate — an agenda
make — terms

f Find the words or phrases which mean:

start (para 2)
get underway

be happening (para 3)
be in progress

argument about a price (para 4)
haggling

impressive speech (para 4)
rhetoric

2 Form new groups with people who read different case studies. Discuss the different attitudes to:

> relationship-building   time   hierarchy   power   interruption
> delegation   technical matters

In which of the three countries would you feel most at home?

2 The groups can be any size you like, but should be made up of at least one member of each of the original groups. They discuss the different attitudes displayed in the case studies to the topics in the box.

Have a class feedback session with groups reporting on what they discussed. Ask them to say in which of the three countries they would feel most at home when doing business.

If you're short of time

Ask students to read the *Fast talking* text at home and make sure they understand it before the next class.

Reading the case studies and answering the vocabulary exercise in *Meeting across culture* could also be done for homework.

Set the Grammar and Lexis links exercises for homework and check the answers at the beginning of the next class.

15 Snail mail

This unit is about office paperwork, particularly letters. Students begin by thinking about the kinds of documents they see in a day and attitudes to paperwork. They read a text about a company which has abolished paperwork and traditional office organisation. This leads them on to consider whether letters are ever necessary and which means of communication students would consider first in a number of situations.

Business letters and common mistakes made in them are examined next and students practise correcting letters. Finally, they work in groups to write and answer letters of complaint and apology.

The grammatical focus is on multi-verb expressions and the lexical focus is on prepositions.

In this first section, the focus is on attitudes to paperwork. The aim is to get students thinking about the kinds of documents they see every day and the best ways to deal with paperwork.

Warm-up

Ask students what they think *snail mail* is and how it got its name. (*Snail mail* is a relatively recent term for mail sent through the postal system rather than by e-mail. A snail is a small animal known for the very slow speed at which it moves. The advent of e-mail has made ordinary mail seem very slow by comparison.)

1   Students work individually to list the documents they see in a typical day. They should list document types like e-mails, faxes, memos, etc. without going into the specific contents. Allow them to compare lists in pairs and small groups. See how many different types the class has come up with by making a class list on the board. This will give students access to more office vocabulary.

Ask students to put a tick next to the items in their lists which they look forward to receiving and a cross next to those which they dread.

2   Students can work individually or in pairs to complete the sentences. When they have finished, check the answers, go over any difficult vocabulary and find out which of the sentences reflect the students' own attitudes.

15 Snail mail

Writing without thinking is like shooting without aiming. Arnold Glasow

1 According to management guru Henry Mintzberg, even in the age of the electronic office most of us still spend a third of our time tied to our desk – doing routine paperwork. What kind of documents cross your desk in a typical day? Write the document types below.

_____ _____

_____ _____

_____ _____

_____ _____

2 Different managers are talking about the paperwork they have to do. Complete what they say below by writing in the documents they are referring to:

> forms   copies   memos   letters   invoices   report   figures
> mail   post-it   contracts   receipts   questionnaires   record
> diagrams   trade journals

a The first thing I do when I get into the office is get myself a coffee and check the morning **mail**.

b Whenever I have important **letters** to write, I usually draft them several times before finally sending them.

c One thing I can't stand is filling in **forms** – they never give you enough space to write your answers!

d I try to read as many **trade journals** as possible – just to keep up with what's going on.

e I work in the legal department, so that means a lot of drafting and drawing up of **contracts**.

f I work for a design firm, so I often find myself faxing **copies** of plans and **diagrams**.

g I have to keep a **record** of all my expenses, so I always ask for **receipts** – I have a pile by the end of the month!

h I try to settle **invoices** as quickly as possible, but I query them immediately if the **figures** don't add up.

i I used to circulate **memos** to other people in the department, but these days I just e-mail them on the Intranet or stick a **post-it** on their desk.

j In my job I have to construct market research **questionnaires**, which usually means putting together some kind of **report** afterwards.

3 Read the first two paragraphs of the article below. What's Oticon's solution to the paperwork problem? *Most paper that comes into the office is scanned electronically and then recycled.*

4 Read the article again and think about the questions on the right. Then discuss them with a partner.

This organization is
disorganization

Adapted from *Fast Company* magazine online (fastcompany.com)

Oticon headquarters is an anti-paper anti-office with mobile workstations and networked computers. There are plenty of workstations, but no one is
5 sitting at them. People are always on the move. One reason employees are free to move around is that they don't have to drag lots of paper with them.

Every morning, people visit the company's
10 second-floor 'paper room' to sort through incoming mail. They may keep a few magazines and reports to work with for the day, but they run everything else through an electronic scanner and throw the originals into
15 a shredder that empties into recycling bins on the ground floor.

It's hard to imagine a more disorganized organization than Oticon. But, over the years, Lars Kolind and his Danish colleagues have
20 built a business so successful that they have captured the imagination of business innovators around the world. At Oticon, teams form, disband and form again as the work requires. The company has a hundred or so
25 projects at any one time, and most people work on several projects at once.

'The most important communication is face-to-face communication,' says Torben Petersen, who led the development of Oticon's
30 new information systems. 'When people move around and sit next to different people, they learn something about what others are doing,' says Poul Erik Lyregaard, Oticon's R&D leader. 'They also learn to respect what those people
35 do. They're not just "those bloody fools in marketing".'

Kolind sums it up: 'To keep a company alive, one of the jobs of top management is to keep it disorganized.'

1 Do you wish you could get away from your desk more?

2 Be honest. How much of your own paperwork is basically just rubbish?

3 Do you like multi-tasking or do you prefer to work on one thing at a time?

4 Do you agree that face-to-face communication is the most effective? Do you think that cross-functional teams work?

5 Can you sum up the article in a sentence?

5 Oticon's approach to office organisation is sometimes called 'hot-desking'. Would this system make your life easier or more complicated?

3 This activity is aimed at training students to scan a text for specific information. They should only be reading the first two paragraphs and finding the answer to the question, so don't allow them too much time and deal with any questions on vocabulary later. Students might notice the American spelling in this text: *organization, disorganization,* etc.

4 Students read the text more carefully and answer the questions on the right. Encourage them to answer the questions on their own first and then to discuss them in pairs. In a class feedback session, find out how much consensus there is and ask for several examples of one-sentence summaries of the article. One-sentence summaries are a very useful way of checking that students have understood a text and of helping them to keep their communications concise and to the point.

5 The term *hot-desking* probably comes from the idea that the desk and chair are still warm from the previous occupant when the next one moves in. The desk is in constant use by somebody and never gets the chance to cool down. Ask students for their views on the advantages and disadvantages of *hot-desking.*

Is a letter necessary?

This section explores how necessary business letters are and what the alternatives are to writing them. Students rearrange some advice on letter writing and discuss how good it is. They then do some work on prepositions, completing office tasks and discussing what their first choice of ways to deal with them would be.

Warm-up

The title of this section echoes the British wartime slogan *Is your journey really necessary?* which was designed to save fuel by making people think twice before they made any kind of car journey. Ask students what would be saved if we cut down on the number of letters we sent (paper, ink, postage, time, Post Office time, etc.).

1   This exercise questions the occasions when sending business letters is really necessary and when other forms of communication are better. You might like to ask students to list the alternatives to sending a letter (an e-mail, a fax, a phone call, a meeting). Students put the text in order to assemble some advice about writing business letters. They should also add appropriate punctuation.

Check by asking one student to start the text, another to add the next section, and so on. Then find out whether or not they agree with the advice.

2   First, students complete the sentences with the prepositions, then look at the bulleted options and decide what they would do first in each of the situations. They discuss each point in pairs or small groups and then report back to the class.

Direct students' attention to the Lexis link on page 108 where they will find more exercises to practise using prepositions and some advice on learning them.

Is a letter necessary?

1 Do you ever get business letters – or is it all e-mails these days? Do you think people take more notice of a formal letter than an e-mail? Put the following advice in the right order. Is it good advice?

Before you write your next business letter, ...

|11| up on discussions for confirmation purposes.
|2| must ask: is a letter necessary? There are many
|8| failed. They are necessary when it is
|10| record of something. They are necessary to follow
|5| call may be the better
|1| there is an important question you
|6| solution. Letters are necessary
|3| occasions when a face-to-face
|7| when face-to-face discussions have
|4| meeting or a telephone
|9| important to have a permanent

> **Lexis link**
>
> for more on prepositions
> see page 108

2 What would you do *first* in situations 1–12 below?
- write a letter
- send a fax
- send an e-mail
- speak to the person face to face
- make a phone call
- arrange a meeting

Complete and discuss each point. Use one of the prepositions from the box.

up	to	about	of	off	on	on	with	with	for
for	for								

You want to ...

1 introduce your company **to** a prospective client.

2 complain **about** the service at a hotel you stayed in.

3 give instructions **on** how to get to your office.

4 confirm an appointment **for** tomorrow morning.

5 sum **up** what was agreed at a recent meeting.

6 deal **with** a complaint from an important customer.

7 follow up **on** a sales presentation you made.

8 raise the subject **of** a salary increase with your boss.

9 thank someone you stayed with **for** their hospitality.

10 ask **for** a signature on a contract.

11 send **off** a job application and CV.

12 share a joke you found on the Internet **with** a friend.

In a rush

1 Read the business letter below. The person who wrote it was in a rush to finish it and made a lot of mistakes. Work with a partner. There are 17 mistakes in all. Try to correct them.

XENON Communications

IN TOUCH WITH TECHNOLOGY

⟵ address

22~~st~~ nd February

Re Enquiry about the DigiCom System

M~~y~~ ~~d~~ear Ms Ramalho, [D]

T ~~T~~hank you for your letter ~~from~~ *of* Feb 9 and for your interest in the new Xenon digital com~~m~~unication system. [M]

I am ~~such~~ sorry you were ~~disabled~~ *unable* to attend our presentation in São Paulo last month, but I am delighted to tell you we are planning another one in Brasilia on April 30.

In the ~~mean time~~ *meantime*, I enclose a copy of our ~~last~~ *latest* catalogue and curr~~a~~nt pri~~z~~e list. [e] [c]

If you have any questions or would like further information~~s~~ concerning our company and its products, please don't hesitate ~~but~~ *to* contact me again.

I look forward~~s~~ to hearing from you.

Yours ~~fatefully,~~ *sincerely [or 'Best wishes']*

Rudolf Kinski

pp Brian Green

XENON Communications Unit 45 Pinewood Industrial Park Oxford OX7 T42

tel (44) (0)1865 356 777 e-mail xenon-communications@virgin.net website www.xenon.co.uk

2 🔲 15.1 The person who wrote the letter asked a colleague with better English to check it for him. Listen to eight extracts from their conversation. Do they make the same corrections you did?

Could I see you a moment?

Fluency Work with a partner to practise checking each other's business letters. Both speakers see pages 120 and 121.

In a rush

In this section, students look at a hurriedly written business letter and identify the mistakes in it. They correct it and then check by listening to the writer's colleague talking to him about the letter.

1 Establish that *in a rush* means the same as *in a hurry*. Students work in pairs to read the letter and find the mistakes. Ask them to make a note of their corrections.

2   📼 **15.1** Play the recording for students to listen and check the corrections they made to the letter in Exercise 1.

Could I see you a moment?

Fluency

This exercise is both a roleplay and an exercise in correcting mistakes in business letters. Students turn to pages 120 and 121 and follow the instructions. Draw their attention to the Useful language box which will help them with ways to describe the mistakes in the letters.

Answers:

December 3rd

Dear Mr Barghiel,

I am writing to confirm our appointment on **December 7th. Of** course, I have your **address**, but **I wonder** if you could **send me instructions** on how to get your office **because** I will be **coming by car**.

Many thanks. **I am very much looking forward** to **meeting** you.

Yours **sincerely**,

May 7th

Dear **Dr Garland**,

With **reference** to your order **(ref No. 606-1), I regret to inform you** that **the DCS1** is **currently** out of stock. May I suggest you consider **upgrading** to the DCS2? **If** you are **interested**, I would be happy to send you **details**.

Let me know if **I can be** of any **further help.**

Yours sincerely,

📼 **15.1**

1
Erm, well, where's the address? You've completely missed the address out. And what's the twenty-twost of February, Rudi? You mean twenty-second. That should be 'nd', right?

2
'My dear Ms Ramalho' is a bit old-fashioned, don't you think? Sounds like a 19th-century love-letter, eh? I don't think you need the 'my'. 'Dear Ms Ramalho' will do. And it's a capital 'T' for 'Thank you'. I know it's after a comma, but it's a capital.

3
So that should be: 'Thank you for your letter *of* February ninth.' Oh, and 'communication' has got a double 'm' Rudi! Try using the spell check.

4
What's this? 'I am *such* sorry'? That's '*so* sorry', isn't it? Actually I don't think you need the 'so'. Just 'I'm sorry' sounds better ... OK ... 'I'm sorry you were *disabled* to attend our presentation'? So this woman arrived in an ambulance, did she? 'Unable', I think you mean.

5
'In the mean time ...' Oh, I think 'meantime' is one word, not two. Yeah, one word. Oh, what's gone wrong here? 'I enclose a copy of our *last* catalogue'? That should be '*latest*'. The last one's the old one not the new one.

6
Erm, 'current' is with an 'e', not an 'a' – c-u-double r-e-n-t. And it's a *price* list, Rudi, not a *prize* list. With a 'c' not a 'z'. We're not running a lottery!

7
'Information' is singular. You don't need the 's'. So, 'If you would like further information ... uh-huh ... please don't hesitate but contact me again.' That should be 'don't hesitate *to* contact me again'.

8
Right, nearly finished. 'I look forwards to hearing from you.' That doesn't sound right to me. Wait a minute, it's 'I look *forward*' not 'forwards'. Yeah. And, er, 'Yours fatefully'. That's 'faithfully' not 'fatefully' – f-a-i-t-h, faithfully ... Actually, it isn't, is it? It's 'Yours sincerely'. Because you've written the woman's name. I'd just put 'Best wishes' if I were you. It's simpler. Er, Rudi, maybe you'd better leave the letter writing to me in future.

What's missing?

In this section, students practise completing some common expressions from business letters, decide what part of the letter they usually come in, and whether they are formal or informal.

Warm-up

Brainstorm some of the expressions that students might expect to find in business letters. They should be able to come up with at least some of those they will meet in this section.

This might be an opportunity to discuss the difference between *Yours faithfully* and *Yours sincerely*. Properly, *faithfully* should be used when you don't know the name of the person you are writing to and have to use *Dear Sir* or *Dear Madam*, whilst *sincerely* should be used if you do know the name, as in *Dear Mr Smith*. However, in recent years the distinction has become blurred and students are likely to see these forms mixed up in native speakers letters and also other endings such as *Best wishes*.

1 Students should work individually to complete the expressions, but allow them to compare notes in pairs before checking with the class.

2 Students decide where in a letter the expressions are likely to come and categorise them according to whether they are formal or informal.

You might like to focus attention on the verb forms in numbers 2 and 10.

Direct students' attention to the Grammar link on page 108 where they will find more information and practice exercises on multi-verb expressions.

What's missing?

1 Replace the missing words in the following sentences from business letters. In sentences 1–7 one word is missing. In 8–14 two words are missing. The first one has been done for you as an example.

1 How are things _with_ you?

2 I apologise _for_ not replying sooner.

3 Further _to_ our telephone conversation yesterday, ...

4 See you _at_ the weekend. Best wishes, Jim.

5 I thought I'd send you a copy _of_ this article.

6 Sorry I wasn't there _to_ meet you when you called.

7 _Yours_ Sincerely, Brian Green

8 Thank you _for_ your letter _of_ May 6.

9 Get back to me soon _as_ _as_ you can.

10 I look forward _to_ hearing _from_ you.

11 With reference _to_ your fax _of_ June 3, ...

12 I am writing _with_ regard _to_ your recent advertisement.

13 I'll be _in_ touch _in_ the next couple of weeks or so.

14 _If_ I can be _of_ any further assistance, do contact me again.

2 Now write the numbers of the sentences in the box below according to whether they usually come at the beginning or end of a business letter and whether they are formal or informal.

Grammar link

for more on multi-verb expressions see page 108

	Formal	Informal
Beginning	2, 3, 8, 11, 12	1, 5, 6
End	7, 10, 14	4, 9, 13

Crossed in the post

Work in groups to practise sending and receiving letters of complaint and apology.
Every ten minutes you will have to 'mail' the letter you have written to another
group and reply to the one you receive. Use the phrases and expressions below as
the basis for your letters, but add extra points if you like.

1 Preparation

In your group invent a defective piece of equipment you recently purchased – it
can be anything you like.

> Product: _____   Problem: _____

When you are ready, write to the manufacturer and complain.

2 A letter of complaint

> writing / complain about ... / recently purchased /
> seem to be having problems with ... / expensive item /
> well within guarantee / repair or replace / look forward / hearing /
> you soon

Mail your letter and reply to the one you receive.

3 A standard response

> thank you for your letter of ... / surprised to hear /
> having problems with ... / always try to ensure / highest quality /
> our products / probably just ... / may we suggest you ...? / if /
> further difficulties / please contact / again or try /
> customer helpline on freephone 0800 505

Mail your letter and reply to the one you receive.

4 A stronger complaint

> again writing / complain about ... / found your response /
> previous letter / quite unsatisfactory /
> clearly a defect requiring urgent attention / customer helpline /
> permanently engaged / afraid / must insist / immediate action /
> otherwise / no alternative / ask for full refund of purchase price

Mail your letter and reply to the one you receive.

5 *Either* A letter of apology

> writing / regard / your letter of ... / very sorry to hear /
> still having problems with ... / please accept / sincere apologies /
> immediately send an engineer / sort out / problem / in addition /
> happy to offer 20% refund or free upgrade

***Or* A dismissive response**

> regard / your letter of ... / I can only say / never had complaints before /
> problem you describe simply cannot happen / not our policy /
> offer refunds / if / return / item / us / happy to check / but / afraid this /
> have to be / your expense

*Mail your letter. If necessary, phone the other group to confirm, alter or complain
about the arrangements.*

Crossed in the post

Warm-up

Ask students if they know the expression *crossed in the post* or if they can guess what it means. (Two items cross in the post when they are sent at the same time and not in response to each other.) The title here is a play on words; the letters the students will send are letters of complaint, so they are from people who are cross.

Students work in groups. Go through the instructions with them carefully and ensure that everyone knows what they have to do. Allow plenty of time for the preparation stage, but once the activity has started, keep a strict eye on the time limit and ask the students to mail their letters as soon as the ten minutes is up.

The activity can be extended by employing the options of phoning the other group to confirm, alter or complain about the arrangements.

If you're short of time

Set the correction of the letter in *In a rush* Exercise 1 and preparation of roles for *Could I see you a moment?* for homework.

Set the Grammar and Lexis links exercises for homework and check the answers at the beginning of the next class.

16 Solving problems

In this unit, students look at ways of solving problems. They begin by identifying the time and place where they generally get their best ideas. They read about a company that encourages employees to make suggestions and rewards the ones which are adopted. Students then practise making their own suggestions to solve specific problems.

In the next section, they listen to a problem-solving meeting and learn a systematic way to identify a problem, the objectives and the possible courses of action. They then learn some problem-solving techniques and a procedure for holding a problem-solving meeting.

They practise giving each other advice on real-life problems and then read about some more creative suggestions for tackling problems.

Finally, they work in groups to roleplay a problem-solving meeting, using the techniques and procedures they have learnt and based on actual case studies of problems that major companies have faced.

The grammatical focus is on conditionals with past reference and the lexical focus is on collocations relating to people and products.

This first section invites students to decide how good they are at problem-solving and where and when they get their best ideas. They learn about a company that rewards its employees' good ideas and have the opportunity to think up solutions to three real-life business problems and compare their solutions to the ones the companies actually used.

1 Students complete the phrases and decide which ones are true for them.

2 Students compare their results with a partner. You might like to have a class feedback session with a show of hands for each situation ticked. Encourage students to give examples of good ideas they have come up with in the various situations.

3 Ask students to try to explain the implications of the Japanese expression in their own words (it is vital for everyone in a company to contribute ideas because if all the ideas are coming from just one person, the wealth of talent possessed by the rest of the staff is wasted).

Focus students' attention on the bulletin board and ask someone to explain what ideas the company is looking for. Emphasise that it is looking for both big and small ways of saving money. In pairs, students brainstorm ideas for ways in which their companies could save money. They then compare their suggestions with others.

4 🔊 **16.1** Play the recording and ask someone to explain what the idea was.

5 Allow plenty of time for students to discuss their ideas for solving the three problems. Encourage them to think of more than one solution to each and allow them to compare with others.

6 🔊 **16.2** Play the recording for students to listen and compare their ideas with the companies' solutions. Then in a class feedback session invite students to comment on the real solutions.

🔊 **16.1**
The first suggestion the company got was a joke really, but it won the $100 bonus. The suggestion was that the bonus be reduced to $50.

🔊 **16.2**
1
After many expensive and unsuccessful attempts to promote the restaurant with posters and T-shirts, the owner, Martha Sanchez, finally came up with a winner. She offered free lunches for life to anyone who agreed to have the name and logo of the restaurant tattooed on a visible part of their bodies. To date, 50 people have become walking advertisements.

2
A lot of time was wasted on electronic devices that could authenticate signatures and on educating customers of the bank to look after their cheque books. Someone suggested using passwords, but people always forgot them. Finally, the bank manager had a different idea – why not simply put a photograph of the account holder on each cheque?

3
The company quickly realised that there *is* no way of making industrial cleaners exciting. Special offers and competitions had limited success. So they tried something silly instead. The company's name was changed to the New Pig Corporation. All products were labelled with the New Pig logo, the hotline was changed to 800-HOT-HOGS and its company address to 1 Pork Avenue. Did it work? Well, growing at a rate of 10% a year, New Pig currently employs more than 300 people and enjoys sales of over $80 million.

16 Solving problems

Problem solving is finding ways of getting from where we are to where we want to be. *Alan Barker, How to Hold Better Meetings*

1 How good are you at problem-solving? Where and when do you get your best ideas? Complete the following phrases and tick those that are true for you.

| meetings | work | desk | drinks | night | shower | holiday |
| daydreaming | course | morning | book | bath | court | music |

a first thing in the **morning**

b in the middle of the **night**

c travelling to and from **work**

d on **holiday**

e at my **desk**

f lying in a nice hot **bath**

g while I'm taking a **shower**

h listening to **music**

i on the golf **course**

j on the tennis **court**

k after a few **drinks**

l relaxing with a good **book**

m in problem-solving **meetings**

n while I'm **daydreaming** !

2 Compare the phrases you ticked in 1 with a partner.

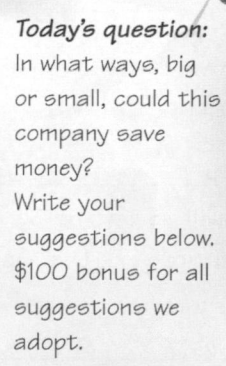

Today's question:
In what ways, big or small, could this company save money?
Write your suggestions below.
$100 bonus for all suggestions we adopt.

3 There is a Japanese expression: *None of us is as smart as all of us.* Following this idea, one American company regularly posts questions on a bulletin board and invites its staff to brainstorm suggestions. Read the bulletin board on the left.

Work with a partner. Think of as many ways as possible your company could save money. Then compare your ideas with the rest of the group.

4 🔲 **16.1** Listen to the first idea the company awarded a $100 bonus to.

5 Now read the problems on the right that three real companies faced. Try to solve them with a partner.

6 🔲 **16.2** Listen and compare each company's solution with yours. What do you think of the real solutions?

1 The owner of a Mexican restaurant in San Francisco faced a dilemma. She wanted to advertise but couldn't afford to pay for space in the local newspaper or for airtime on the local radio station.

2 The manager of a bank in the UK had become alarmed at the number of stolen cheques being cashed. Signatures were simply too easy to forge. Something had to be done.

3 A company that makes industrial cleaners and sells them by direct mail had an obvious problem — boring product, boring market. The question was: how could they get noticed?

Suggestions

1   Problem-solving meetings should start with clear objectives and end with clear actions. Look at the problems and objectives in the box. Complete the suggestions in column 3 using the phrases below.

    a to shift production to somewhere like South-East Asia
    b to sell it direct online
    c delay the new product launch
    d offered it on a sale or return basis
    e encrypting our most confidential information

    f sell it off at a discount
    g raising prices
    h we involved the police
    i bought the company out
    j just manufacture our own components

What's the problem?	What's our objective?	What action can we take?
1 We can't get retail outlets to stock our new product.	to get access to the customer	What if we _d_ ? Another option would be _b_ .
2 Our sole supplier is about to go bankrupt!	to get the supplies we need	Supposing we _i_ ? Alternatively, we could _j_ .
3 Rising labour costs are reducing profits.	to maintain our profit margins	How about _g_ ? The answer could be _a_ .
4 Old unsold stock is starting to pile up in the warehouses.	to create space for new product	Why don't we _c_ ? Couldn't we just _f_ ?
5 Someone in the company is passing on information to the competition!	to protect our competitive advantage	What about _e_ ? Maybe it's time _h_ .

2   [cassette] 16.3 Listen to extracts from the meetings above and check your answers.

3   Listen again and answer the following questions:

    Extract 1 Which of the two suggestions is better received? _b_

    Extract 2 What will happen if a solution isn't found? _They will go out of business._

    Extract 3 Why isn't a price increase an option? _It's a very price-sensitive market._

    Extract 4 How is product development affecting the stock situation?
    The product development cycle is short so old stock piles up.

    Extract 5 What do you think the last speaker means when he says 'Perhaps we can even turn the situation to our advantage'? _They can use the spy to feed false information to the competition._

4   For each problem, add one more suggestion of your own. Compare with the other members of your group. Have you ever experienced similar problems yourself?

Collocations

Lexis link

for more on the vocabulary of people and products see page 110

5   Go back and underline the five most useful collocations in 1 (eg. *retail outlet, stock a product, labour costs*). What are the equivalent expressions in your own language?

Suggestions

This section looks at problem-solving meetings and language for making suggestions.

1 The box divides the process of solving a problem into identification of the problem, assessment of the objective and suggestions for possible action. Students complete the action column with the phrases given. Do not check answers at this stage.

2 🔊 **16.3** Play the recording for students to check their answers.

3 Play the recording again. Students should make notes on their answers to the questions. Pause the recording between extracts to allow them time to do this. Check the answers with the class.

4 Students work individually to think up one more solution for each of the problems in Exercise 1. They then compare ideas with others. Ask anyone who has experienced similar problems to tell the class about it.

Collocations

5 Encourage students to compare the collocations they have underlined with a partner and discuss the equivalent expressions in their own language(s).

Direct students' attention to the Lexis link on page 110 where they will find more useful collocations for talking about people and products.

🔊 **16.3**

Extract 1

A: OK, we both know the problem. Basically, we can't get retail stores to stock our new product. They say it's too expensive. So the question is: how do we get access to the customer?

B: **What if we offered it on a sale or return basis?**

A: No, I don't think so. If we did that, we'd just create cashflow problems for ourselves.

B: Hm. Well, **another option would be to sell it direct online**.

A: It's a possibility, but I really don't think we know enough about e-commerce to take the chance. And if we start bringing in Internet specialists, we could end up spending a fortune.

B: Of course, **we wouldn't have this problem if we'd priced the product more sensibly in the first place.**

Extract 2

A: Right, our objective for this meeting is to think of ways we can get the supplies we need. As I'm sure you've all heard our sole supplier is about to go bankrupt!

B: Hopefully, it won't come to that, but if it does, we'll certainly have to act fast. **Supposing we bought the company out?**

A: What, and took on all their debts? I don't think so!

C: **Alternatively, we could just manufacture our own components**. I've spoken to our technical department. They say they can do it.

A: Yes, but do you have any idea how long it would take to get an in house production facility operational?

C: Well, what choice do we have? Unless we do something, we'll be out of business within six months!

D: What I want to know is why our suppliers didn't tell us they were in trouble. **If we'd known this was going to happen, we could have had our own production plant up and running by now.**

Extract 3

A: What I want to know is: how do we maintain our profit margins with labour costs rising the way they are?

B: Well, it seems obvious, but **how about raising prices?** I mean, even with a 2% price rise, we'd still be very competitive.

C: No, I'm afraid that's not an option. This is an extremely price-sensitive market.

B: I know that, but what else do you suggest? If we don't cover our costs, we'll soon be running at a loss.

A: Now, let's not panic. **The answer could be to shift production to somewhere like South-East Asia**. We've talked about it before.

C: And close down our plants here? Wouldn't it be easier if we just tried to renegotiate with the unions – get them to accept a lower pay offer?

A: **If we'd been able to get the unions to accept a lower pay offer, John, we wouldn't be considering outsourcing to Asia.**

Extract 4

A: Now, what on earth are we going to do about all this unsold stock piling up in the warehouses? If we don't move it pretty soon, there'll be no space for new product. And we'll be left with a lot of old product nobody wants! So, ideas? Anybody?

B: Well, in my opinion, our product development cycle is way too short. **Why don't we delay the new product launch** to give us time to sell existing stock?

A: This is a technology-driven business, Robert. If we don't continually upgrade our product, the competition will.

B: And if we didn't all keep upgrading every three months, we wouldn't have this problem!

C: Wait a minute, wait a minute! This old stock, **couldn't we just sell it off at a discount** to create space for the new stuff? Say, 15%?

A: I'd rather not start talking about a 15% discount at this stage, if you don't mind.

C: **Well, if we'd discounted it sooner, we wouldn't have had to be so generous.**

Extract 5

A: Now, I've brought you all here to discuss a very serious matter. Someone in the company – we don't know who – is passing on information to the competition. I'm sure I don't need to tell you that in a business like ours it is essential we protect our competitive advantage. So, ... what do we do?

B: Are you telling us we have a spy amongst us?

A: If I wasn't, Simon, we wouldn't be here now.

C: Well, let's think. We already restrict access to important files, but **what about encrypting our most confidential information** as well? It's common practice in most companies these days. I'm surprised we don't do it already.

A: I'm afraid it's more serious than just downloading data off the company server. This person seems to be recording meetings and private conversations as well.

B: You're joking!

A: (coughs)

B: Erm, sorry, it's just that I can hardly believe this.

C: Well, **maybe it's time we involved the police**. Clearly a crime is being committed here.

A: It most certainly is. And **I would have called the police in already if I'd thought it would do any good**. But, I don't want our spy, whoever it is, to know we know. So, unless we have to, I'd rather see if we can deal with this ourselves first. And who knows? Perhaps we can even turn the situation to our advantage ...

6 Students should be able to complete the sentences without listening to the recording again, but be prepared to play it if necessary or as a way of checking the answers. Then ask them to identify which sentences refer to the past and present and which only to the past. Allow them to discuss this in pairs before checking with the class.

Direct students' attention to the Grammar link on page 110 where they will find more information on conditionals with past reference and practice exercises.

Problem-solving techniques

1 Allow students to work in pairs or small groups to complete the checklist. Ask them to comment on how useful they think the checklist is.

2 In the same pairs or groups, students match the sentences to the steps in the problem-solving process. Check the answers with the class and deal with any difficult vocabulary.

6 Complete the sentences. They were all in the extracts you just listened to.

> 'd discounted + wouldn't have   'd been + wouldn't be
> wouldn't have + 'd priced   would have + 'd thought
> 'd known + could have

1 We <u>wouldn't have</u> this problem if we <u>'d priced</u> the product more sensibly in the first place.

2 If we <u>'d known</u> this was going to happen, we <u>could have</u> had our own production plant up and running by now.

3 If we <u>'d been</u> able to get the unions to accept a lower pay offer, John, we <u>wouldn't be</u> considering outsourcing to Asia.

4 If we <u>'d discounted</u> it sooner, we <u>wouldn't have</u> had to be so generous.

5 I <u>would have</u> called the police in already if I <u>'d thought</u> it would do any good.

Which of the sentences above refer

a to the past and present? ☐1 ☐2 ☐3   **b** only to the past? ☐4 ☐5

Grammar link

for more on conditionals (past reference) see page 110

Problem-solving techniques

1 Do you have a special procedure for dealing with more complex problems? Complete the checklist below using the verbs in the boxes:

> **1 – 4** review   define   select   brainstorm
> **5 – 12** invite   assign   break   explore   draw up   restate
> eliminate   criticise

Step One: <u>define</u> the basic problem (1)	<u>break</u> the problem down into parts (5)
	<u>restate</u> the problem as a challenge (6)
Step Two: <u>brainstorm</u> ideas (2)	<u>invite</u> everyone to speak (7)
	<u>criticise</u> nothing at this stage (8)
Step Three: <u>review</u> your ideas so far (3)	<u>explore</u> the possibilities of each idea (9)
	<u>eliminate</u> impractical suggestions (10)
Step Four: <u>select</u> the best solution (4)	<u>draw up</u> an action plan (11)
	<u>assign</u> different tasks to different people (12)

2 The following sentences were used in a problem-solving meeting. Decide at which step in 1 each sentence was used.

a Now, what we need are as many ideas as possible. **2**

b How could we make this idea work? **9**

c On balance, I think we should go with this idea. **4**

d Let's think about what we **can** do, instead of what we **can't**. **6**

e I'd like to hear what you all have to say. **7**

f OK, basically, the problem is this. **1**

g OK, let's see what we've got so far. **3**

h I think we'll have to reject this idea for now. **10**

i Now, how do we implement this? **11**

j OK, that's a nice idea. **8**

k Joanne, can I leave the details to you. **12**

l I think there are three main aspects to the problem. **5**

Everyday problems

Giving advice

1   Work in groups. What sort of everyday problems do you face at work? Write down on separate slips of paper two or three of the toughest problems you have to deal with. Be specific.

2   Swap papers with another group. Read out the problems one by one and discuss with your group how they could be solved. Write down any suggestions on the back of the papers.

3   Return the papers to their original owners. Was any of the advice useful?

Creativity

1   How important is creativity in problem-solving? Work in groups. Each group reads a different piece of advice on how to solve problems creatively.

How to solve **problems**

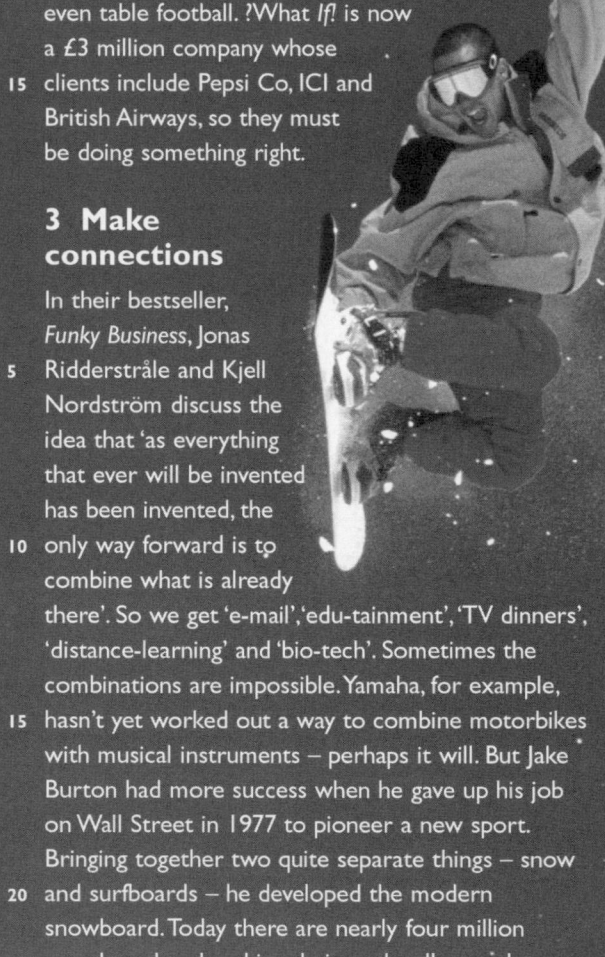

1 Change your perspective

A lot of problems can be solved simply by looking at them in a different way. Try problem reversal. Don't ask how you can sell more of your products. Ask
5   how you could sell fewer and see where that idea takes you. Perhaps you could create a totally new market where exclusivity was more important than sales volume. As marketing and communications specialist Ros Jay points out: 'Many companies have
10 done well out of problem reversal. Businesses like Apple Computers have looked at the market and, instead of saying "how can we compete with all these big players", have asked themselves "what can we do that all these other companies aren't doing?"'
15 In the late 90s the mighty IBM's slogan was 'Think'. Apple's was 'Think different'.

2 Be playful

Must work always feel like work? John Quelch, Dean of the London School of Business, asks: 'How many times a day does the average five-year-old laugh?
5   Answer: 150. How many times a day does the average 45-year-old executive laugh? Answer: five. Who is having more fun? Who is, therefore, likely to be more creative? Need we ask?' At ?What If!, a London-based innovation consultancy, they've
10 worked out that most people get their best ideas away from the office, so they've made the office look like home, complete with armchairs, kitchen and

even table football. ?What If! is now a £3 million company whose
15 clients include Pepsi Co, ICI and British Airways, so they must be doing something right.

3 Make connections

In their bestseller, *Funky Business*, Jonas
5   Ridderstråle and Kjell Nordström discuss the idea that 'as everything that ever will be invented has been invented, the
10 only way forward is to combine what is already there'. So we get 'e-mail', 'edu-tainment', 'TV dinners', 'distance-learning' and 'bio-tech'. Sometimes the combinations are impossible. Yamaha, for example,
15 hasn't yet worked out a way to combine motorbikes with musical instruments – perhaps it will. But Jake Burton had more success when he gave up his job on Wall Street in 1977 to pioneer a new sport. Bringing together two quite separate things – snow
20 and surfboards – he developed the modern snowboard. Today there are nearly four million snowboarders breaking their necks all over the world in the name of fun!

2   Form groups with people who read different texts. Give each other a summary of what you read. Which is the best advice? Do you know of other companies which successfully use these methods?

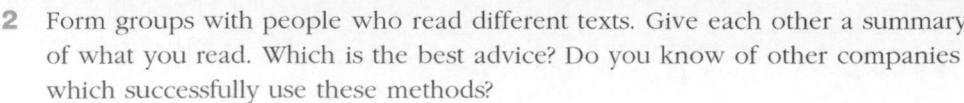

Everyday problems

This section gives students practice in taking real-life problems and making suggestions for ways of solving them. Because the problems come from the students themselves, this will seem more authentic and they should be motivated to try to solve the problems.

Giving advice

1 Make sure the problems that groups write down are quite specific but clearly explained, particularly if they deal with technical matters in industries which students in other groups may be unfamiliar with.

2 When students are writing down advice, remind them of the structures in the action column in the chart on page 68 which they might find useful for making suggestions and giving advice.

3 In a feedback session, find out if students thought any of the advice was useful.

Creativity

In this section, students read about some creative ways of solving problems. They summarise what they have read and discuss whether any of the advice is likely to be successful.

1 Establish that *creativity* is the ability to do things in an imaginative and original way. Creative problem-solving involves thinking of a problem in a different way in order to come up with a new solution.

Divide the class into groups and make sure that each group reads a different section of the text or, if you have more than three groups, that every section of text is read by at least one group.

2 Each new group should have at least one member who read each section of the text. They take turns to give the other members of the group a summary of the section they read.

They then discuss which they think is the best advice and whether they can give any examples of companies who have successfully used these methods.

Case studies

Again working in groups, students choose a case study and hold a problem-solving meeting following the procedure they have already looked at. They then listen to a recording of what the companies actually did.

1   Remind students of the four-step procedure they studied on page 69. Divide them into groups of four to six people and allow them to make their choice between the case studies. Try to ensure that at least one group chooses each case study, though this is not essential.

Students work through the steps given here, conduct their problem-solving meeting and then summarise the problem and their proposed solutions for the rest of the class.

This will take quite a lot of time, so you might want to set some of the preparation for homework.

2   ▭ **16.4** Play the recording for students to listen and compare their solutions with what the companies actually did. Ask them to say if anything is relevant to their own lines of business and to explain in what way.

If you're short of time

Get students to do their preparation work for *Case studies* at home and to come to the next class prepared to discuss their ideas and suggestions.

Set the Grammar and Lexis links exercises for homework and check the answers at the beginning of the next class.

▭ 16.4
Case study 1: Harley-Davidson
Harley chief, Richard Teerlink, was quick to realise that the company's greatest asset was its customers. So the first thing he did was build up the Harley Owners' Club which now has nearly half a million members. He also recognised the trend towards higher-income customers, for whom a Harley was a status symbol. These yuppies, rich urban bikers or Rolex riders, as they were sometimes called, were clearly the key to the company's survival. By creating an extended family of Harley enthusiasts fighting to save a great American legend from Japanese attack, Teerlink was able to work effectively on the emotions of his target market.

But Teerlink was a practical businessman, too. He knew that he couldn't ignore the technical side. So Harley executives were sent to Japan to learn some of the Japanese quality assurance techniques. More significantly, Harley-Davidson immediately got rid of all of its executive vice-presidents and replaced them with three self-directed teams: one to create demand; one to manufacture the products; and one to provide customer support. The next step was to set up the Harley Institute which offers every employee up to eighty hours of training a year.

In a final masterstroke, Teerlink persuaded the International Trade Commission to increase the tax on imported Japanese motorbikes over 700ccs from 4.4% to an enormous 49.4% for a fixed period of time to give American manufacturers time to recover.

And recover they did. By 1988, when Harley-Davidson threw its 85th birthday party in Milwaukee, 40,000 Harley lovers had come from all parts of the United States to attend with Harley executives riding at the head of each convoy. By 1989, Harley was again the number one heavyweight bike company in the US with 59% of the market. Today it's still growing by 8 to 10% a year and enjoying record sales of around $2 billion.

Case study 2: Hennessy Cognac
It's close to midnight and you're relaxing after a long, hard day at the office. The barman's waiting to take your order. You don't know what to have. You look at a table in the corner where an attractive group in their early twenties seem to be having fun. 'What are *they* drinking?' you ask the barman. 'Hennessy martinis, madam. They're the latest thing. Would you like to try one?' You've never heard of it. 'Sure,' you reply. The barman pours the dark golden drink into a cocktail glass. 'Hey, this isn't at all bad!' you say. You order a couple more and can't wait to tell your friends about your new discovery.

What you don't know is that those rich kids in the corner are getting paid to drink this stuff. They're part of an ingenious campaign dreamt up by the Hennessy marketing department to influence people's choice of drinks in bars all over the States. 'Stealth marketing' they call it. Over the past six months Hennessy have been interviewing and recruiting young, good-looking people to go into bars in New York, Chicago, San Francisco, L.A. and Miami and order Hennessy cocktails, tell bar staff how to make them if they don't know and buy drinks for anyone they like. Hennessy pays for their drinks and they get $50 a night for the job.

Clever. But does it work? Yes, brilliantly! Hennessy sales have increased ever since the campaign. In 1997, Hennessy finally broke the one-million-case-a-year barrier in the US. And today Hennessy sponsors party nights all over the world from Paris to Kuala Lumpur. Of course, the secret is out now. But that hasn't stopped other companies copying the strategy to influence those customers who believe they cannot be influenced.

Case studies

1 Work in groups. Choose a chairperson. Using the procedure on page 69, hold a meeting to solve the problem in **either** Case study 1 **or** Case study 2 below.

- Read paragraph one. What else do you know about this business?
- Read paragraph two. What's your immediate response to the problem?
- Read paragraph three. It should give you some extra ideas on how to solve the problem.
- Conduct a problem-solving meeting with your group.
- Summarise the problem and your solutions for the other group or groups. Find out if they agree with you.

2 ▭ 16.4 Listen to the cassette to find out what the companies actually did. Were your suggestions similar? Is there anything in the case studies which is relevant to your own line of business?

Case study 1

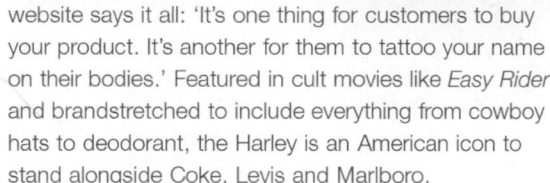

A quality problem at Harley-Davidson

The company
Harley-Davidson is more than
5 just a motorcycle company.
It's a legend. The firm's
website says it all: 'It's one thing for customers to buy
your product. It's another for them to tattoo your name
on their bodies.' Featured in cult movies like *Easy Rider*
10 and brandstretched to include everything from cowboy
hats to deodorant, the Harley is an American icon to
stand alongside Coke, Levis and Marlboro.

The challenge But in the mid 80s the company
was in big trouble. Faced with strong competition from
15 Japan and unable to keep costs down without affecting
quality, Harley was steadily losing market share to
copycat models manufactured by Honda, Yamaha and
Kawasaki. Thanks to just-in-time production methods
and a simpler management structure, it seemed that
20 everything the Americans could do the Japanese could
do better and more cheaply. A flood of Japanese
imports was even starting to worry the Reagan
administration in Washington. New Harley-Davidson
CEO Richard Teerlink had to come up with a rescue
25 plan – and fast!

The opportunity One thing Teerlink knew was
that the average age of the Harley rider was increasing.
It was no longer a young blue-collar worker's bike. High
prices had seen to that. Now middle-aged bankers,
30 accountants and lawyers wanted to swap their
business suits for biker leathers at the weekend and go
in search of freedom. These people weren't in a hurry
to take delivery of their bikes, as long as it was worth
the wait, and 75% of them made repeat purchases.
35 They admired the superior engineering of the Japanese
bikes, but they really didn't want to buy Japanese –
they just needed a good reason not to.

Case study 2

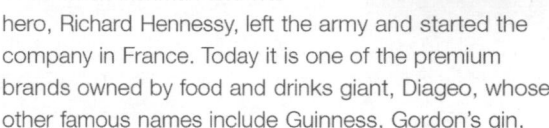

An image problem at Hennessy Cognac

The company
Hennessy Cognac has a long and
5 colourful history going back to
1765 when Irishman and war
hero, Richard Hennessy, left the army and started the
company in France. Today it is one of the premium
brands owned by food and drinks giant, Diageo, whose
10 other famous names include Guinness, Gordon's gin,
Dom Perignon champagne and Johnnie Walker's whisky.

The challenge But in America in the mid 90s
Hennessy had a serious image problem. Perhaps
because of its great tradition, Hennessy was regarded
15 as an after-dinner drink for old men, bores, snobs –
everything the young ambitious American professional
definitely did not want to become. Compared with the
ever-popular gin and tonic and other more exotic
cocktails, sales of Hennessy looked positively horizontal.
20 Conventional advertising and point-of-sale promotions
seemed to have little effect. The marketing team at
Diageo needed to devise a truly original campaign if
they were going to reverse a slow decline in sales.

The opportunity You're not paying attention.
25 Nobody is. These days there's so much marketing hype
it's impossible to take it all in. It's estimated that we all
see around 3,000 advertising messages every day from
billboards to T-shirts, bumper stickers to webpage
banners, and the net result is that we take no notice at
30 all. Particularly in sophisticated luxury goods markets,
straight advertising just doesn't work anymore. What
does seem to work is peer pressure – seeing what our
friends and colleagues are doing and doing the same.
Busy people, especially, don't like their lives being
35 interrupted by stupid commercials. But that doesn't
mean they can't be persuaded, as Diageo discovered.

17 Global village

A man's feet must be planted in his country, but his eyes should survey the world.
George Santayana, philosopher and writer

1   Read the list below. What point are they all making about national cultures?

Did you know that ...

*   there are more Manchester United football supporters in China than there are in Manchester?
*   France's biggest tourist attraction is not the Eiffel Tower, but Disneyland?
*   Romania's biggest tourist attraction is not Dracula's castle, but a replica of the ranch in the TV series, *Dallas*?
*   in Britain more people work in Indian restaurants than in steel, mining and shipbuilding combined?
*   the theme song for Iraqi leader Saddam Hussein's 54th birthday party was Frank Sinatra's *My Way*?

Is this what we mean by globalisation?

Discussion
2   Discuss the following two opinions with a partner. Which one is closer to your own point of view?

a   'As business and the media globalise, and we all eat the same food, wear the same clothes and watch the same films, we are all in danger of becoming the same as everyone else.'

b   'Globalisation is just about selling products and services to a connected world market. It's not about culture. A Chinaman is no less Chinese because he wears Nikes and eats KFC.'

3   Work in groups of four. Each group reads a different article on page 73. Choose the best title for your article by combining one word from **a** and **b** in the box.

a	New	Global	Divided	Forgotten	Borderless	Equal
	Emerging	Culture	Youth	Media		
b	World	Billions	Culture	Capitalism	Reaction	
	Opportunities	Shock	Myth	Power	East	

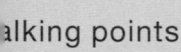

17 Global Village

This is a discussion unit about the effects of global trade on national cultures.

It begins by giving some surprising information about the spread of cultural icons around the world and asks students to discuss whether or not world trade is destroying national cultures. Students then read a series of articles reflecting different views on globalisation. They give these articles titles and discuss how far they agree or disagree with the views expressed.

Finally, they each prepare a short talk on how globalisation affects their companies.

This first section explores the influence of one culture on another and whether trade between countries enhances or damages the cultures involved.

Warm-up

Write the expression *global village* on the board. Ask students if they have come across it before and what they think it means. (The expression refers to the fact that advances in technology and communications in recent years seem to have reduced the world to the size of a village. It is now possible to travel from one side of the globe to another in a matter of hours or pick up the phone and do business with someone on another continent in seconds. The expression may also be seen to refer to the increase in trading links between all the countries of the world so that it sometimes appears that there is one global marketplace where everyone can buy and sell their products, just like in a traditional rural village.)

1 Ask individual students to read out different items from the list. Elicit that the point that they are making is that cultural icons of different countries have spread so widely round the world that they can sometimes supersede another country's own traditional icons. Ask if this is what students understand by *globalisation*. You might like to ask them which of the items in the list surprised them most and if they can give any similar examples from their own countries.

Discussion

2 Students read and discuss two opposing viewpoints about the effects of international trade on national cultures. In a class feedback session, find what proportion of the class finds each of them closer to their own point of view. Encourage them to say on what points they differ.

3 Try to ensure that at least one group reads each of the articles. Students will go on to talk to a new group about what they have read, so it might be a good idea to get these original groups to prepare a summary of their article together before they split up.

4   Make sure each group has at least one member who has read each article. They explain their choice of title and summarise what they read for the other members of the group.

Suggested titles:

> Article 1 *Borderless World, Emerging East, Global Capitalism*
> Article 2 *Youth Reaction, Equal Opportunities, New World*
> Article 3 *Global Myth, Divided World, Forgotten Billions*
> Article 4 *Youth Culture, Media Power, Culture Shock*

For further exploitation of the texts, write the following words on the board and ask students to make as many two-word collocations as they can using them. Many of the collocations are in articles 1 and 2. Encourage students to make sentences using them.

> international opinion global areas culture
> businesses national growth market economy
> media competition public unfair choice
> modern consumer trade reforms coverage
> private socialist

5   Still in their groups, students complete the sentences individually and then read them out to the other members. Encourage the asking of questions.

6   Preparation for these short talks could be done for homework. Point out that the expressions in the box are useful ones for structuring a talk and helping the audience follow what you are saying.

If you're short of time

Ask students to read the articles at home and come to class prepared to discuss them in groups and provide titles for them.

Set the preparation for the short talks on how globalisation has affected their businesses for homework.

Article 1

According to Chai-Anan Samudavanija, director of the Chaiyong Limthonghul Foundation, a private think-tank in Bangkok, 'No modern economy can any longer be limited
5 to its country's borders.' These days capital, goods and labour move freely across borders. During the last forty years international trade has increased by 1500% as tariffs have fallen from 50% to less than 5%. That's why companies like Exxon do two-thirds of their business outside the US
10 and components for the new Ford Escort come from fifteen different countries.

The biggest effect of globalisation has been in the East. The end of the Cold War and the decision to speed up market reforms has resulted in Asia's new growth areas: the
15 highlands of south-west China, Myanmar, Laos, Thailand and Vietnam. Article 11 of the Chinese constitution has even been rewritten. It now reads: 'Private businesses are an important part of the country's socialist market economy.' And in Russia some companies say they no longer hire
20 Westerners because they don't think they're Capitalist enough!

Article 2

Several years ago at the first anti-globalisation protest in Seattle, 50,000 students famously succeeded in closing down a meeting of the World Trade Organization. Since
5 then, similar protests have been held in Washington, London, Genoa, Prague, Melbourne and elsewhere. Thanks to global media coverage, the protesters have been remarkably successful in forming public opinion. They say global companies create unfair competition, reduce
10 consumer choice and destroy national culture.

But Pankaj Ghemawat of the Harvard Business School says it's the opposite: globalisaton opens up markets and cultures to everyone. In a truly global market even the smallest companies can compete. In an interview with *Time*
15 magazine, Slavo Zizek of the Institute for Social Studies in Ljubljana, Slovenia, points out that it's the bigger countries like France and Germany who have more to fear from globalisation than smaller ones like Slovenia. One of the benefits of globalisation, Zizek claims, is that powerful
20 nations actually lose power to the weaker ones.

Article 3

Almost every major company now likes to call itself 'global'. But globalisation is a lie. The fact is that less than 2% of executives ever work abroad. Both Microsoft and Intel do
5 70% of their business in the United States. 38 million people may eat at McDonald's every day, but, as the company itself points out, that's only about half a per cent of the world's population. Nine out of ten PCs may run on MS-DOS, but only one per cent of the world owns a
10 computer. 60–70% have never even made a phone call!

More shocking still, 80% of the world lives in sub-standard housing, 70% is unable to read and 50% suffers from malnutrition. If you have a little money in the bank, cash in your wallet and a bit of spare change in a dish
15 somewhere, you are already among the top 8% of the world's people. Even in industrialised countries like the Czech Republic and Brazil, there is a big difference between the 'globalised' rich and the local poor. Looked at in proper perspective, the global village is a very small one.

Article 4

The global village is a product of the media. CNN World Report has 130 reporters covering 200 different countries 'the American Way'. According to *Asia Week*, the head of
5 News Corporation, Rupert Murdoch, is the fourth most powerful man in Asia. Murdoch owns eight international newspapers and many of the world's biggest film, television and Internet companies. The *Washington Post* called him 'the global village's communications minister'.
10 Satellites do not respect national borders. MTV has gone where the CIA never could – into 400 million homes globally. Its influence on young consumers is huge. 200,000 Russian youths gathered in Moscow's Red Square to listen to bands sponsored by The GAP, Ericsson and Shiseido.
15 One four-week sales promotion on the music channel resulted in an amazing 30% rise in sales for Levis. MTV's Bill Roedy says 'We're always trying to fight the stereotype that MTV is importing American culture.' At the same time, he adds: 'We want MTV in every home.' Polish president,
20 Aleksandr Kwasniewski, sums it up: 'We have to realise that MTV is more powerful than NATO.'

4 Form new groups with people who read different articles. Explain your choice of title.

5 Complete the following with your ideas about the article you read. Read your statements out to your group and take questions if necessary.

> I basically agree with the point about ...   I totally disagree with the point about ...   I can't believe the point about ...

6 Prepare to talk for a minute or two to the class about how globalisation has affected or may affect the company you work for.

> So far, ...   Up till now, ...   Over the last few years, ...   Looking ahead, ...
> In the future, ...   Over the next few years, ...

18 Eating out

Conversation is the enemy of good wine and food. Alfred Hitchcock, film director

Discussion 1 Work with a partner and discuss the following questions.

a Is lunch an important meal for you?

b Do you ever have business lunches?

c Which of the following are you most likely to say to a foreign colleague visiting your country?

I thought you might like to try some of our local cuisine.

I thought we could just grab a quick pizza or something.

I thought we'd just work through lunch and eat later.

Sentence-building 2 What kind of restaurants do you like? Add the phrases in the box to the diagram below to make twelve useful expressions.

specialises in fish	you can get fresh oysters	they know me
a fantastic view of the city	I sometimes go	down the road
round the corner	does an excellent lasagne	a superb menu
five minutes from here	you might like	a very pleasant atmosphere

There's a (really nice / pretty good / great new) place

just
a down the road
b round the corner
c five minutes from here

which
d specialises in fish
e does an excellent lasagne
f you might like
g you can get fresh oysters

where
h they know me
i I sometimes go

with
j a fantastic view of the city
k a superb menu
l a very pleasant atmosphere

18 Eating out

This is a unit on eating out with business colleagues and clients. The aim is to give students some useful language to use when they are either the hosts or the guests at a business meal and to encourage discussion of cultural differences in expectations and manners when it comes to food.

The grammatical focus is on the passive and the lexical focus is on collocations relating to food and drink.

This first section encourages students to discuss their experiences of business lunches and to talk about the kinds of restaurants they like. They also try to identify food from a photograph.

Warm-up

Ask students to tell you about the last business meal they had, describing the food, the place and the people present.

Direct their attention to the quotation from Alfred Hitchcock and ask them to explain in their own words what it means (if people talk during a meal, they don't notice the quality of the wine and the food, so it is wasted).

Discussion

1 Point out to students that using *I thought* is a way of making a suggestion more indirect. It gives the other person space to decline the offer or make a different suggestion, so it is more polite.

Sentence-building

2 When students have completed the diagram, they will have twelve useful expressions for talking about their favourite restaurants. If you have time, you could ask students to practise them in pairs, taking turns to invite the other out for a business lunch, using one of the expressions to describe where they are going.

You could use the stimulus of the picture to start a discussion of the role of café life in the countries represented. Are cafés useful as informal places for a business discussion? Where do short informal discussions normally take place? This can then naturally lead into Exercise 3.

3 Students discuss their favourite places in pairs and then report back to the class.

Ask what catering facilities students' companies provide for business meetings. Is it acceptable to invite a client to eat in their company canteen?

4 Demonstrate the activity by focusing students' attention on the picture and questioning them about some of the items, using the expressions from the box. Then put them in pairs to continue the discussion. Go round offering help and encouragement and explain any unknown expressions.

Ask students if there are any foods that they would avoid suggesting or serving to clients. Elicit the sorts of food that might cause offence and the reasons why they are best avoided.

Who said it?

In this section, students learn expressions that they will find useful when having a business lunch with a colleague.

Warm-up

Brainstorm some of the expressions students think they are likely to say or hear during a business lunch.

1 Go through the instructions with the class. Point out that some of the things could be said by either the host or the guest, depending on the circumstances, but are most likely to be said by one rather than the other.

To make checking the answers more interesting and lively, read out the utterances and ask the students to point left (host), right (guest) or both ways at once (either) to indicate who they think probably said each one.

2 📼 **18.1** Play the recording for students to listen and compare with their own answers. Make sure they realise that the man is the host.

📼 **18.1**

A: So, here we are. Hm, it's a bit more crowded than usual.
B: **Nice place. Do you come here often?**
A: Mm, yes. It's very convenient and the food is excellent, but it looks like we may have to wait for a table today. This place is getting more and more popular.

A: Our table's going to be a couple of minutes, I'm afraid, but we can sit at the bar if you like.
B: Oh, OK. I see what you mean about this place being popular.
A: Well, we shouldn't have to wait too long. **Now, what would you like to drink?**
B: Oh, just a fruit juice or something for me.
A: OK ... er, excuse me.

B: ... So, I'm not really sure how I ended up in financial services.
A: Me neither. I studied law at university, but I never wanted to work for a bank. Right. **I'll just see if our table's ready.**

A: **OK, this is their standard menu ...**
B: Mm. **It all looks very good.**
A: **... and those are the specials. Let me know if you want me to explain anything.**
B: Thanks. I may need some help. **So, what do you recommend?**
A: **Well, they do a great lasagne.** But perhaps you'd like something more typically English.
B: Mm, yes. And perhaps something a bit lighter.
A: **Is there anything you don't eat?**
B: No, not really. **I'm allergic to mussels**, that's all.
A: Oh, that's a pity. The mussels are a speciality. But, erm, **you could try the lamb. That's very good here.** It comes with potatoes and a salad.
B: Mm. **That sounds nice.** But isn't it a little too heavy?
A: Well, you could have it without the potatoes. Or perhaps you'd prefer the cod ...

A: **Shall we order a bottle of the house red?**
B: Well, maybe just a glass for me.
A: Oh, let's get a bottle. We don't have to finish it.
B: Oh, well, I suppose not. **Could we order some mineral water too?**
A: Sure. Sparkling or still?

B: **This is absolutely delicious. How's yours?**
A: Not bad at all. More wine?
B: Not for me, thanks. So, how do you think the meeting went this morning?
A: Quite well, I think. Of course, we still have a lot of things to discuss ...

A: **Now, how about a dessert?**
B: Oh, **better not. I'm on a diet**.
A: Me too. But it doesn't stop me. How about peaches in wine? That's not too fattening.
B: More wine! James, we have another meeting this afternoon, remember.

B: Right. **I'll get this.**
A: Oh, no, you don't. I'm paying.
B: But you paid yesterday, James. It's my turn.
A: **No, no, I insist. You're my guest.**

3 Do you have a favourite place where you take clients and colleagues? If so, tell a partner about it.

4 Look at the buffet in the photograph. How many of the dishes can you name? Discuss the food with a partner. Use the phrases and expressions below to help you.

> What's that?   It looks like a kind of ...   What are those?
> Some sort of ..., I think.   That looks nice.   Hm. I don't fancy it.
> It doesn't look very ...   I wonder what it's like.
> It looks a bit like ...,   ... only more ...   ... only not as ...
> I wonder what's in it.   I think it's made of ...   So, what are you having?
> I'm not sure. How about you?

Who said it?

1 The following things were said during a business lunch. Who do you think probably said them – the host, the guest or could it be either? Write H, G or E next to each sentence.

1 Nice place. Do you come here often? **G**

2 Now, what would you like to drink? **H**

3 I'll just see if our table's ready. **H**

4 This is their standard menu. **H**

5 It all looks very good. **E** (G more likely)

6 And those are the specials. **H**

7 Let me know if you want me to explain anything. **H**

8 So, what do you recommend? **G**

9 Well, they do a great lasagne. **H**

10 Is there anything you don't eat? **H**

11 I'm allergic to mussels. **E** (G more likely)

12 You could try the lamb. That's very good here. **H**

13 That sounds nice. **E** (G more likely)

14 Shall we order a bottle of the house red? **E** (H more likely)

15 Could we order some mineral water too? **G**

16 This is absolutely delicious. How's yours? **E**

17 Now, how about a dessert? **H**

18 Better not. I'm on a diet. **E**

19 I'll get this. **E** (H more likely)

20 No, no, I insist. You're my guest. **H**

2 🔲 18.1 Now compare your answers with the conversation in the restaurant. The man is the host.

Table manners

1 In Russia they sit down at cocktail parties. In China the most important guest is seated facing the door. In Japan a tip is not expected; in France it is an insult not to leave one. How culturally aware are you at the table? Try the quiz below. <u>Underline</u> the correct information.

Cross-cultural quiz

1 In *Greece / Finland* people frequently stop for lunch at 11.30 in the morning.

2 In *Switzerland / Brazil* it's common to be up to two hours late for a party.

3 In *Portugal / the USA* a business lunch can last up to three and half hours.

4 In *Japan / Russia* the soup (is often eaten) at the end of the meal.

5 In *France / Britain* cheese (is normally served) after the dessert.

6 In *American / German* restaurants you (may be asked) if you want a bag for the food you can't eat.

7 In *Arab / Asian* countries you must wait for your host to serve you the main meat dish.

8 In *Mexico / Belgium* you should keep both hands on the dinner table where they (can be seen.)

9 At a *Turkish / Chinese* dinner table it is extremely impolite to say how hungry you are.

10 The *Japanese / British* sometimes (need to be offered) more food three times before they will accept.

11 *American / Latin* executives like (to be invited) to your home for dinner.

12 In *Belgium / Spain* an 11 o'clock dinner is quite normal.

13 In *Asian / Arab* countries food (is usually eaten) with just three fingers of the right hand.

14 In *Poland / Japan* you should keep filling other guests' glasses until they turn them over.

15 In *African / Asian* countries it is the host who decides when the guests should leave.

2 Find seven examples of the passive in the quiz in 1.

(circled)

Sticky situations

Grammar link

for more on the passive see page 112

🔲 18.2 Listen to business people from different countries chatting over lunch and answer the questions.

Conversation 1

1 What is Seiji worried about?
Fugu can be poisonous

2 Seiji uses different expressions to stop his colleague choosing the *fugu*. Complete them.

a It's rather **unusual** .

b It's a little **exotic** .

c You may **not like it** .

d I think you'd **prefer something else** .

e Really, I think you should **try something else** .

3 What does David say when he decides to change his mind?
Maybe I'll have the tempura instead.

Conversation 2

1 What is Hans's problem?
He doesn't want to try squid.

2 The Spaniards use different expressions to encourage Hans to try the squid. Complete them.

a We thought you might **like to try the local speciality**

b You'll **love it** .

c You'll really **enjoy this** .

d This is something **really special** .

e It's really **very good** .

3 What does Hans say when he refuses the Spaniards' offer?
I hope you don't mind, but could I just have something a bit simpler?

Conversation 3

1 Why does Louise have a problem choosing what to eat? **She's on a special diet.**

2 Jean-Claude and Louise mention lots of different cooking methods. Complete them.

a fr**ied**   d gr**illed**

b b**oiled**   e ba**ked**

c ro**ast**

3 Complete these extracts from the conversation:

a ... nothing made **of** pastry.

b ... nothing cooked **in** oil.

c It comes **with** potatoes and fresh vegetables.

4 Have you ever had lunch with anyone like Louise?

Table manners

This section introduces some cultural differences related to eating out.

Warm-up

Ask students what they understand by the expression *table manners* and to give examples of good and bad table manners in their country. Start them off with a few examples, e.g. in Britain it is bad manners to put your elbows on the table; it is good manners to wait until everyone is served before you start eating.

Quiz

1   Allow students to discuss their answers to the quiz in pairs or small groups, but discourage them from looking at the answers until they have finished. Find out if anyone knew any of the information already or if they just guessed.

Ask them to tell the class about any other customs they are aware of that are different in different cultures.

2   Elicit the meaning of *passive* and an example of it. If students need more work on this, you might like to go through the form of the passive in the Grammar link on page 112 and do some of the practice exercises before asking them to identify the passives in the quiz.

Sticky situations

This section is about how to deal with food that, for one reason or another, you can't or don't want to eat. Students learn some polite ways to decline food and ways to offer certain dishes or discourage people from choosing them.

Warm-up

Ask students to work in pairs to come up with the most disgusting combinations of food that they can imagine. These should be real foods but combined in very unappetising ways, e.g. chocolate-covered oysters in curry sauce. Perhaps ask them for a complete menu with starter, main course and dessert. Then have a class vote on which meal they would least like to eat.

Encourage students to read through the table first so they have some idea of what each conversation is about and what questions they will have to answer.

🔲 18.2 Play the recording. You may like to pause it after each section to give students a chance to note down their answers to the questions before moving on. Allow them to discuss their answers in pairs or small groups before checking as a class.

Get students to practise the language for offering and declining food by offering each other some of the disgusting dishes they produced in the Warm-up activity. You could find out who is best at persuading others to try something new and who is best at politely avoiding having to eat something they really don't want.

🔲 **18.2**

Conversation 1
A: ... So, Seiji. What's this fugu? It's a kind of fish, isn't it?
B: Ah, yes. Er, **it's rather unusual**, er ...
A: Traditional Japanese dish, eh?
B: Yes, but, er, **it's a little exotic. You may not like it.**
A: No, no, I like trying new things. Fugu sounds good to me.
B: **I think you'd prefer something else.** Fugu can be ... a little dangerous.
A: A bit spicy, you mean? Ah, don't worry about that. I love spicy food.
B: No, not spicy. It's, er ... It's poisonous.
A: It's what?
B: Poisonous.
A: Poisonous?
B: If it isn't cooked the right way, yes.
A: Well, I ...
B: Some people love it. And this is a very good restaurant, but thirty people die every year from bad fugu. **Really, I think you should try something else.**
A: Yeah, well, sure. I think you're probably right. **Maybe I'll have the tempura instead.**
B: Yes, tempura. Much better idea, David.

Conversation 2
A: Now, Hans, **we thought you might like to try the local speciality.**

B: Ah, yes?
C: Yes, it looks a little strange at first. But **you'll love it.** You like shellfish, don't you?
B: Well, I like prawns. And the mussels we had the other day were excellent.
C: Then **you'll really enjoy this.** It's squid.
B: Squid?
C: Yes, like octopus, you know?
B: Yes, I know what squid is.
C: Ah, but this is not just squid.
B: No?
A: No, **this is something really special.** It's served in its own ink – as a sauce.
B: It's served in ink?
A: Yes, you know, the black liquid that squid make.
B: Erm, yes. It sounds a bit ... . Actually, **I hope you don't mind, but could I just have something a bit simpler?**
C: Well, if you're sure you don't want to try it. **It's really very good.**
B: Yes, I'm sure it is, but, erm ...

Conversation 3
A: Now, is there anything you don't eat, Louise?
B: Well, I am **on a special diet** at the moment, Jean-Claude. I hope that's not a problem.
A: No, of course not. This is a very good menu. I am sure we can find something

you'll like. What can't you eat?
B: Well, I can't eat anything **fried**. In fact, no fat at all. **Nothing made of pastry** or **cooked in oil.** No red meat, of course. Not too much sugar. I can eat white fish but only **boiled**.
A: What about the chicken here? That's very plain and simple.
B: Is there a sauce on it?
A: Yes, it's a delicious cream and wine sauce.
B: No cream, I'm afraid.
A: No cream?
B: Or wine. I'm not allowed any alcohol at all. Not that I drink much anyway.
A: I see. Well, I'm sure they'll serve it without the sauce.
B: Hm. How's the chicken cooked?
A: Er, it's **roast** chicken, I imagine.
B: I can only have **grilled**.
A: I'll ask them to grill it.
B: Hm. I'd prefer fish really.
A: Well, how about the trout?
B: Is it boiled?
A: No, **baked** in the oven.
B: Hm. I may not like it. What does it come with?
A: **It comes with potatoes and fresh vegetables**.
B: Oh, I can't eat potatoes. All that carbohydrate! Vegetables are OK. But no beans and ...

A healthy diet

This section looks at the issue of what kinds of food are best for you. It gives students a wide range of vocabulary for food and drink items.

Students work individually to categorise the food. Allow them to compare their completed charts in pairs or small groups.

Direct students' attention to the Lexis link on page 113 where they will find useful adjectives for describing food and drink items in more detail.

Out to lunch

In this final section, students put together everything they have learnt in this unit to roleplay a business lunch. Go through the instructions carefully and make sure that both partners complete the menus carefully. If possible, have pairs made up of students of different nationalities so that they are genuinely not familiar with the dishes they are being offered. Ask some pairs to perform their roleplays for the class.

If you're short of time

Set the section *A healthy diet* for homework.

Set the Grammar and Lexis links exercises for homework and check the answers at the beginning of the next class.

A healthy diet

Do you watch what you eat or eat what you like? Categorise the food and drink below according to whether:

	It's good for you	It's bad for you
You like it		
You don't like it		

Lexis link

for more food and drink vocabulary see page 113

grilled chicken   a cup of tea   roast beef   baked ham   a brandy
ice-cream   a vodka and ice   smoked salmon   a fruit juice
fillet steak   apple pie and cream   lamb chops   duck paté and toast
a glass of port   baked trout   local seafood   a whisky and soda
boiled vegetables   a coke   chips   a green salad   still mineral water
a hot curry   fresh pasta   a beer   a cheeseburger   a black coffee
a salami sandwich   a liqueur   pork sausages   fresh fruit   raw fish
a slice of chocolate gateau   cheese and biscuits   a glass of wine
fried rice   a gin and tonic   veal

Out to lunch

Work with a partner. You are having a business lunch together. Take turns to be the host and help your guest choose something to eat and drink from your menu.

On the menu, write down the names of three different starters and main dishes which are typical of your country or region.

The first dish should be something you dislike and never recommend to anyone.

The second dish should be something you really like and think everyone should try.

The third dish should be something which is quite difficult to describe.

If you want, add a couple of wines to the wine list.

MENU

STARTERS

1 _____
2 _____
3 _____

MAIN DISHES

1 _____
2 _____
3 _____

WINE LIST

1 _____
2 _____

When you are both ready, use Speaker A's menu first.

Speaker A (the host): help your guest to choose a meal, describing the dishes if necessary and recommending some dishes (or not).

Speaker B (the guest): find out as much as you can about the dishes before you choose. Don't be too easily persuaded or dissuaded.

Then change over and use Speaker B's menu. Speaker B is now the host, Speaker A the guest.

19 Messaging

Communication is the soul of management. *Dianna Booher, CEO of Booher Consultants Inc.*

1 Read the following statistics and discuss the questions with a partner.

At the end of the 20th century 90% of the world's telecommunications were phone calls. According to *Newsweek* magazine, that figure will soon drop to less than 10% as we all switch to e-mail and other forms of digitally transmitted data.

a *Are you getting more e-mail than phone calls these days?*

b *Do you think the shift towards e-mail is a good thing?*

Online retailer Amazon.com currently stocks 213 books on 'netiquette' or how to write your e-mail. You can even buy a course on 'cyber-grammar'!

a *Is this all really necessary?*

b *Is e-mail really that difficult?*

Communication experts repeatedly tell us that 60% of communication is how you look, 30% how you sound, and only 10% what you actually say.

If this is true, does it mean that phone calls are only 40% and e-mails only 10% effective?

2 Read the following extract from a book. What's the main point it's making?
E-mail has brought an informality and spontaneity to business communication that most people appreciate.

Glossary:

suppress = hide
dig out = look for
cc = send a copy to
fire off = send quickly
font = style of type
margin = blank space at
the side of a page

We have been trained throughout our business careers to suppress our individual voice and to sound like a 'professional' – that is, to sound like everyone else. If you need to hear how the professional voice sounds, dig out a
5 memo you wrote four years ago and compare it with how you'd write an e-mail about it now. A professional memo obeys rules such as one page is best, no jokes, spell-check it carefully and send it to as few people as possible.

Now we write e-mails. They're short, they're funny; they sound
10 like us, and we cc the CEO whenever we feel like it. E-mail is a more immediate medium than paper. My expectation of the response time to many messages I send is today, not tomorrow or a week from now. This urgency means I'm more likely to write quickly and conversationally when I respond to a message. A lot of the
15 spontaneity in e-mail messages comes from writers breaking through their natural caution and reserve, rushing the writing process, giving themselves permission to be blunt, honest and sincere in response to a query.

That's why most of us don't want to use a word processor
20 to write our e-mails. We want to be free of the expectation that we've spell-checked it or even re-read it before firing it off. We certainly don't want to waste our time messing about with fonts and margins.

Adapted from *The Cluetrain Manifesto* by R Levine, C Locke, D Searls & D Weinberger, FT.com

Messaging can refer to sending e-mails or leaving voice messages and there is work on both in this unit.

Students first discuss a text about the freedom of expression that e-mails give us and listen to some people giving their views on the opinions expressed.

They then read an exchange of e-mails, put them in the right order and examine some of the language used in them. Next, they listen to some voice mail messages and take notes.

Finally, they work with both e-mails and voice mail, sending a selection of each to another group to deal with.

The grammatical focus is on reported speech.

In this first section, students read some statistics about e-mail and answer questions. They then read a text about the freedom e-mail gives us to express our own voices, and be honest, blunt and sincere. They listen to some business people giving their reactions to the text and practise voicing their own opinions.

Warm-up

Focus students' attention on the quotation of Dianna Booher. Why does she use the word 'soul'? (Communication humanises management; without it management is 'dead'). What and how should management communicate? Who should communicate with whom?

1 Students work in pairs to read the statistics and answer the questions. Elicit answers and ask which statistics surprised them the most.

2 The question here is intended to encourage students to read for gist simply to find out what the main point of the text is. Encourage them to read it quickly and answer the question.

Give students time to look at the text in more detail. The main point of the text is that e-mail frees us from the restrictions imposed by more formal letters and memos and allows us to respond in a more personal, spontaneous and honest way to questions. E-mails are often badly spelt and the layout unbusinesslike, but nobody would want to change this because it would destroy the freedom that we now enjoy.

If time permits, you might like to revise with the students the grammatical and stylistic short cuts that we use in e-mails that we would not use in a letter (abbreviations, verbless sentences, wry comments, exclamations, lack of paragraphing, etc.). Refer to page 45 of the Student's Book, if necessary.

3 ▭ **19.1** Go through the instructions with the class and make sure they understand that they have to match two points to each speaker, and put numbers in the boxes. Have individual students read out the points before playing the recording so they know what they are listening for. Then allow them to compare answers in pairs before checking with the class.

4 Students discuss the points made in Exercise 3 and decide whether they agree or disagree. Draw their attention to the useful expressions in the box.

Ask students for their own preferences when writing and receiving e-mails. Do particular things annoy them? What e-mail writing conventions have emerged in their own countries?

Focus attention on the cartoon. Ask students if anyone in their company is like Wally's boss, i.e. computer illiterate, technophobic.

▭ **19.1**

1
Erm, I couldn't disagree more, actually. Just because e-mail is quick to send doesn't mean it's quicker to write or read. Bad spelling, grammar and layout look just as bad on a screen as on a piece of paper. People forget that e-mails can be sent on to other people or printed out and kept on file for years. Poorly written ones reflect badly on your professionalism.

2
Well, I think it depends on who you're e-mailing and why. If it's someone I don't know, my e-mail will look pretty much like a standard business letter. But if it's someone I e-mail every day, then I just get straight down to business. Most of these e-mails are just replies to other e-mails, anyway. So I may not even bother to write the other person's name. If it's someone I know well but haven't been in contact with for a while, I always start off with a few pleasantries.

3
Erm, people are much too informal in most e-mails, if you ask me. And disorganised. You can tell they're actually thinking through what they want to say as they write. A lot of the e-mails I get are about as ineffective as a phone call. First we get all the 'How are things? It was good to talk the other day' stuff. And when they finally get down to business, it's often something trivial they could have sorted out themselves. And they forget to add the attachment!

4
In the past we were sent on courses to develop a professional telephone manner, an appropriate business writing style and so on. But I think it makes more sense now just to talk about messaging rather than phoning, faxing, e-mailing. And the language is very similar these days no matter what medium of communication you're using. As a matter of fact, my company pays a monthly fee for me to have something called a unified messaging service. That means all my voice mails, e-mails and faxes go to a central

inbox and I can get them any time I like in any way I like through my mobile, my laptop or my electronic organiser. I can even read my voice mail and listen to my e-mail. It's great!

5
Well, frankly, I always hated all that 'Dear Sir or Madam', 'with regard to your letter of', 'don't hesitate', 'yours sincerely' kind of rubbish. Thank God we can just write like normal human beings now. E-mail's great strength is its simplicity and directness. You don't need to learn any special expressions or worry about where you're going to put the date. As if anyone cared! In some ways e-mail's a lot like voice mail – you just talk through a computer keyboard instead of a phone. You keep it short and friendly. Do it once and send it. People who go on about 'netiquette' drive me nuts. They're just trying to make e-mail as over-complicated as business letters used to be.

3 🔊 **19.1** Listen to five business people giving their reactions to the text in 2. They each make two main points. Take notes and match the people to the points they make.

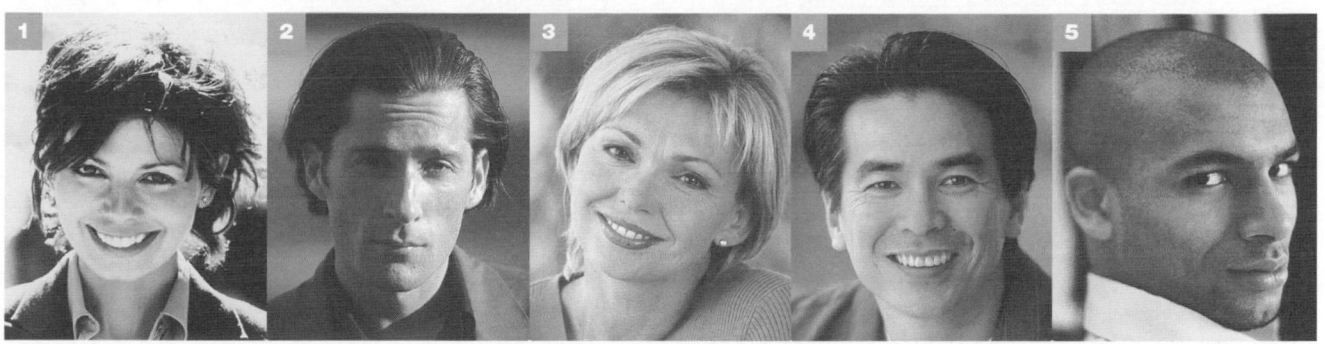

a You have to adjust your writing style to the person you're e-mailing. ☐2

b People used to think you had to have special training to answer the phone and write business correspondence. ☐4

c People waste too much time on social chit-chat. ☐3

d Impressions count with e-mail as much as mail. ☐1

e Having to learn formal letter-phrases used to be a real pain. ☐5

f When replying to another e-mail, just get straight to the point. ☐2

g These days you can send and receive messages using many different media. ☐4

h Most e-mails are badly planned. ☐3

i There's no such thing as a special way of writing e-mails. ☐5

j You don't know who might read your e-mail. ☐1

4 Work with a partner. Which of the points the speakers made in 3 do you agree or disagree with? Use the phrases in the box if you like.

> I agree with the point about ...
> I agree in some ways with the point about ...
> But I'm not so sure about ...
> I don't go along with the point about ...

An urgent matter

1 A management consultancy is putting together a proposal for a major new client, pharmaceutical giant, Hoechst. Put the following e-mails between two of their consultants into the correct order. Read all the e-mails first – **a** and **h** are in the right place.

1

a Subject: Hoechst report – progress?
Attachments: none

Sam
This is just a quick reminder to let you know that the Hoechst report was due yesterday. E-mail me if you're having problems.

Jonathan

6

b Subject: Costing for Hoechst
Attachments: none

Jonathan
I see your point. Estimates would give us more room to negotiate on fees, but I think the client will appreciate that we've fully itemised all the costs.

Sam

5

c Subject: So you are alive after all!
Attachments: none

Sam
Thanks for the report. At last! Actually, you've done a great job on it. Just one thing. Should we be quoting precise figures at this stage or just giving a rough estimate?

Jonathan

4

d Subject: Hoechst report
Attachments: HoechstRep
            CostBrkdn

Jonathan
Sorry for the delay in getting back to you. Our server's been down again. I'm sending a first draft of the report as an attachment together with a detailed breakdown of costs for the whole project. Could you have a look at them and tell me if there's anything you want changing?

Sam

3

e Subject: HELLO?
Attachments: none

SAM!
Haven't you received my previous two e-mails? This is getting urgent. I've tried to phone, but you're never in. Look, I'm under a lot of pressure from head office to get this proposal in on schedule. Don't let me down, Sam.

Jonathan

7

f Subject: Costing for Hoechst
Attachments: HoechstRepAlt

Sam
Yeah, you're probably right. It looks better if we show that we can set and stick to a budget. Can you just make a few alterations (see attachment) and then e-mail me another copy? Oh, and cc one to Lisa as well. Thanks.

Jonathan

2

g Subject: Hoechst report – update please
Attachments: none

Sam
Just had a call from Lisa. She wants to know what the hold-up is with the Hoechst report. Did you get my last e-mail? Please let me know what the position is asap.

Jonathan

8

h Subject: Revised Hoechst Report
Attachments: HoechstRep2
            ConJoke

Jonathan
Here's the revised version of the report. OK, so I just missed the deadline, but only two days late. Give me a break. By the way, I found a joke on the Internet the other day that might appeal to your sense of humour: You could use it in your presentation to Hoechst:
Why are they using consultants instead of rats in laboratory experiments these days? See attachment for answer :)

Sam

An urgent matter

In this section, students read an exchange of e-mails between two colleagues in a management consultancy. They have to read them and number them in the correct order. They then examine some of the language used in these e-mails.

1   When checking answers, have two different students read the e-mails out (one as Jonathan and the other as Sam) so that they can hear the flow of the communication.

You might like to draw students' attention to the effect of the capital letters in e-mail e. Jonathan's previous two e-mails have not been responded to and he is getting desperate. The capital letters make words stand out and are the e-mail equivalent of shouting.

Also check that students understand the symbol at the end of e-mail h. This is an *emoticon*, a symbol made up of items from the keyboard which gives the receiver an indication of the sender's mood. This one is a smiley face (when turned round) to show that the sender is happy. Ask what other emoticons students are familiar with. You could extend the discussion to text-message abbreviations.

2 Before they look at the answer, see how many ideas students can come up with for punchlines to Sam's joke. (The beginning of the joke is the last paragraph in e-mail h on page 80.)

A lot of jokes are sent around the world by e-mail. Ask students if they have received any good ones and, if so, to tell them to the rest of the class.

3 This exercise focuses on some common expressions found in e-mails. Encourage students to do the matching without looking back at the e-mails in Exercise 1, but allow them to do this if they need to.

Point out that this is a useful bank of language that they can use later on in the unit when they write their own e-mails.

Relaying messages

This section widens the subject of messages to include voice mail. Students practise listening to voice mail messages and writing summaries of what they hear. They then reply to one of the messages by writing an e-mail.

1 **19.2** Go through the instructions with the class before playing the recording. Students then discuss who they think the famous people are supposed to be.

2 Students choose one of the voice messages. Try to ensure that each message is chosen by at least one pair. Play the recording again, several times if necessary. Students listen for their chosen message and take notes. Make sure students are silent during the other messages so that they do not disturb other students taking notes.

3 Students work together to write a summary of their chosen message. Notes are provided to help them, but they can add to these as they wish. The summary notes encourage the use of reported speech.

Direct students' attention to the Grammar link on page 114 where they will find more guidance on reporting what people say and some useful practice exercises. You may want to go through these in class first.

4 Students read out their summaries.

5 This could be done for homework if you are short of time. The e-mails could be displayed in the classroom for other students to read and enjoy.

19.2
Message 1
Message received today at 9.37.
Hello, this is Bill calling from Seattle. Sorry for not getting back to you sooner, but I only just got your e-mail. I'm having a few problems with this new Outlook Express program. Just can't get the damn thing to work! Anyway, I've been thinking about what you said at our last meeting and I think I may have the answer. Why don't we simply buy the Internet? It would certainly solve a lot of problems. Think about it and call me back later today.
To repeat the message, press one; to delete the message, press two; to save the message, press three. Message erased.

Message 2
Message received today at 9.56.
Hi, Richard here. You won't forget those figures for our meeting in New York tomorrow morning, will you? I booked you both onto Virgin flight 776 from Heathrow, economy class. Sorry, I couldn't get us all a seat in upper class. Believe me, I tried everything. So I won't actually be with you during the flight. But I can give you a lift to the airport if you like. I'm going ballooning this afternoon, so phone me back after 4.30 if you want to fix something up. Speak to you later.
To repeat the message, press one; to delete the message, press two; to save the message, press three. Message erased.

Message 3
Message received today at 10.04.
Hello, it's Anita. I'm just phoning to say how much I loved the 'Beauty without Cruelty' campaign you ran for us and to see if you'd like to come to the launch of our new cabbage and banana shampoo. I realise it's rather short notice, but would one of you be prepared to give a little speech? You were so good last time. There'll be a lot of celebrities there and we're donating all the profits from ticket sales to Save the Squirrel. I'm in Papua New Guinea right now so call me on the satellite phone. Bye.
To repeat the message, press one; to delete the message, press two; to save the message, press three. Message erased.

Message 4
Message received today at 10.21.
Luciano here. I'm calling to say I'm very unhappy about the direction you are trying to take my company in. God knows it's a difficult enough business to begin with. You try selling low-budget T-shirts and pullovers in today's market! As you know, we have a reputation for dramatic and controversial television commercials and your suggestion that we use some ageing rock group to promote our product is frankly pathetic. I want a fresh proposal on my desk by tomorrow morning or I'll call in another group of consultants. Phone me the minute you get in.
To repeat the message, press one; to delete the message, press two; to save the message, press three. Message erased. No more messages.

2 What do you think the punchline to Sam's joke is? See below for the answer.

3 Match up the words and phrases below to make fifteen complete expressions. If you need to, refer to the e-mails you read in exercise 1, where they all appeared in the same order as here.

a	this is just	if you're having	problems
b	the report	to negotiate	costs
c	e-mail me	was due	reminder
d	room	itemised	on fees
e	fully	a quick	yesterday
f	quote	the delay in	estimate
g	give	precise	report as an attachment
h	sorry for	a rough	getting back to you
i	send a	breakdown of costs	figures
j	a detailed	first draft of the	for the project
k	be under	proposal in	a budget
l	get a	stick to	head office
m	set and	missed	the deadline
n	let me	pressure from	position is asap
o	I just	know what the	on schedule

Relaying messages

1 🔲 19.2 You and a partner both work for a top management consultancy in London. Listen to four voice mail messages famous business people *might* have left you (but didn't!). Who do you think the callers are supposed to be?

2 With your partner, listen to one of the messages again and take notes.

3 Write a brief summary of the message you listened to. Use the notes below to help you.

Message 1: (*Name*) rang to apologise for ... . Apparently, he's ... . He said ... and suggested ... . He asked us to ... .

Message 2: (*Name*) rang to remind us to ... . Unfortunately, he said he couldn't ..., but he offered to ... and told us to ... .

Message 3: (*Name*) rang to thank us for ... and to invite us to ... . She admitted ..., but was wondering if ... .

Message 4: (*Name*) rang to complain about ... . He threatened to ... if we don't ... . He insisted we ... .

Grammar link

for more on reporting see page 114

4 Read out your summary to the rest of the class and listen to theirs.

5 Write a short e-mail in reply to one of the voice mail messages.

Dealing with messages

1 Work in groups to produce a short profile of a company, a department in that company and an executive who works in that department. Invent the whole thing or use the names of real people and companies if you prefer.

PROFILE

Name of company:

_____

Location:

_____

Main business activity:

_____

Department:

_____

Name of executive:

_____

Position in company:

_____

2 Prepare five e-mail messages and (if you can) five voice mail messages that the executive you invented might receive on a typical (or not so typical) working day. Keep each message fairly short. Include personal ones if you like.

Message ideas:
good news
an offer
a complaint
a crisis
an apology
an invitation
a request
bad news
a rumour
a reprimand
an ultimatum

3 When you are ready, write out your e-mail messages or print them off on a PC. Record your voice mail messages onto a cassette.

4 Swap your profile, voice mail cassette and e-mails with another group.

5 Read and listen to the messages the other group gave you and decide how you are going to respond to each. Classify the messages as 'important', 'urgent', 'postpone', 'delegate' or 'bin'.

6 Write replies to the messages and return them to the group you swapped with.

7 Report back to the class how you dealt with the messages you received.

Dealing with messages

In this section, students put together everything they have learnt in this unit to practise sending and responding to e-mails and voice mail messages.

Fluency

1 You will need to allow plenty of time for the activities in this section, but it is worth doing as it practises a range of skills and language that students have learnt. Remind students that they can make up all the information for their profiles or use real names if they prefer.

2 Point out that there are some suggested ideas for messages, but students are free to use their own topics if they wish.

3 If you don't have facilities for students to record voice mail messages, they could write these on paper and mark them 'voice mail'. However, providing facilities for them to record their voice mail messages and print out their e-mails will pay dividends. The activity will seem much more real, and so students will participate more enthusiastically.

4 Groups swap profiles and messages.

5 The groups read, listen to and discuss the messages they receive. They then work together to decide how they are going to respond to each.

6 Allow plenty of time for students to prepare their replies and for the original group to read them.

7 In a class feedback session, find out how successfully the messages were dealt with.

If you're short of time

Set ordering the e-mails in *An urgent matter* Exercise 1 and matching up the words and phrases Exercise 3 for homework.

Set the Grammar link exercises for homework and check the answers at the beginning of the next class.

20 Negotiating

This unit begins by reminding students that negotiating is something we do all the time with people we meet and know – it isn't confined to business board rooms.

Students discuss what makes a good negotiator and listen to four business people sharing their views on the subject.

The focus then changes to the kind of language used in negotiations. Students practise identifying and using softening techniques to make statements less direct and more diplomatic.

The next section also focuses on language and students listen to some extracts from different negotiations.

In the final section, they read a text about the business side of football. They then use all the skills and language they have learnt in the unit to prepare and perform a guided roleplay negotiation of a football transfer.

The grammatical focus is on the grammar of diplomacy and the lexical focus is on collocations and expressions relating to negotiating.

In this first section, students read an extract from one of William Ury's books on negotiating and discuss the situations described in it. They formulate some advice for the person described and decide what they think a good negotiator is. They then listen to business people talking about how to negotiate and answer questions analysing what was said. Finally they examine some common collocations concerned with negotiation.

Warm-up

Ask students to list the situations in the past week in which they have had to negotiate. Tell them to include situations with family members and colleagues on everyday matters as well as any actual business negotiations they have been involved in. Ask them to tell the class about any of these situations and how well they think they succeeded in negotiating.

Focus students' attention on the quotation of Aristotle Onassis. Do they know about any of his business deals or love affairs? (Maria Callas and Jackie Kennedy Onassis).

Elicit from them that the best outcome of a negotiation is a 'win–win' situation, where both sides leave the negotiation with some degree of satisfaction. How can this be true of battles or love affairs?

1   Read the instructions and find out if any of the students have read either of the books mentioned. Then ask them to read the text and say if any of the situations are familiar.

20 Negotiating

Never begin a deal, a battle or a love affair if the fear of losing overshadows the prospect of winning. *Aristotle Onassis, shipping tycoon*

1 William Ury is co-author of the world's most famous book on negotiating, *Getting to Yes*. Read the following extract from his best-selling sequel, *Getting Past No*. Which of the situations remind you of something that's happened to you?

Daily life is full of negotiations that can drive you crazy. Over breakfast you get into an argument with your spouse about buying a new car. You think it's time, but your spouse says: 'Don't be ridiculous! You know we can't afford it
5 right now.'

A morning meeting with your boss. You present him with a carefully prepared proposal for a new project, but he interrupts you after a minute and says: 'We already tried that and it didn't work. Next item.'

10 During your lunch hour you try to return a defective toaster-oven, but the salesperson refuses to refund your money because you don't have the sales slip: 'It's store policy.'

In the evening you need to return some phone calls, but the line is tied up by your thirteen-year-old daughter. Exasperated, you
15 ask her to get off the phone. She yells: 'Why don't you get me my own phone line? All my friends have them.'

Adapted from Getting Past No by William Ury

2 a In order to give the person in the extract in 1 advice, what else would you need to know about each situation?

b What would you say in response to each of the people in the text?

Compare your ideas with a partner.

3 Complete the following sentence in not more than five words: 'A good

negotiator _____,'

Compare sentences with other people in the class.

4 🔘 **20.1** Listen to four business people sharing their views on how to negotiate and answer the questions below.

a Put the following stages in a negotiation into the order Speaker 1 mentions them.

have lunch 5	create rapport 1
agree on a procedure 2	set out proposals 3
bargain 7	agree terms 8
close 9	celebrate 10
listen and take notes 4	make counter-proposals 6

b Speaker 2 refers to the following acronyms. What do they mean?

OP *opening position*

TP *target position*

WAP *walk-away position*

FBP *fall-back position*

BATNA *best alternative to a negotiated agreement*

c According to Speaker 3, why doesn't 'win-win' usually work?
Most people have an 'I win – you lose' mentality.

d What five pieces of advice does Speaker 3 offer?
Don't get personal.

Don't agree to anything until you've discussed everything.

Don't make any concessions without asking for something in return.

Ask lots of questions.

Don't give in to pressure.

e According to Speaker 4, what's the worst thing you can do to a

negotiator? *accept his first offer*

What's the difference between tactics and dirty tricks? *tactics are your strategies; dirty tricks are your opponent's*

What examples does he mention? *Shock with your opening offer; deliberately misunderstand them, using English as an excuse; kill them with silence; use emotion to your advantage; at the end, say you haven't got your boss's ok or make a last-minute demand.*

Collocations 5 Match up the halves of the following collocations. All of them have appeared in the unit so far.

a initial	deal	**e** critical	process
b long-term	offer	**f** win-win	demand
c dirty	relationship	**g** negotiating	phase
d one-off	tricks	**h** last-minute	negotiation

2   Students work individually to decide what further information they would need in order to give advice and what they would say in response to each of the people in the text. They compare their ideas with a partner.

In a class feedback session, find out how much consensus there is about the best way to deal with each situation.

3   Again students work alone to complete the sentence and then compare their ideas around the class.

4   📼 **20.1** Allow students time to look at questions a–e so they know what they are listening for. Check that they know what an acronym is. Pause the recording between speakers to allow students time to write down their answers. You may need to play the recording several times. Allow students to compare notes in pairs or small groups before checking the answers with the class.

Collocations

5   Check the answers by asking one student to read out the first part of a collocation and another to supply the second part.

Students could write sentences, newspaper headlines or book-titles to illustrate the use of these collocations.

📼 **20.1**

Speaker 1
Spend as much time as possible at the outset getting to know exactly who you're dealing with. Inexperienced negotiators tend to go straight in there and start bargaining. That may be OK for a small, one-off deal, but it's no way to build a long-term business relationship. So create rapport first. This could take several hours or several months! When you're ready to start negotiations make sure you agree on a procedure before you begin. And while they're setting out their proposals, don't interrupt. Listen. And take notes. Then have lunch! Don't be tempted to make your counter-proposals and enter the bargaining phase until after a good long break. You'd be surprised how much you can find out over a decent meal. Bargaining, of course, is the critical phase, but it can be surprisingly quick. If it isn't, break off and fix another meeting. Don't try to run marathons. When you do finally get to the agreement stage, agree the general terms, but leave the details to the lawyers – that's what they're there for. Close on a high note and remember to celebrate!

Speaker 2
Prepare thoroughly. If you don't, you won't know whether to accept an offer and may end up actually arguing with your own side, which is suicide in a negotiation. So, make sure you establish all the points you're going to negotiate and have a clear idea of your opening, target and walk-away position on each. Your opening position or OP is your initial offer – on price or whatever. Your TP, your target position, is what you're realistically aiming for. And your WAP or walk-away position is the point at which you walk away from the negotiating table. Always be prepared to do that. Know what your fall-back position or FBP is – what you'll do if you don't reach an agreement. Some people call this your BATNA, your best alternative to a negotiated agreement. You nearly always have a BATNA, however undesirable. But if you really haven't got one, you'd better be good at bluffing or you going to lose big time!

Speaker 3
Ideally, a successful negotiation is a kind of joint problem-solving meeting, where we identify each other's interests, wants and needs and then explore the different ways we could satisfy those. I say 'ideally', because it hardly ever is like that. Win–win negotiation is a great idea, but most people have a simple 'I win – you lose' mentality. So what do you do with the person who simply won't listen, who keeps interrupting, who becomes aggressive, who makes last-minute demands, who won't make a decision? I must have read dozens of books on negotiation tactics. The problem is, so has everybody else. So they don't really work. My only advice is: don't get personal – ever; don't agree to *anything* until you've discussed *everything*; don't make any concessions without asking for something in return; ask lots and lots of questions; and don't give in to pressure. Remember, if the answer must be now, the answer must be 'No'.

Speaker 4
I think it was the negotiations trainer and writer, Gavin Kennedy, who said the worst thing you can do to a negotiator is to accept his first offer. You may think that's exactly what he wants, but that's where you'd be wrong. If you accept his first offer without a fight, your opponent will think he could have got a lot more out of you. He won't be happy at all, and you don't want that. So play the game. And don't worry about dirty tricks. They're only dirty tricks when your opponent uses them. When you use them, they're tactics! So use them. Shock them with your opening offer; use your English as an excuse to deliberately misunderstand them; kill them with silence; use your emotions when it's to your advantage; right at the end, say you have to get the OK from your boss or make another last-minute demand.

Directness

This section looks at the issue of how direct you should be when negotiating. Cultural differences are examined and ways of making statements more diplomatic are identified and practised.

1   Allow students time to read the joke and discuss it amongst themselves.

Then ask if they think there is a lesson to be learned from it: how we word our requests to other people has a great effect on what their response will be.

2   Students work individually to decide where on the line they would put themselves and most people from their own culture.

3   Students work with people who put themselves on the other side of the line. When they try to persuade each other, remind them of the language they have learnt in earlier units for expressing your point of view.

4   Make sure students understand that the first statement in each case is what the negotiators actually thought. However, what we think is not always what we say. Elicit that what we say is usually softer, politer, more diplomatic than what we think.

Their task is to write what the negotiators actually said using the prompts. If students are finding this difficult, direct their attention to the Grammar link on page 116 where they will find an explanation of the grammar of diplomacy. They could do the practice exercise on page 117 before tackling this exercise.

5   Ask students to consider the role of adverbials, verbs, tenses, modals and adjectives in tempering the direct approach. How does a question alter the tone?

Ask individual students to give their opinions or have a show of hands from the whole class on which version they prefer.

Directness

1 Read the joke. Is there a lesson to be learned from it?

> Two priests were so addicted to smoking that they desperately needed to puff on cigarettes even while they prayed. Both developed guilty consciences and decided to ask their superior for permission to smoke.
> The first asked if it was OK to smoke while he was praying. Permission was denied. The second priest asked if he was allowed to pray while he was smoking. His superior found his dedication admirable and immediately granted his request.

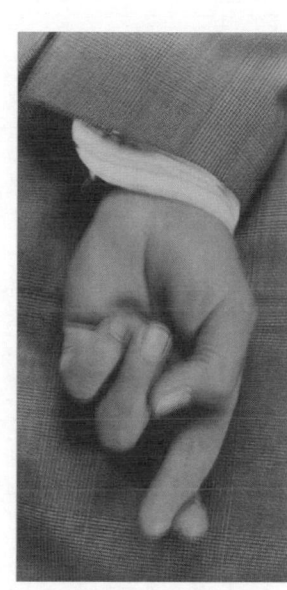

2 How direct you want to be in a negotiation is a matter of both cultural background and personal choice. On which side of the line below would you place people from your own culture? How about you personally?

prefer the diplomatic approach ◄──────┼──────► prefer straight-talking

3 Find someone in your group who put themselves on the other side of the line from you. Try to persuade each other that your side is better.

4 The following thoughts passed through the minds of two negotiators during a negotiation. Use the words and phrases in brackets to reproduce what they actually said.

a That's impossible.

(*unfortunately / would not / possible*) <u>Unfortunately, that would not be possible.</u>

b We can't go higher than 7%.

(*would find / quite difficult*) <u>We would find it quite difficult to go higher than 7%.</u>

c We won't accept less than $5 a unit.

(*afraid / not in a position / this stage*) <u>I'm afraid we're not in a position to accept less than $5 a unit at this stage.</u>

d You'll have to pay more if you want that.

(*may / slightly*) <u>You may have to pay slightly more if you want that.</u>

e We need a commitment from you now.

(*would / some kind*) <u>We would need some kind of commitment from you now.</u>

f We should spend more time looking for a compromise here.

(*shouldn't / little?*) <u>Shouldn't we spend a little more time looking for a compromise here?</u>

g It would be a good idea to agree on a price before we go any further.

(*wouldn't / better?*) <u>Wouldn't it be better to agree on a price before we go any further?</u>

h We hoped you'd pay a deposit today.

(*were hoping / able*) <u>We were hoping you'd be able to pay a deposit today.</u>

i It will be difficult to get my boss to agree to this.

(*might not / very easy*) <u>It might not be very easy to get my boss to agree to this.</u>

j That's as far as we can go.

(*think / about / the moment*) <u>I think that's about as far as we can go at the moment.</u>

Grammar link

for more on the grammar of diplomacy see page 116

5 What do the negotiators do to make their statements more diplomatic? Do you prefer the direct or diplomatic versions?

They use less direct language.

The language of negotiations

1 The following expressions are all useful in negotiations, but some letters are missing from the final words. When you have completed them, the letters in the box spell out some good advice for a negotiator.

a	Perhaps we should begin by outlining our initial ...	P O S I T I O N
b	Can I make a ...	S U G G E S T I O N?
c	What if we offered you an ...	A L T E R N A T I V E?
d	Let me get this quite ...	C L E A R
e	Would you be willing to accept a ...	C O M P R O M I S E?
f	I'm afraid this doesn't really solve our ...	P R O B L E M
g	We may be in a position to revise our ...	O F F E R
h	I think that's about as far as we can go at this ...	S T A G E
i	Are these terms broadly ...	A C C E P T A B L E?
j	Let me just check I understand you ...	C O R R E C T L Y
k	I'm afraid we could only accept this on one ...	C O N D I T I O N
l	What sort of figure are we talking ...	A B O U T?
m	Could you give us an idea of what you're looking ...	F O R ?
n	What sort of time-scale are we looking ...	A T ?
o	We'd like to see some movement on ...	P R I C E
p	Can we just run through the main points once ...	M O R E?
q	At the moment, we do not see this as a viable ...	O P T I O N
r	We seem to be nearing ...	A G R E E M E N T
s	Well, that's it. I think we've earned ourselves a ...	D R I N K!

Lexis link

for more on the vocabulary of negotiations see page 117

2 ▭ 20.2 Listen to extracts from two different negotiations and tick off the expressions in 1 as you hear them. Which two are not used? a, g

3 Listen again and complete the following notes:

Mammoth Construction plc

Schumann Tender

Our original bid: 7.8m euros

Client counter-offer: 7m euros

Project to be completed within 18 months

Plant to be operational by next September

Our revised bid:

2m euros in advance

2m euros mid-contract

3.2m euros on completion

TOTAL: 7.2m euros

Schedule overrun penalty: 25,000 euros per week

Smart Move plc
THE COMMUNICATION SKILLS SPECIALISTS

Telesales training (2-day seminar)

no. seminars: 8 over 6 -month period

no. trainers 3

materials to be approved

max. no. participants per seminar: 16

Full fee: £ 24,000

Discount: 15 % = £ 3,600

Final fee: £ 20,400

25 % non-refundable deposit = £ 5,100

The language of negotiations

This section provides students with more language which they can use in negotiations. They complete a crossword and then listen to extracts from negotiations and tick the expressions as they hear them. They then complete notes on the positions of two companies involved in a negotiation.

1   When students have completed their crosswords, check the answers and ask for the good advice spelt out in the box: never lose your temper.

2   📼 **20.2** This exercise gives students an opportunity to hear the expressions they have just learnt. Play the recording for them to tick the expressions as they hear them and then ask which two were not used.

Direct students' attention to the Lexis link on page 117 where they will find more exercises on the vocabulary of negotiations.

3   Give students a chance to read through the notes before you play the recording again.

📼 **20.2**

Extract 1

A: Now, the next thing is: **we'd like to see some movement on price**. We had a rather lower figure in mind than the one you've quoted us.

B: OK. **What sort of figure are we talking about?**

A: Well, something nearer to seven million euros.

B: Now, **let me just check I understand you correctly**. You're offering us seven million for the whole construction contract?

A: That's right.

B: And **what sort of time-scale are we looking at?**

A: We would expect you to complete the project within 18 months.

B: How flexible can you be on that?

A: Not very. We were hoping to have the plant fully in operation by next September.

B: I see ... **Can I make a suggestion?**

A: Go ahead.

B: Well, **would you be willing to accept a compromise?**

A: That depends on what kind of compromise you had in mind.

B: Well, **what if we offered you an alternative?** What if you paid us two million in advance, two million mid-contract, and another 3.2 million on completion.

A: On schedule?

B: On schedule. 18 months ... Or thereabouts.

A: Hm. So that's 7.2 million euros in all.

B: Correct.

A: And what if you run over schedule?

B: Then there would be a penalty. Let's say

25 thousand euros for each week we ran over schedule.

A: Hm. **I'm afraid this doesn't really solve our problem**. What we need from you is a guarantee that the project will be finished on time.

B: And, as you know, I can only give you that guarantee by bringing in more outside contractors.

A: Which ups the price to your original bid of 7.8 million euros?

B: Yes.

A: **At the moment we do not see this as a viable option.**

B: 7.8 million really is my best price on that.

A: Well, in that case, **I think that's about as far as we can go at this stage.**

B: Now, wait a minute. We're not going to lose this deal for 600,000 euros, surely ... How about this ...?

Extract 2

A: Right. **We seem to be nearing agreement**. But, erm, before we finalise things, **can we just run through the main points once more?**

B: Sure.

A: Now, you'll provide a series of eight two-day in-company seminars for our telesales team over the next six months. You yourself will be conducting most of the sessions with two other trainers, using materials specially designed to meet our specific needs and approved by us four weeks prior to the first seminar?

B: That's correct.

A: And, er, **let me get this quite clear**, each seminar is to have no more than 16 participants, is that right?

B: Yes. We find the seminars are much more effective with smaller groups.

A: Hm, I suppose you're right. It does also

mean running more courses, but OK. Now, since we are booking eight seminars, we'll obviously expect a reasonable discount on your usual fee.

B: Erm, yes. **Could you give us an idea of what you're looking for?** Because with this particular course ...

A: I would have thought a 15% discount was fair. So that's eight times £3,000 is £24,000 minus 15%, which is, erm, £3,600. And that would come to a total fee of £20,400. And you'd invoice us on completion of the whole series of seminars. **Are these terms broadly acceptable?**

B: Er, well, just a moment. We haven't actually agreed on the discount yet. As I was about to say, with this particular course there wouldn't normally be such a large discount. We offer 10% on five or more of our standard seminars, but this is a specially designed course for your personnel only. Obviously, we have to cover our development costs.

A: I should think you could cover them quite easily on just over £20,000, Mr Smart. No, my mind's made up. 15% – take it or leave it.

B: Well, now, **I'm afraid we could only accept this on one condition**.

A: Which is?

B: Erm, we'd want a 25% non-refundable deposit in advance ...

A: Done.

B: You see, ... erm, sorry?

A: 25% deposit – no problem. I'll get accounts to make you out a cheque for, let me see, £5,100 ... **Well, that's it. I think we've earned ourselves a drink!**

B: Erm, well, yes. Nice doing business with you.

The transfer

This section leads up to a guided roleplay of a negotiation about a football transfer deal. It begins with a text about Manchester United which demonstrates that football is big business and the football transfer system allows players to be traded for millions of pounds.

Students then divide into teams to negotiate the transfer of a football player from his present club to Manchester United. They use the language and skills they have practised in this unit to carry out the negotiation.

Warm-up

Find out what sports the students are interested in and whether the players command large salaries. Encourage discussion of sports other than football as this will be covered in later exercises. Find out what the students views on sports sponsorship are and, for example, whether they think cigarette companies should be allowed to sponsor sporting events and advertise their products at them.

1 Elicit that 'footballers are today's rock stars' means that footballers are known for getting high salaries just as rock stars were in the past.

   Students may know similar journalistic expressions such as 'grey is the new black' (grey is the colour in fashion now to replace black which used to be in fashion). Check the collocations before students go on to read the article.

2 Elicit various opinions on what the title means.

   If you have time and wish to exploit the text further, you could put the following figures on the board and ask students to find them in the text and explain their significance: 1990, 1991, 1993, 2000, 1500, £30m.

3 Invite some pairs to perform their conversations for the class. If all your students are interested in football (or if none of them are) allow them to persuade each other to go to other sporting events.

4 ▭▭ **20.3** This roleplay will take some time to set up and perform, so allow enough time. Go through the instructions with the class. Listening to the details of a football transfer and taking notes will be quite challenging for weaker students. In order to give students

a structure for their notes, put the following guidance on the board, have it ready on an overhead transparency or make photocopied handouts. Ask them to fill it in as they listen.

Points to be negotiated

What the team gets

Transfer fee: money one team pays to another for a player

- Young player: £ _____
- International star: £ _____

What the player gets

(represented by FIFA agent who negotiates)

Weekly wage + annual fee

- Average basic weekly wage: £ _____
  (more for internationals and _____ players)
- Annual fee: £ _____

Details of contracts

- Usually for two, _____ or _____ years
- Penalty of around £ _____ for leaving before end of contract
- Merchandising percentage of profits from sales of things with the _____ on them
- Extras for foreign players
  _____

Students then divide into two teams and turn to their respective pages to find the instructions for their side of the negotiation.

Go round as students prepare, ensuring that they have understood what they have to do.

If you're short of time

Allow students to read the recording script describing how football transfer deals are put together and refer to it as they prepare for their negotiation.

Set the Grammar and Lexis links exercises for homework and check the answers at the beginning of the next class.

▭▭ **20.3**

Right, well, when a team wants to sell a player, they agree a transfer fee. That's the price other clubs have to pay them if they want to buy that player. These vary a lot. For a young, talented player with lots of potential the transfer fee could be around three or four million pounds. Obviously, for a real international star, it could be anything up to twenty million. For a team like Manchester United that equals the club's annual profit. So buying a player is a big decision.

That's what the player's club gets, but what about the player? Well, every professional player has a FIFA agent. FIFA's the governing body for world football. And the agent's job is to negotiate terms with teams

who want to buy the player. The average weekly wage in the UK Premier League is about £5,000, or £250,000 a year. Internationals get more and so do foreign players sometimes – it encourages them to come and live in England. So, basically, the wage for all the players is the same, with the stars getting maybe 10 or 15% more.

But, of course, the players don't just get a wage, they also get an annual fee, which is usually much, much more than the basic wage. Superstars can get anything from a one to four million pound annual fee. The fee is really just to stop them going to another team and it's their main source of income.

OK, contracts. Players' contracts can be for two, three or five years, and if a player

wants to leave before his contract expires, he has to pay a penalty – maybe five million pounds or something ridiculous like that. But they usually work something out. There's no point having players who don't want to play for you any more.

So, those are the main points to negotiate in a transfer. Other things might include a percentage of merchandising profits – from sales of shirts, caps, boots with the player's name on – and foreign players will often want a house and car provided as well, since they may only stay a few years. Some ask for free flights home to visit family. Oh, by the way, all those figures I've mentioned are net, not gross. Footballers don't like to worry about how much tax they're going to have to pay!

The transfer

1 Footballers are today's rock stars and some of the most spectacular negotiations lead to multi-million dollar packages for the world's top players. But has soccer become too much of a business for the good of the game? Match up the collocations below and read the article.

a market — industry
b corporate — value
c money-making — image

d stock market — coverage
e media — outlets
f merchandising — flotation

g bluechip — time
h sponsorship — deal
i air — company

Different goals

There was a recent news report about an anthropologist who discovered a lost tribe in the Amazon whose way of life had hardly changed since the Stone Age and who had never seen a car or met a foreigner. What shocked her most about
5 the natives, however, was not their strange social customs or mysterious religious rituals, but the fact that several of them were wearing Manchester United football shirts!

Whether or not that report is true, what is certain is that Manchester United stopped being just a famous football
10 team several years ago and became a highly successful multinational corporation. The words 'football' and 'club' were actually dropped from the players' badges in 2000 in an effort to strengthen corporate image. With a successful stock market flotation in 1991 and a market value, according
15 to City accountants Deloitte & Touche, of over £110m, Manchester United is as much a triumph of the media as of great soccer.

Since 1990 the club has won – to date – four League titles, a League Cup, three FA Cups, A European Cup
20 Winners Cup and a European Super Cup. But it was the media coverage of the 1990 World Cup and the arrival of SkyTV in 1993 that really transformed the game into the money-making industry it is today. 'Top clubs have grown on the back of television contracts,' says Richard Baldwin of
25 Deloitte & Touche. Teams like Bayern Munich, Arsenal, Real Madrid and Galatasaray turn profits many bluechip companies would envy.

'It's an oil well,' says Manchester United's former head of merchandising. He should know. The team's
30 megastore at Old Trafford, which stocks 1,500 different items, is constantly packed, and merchandising outlets as far away as Singapore, Hong Kong and Sydney attract thousands of fans who couldn't even tell you where Manchester is on the map. 'United
35 look and behave very much like a traditional business from a corporate point of view,' says Nigel Hawkins, a financial analyst at Williams de Broë.

'They have a strong brand and they have worked to maximise it by bringing in good people.' They certainly have.
40 One sponsorship deal alone – with Vodaphone – netted Manchester £30 million.

But not everyone is so enthusiastic about the branding of soccer. Many of the small clubs, for example, whose matches never get air time, struggle to survive. Since that's where
45 tomorrow's stars will come from, that could be very bad for the game's future. And some people are also concerned about the number of foreign players bought by the top clubs to make sure they keep winning trophies. No wonder the England team does so badly, they say, when most of the best
50 players in the English Premier League have foreign passports!

Recently, even some of the stars themselves have complained about contracts that permit them to be traded for millions like thoroughbred
55 racehorses. Imagine, said one player, you worked for IBM and not only did they insist you appear in all their TV commercials, but when you
60 wanted to move to Hewlett-Packard, they demanded ten million dollars from your new employer! He may have
65 a point. But systems analysts don't make headlines and not even IBM has its logo in the Amazon rainforest.

2 What do you think the title 'Different goals' means?

3 Do you support a football team? Find someone who doesn't and try to persuade them to go to a match with you.

Fluency **4** 🔊 20.3 You are going to work in two teams to negotiate an international transfer deal. First, listen to a brief description of how such deals are put together and take notes. When you're ready, Team 1 see page 121. Team 2 see page 123–4.

Present Simple

About half of all spoken English is in the Present Simple. You use it to talk about actions and states which are always or generally true.

Affirmative	
I you we they	work
he she it	works

Negative	
I you we they	don't work
he she it	doesn't work

Interrogative		
do don't	you we they	work?
does doesn't	he she it	work?

Spelling changes	
verb	**he/she/it**
go	goes
watch	watches
push	pushes
miss	misses
fax	faxes
try	tries

Practice 1 Correct the following using the information above.

1   A   ~~Works he~~ *Does he work* for the BBC?
    B   No, he ~~don't~~ *doesn't* work for them anymore. He work*s* for CNN.

2   A   Where ~~work you~~ *do you* work?
    B   I work for a design company in Frankfurt.

3   At our firm, we ~~doesn't~~ *don't* work on Friday afternoons.

4   On Mondays our CEO usually ~~flys~~ *flies* to Oslo.

Practice 2 Translate the following conversation into your language.

A   Excuse me, do you work here?
B   No, I don't.
A   Don't you?
B   No, but she does.

Practice 3 Match sentences 1–8 with their functions a–d below.

1   I live just outside Munich.
2   He runs 5km every day.
3   Your presentation is this afternoon.
4   The United States has the world's strongest economy.
5   That's a good idea!
6   She works Saturdays.
7   I love Vienna at Christmas.
8   My train leaves at 7.30.

Which sentences above mainly

a   describe habits and routines?   2   6
b   refer to schedules and timetables?   3   8
c   express thoughts, feelings and opinions?   5   7
d   refer to long-term situations or facts?   1   4

Present Continuous

You use the Present Continuous to talk about current situations in progress and future arrangements.
They're staying at the Hilton.
He's giving a talk on globalisation at 3 o'clock.

Affirmative	
I'm	
you're we're they're	working
he's she's it's	

Negative	
I'm not	
you aren't we aren't they aren't	working
he isn't she isn't it isn't	

Interrogative		
am aren't	I	
are aren't	you we they	working?
is isn't	he she it	

Spelling changes	
verb	**-ing form**
make	making
come	coming
run	running
drop	dropping
forget	forgetting
lie	lying

Practice 4 Correct the following using the information above.

1   A   Are you mak~~i~~ng any progress?
    B   Not much.
2   A   They're drop*p*ing the product.
    B   They can't do that!
3   A   He's a total genius!
    B   Who are you refe*r*ing to?
4   A   Are you forge*tt*ing we have a meeting at 10?
    B   No, I'm just com~~e~~ing.
5   A   He says we're ge*tt*ing a pay increase.
    B   He's ~~licing~~! *lying*

Practice 5 Read the conversation.

A   Alison?
B   Yes. Who's calling? (1)
A   It's Paco … About our appointment, we're meeting (2) on Thursday, right?
B   That's right. Are you flying (3) to Heathrow?

A No. I'm working (4) in Zaragoza this month. So Gatwick's easier for me.

B Fine. Oh! The batteries are going (5) on my mobile. Can I call you back?

In the conversation above, find examples of

a something happening right at this moment. ☐1 ☐5

b something happening around the present time. ☐4

c a future arrangement. ☐2 ☐3

Present Simple or Continuous?

Some verbs are not 'action' verbs, and are not usually used in the continuous form.

> be know understand see hear think
> believe like seem need mean want

Practice 6 Choose the best alternatives in the following conversation.

A What <u>do you do</u> / are you doing?

B <u>I'm</u> / I'm being an electrical engineer for Siemens.

A Really? Here in Munich?

B That's right. <u>Do you know</u> / Are you knowing Munich?

A Oh, yes, great city. So, how do you enjoy / <u>are you enjoying</u> the conference so far?

B Well, it's all right, <u>I guess</u> / I'm guessing. Do you give / <u>Are you giving</u> a talk?

A No, no. <u>I only come</u> / I'm only coming to these things to get out of the office for a few days. Where do you stay / <u>are you staying</u>, by the way?

B At the Avalon. <u>I usually stay</u> / I'm usually staying at the Bauer Hotel in Münchenerstrasse but it was full.

A Well, if you don't do / <u>you aren't doing</u> anything later, do you want to go for something to eat?

Lexis: Conferences

Collocations Complete the following by writing the nouns and noun phrases in the right-hand boxes. They are all things you might do at a conference.

> other delegates   a committee   useful contacts
> a talk   business cards   the bar

make / establish	useful contacts	meet in / hang around	the bar
go to / give	a talk	sit on / elect	a committee
exchange / give out	business cards	network with / flirt with	other delegates

Talking shop When business people get together they often just talk about work. This is called 'talking shop'. Write in the missing pairs of words below.

> in + distributor   out + product   up + plant
> down + factory   with + supplier   to + office
> for + contract   off + workers   of + job
> under + takeover

1 A I hear GEC are setting <u>up</u> a new <u>plant</u> in Warsaw.

   B Warsaw? I thought it was Prague.

2 A I understand you're <u>in</u> talks with a local <u>distributor</u> in Naples.

   B Yeah, that's right. In fact, we've already reached an agreement.

3 A They say GM are laying <u>off</u> 5,000 <u>workers</u> in the UK.

   B Is that right? Well, I knew they were downsizing.

4 A Someone told me Sony are bringing <u>out</u> a new <u>product</u> in December.

   B Yes, I heard that too. Some kind of multi-media entertainment system.

5 A I hear you're thinking <u>of</u> leaving your <u>job</u> at Hewlett-Packard.

   B Well, yes. Just between us, I'm moving to Cisco Systems.

6 A I understand you're being transferred <u>to</u> head <u>office</u> in Stockholm.

   B Well, it's not official yet, but yes, I'm going just after Christmas.

7 A They say they're <u>under</u> threat from a hostile <u>takeover</u> bid.

   B Really? It's the first I've heard of it.

8 A Someone told me they're doing a deal <u>with</u> a <u>supplier</u> in Tel Aviv.

   B Well, that makes sense. They do most of their business there.

9 A I hear you're bidding <u>for</u> a new <u>contract</u> in Singapore.

   B Yeah, we are. The negotiations are going quite well, in fact.

10 A Someone told me they're closing <u>down</u> the Liverpool <u>factory</u>.

   B It doesn't surprise me. From what I heard, they're trying to centralise production.

3 Making calls

Past Simple

You use the Past Simple to talk about completed, past events. Most verbs are regular, but there are about 100 important irregular verbs that are useful to learn.

Affirmative	
I you he she it we they	worked

Negative	
I you he she it we they	didn't work

Interrogative		
did didn't	I you he she it we they	work?

Spelling changes	
verb	**past simple**
study	studied
prefer	preferred
stop	stopped
admit	admitted

To be

Affirmative	
I he she it	was
you we they	were

Negative	
I he she it	wasn't
you we they	weren't

Interrogative	
was wasn't	I? he? she? it?
were weren't	you? we? they?

Practice 1 Correct the following using the information above.

A ~~Phoned~~ *Did* Enrique *phone* about those figures?
B No. I wait*ed* all morning, but he phoned ~~not~~ *didn't*.
A Typical! And I suppose he didn't *do* the report either.
B No. Did he ~~went~~ *go* to the meeting yesterday?
A No, but I ~~not~~ *didn't* expected him to.

Practice 2 Write the Past Simple of the verbs below.

hurry **hurried**	play **played**
occupy **occupied**	enjoy **enjoyed**
refer **referred**	offer **offered**
confer **conferred**	suffer **suffered**
drop **dropped**	develop **developed**
flop **flopped**	visit **visited**
commit **committed**	
transmit **transmitted**	

Why don't the verbs on the right follow the same spelling changes as the verbs on the left?

Practice 3 Time adverbs help us to be more specific about the past. Using the time adverbs in the box, complete this short presentation about the development of a new product.

for	in	during	ago	over	before

As you know, we first got the idea for the new product a year (1) **ago** , but (2) **before** we could go to market with it, there was a lot of work to do. (3) **For** six months the product was in development at our research centre in Cambridge. We then ran tests (4) **over** a three-month period. (5) **During** that time we also conducted interviews with some of our best customers to find out what they wanted from the product. (6) **In** March we were finally ready for the launch.

Practice 4 Complete the joke using the Past Simple of the verbs in brackets.

A businessman (1) **wanted** (want) to interview applicants for the position of divisional manager. There (2) **were** (be) several strong candidates, so he (3) **decided** (decide) to devise a simple test to select the most suitable person for the job. He (4) **asked** (ask) each applicant the simple question, 'What is two and two?'

The first applicant (5) **was** (be) a journalist. He (6) **lit** (light) a cigarette, (7) **thought** (think) for a moment and then (8) **said** (say) 'twenty-two'.

The second applicant (9) **had** (have) a degree in engineering. He (10) **took** (take) out his calculator (11) **pressed** (press) a few buttons, and (12) **showed** (show) the answer to be between 3.999 and 4.001.

The next applicant (13) **worked** (work) as a corporate lawyer. He (14) **stated** (state) that two and two (15) **could** (can) only be four, and (16) **proved** (prove) it by referring to the well-known case of Gates v Monopolies Commission.

The last applicant (17) __turned__ (turn) out to be an accountant. The businessman again (18) __put__ (put) his question, 'What is two and two?'

The accountant (19) __got__ (get) up from his chair, (20) __went__ (go) over to the door, (21) __closed__ (close) it, then (22) __came__ (come) back and (23) __sat__ (sit) down. Finally, he (24) __leaned__ (lean) across the desk and (25) __whispered__ (whisper) in a low voice, 'How much do you want it to be?'

Practice 5 Read the conversation and answer the questions.

Anne Who did you tell?
Bengt Just Claire.
Anne And who told you?
Bengt Stefan.
Anne And nobody else knows?
Bengt Only you.
Anne Well, of course, I do. I told Stefan.

1 Who knew first?
   ⓐ Anne **b** Bengt **c** Claire **d** Stefan
2 How did Bengt find out? _Stefan told him._
3 Who was the last to know?
   a Anne **b** Bengt ⓒ Claire **d** Stefan
4 Read these two questions and <u>underline</u> the subject in each. *Who did <u>you</u> tell? Who told <u>you</u>?*

Practice 6 Correct the six errors in these conversations.

1 **A** They're moving us to a new office.
   B Who ~~did say~~ *said* so?
   A The boss. I spoke to him this morning.
   B Oh. So where ~~said~~ he *did say* we're moving to?

2 **A** Well, I went to the interview.
   B And? What ~~did~~ happen*ed*
   A I got the job!
   B What ~~said I~~? I knew you'd get it. Congratulations!
      did I say

3 **A** I spoke to Amy at the meeting about our idea.
   B And what ~~thought she~~? *did she think*
   A She liked it.   *came*
   B Good. So who else ~~did come~~ to the meeting?

Lexis: Telephone expressions

To the caller, the person who answers the phone *is* the organization.
Telephone Behaviour training film, Video Arts

Dealing with difficulties and distractions In business, phone calls are often interrupted. Look at the difficulties and distractions on the left. Match each one to an appropriate response on the right.

1 Your colleague comes in and wants you to sign something.
2 Your colleague leaves a few seconds later.
3 There's a terrible noise right outside your office. You can't hear yourself think!
4 Your boss wants a word with you – now!
5 Someone else is trying to call you.
6 The other person gives you their name – it's unpronounceable!
7 You think you misunderstood the information the other person just gave you.
8 You gave the other person a lot of information very quickly.
9 The other person just won't stop talking!

a Sorry, could you speak up a little?
b Look, I've got someone on the other line. Can I call you back?
c OK? Did you get all that?
d I'll have to go, I'm afraid. Something's come up.
e Sorry about that. Where were we?
f Anyway, I won't keep you any longer. Speak to you soon.
g Excuse me a moment.
h Sorry, could you spell that for me, please?
i Can I just check that with you?

1	g	2	e	3	a	4	d	5	b	6	h	7	i	8	c	9	f

4 Keeping track

Comparatives and superlatives

Type	adjective	comparative	superlative
1	cheap	cheap**er**	the cheap**est**
2	safe	saf**er**	the safe**st**
3	big	big**ger**	the big**gest**
4	early	earl**ier**	the earl**iest**
5	important	**more/less** important	the most/ the least important
6	good	**better**	the best

Practice 1 Classify the adjectives below as type 1–6.

clever	1	high	1	sad	3
hot	3	global	5	thin	3
dirty	4	bad	6	fat	3
helpful	5	wealthy	4	late	2
hard	1	easy	4	effective	5
heavy	4	rich	1	reliable	5

What generalisations can you make about one-syllable, two-syllable and three-syllable adjectives?

Practice 2 Use your own personal experiences to complete the following sentences. If necessary, use a dictionary to help you choose the right adjectives.

a The job I've got now is a lot _____ than my previous one. On the other hand, it's not quite as _____.

b I found _____ to be a fairly _____ city, but I think _____ is even _____.

c To be honest, I don't really like _____ music. I prefer something a bit _____.

d I'll never forget the view from _____. It's even _____ than the one from _____.

e I find _____ food fairly _____, but it's not quite as _____ as people think.

f I think the _____ building I've ever seen must be _____. Either that or _____, which was just as _____, but in a different way.

g The people in _____ are some of the _____ I've ever met – apart from the _____, who are even _____.

h I drive a _____ these days. In terms of _____, it's the _____ car I've ever had, but it's not as _____ as the _____ I used to have.

Practice 3 Complete the following humorous article using the comparative and superlative expressions in the box.

a – g		
a lot more	by far the lowest	
world's highest	little safer	much better
compared with	even worse	

h – n		
half as many	10% longer	one of the best
as famous as	twice as likely	
significantly happier	a little more	

How to live forever: 8 golden rules

Rule 1 Don't live in Iceland. With long dark winters, sub-zero temperatures and active volcanos, it has the

(a) *world's highest* suicide rate. Move to Palm Beach, Florida, where you have a

(b) *much better* chance of living to be over a 100 – like the rest of the residents.

Rule 2 Don't go to Johannesburg. It's the murder capital of the world. Statistically, it's

(c) *a lot more* dangerous than São Paolo or New York. Milan's a

(d) *little safer* but try not to breathe. The pollution's (e) *even worse* than in Mexico City.

Rule 3 Don't get sick in Equatorial Guinea. There's only one doctor to every 70,000 patients and no anaesthetic. If you have to be ill, be ill in Kuwait. It has (f) *by far the lowest* death rate in the world. Only 3.1 people per thousand die annually,

(g) *compared with* 11.2 in Britain.

Rule 4 If you're a man, think of becoming a woman. On average, women live (h) *10% longer* than men. If you're a woman, stay single. Crime figures show women are (i) *twice as likely* to be killed by their partner than anyone else.

Rule 5 Smoke one cigarette a day. It won't do you much harm and, according to some doctors, it's

(j) *one of the best* ways of avoiding senility in old age.

Photocopiable In Company Intermediate Teacher's Book © Macmillan Publishers Limited 2002

Rule 6 Drink red wine – in moderation.

(k) _Half as many_ red wine drinkers suffer from heart conditions as white wine and beer drinkers. Drinking all three is not an option!

Rule 7 Become a 'chocoholic'. Chocolate isn't good for you, but it releases chemicals in the brain that make you

(l) _significantly happier_. And it's a medical fact that happiness prolongs life.

Rule 8 Die young and famous – like Elvis, James Dean and John Lennon. People will keep believing you're still alive. Even if you can't be (m) _as famous as_ Marilyn Monroe or Kurt Cobain, you can be

(n) _a little more_ careful than they were. No sex, no drugs, no rock 'n' roll. You won't actually live longer. It will just seem like it!

Lexis: Business phrasal verbs

If at first you don't succeed, try, try again. Then give up. No use being a damn fool about it. *WC Fields*

Complete each dialogue using one of the five words in the box. Then match each phrasal verb in the dialogue to a verb similar in meaning.

up	down	off	on	out

The project meeting

A OK, that's item two. Let's move [on] to item three: new projects.
B Now, just hold [on] a minute, Sylvia.
A Kim, I'm counting [on] you to get us the Zurich contract.
B But this is not the time to be taking [on] more work.

continue = _move on_   accept = _take on_   rely = _count on_   wait = _hold on_

The troubleshooting meeting

A Right. Have you managed to sort [out] the problem with our computers?
B To be honest, we haven't really found [out] exactly what the problem is yet.
A Well, can I just point [out] that it's now affecting everyone on the first floor?
B Yes, I know. We're carrying [out] tests on the system now. Give us a couple of hours.

say = _point out_   discover = _find out_   do = _carry out_   solve = _sort out_

The union negotiation

A The question is, will you agree to call [off] the strike?
B Not if you're still planning to lay [off] a quarter of the workforce, no.
A I'm afraid that's a decision we can't put [off] any longer.
B Then, I'm sorry, we shall have to break [off] these negotiations.

fire = _lay off_   end = _break off_   cancel = _call off_   postpone = _put off_

The marketing meeting

A We really must fix [up] a meeting to discuss our pricing strategy.
B Our prices are fine. We're trying to build [up] market share, Otto. Profits can wait.
A Yes, but our overheads have gone [up] nearly 20% over the last eighteen months.
B I know, but that's no reason to put [up] prices. We'll just lose customers.

rise = _go up_   raise = _put up_   arrange = _fix up_   develop = _build up_

The budget meeting

A I'm afraid they've turned [down] our application for a bigger budget.
B That's because group turnover's gone [down] again. So where are we supposed to make cuts?
A We could start by cutting [down] the amount of time we waste in these meetings!
B Now, calm [down] everybody. We need to be practical.

reduce = _cut down_   relax = _calm down_   reject = _turn down_   decrease = _go down_

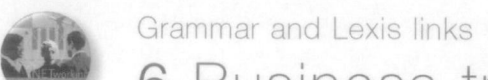
Polite question forms

When you make enquiries and requests, polite question forms and indirect questions are often more polite than imperatives and direct questions.

Imperative / direct question

Where's the nearest taxi rank? (enquiry)
Why is the flight delayed? (enquiry)
Can I open the window? (request)
Help me with my bags! (request)

Polite question form / indirect question

Could you tell me *where the nearest taxi rank is?*
Do you think you could tell me *why the flight is delayed?*
Could I *open the window?*
Do you mind if I *open the window?*
Would you mind if I *opened the window?*
Could you *help me with my bags?*
Would you *help me with my bags?*
Would you mind *helping me with my bags?*

Practice 1 You've just got a new boss. Your old boss was rude and a nightmare to work for. Fortunately, your new boss is much nicer. Look at some of the things your old boss used to say to you below and change them into what your new boss would probably say using a polite question form. Think carefully about word order and grammar.

1   *Coffee!*
2   *Remember to use the spell check in future!*
3   *I want a word with you in private!*
4   *Where do I plug this mobile in?*
5   *Check these figures again!*
6   *How does this damn computer work?*
7   *What's the phone code for Greece?*
8   *You'll have to work overtime this evening.*

1   Could you _make me a coffee, please?_
2   Would you please _use the spell check in future?_
3   Could I _have a word with you in private?_
4   Is there somewhere _I can plug this mobile in?_
5   Would you mind _checking these figures again?_
6   Could you tell _me how this computer works?_
7   Do you happen _to know the phone code for Greece?_
8   Do you think I could ask _you to work overtime this evening?_

Practice 2 When you're rushing around on business, it's easy to sound more aggressive than you mean to. The business traveller on the right is rather stressed. Use polite question forms or indirect questions to make him sound more polite.

a I want a window seat. Could I have a window seat, please?

b Help me with my bags! Could you help me with my bags?

c Where's a cashpoint? Could you tell me where there's a cashpoint?

d Change this twenty-pound note! Would you mind changing this twenty-pound note?

e Don't drive so fast! Would you mind not driving so fast?

f Lend me your mobile! Do you think you could lend me your mobile?

g I need to recharge my laptop somewhere. Do you know if there's somewhere I could recharge my laptop?

h You'll have to give me three separate receipts. Would you mind giving me three separate receipts?

i What time is it? Could you tell me the time, please?

j How far is it to the airport? Do you happen to know how far it is to the airport?

Lexis: Business trips

If you look like your passport photo, you're far too ill to travel. *Stuart Crainer, business journalist*

1 Think about the business trips you've been on in the past. Complete the collocations below using the words in the box.

control	flight	the airport	lounge
shopping	destination	sleep	movie
check-in	plane		

☐ confirm your **flight**

☐ board the **plane**

☐ arrive at your **destination**

☐ try to get some **sleep**

☐ go through passport **control**

☐ wait in the departure **lounge**

☐ take a taxi to **the airport**

☐ queue at **check-in**

☐ do some **shopping**

☐ watch the in-flight **movie**

2 Now do the same with these:

arrivals	your things	hotel
a meal	in the traffic	the office	bags
night	breakfast	a cab	customs

☐ collect your **bags**

☐ go out for **a meal**

☐ be met in **arrivals**

☐ unpack **your things**

☐ go through **customs**

☐ skip **breakfast**

☐ get stuck **in the traffic**

☐ check into your **hotel**

☐ hail **a cab**

☐ phone **the office**

☐ get an early **night**

3 Think about the business trips you've been on in the past. Put the expressions in 1 and 2 into the order they normally happen by numbering the tick boxes. Use them to write the story of one of your trips.

7 Handling calls

Will

Will is a modal verb (like *can, must* and *should*).

Affirmative		
I you he she it we they	will ('ll)	work

Negative		
I you he she it we they	will not (won't)	work

Interrogative		
will won't	I you he she it we they	work?

Practice 1 Correct the following sentences using the information above.

a Do you will help me?

<u>Will you help me?</u>

b Stop making personal calls or I'll to charge you for them.

<u>Stop making personal calls or I'll charge you for them.</u>

c I expect the company will to do well.

<u>I expect the company will do well.</u>

d I don't will accept anything less than 2%.

<u>I won't accept anything less than 2%.</u>

e Don't worry, he wills phone you back within the hour.

<u>Don't worry, he'll phone you back within the hour.</u>

f I'll to take that call, if you like.

<u>I'll take that call if you like.</u>

g I'll sending the figures right away.

<u>I'll send the figures right away.</u>

Practice 2 Match the corrected sentences in 1 to their functions below.

1 a prediction about the future <u>c</u>

2 a spontaneous decision/reaction <u>g</u>

3 an offer <u>f</u>

4 a request <u>a</u>

5 a promise <u>e</u>

6 a refusal <u>d</u>

7 a threat <u>b</u>

Practice 3 Match the following to make five short conversations.

1 A I really need that report today.

2 A My plane gets in at seven.

3 A I'm just off to a meeting.

4 A Eva's off sick today.

5 A She wants to see you – now!

B I'll have to speak to her, I'm afraid.

B I'll be right there.

B I'll finish it this morning.

B I'll phone you later, then.

B I'll come and meet you at the airport.

A Good. I'll tell her you're on your way.

A Fine, I'll just give you my mobile number.

A OK, I'll see if I can reach her at home.

A Great. I'll see you there, then.

A OK, I'll look forward to seeing it.

You can often qualify sentences containing **will** with **if**.

I'll *try to get you onto an earlier flight* **if** *I can.*

If *you've got time,* ***I'll*** *show you round the factory.*

I'll *send you a copy of our brochure* **if** *you like.*

If *you prefer,* ***I'll*** *meet you at the station.*

Practice 4 Complete the conversation using the pairs of words in the box.

wait + details   busy + later   leave + OK
try + time   give + right   desk + look
nothing + away   make + know

József knocks on his boss's door and goes in. Tom is working hard at the computer and doesn't look up.

József: Oh, sorry. If you're (1) <u>busy</u>, I'll come back <u>later</u>.

Tom: No, no, come in, József. If you (2) <u>give</u> me two minutes, I'll be <u>right</u> with you. ... I'll just save what I'm doing. ... Now, what can I do for you?

József: Well, I just need you to check and sign these documents for me.

Tom: Sure. If you leave them on my (3) <u>desk</u>, I'll have a <u>look</u> at them this afternoon.

József: Fine. I'll just put them here, then.

Tom: By the way, it's not urgent, but did you call Budapest about next week's meeting?

Photocopiable In Company Intermediate Teacher's Book © Macmillan Publishers Limited 2002

József: Er, no. I'll (4) <u>try</u> and do it before lunch if I have <u>time</u>.

Tom: OK.

József: And I'll get someone to (5) <u>make</u> the travel arrangements if you let me <u>know</u> how many people are coming.

Tom: Oh, right. I think it's four. If you (6) <u>wait</u> a second, I'll give you the <u>details</u>. ... Yeah, here we are. They're sending their unit manager and three sales executives.

József: OK, I'll see to it.

Tom: Good. And I'll (7) <u>leave</u> it to you to sort out the conference room, if that's <u>ok</u>. We'll need the usual AV equipment and refreshments.

József: Of course. Well, if there's (8) <u>nothing</u> else, I'll get on with it right <u>away</u>.

Tom: Thanks, József.

Lexis: Office life

A desk is just a wastebasket with drawers.
Anonymous

Complete the poem about a day at the office using the verbs on the right. Use the rhyme to help you.

To do today

First, there's a report to <u>do</u>.	check
Then I'll <u>fax</u> those figures through.	get
Flight details.	do
<u>check</u> e-mails.	fax
Don't worry, I'll <u>get</u> back to you.	

A memo now to <u>circulate</u>.	update
Nasty jobs to <u>delegate</u>.	circulate
Travel miles.	running
<u>Update</u> files.	delegate
Can't stop now! I'm <u>running</u> late.	

<u>Hold</u> my calls till half past ten.	cleared
Should have <u>cleared</u> my desk by then.	grab
<u>Print</u> a copy.	hold
<u>Grab</u> a coffee.	cancel
<u>Cancel</u> English class again!	print

Messages to <u>listen</u> to.	meet
One moment, please, I'll <u>put</u> you through.	arrange
<u>Meet</u> at three.	listen
<u>Crash</u> PC!	put
<u>Arrange</u> another interview.	crash

<u>Pick</u> up clients at the station.	give
<u>Give</u> a formal presentation.	make
<u>Make</u> a list	break
Of deadlines <u>missed</u>.	missed
<u>Break</u> off the negotiation!	pick

<u>Contact</u> supplier in Milan –	postpone
<u>Fix</u> an appointment if you <u>can</u>.	get
<u>Get</u> that phone!	contact
Must <u>postpone</u>	fix
The teleconference with Japan.	can

<u>Finish</u> work at half past eight.	phone
Must <u>phone</u> home – I may be late.	hit
<u>Leave</u> the car.	celebrate
<u>Hit</u> the bar.	finish
Damn it – why not <u>celebrate</u>?	leave

So, you <u>blew</u> the presentation!	draft
<u>Screwed</u> up the negotiation!	hand
<u>Feeling</u> better?	screwed
<u>Draft</u> a letter.	blew
Now <u>hand</u> in your resignation!	feeling

Is your office anything like this?

8 Making decisions

Conditionals (future reference)

You can connect two related ideas in one sentence using *if*. Look at the dialogue below.

A **_If we take on another project_**, *we'll need more staff.*

B *But we'll need a bigger office* **_if we employ more people_**.

C *No, not* **_if we hire teleworkers_**, *we won't.*

The sentences on the left are examples of conditionals. The *if*-clause (underlined) introduces a possibility (e.g. we take on another project). The main clause shows what the speaker thinks the result of that possibility will be (e.g. we'll need more staff).

The *if*-clause can come at the beginning or end of a sentence. When it comes at the end, there is no comma (,) after the main clause.

Practice 1 Match the sentence halves in the following extracts from a meeting about a product that is still in development.

Extract 1

A Look, Jean, the product is still in development. If we rush the launch through,

B I realise that. But if I gave you another six weeks,

A Well, we might be able to

B Ian, you know if I give *you* more people,

A Well, if you can't give me any more staff,

B You realise we may lose our technological lead,

A Yes, but I'd prefer to be second or third onto the market

B Hm. You wouldn't say that

a could we have it ready for the Seoul Trade Fair?

b if it means we make a superior product.

c if we don't get this product out before our competitors?

d we won't have time to run the final tests.

e if we had more people working on the project.

f there's no way we're going to be ready, Jean. I'm sorry.

g if you had to deal with the marketing department!

h I'll have to take them off other projects. And I can't do that.

Extract 2

A Well, if we're going to meet our deadline without extra staff,

B OK, fair enough. And if I get you that bigger budget,

A I promise. But if we spent more,

B We'll let Finance worry about that. If we can solve this problem with a bit of overtime,

A Excellent. Because we're missing the publicity event of the year

B You're telling me! If we didn't have a stand at the Fair,

A OK. That's decided then. I'll get us to the launch stage on time

B Great. Now, if you're not rushing off home,

a it would be a disaster.

b if we're not at Seoul.

c can you promise me we'll be ready on schedule?

d I'll buy you that drink I owe you!

e I'll do what I can to get you the budget for that.

f wouldn't that affect our profit margins?

g I'm going to need a bigger budget, Jean so I can pay my people overtime.

h if you get head office to OK a budget increase.

Practice 2 Look again at the extracts in Practice 1. Which of the grammatical structures below come in the *if*-clause, which in the main clause and which in both?

present simple	present continuous
past simple	going to + infinitive
will + infinitive	would + infinitive
may + infinitive	might + infinitive
can + infinitive	could + infinitive

if-clause	main clause
present simple	will + infinitive
past simple	could + infinitive
can + infinitive	might + infinitive
going to + infinitive	present simple
present continuous	may + infinitive
	would + infinitive
	going to + infinitive
	can + infinitive
	present continuous

Photocopiable

As well as *if*, we can use other words to connect two related ideas in a conditional sentence.

Unless *we reach a decision by this afternoon, it may be too late.* (= If we don't reach a decision ...)

The product will be ready in time **provided/providing (that)/as/so long as** *everyone does overtime.* (= ... if, but only if, everyone does overtime.)

Suppose/Supposing *the tourist industry is affected, what'll we do then?* (= What if the tourist industry ...)

Practice 3 Rephrase the sentences below using the word(s) in brackets.

a If they offer you a promotion, what will you do? (supposing)

<u>Supposing they offered you a promotion, what</u> ...

b We'll go ahead with the new design, but only if the market research is positive. (provided that)

<u>Provided that the market research is positive,</u> ...

c We'll lose the contract if we don't lower the price. (unless)

<u>Unless we lower the price, we'll</u> ...

d You can go to the conference, but only if you give a talk. (as long as)

<u>... as long as you give a talk.</u>

Lexis: Money and markets

Having money is rather like being a blonde. It's more fun, but not vital. *Mary Quant, fashion designer and brunette*

If the price is right

1 All the verbs and adjectives in the box can be used to talk about bigger or smaller increases and decreases in prices. Fit them into the diagram.

~~cut~~ rising stable raise slash falling
freeze soaring plunging hike

	Verbs		**Adjectives**	
+ ↑	**a** <u>hike</u>		**f** <u>soaring</u>	
	b <u>raise</u>		**g** <u>rising</u>	
0	**c** <u>freeze</u> prices		**h** <u>stable</u> prices	
	d cut		**i** <u>falling</u>	
− ↓	**e** <u>slash</u>		**j** <u>plunging</u>	

2 Put the two sets of adjectives below in order of scale from the smallest to biggest.

~~reasonable~~ ~~record~~ ~~huge~~ modest

The company made a <u>modest</u> profit.
<u>reasonable</u>
<u>huge</u>
<u>record</u>

heavy slight moderate crippling

The company suffered <u>slight</u> losses.
<u>moderate</u>
<u>heavy</u>
<u>crippling</u>

The marketplace

1 Make collocations containing the word 'market' by writing the following words before or after it.

growing leadership niche ~~break into~~
declining share enter competitive
be forced out of forces ~~research~~
saturation flood mass dominate
challenger supply

break into (the)		research
growing		leadership
niche		share
declining		forces
enter (the)	market	saturation
competitive		challenger
be forced out of (the)		supply
flood (the)		
mass		
dominate (the)		

2 Complete the following sentences using some of the collocations you made in 1.

a Market <u>saturation</u> occurs when the demand for a product is satisfied but you continue to <u>flood</u> that market.

b Even a very small or <u>niche</u> market can be profitable if you totally <u>dominate</u> it.

c Pepsi has always been the No 2, the market <u>challenger</u> threatening Coke's global market <u>leadership</u>.

d The PC market has been so fiercely <u>competitive</u> that many European firms have <u>been forced out of</u> it altogether.

Economic indicators Are the following newspaper headlines good or bad news? Write G or B.

Deeper into recession <u>B</u> Housing boom <u>G</u>
Retail price index up <u>G</u> Markets buoyant <u>G</u>
Signs of recovery <u>G</u> Economic downturn <u>B</u>
Dole queues lengthen <u>B</u> Slump imminent <u>B</u>
Inflation hits all-time low <u>G</u>

10 Small talk

Past Simple or Present Perfect

The Present Perfect is a present tense. You use it to talk about

- things that start in the past and continue up to the present.
  We haven't seen much cricket this summer.
- people's experiences, no matter when they happened.
  I've tried green tea before.
- things that have an obvious connection to the present.
  Dr Winter has come over from the Atlanta office.
  (= he's here now)

Affirmative	
I you we they	have
――――― he she it	worked has

Negative	
I you we they	haven't
――――― he she it	worked hasn't

Interrogative	
I have haven't	you we they
――――― has hasn't	he she it
	worked?

Practice 1 Read the three sentences below.

The Thomke family (came to America) *from Switzerland forty years* **ago** *and* (started a business) (a)
Since *the 1980s they* **have been** *extremely successful.* (b)
In fact, **for** *the last five years they* **have been** *the market leader in their field.* (c)

1 Which of the sentences above refers to
   a point in time? |a| a period of time? |c| both? |b|

2 Which two pieces of information are basically
   history? (circled)
   Which tense is used? _past simple_

3 Which two pieces of information are most relevant
   to the family's **current success**? _underlined_
   Which tense is used? _present perfect_

Practice 2 Look at the following time expressions and decide which are used before *ago*, after *for* and after *since*. Fill in the table.

a week	Thursday	a couple of days
2001	last month	the day before yesterday
over an hour	the 1990s	Christmas	years
a long time	half past four	the oil crisis

___ ago	for ___	since ___
a week	a week	Thursday
a couple of days	a couple of days	2001
over an hour	over an hour	last month
years	years	the day before yesterda
a long time	a long time	the 1990s
		Christmas
		half past four
		the oil crisis

Practice 3 Using the rules you've worked out so far, try the following quiz about the people who said these sentences. Write *yes, no* or *maybe*.

a *I lived in Lisbon.*
   Does he live there now? _No_
b *I lived in Helsinki for six months.*
   Does she live there now? _No_
c *I've lived in Toronto.*
   Does he live there now? _No_
d *I've lived in Taipei for three years.*
   Does she live there now? _Yes_
e *I've been in all morning and she hasn't phoned.*
   Is he in now? _Yes_ Is it still morning? _Yes_
f *I was in all morning and he didn't phone.*
   Is she in now? _Maybe_ Is it still morning? _No_

Practice 4 Complete the conversation using the items in brackets in either the Past Simple or Present Perfect.

Tibor, a sales manager, is planning to send his staff on a team-building survival course.

Tibor: Right now (1) _did_ you all _get_ (*get*) my
e-mail yesterday about the training course?

Fydor: Er, yes ... (2) _was_ (*be*) it a joke?

Tibor: I certainly (3) _didn't mean_ (*not mean*) it to
be a joke, Fydor. No, I (4) _have noticed_
(*notice*) recently that we need to work as a
team more. Last year's interpersonal skills
course obviously (5) _wasn't_ (*not be*) as
successful as I (6) _hoped_ (*hope*), and so I
(7) _have now decided_ (*now decide*) to send
you all on a management survival course.

In Company Intermediate Teacher's Book © Macmillan Publishers Limited 2002

Fydor: At the *Death or Glory Training Camp*.

Tibor: That's right. (8) <u>Have</u> you <u>heard</u> (*hear*) of it?

Fydor: No.

Eva: Erm, you (9) <u>said</u> (*say*) in your e-mail, Tibor, that you won't be coming on the course with us yourself. Is that right?

Tibor: Er, unfortunately, yes. Obviously, I (10) <u>wanted</u> (*want*) to join you, but I'm going to be much too busy, I'm afraid. For one thing, I still (11) <u>haven't done</u> (*not do*) the quarterly sales figures.

Ivan: Tibor, why (12) <u>didn't you tell</u> (*not tell*) us about this at the departmental meeting last week?

Tibor: Well, I (13) <u>didn't make up</u> (*not make up*) my mind until today. But I, er, (14) <u>thought</u> (*think*) it would bring us all together.

Fydor: It (15) <u>has already brought</u> (*already bring*) us together. None of us wants to go!

Tibor: Now, look, Fydor, don't be so negative. Wait until you (16) <u>have had</u> (*have*) a chance to think about it. I (17) <u>haven't</u> even <u>shown</u> (*not show*) you the course brochure yet. Anyway, what do the rest of you think?

Eva: I think it's the most ridiculous thing you (18) <u>have ever asked</u> (*ever ask*) us to do. And, god knows, the interpersonal skills training (19) <u>was</u> (*be*) bad enough. I am not being dumped on a freezing hillside by some sadistic ex-commando, stripped to my underwear and told to find my way back to civilisation with a fruit knife, a chocolate bar and a ball of string!

Lexis: Conversation

A 30-second elevator exchange can be as productive as a one-hour meeting.

William Raduchel, Sun Microsystems

Changing the topic In conversation we often want to describe our experiences. What do the following adjectives describe? Choose nouns from the box.

| ~~city~~ people sport film clothes |
| weather economy |

historic/sophisticated/cosmopolitan/industrial <u>city</u> (1)

marvellous/beautiful/changeable/miserable <u>weather</u> (2)

exciting/competitive/dangerous/national <u>sport</u> (3)

healthy/depressed/strong/weak <u>economy</u> (4)

trendy/smart/scruffy/designer <u>clothes</u> (5)

friendly/proud/hard-working/enterprising <u>people</u> (6)

exciting/classic/unforgettable/gripping <u>film</u> (7)

| food car holiday hotel book |
| news job |

great/shocking/tragic/latest <u>news</u> (8)

difficult/secure/challenging/well-paid <u>job</u> (9)

economical/powerful/luxury/flashy <u>car</u> (10)

fabulous/relaxing/beach/sightseeing <u>holiday</u> (11)

delicious/awful/simple/healthy <u>food</u> (12)

comfortable/poor/luxurious/four-star <u>hotel</u> (13)

dull/entertaining/brilliant/well-written <u>book</u> (14)

Exaggeration and understatement Are you the sort of person who tends to exaggerate or are you a master of understatement?

Exaggeration

A *I hear it was a fairly dirty hotel.*

B *Yeah, **it was absolutely filthy**!*

Understatement

A *I hear it was a fairly dirty hotel.*

B *Well, **it wasn't exactly the cleanest** I've ever stayed in.*

1 Respond to the following statements using the words in brackets to exaggerate.

1 A I suppose Helsinki was pretty cold.
   B (freezing) <u>Yes, it was absolutely freezing!</u>

2 A Thailand is an interesting country.
   B (fascinating) <u>Yes, it's absolutely fascinating!</u>

3 A So, he's got a big house in the country?
   B (enormous) <u>Yes, it's absolutely enormous!</u>

4 A It's actually a very small place.
   B (tiny) <u>Yes, it's absolutely tiny!</u>

5 A She's quite a beautiful woman.
   B (gorgeous) <u>Yes, she's absolutely gorgeous!</u>

6 A Of course, Turkey's hot in summer.
   B (boiling) <u>Yes, it's absolutely boiling!</u>

2 Now do the same to understate.

1 A It's a dull book, isn't it?
   B (interesting / read) <u>Well, it isn't exactly the most interesting I've ever read.</u>

2 A So it was quite an ordinary meal?
   B (amazing / had) <u>Well, it wasn't exactly the most amazing I've ever had.</u>

3 A Well, that was a boring party!
   B (exciting / been to) <u>Yes, it wasn't exactly the most exciting I've ever been to.</u>

4 A It's been a stressful week.
   B (relaxing / had) <u>Yes, it hasn't been the most relaxing I've ever had.</u>

5 A It was a pathetic joke.
   B (funny / heard) <u>Well, it wasn't the funniest I've ever heard.</u>

6 A Isn't Chicago dangerous?
   B (safe place / been to) <u>Yes, it isn't the safest place I've ever been to.</u>

11 E-mail

Future forms

In English there are many ways of talking about the future. The differences between them have less to do with time than with the speaker's attitude to the future event. Study the following examples, all of which refer to the same point in time: next Sunday.

I'm forty on Sunday. (1)
I fly home on Sunday. (2)
I'll let you know on Sunday. (3)
You won't have a problem getting a taxi on Sunday. (4)
I'm going to a wedding on Sunday. (5)
No! I'm not working on Sunday! (6)
It's going to snow on Sunday. (7)
I'm going to have a good rest on Sunday. (8)

The form we choose can depend on such things as:
- whether we are talking about a fact or an opinion
- how sure we are
- whether we have already made plans or arrangements
- how determined we are
- whether we want the thing to happen

Practice 1 Match sentences 1–8 above to their main function.

a   a fixed arrangement ☐ 5

b   a scheduled or timetabled event ☐ 2

c   an informed prediction ☐ 4

d   an offer or promise ☐ 3

e   a plan, intention or decision ☐ 8

f   an indisputable fact ☐ 1

g   a refusal ☐ 6

h   an opinion about the future ☐ 7

In practice, the difference in meaning between certain future forms is often very small.

Practice 2 Match sentences 1–8 above to those below which are similar in structure and function.

a   My plane leaves at five. ☐ 2

b   I'm going to go on a diet. ☐ 8

c   It's going to be a difficult meeting. ☐ 7

d   It's Christmas in three weeks. ☐ 1

e   I'll get back to you within the hour. ☐ 3

f   We're getting a new car on Friday. ☐ 5

g   There'll be a lot of traffic on the roads. ☐ 4

h   I'm not giving someone like him the job. ☐ 6

He's visiting some clients in London next week. (a fixed arrangement – it's likely that he has made an appointment with them)
He's going to visit some clients in London next week. (a future intention – he may or may not have made an appointment with them)
He'll visit some clients in London next week. (a prediction)

My daughter's sixteen tomorrow. (a fact)
My daughter will be sixteen tomorrow. (a certainty)
My daughter's going to be sixteen tomorrow. (a prediction based on certain knowledge!)

Practice 3 Look at the following structures for expressing intention. Put them in order of certainty.

going to	aiming to	planning to
intending to	hoping to	

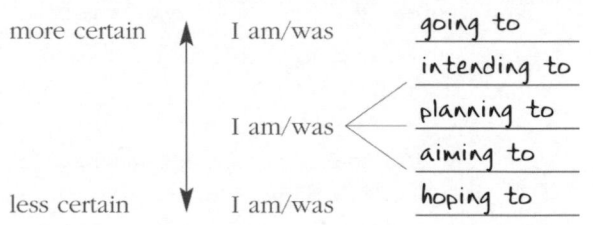

more certain   I am/was   going to
                            intending to
                I am/was   planning to
                            aiming to
less certain   I am/was   hoping to

Practice 4 <u>Underline</u> the most appropriate verb forms in the conversation below.

It's 8pm. Cleo is just leaving work, when she sees the light on in Eric's office.

Cleo: Hello, Eric. Are you still here?

Eric: Hi, Cleo. Yeah, I'm just checking everything for my talk tomorrow.

Cleo: Oh yes, (1) **you'll give / <u>you're giving</u>** your presentation to the board.

Eric: That's right.

Cleo: Are you nervous?

Eric: Not yet. But (2) **<u>I will be</u> / I am** if I don't get this PowerPoint thing to work properly.

Cleo: Oh, I use PowerPoint a lot. (3) **<u>I'll help</u> / I'm going to help** you if you like.

Eric: Thanks, but I think I've had enough for tonight. The presentation (4) **isn't being / <u>isn't</u>** till 11, so (5) **<u>I'll still have</u> / I'm still having** a couple of hours tomorrow morning to get things ready.

Cleo: Well, some of us (6) **will go / <u>are going</u>** out for a Chinese meal and then maybe to that new club if you want to join us.

Eric: Hm, sounds (7) like **you're having / <u>you're going to have</u>** a pretty late night. I think (8) **I'll**

give / I'm giving it a miss this time.

Cleo: Well, (9) **we have / we're having** a drink first in the bar over the road. Why don't you come? (10) **It'll take / It's going to take** your mind off tomorrow.

Eric: Well, maybe you're right. Look, (11) **I'm just checking / I'm just going to check** this thing one last time and (12) **I'm / I'll be** right with you.

Cleo: OK. See you there.

Lexis: Computers

A computer lets you make more mistakes faster than any invention in human history – with the possible exceptions of handguns and tequila. *Mitch Ratliffe, American comedian*

1 Combine the words in the box into at least ten computer terms. Some are written as two words and some as one.

> key site search page data web sheet
> desk menu hard home board spread help
> top ad engine disk base banner

keyboard	website	search engine
homepage	database	spreadsheet
desktop	hard disk	help menu
banner ad		

2 Match each verb on the left with the item on the right that it collocates most strongly with.

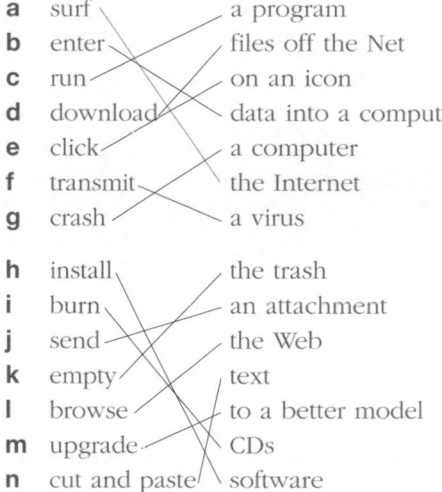

a	surf		a program
b	enter		files off the Net
c	run		on an icon
d	download		data into a computer
e	click		a computer
f	transmit		the Internet
g	crash		a virus

h	install		the trash
i	burn		an attachment
j	send		the Web
k	empty		text
l	browse		to a better model
m	upgrade		CDs
n	cut and paste		software

3 All the verbs below collocate with 'file', but the vowels are missing. Write in the vowels.

open
damage   close
backup   duplicate
update ——→ **a file** ←—— create
convert   save
access   delete
compress

4 Complete the song about computers using the verbs on the right. Use the rhyme and rhythm to help you. Have you experienced similar problems?

My PC is Giving Me Problems

(to the tune of *My Bonnie Lies Over the Ocean*, traditional)

My PC is giving me problems.
My PC is giving me hell.
It says it's got Intel inside it.
But its Intel inside is not well.

Chorus
Bring back, bring back, oh bring back my typewriter, please, oh please.
Bring back, bring back, oh bring back my typewriter, please.

It **crashed** on me three times this morning.	virus
And wouldn't connect to the **Net**.	Net
It **emptied** my trash without warning.	crashed
It's some kind of **virus**, I bet.	emptied

I **e-mailed** head office a memo	attachment
And sent an **attachment** in Word,	error
But HQ's computers are Apple	occurred
And that's when an **error** **occured**.	e-mailed

I **clicked** on an icon to **download**	program
A **program** that iMacs can read	files
But lost half the **files** on my hard disk	download
So somehow I must have miskeyed.	clicked

Now my spreadsheet has lost all its **data**.	upgrade
And sadly no **backups** were made.	helpline
I phoned up the **helpline** at Compaq.	data
They told me I need to **upgrade**.	backups

They finally sent a **technician**,	type
Who debugged my **desktop** with ease,	printer
But something's gone wrong with my **printer**,	technician
'Cause when I **type** 'd's it prints 'c's.	desktop

I guess I'm **computer** illiterate –	keyboard
I don't know my **ROM** from my RAM.	spam
My **keyboard** skills are a disaster	computer
And my e-mail has filled up with **spam**.	ROM

I think I should **shut** down my PC.	Resources
Admit that I'm going **insane**.	retrain
Arrange to see Human **Resources**	shut
And tell them I want to **retrain**!	insane

In Company Intermediate Teacher's Book
© Macmillan Publishers Limited 2002

Photocopiable

Past Continuous

Affirmative		
I		
he		
she	was	
it		
————————		working
we		
you	were	
they		

Negative		
I		
he		
she	wasn't	
it		
————————		working
we		
you	weren't	
they		

Interrogative		
	I	
was	he	
wasn't	she	
	it	
————————		working?
	we	
were	you	
weren't	they	

Practice 1 Match the examples of the Past Continuous below to what they describe.

*I met my wife while I **was working** as a teacher in Barcelona.* (1)
*He **was studying** to be a doctor when he dropped out of university and decided to go into business instead.* (2)
*We **were going** to Vienna for a training weekend, but it was cancelled.* (3)
*You **were** always **working** late when you had that job in the City.* (4)

a a past action which was interrupted or not completed ☐2

b the background to a more important event ☐1

c repeated actions in the past ☐4

d previous plans ☐3

Practice 2 Correct the following conversation. Three of the verbs in the Past Continuous should be in the Past Simple and vice versa.

Inge: Ah, Peter. I was wondering if I could have a word with you?

Peter: Hello, Inge. Er, sure. I ~~just went~~ *was just going* out for lunch, but, er, what was it about?

Inge: Well, I ~~was seeing~~ *saw* Dieter the other day and he told me you're leaving.

Peter: Oh, well, yeah, that's right. Actually, I ~~was deciding~~ *decided* a month ago, but I didn't think anybody ~~was knowing~~ *knew* about it yet.

Inge: Oh, yes. The whole department ~~talked~~ *was talking* about it when I came in this morning. They ~~still talked~~ *were still talking* about it when I left.

The Past Continuous can suggest a continuing feeling or attitude, so you can use it when you want to put gentle pressure on someone to do something.

*I **was wondering** if you could help me.* (And I still am. So will you help me?)
*I **was looking** for something cheaper.* (And I still am. So have you got anything cheaper?)
*We **were hoping** for a bigger discount.* (And we still are. So how about a bigger discount?)

Practice 3 Change the following sentences so that the response to them is likely to be more positive.

a Mr Kanazawa, we hoped to reach a deal by today.

   Mr Kanazawa, we were hoping to reach a deal by today.

b I expected something better from you, Leon.

   I was expecting better from you, Leon.

c Angela, I assumed you would agree to this.

   Angela, I was assuming you would agree to this.

Past Perfect

Affirmative		
I		
you		
he		
she	had	worked
it		
we		
they		

Negative		
I		
you		
he		
she	hadn't	worked
it		
we		
they		

Interrogative		
	I	
	you	
	he	
had	she	worked?
hadn't	it	
	we	
	they	

*By the time I arrived at the party everyone **had left**.* (1)
*I was halfway to the airport before I realised **I'd forgotten** my passport.* (2)

Practice 4 Look at the examples above.

a What happened first: my arrival *or* everyone's else's departure? *everyone else's departure*

b Put the events in chronological order: getting ②
halfway to the airport, forgetting your passport, ①
realising your mistake. ③

The Past Perfect is often used to look back from a time in the past to an earlier time.

Past Simple, Past Continuous or Past Perfect?

Practice 5 Complete the following anecdote by underlining the most appropriate verb forms. Read the whole sentence before you make your choice.

'Apparently, there was this guy working for a financial services company in the City. Anyway, it (1) **was being** / **had been** a really tough year, so he (2) **decided** / **was deciding** to take a nice long holiday. He (3) **just cleared** / **was just clearing** his desk, when he (4) **suddenly remembered** / **had suddenly remembered** what (5) **was happening** / **had happened** the last time he (6) **was** / **was being** off work. He (7) **was coming** / **had come** back to an inbox containing hundreds of e-mails. So this time he (8) **came up** / **had come up** with a bright idea to prevent it happening again.

What he (9) **did** / **was doing** was this: he (10) **set** / **had set** his computer to automatically send a message to anyone e-mailing him, telling them that he (11) **was** / **had been** in the Caribbean for two weeks and not to e-mail him again till he (12) **got back** / **was getting back**. Then, just as he (13) **was leaving** / **had left** the office, he (14) **thought** / **was thinking** he would e-mail his best friend and tell him all about his holiday plans.

Unfortunately, his best friend, who (15) **was going** / **had gone** on holiday the day before, (16) **was setting up** / **had set up** his computer in exactly the same way. So the two PCs (17) **proceeded** / **were proceeding** to e-mail each other every few seconds for the whole fortnight, while these two guys (18) **were enjoying** / **had enjoyed** themselves on holiday, totally unaware. I (19) **heard** / **had heard** that so many messages (20) **were finally building up** / **had finally built up** on the company's server that it (21) **crashed** / **was crashing**, costing the firm millions! True story. Austin in accounts told me.'

Lexis: Presentations

The best audience is intelligent, well-educated, and a little drunk. *Alben W Barkley, ex-US vice-president*

Communication skills Complete the collocations by writing the nouns in the right-hand boxes. They are all things you might do in a presentation.

| an issue | questions | a graph | figures |
| a point | jokes | | |

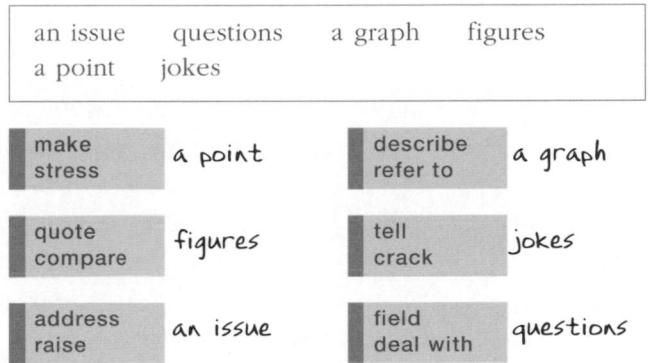

make stress	a point	describe refer to	a graph
quote compare	figures	tell crack	jokes
address raise	an issue	field deal with	questions

Check the meaning in a dictionary, if necessary.

The language of presentations The following expressions are all useful in presentations, but some letters are missing from the final words. When you have completed them, the letters in the box should make a good piece of advice for a presenter.

1	Can everybody hear me ...	O K ?
2	Right, let's get ...	S T A R T E D
3	Let me introduce ...	M Y S E L F
4	I've divided my presentation into three main ...	P A R T S
5	Just to give you a brief ...	O V E R V I E W
6	I'll be saying more about this in a ...	M I N U T E
7	I'm sure the implications of this are clear to all of ...	U S
8	There's an important point to be made ...	H E R E
9	OK, let's move ...	O N
10	I'd like you to look at this ...	G R A P H
11	As you can see, the figures speak for ...	T H E M S E L V E S
12	To go back to what I was saying ...	E A R L I E R
13	Are there any questions you'd like to ask at this ...	P O I N T
14	I'd like to look at this in more ...	D E T A I L
15	Let's just put this into some kind of ...	P E R S P E C T I V E
16	Perhaps I should expand on that a ...	L I T T L E
17	To digress for a ...	M O M E N T
18	So, to sum ...	U P
19	That brings me to the end of my ...	T A L K
20	Thank you. I'm sure you have many ...	Q U E S T I O N S

Modal verbs

| can | could | may | might | will | would | shall | should | must | | ought to | need | dare |

You don't add an _s_ in the 3rd person singular.

Modal verbs are followed by the infinitive without _to_. (NB After _ought_, use _to + infinitive_: She ought to go.)

Couldn't he attend the meeting?

You don't use _do_ or _does_ to make questions.

You don't use _don't_ or _doesn't_ to make negatives.

You use modal verbs to express many different functions. (See Practice 1)

| be able to | have to | be allowed to |

Be able to, have to and _be allowed to_ are often used in place of modal verbs. You use these verbs to express concepts that are not possible with modal verbs.

Will you **be able to** finish the report tomorrow? (_will you can_ is not possible)
I **had to** attend a meeting last night. (_must_ has no past form)

Practice 1 Modal verbs say as much about the speaker's attitude as about the factual content of the sentence. Match the modal verbs in **bold** to their **main function**.

A They **should** be here by now. (a)
B I**'ll** phone and check. (b)
A No, wait a minute, that **must** be them. (c)

A **Could** I leave early tomorrow, do you think? (d)
B Well, I **might** need you to check the monthly figures. (e)
A But I **have to** pick up the kids from school. (f)

expressing obligation **f**
expressing certainty **c**
asking for permission **d**
expressing possibility **e**
expressing probability **a**
taking the initiative **b**

Now do the same with these:

A You **mustn't** load that software onto your company PC! (g)
B But I **can't** do this job without it. (h)
A Well, you **ought to** speak to IT, then. (i)

A I'm getting a drink from the machine. **Can** I get you anything? (j)
B Oh, thanks. **Could** you get me a Coke or something? (k)
A Sure. What's this? You **don't have to** give me the money! (l)

giving advice **i**
saying something isn't necessary **l**
expressing inability **h**
making a request **k**
prohibiting something **g**
making an offer **j**

Practice 2 Try to complete the following modal verbs quiz in under five minutes.

1 _You mustn't do that._
    Will there be trouble if you do it? **Yes**

2 _You don't have to do that._
    Will there be trouble if you do it? **No**

3 Put these sentences into the past:

a I can't talk to you now.
    I couldn't talk to you then.

b I hope we'll meet again.
    I hoped we'd meet again.

c I must fly to Geneva.
    I had to fly to Ganava.

4 What's the opposite of _That can't be right?_
    That must be right.

5 What does _She should be here at nine_ mean?
a She's supposed to be here at nine.
b I expect she'll be here at nine.
c Either.

6 _I could do it_ refers to
a the past.   **c** the future.
b the present.   **d** it depends.

7 _They needn't have done it._ Did they do it? **Yes**

8 _They didn't need to do it._ Did they do it? **No**

9 Are these two sentences possible? _yes_
  a *I could swim by the age of two.*
  b *I was able to swim by the age of two.*
10 Are these two sentences possible? _only 'b' is._
  a *I took the exam three times and finally I could pass.*
  b *I took the exam three times and finally I was able to pass.*

Practice 3 There are modal verbs in a lot of everyday expressions. It is best to learn these by heart. Complete the expressions using the words in the boxes.

wouldn't	couldn't	should	can	may

1 **A** What we need is a holiday.
   B You _can_ say that again!
2 **A** Will it be all right if I just send them an e-mail?
   B I _should_ think so.
3 **A** There are bound to be changes under the new management.
   B I _wouldn't_ be surprised.
4 **A** This strong pound is terrible for business.
   B I _couldn't_ agree more.
5 **A** How are we going to start our own business when we can't even run this one?
   B You _may_ have a point there.

won't	can't	might	have to	must

6 **A** I'll _have to_ be going.
   B Hey, don't rush off just yet!
7 **A** I _won't_ be a minute.
   B OK, I'll wait for you here.
8 **A** You _must_ be joking!
   B I've never been more serious.
9 **A** I _might_ have guessed.
   B Yes, I think we both knew this was going to happen.
10 **A** You _can't_ be serious!
   B No, just kidding!

Lexis: Meetings

Don't call a meeting in your office – it scares people. Go and see them in their offices. *David Ogilvy, advertising guru*

Complete the collocations by writing the nouns and noun phrases in the right-hand boxes. They are all things you might do before, during or after a meeting.

agreement	a decision	comments
the agenda	an opinion	details
an action plan	ideas	a point

set / stick to	the agenda		reach / be in	agreement
brainstorm / exchange	ideas		make / invite	comments
hold / express	an opinion		draw up / implement	an action plan
raise / clarify	a point		go into / sort out	details
			come to / reconsider	a decision

Comments & opinions In meetings, certain expressions help you to introduce your comments and indicate your opinions more clearly. Look at the following five extracts from meetings. Replace the expressions in **bold** with ones in the box which have a similar meaning.

Frankly   Clearly   If you ask me   In short
Incidentally   Strangely enough
As a matter of fact   In theory   Luckily
Overall   Essentially   On the other hand

A **Personally**, / _If you ask me,_ I think this whole project has been a waste of time.
B **To be honest**, / _Frankly,_ I tend to agree with you.
A **However**, / _On the other hand,_ we've put too much money into it to cancel it now.

A **By the way**, / _Incidentally,_ did you get in touch with our agent in Warsaw?
B **Actually**, / _As a matter of fact,_ *she* phoned *me*. I'll talk to you about it later.

A **Obviously**, / _Clearly,_ we don't want to have a strike on our hands.
B **Fortunately**, / _Luckily,_ we may not have to. I spoke to the union representative this morning.

A **In general**, / _Overall,_ did people like the idea of open-plan offices?
B **Funnily enough**, / _Strangely enough,_ they didn't. We may have to rethink our proposal.

A **To sum up**, / _In short,_ by year-end we should be nearing the break-even point.
B **Basically**, / _Essentially,_ then, we're going to make a net loss?
A **Technically**, / _In theory,_ yes. But that's because we're channelling so much money back into the business.

Multi-verb expressions

When we combine two verbs in a sentence, the second verb can follow several patterns:

1 Modal verbs are followed by the infinitive without *to*:
- *We **must make** a decision on this today.*

2 Non-modal verbs are followed either by the infinitive with *to*:
- *We **agreed to review** the situation in a month.*

or by the *-ing* form:
- *They **regretted borrowing** the money.*

If in doubt, use the infinitive with *to*. It's much more common.

3 Some verbs, normally followed by the *-ing* form, change when there's an indirect object:

- *I **advise repackaging** the product.*
- *I **advise you** to repackage the product.*
- *I **suggest breaking** off the meeting here.*
- *I **suggest we** break off the meeting here.*

4 Some non-modal verbs can be followed by both the infinitive with *to* and the *-ing* form. But be careful. The meaning often changes – sometimes completely – as in these examples:

- *They **stopped to talk**.* (= they stopped doing something else so that they could talk)
- *They **stopped talking**.* (= the talking stopped)
- *I **didn't remember to e-mail** you the report.* (= there was no e-mail)
- *I **don't remember e-mailing** you the report.* (= I may have e-mailed it to you, but I don't remember)

5 When a verb is followed by a preposition other than *to*, the *-ing* form is usually used:
- *We **succeeded in getting** the loan.*
- *I'm **thinking of changing** my job.*

When it isn't, the meaning changes:
- *He **went on talking** for over an hour!* (= he wouldn't shut up)
- *He **went on to talk** about profits.* (= he changed the subject)

Practice Study the information above and complete the following advice on how to produce professional letters and faxes by combining the verbs, prepositions and pronouns in brackets.

a Reply to incoming mail promptly. Don't <u>put off writing back</u> for more than a couple of days. (put off / write back)

b Always <u>remember to open</u> with a proper salutation. (remember / open)

c Don't <u>forget to include</u> a subject line. (forget / include)

d <u>Forget about spending</u> a lot of time on social chit-chat at the beginning of the letter. (forget about / spend)

e Most writing experts <u>recommend using</u> lots of subheadings and bullet points to make your message clearer. (recommend / use)

f But they don't <u>suggest you use</u> a lot of old-fashioned formal expressions. (suggest you / use)

g Ideally, you <u>should aim to sound</u> neither too formal nor too friendly. (should / aim / sound)

h You <u>should try to keep</u> your sentences short and simple. (should / try / keep)

i Some people <u>advise you not to exceed</u> 10–15 words per sentence. (advise you / not exceed)

j Also <u>avoid using</u> long complicated words when short ones will do. (avoid / use)

k If you have a lot of information, <u>consider enclosing</u> a separate document. (consider / enclose)

l Beware the spell check! You really <u>can't trust it to pick up</u> all your mistakes. (can't / trust it / pick up)

m Grammar checks are even worse. You'll certainly <u>regret relying</u> on them. (regret / rely)

n If you <u>can manage to get</u> your whole message into less than 200 words, you've done well. (can / manage / get)

o Reread before you send. <u>Imagine receiving</u> your own letter – what impression would it give? (imagine / receive)

p <u>Think about redrafting</u> a difficult letter several times before you send it. (think about / redraft)

Lexis: Prepositions

Size isn't everything. *Anonymous*

Prepositions (*in, at, of, for, through* etc.) are a restricted group of short words, each having many different purposes. They usually take their precise meaning from the words around them.

Apart from their standard uses to refer to time, place and movement, prepositions also combine with verbs, nouns and adjectives to form a lot of useful phrases and expressions. Such phrases are best learned 'whole' as items of vocabulary.

Photocopiable

Prepositional phrases Twenty-three prepositions are missing from the following letter. Write them in.

Dear Mr Savage

Thank you [for] your letter [of] 12th April. I'm very sorry [about] the difficulties you've had [in] getting one [of] our engineers [to] come and repair the alarm system we installed [in] January. Please accept my apologies. I am as concerned [about] the delay as you are.

The manager who is responsible [for] our after-sales service is new [to] the department and not yet familiar [with] all our procedures, but this is no excuse [for] such a long delay. Rest assured, he is now aware [of] the problem and will arrange [for] an engineer [to] call [at] whatever time is most convenient [for] you. Obviously, this will be free [of] charge. I have also authorised a 10% refund [of] the purchase price.

If you are still not fully satisfied [with] the system, please contact me personally and I shall be happy [to] supply you [with] a replacement.

My apologies once again [for] the inconvenience this has caused you.

Preposition + noun Two negotiators are discussing terms. Complete what they say using the pairs of prepositions in the box.

on + in	in + to	by + at	in + on	
in + in	on + at	in + under	in + at	
on + within				

A Normally, we insist on payment (1) **in** advance or **on** delivery.

B Well, we'd prefer to have the product (2) **on** 20 days' approval first and pay **in** arrears.

A I see. Well, perhaps we could arrange for you to pay (3) **in** instalments. But then we'd ask you to cover the insurance while the goods are **in** transit.

B Hm. If we agreed to that, could you guarantee that the goods would be delivered (4) **on** schedule? For us that means **within** seven working days.

A That shouldn't be a problem. Of course, if you order (5) **in** bulk, say 100 units, we deliver free of charge – unless you cancel **at** short notice.

B (6) **In** which case, I suppose there's a cancellation charge. Fair enough. But what if the goods we received were not **to** our satisfaction?

A If, (7) **by** some chance, the goods were damaged, then we would send replacements **at** our expense.

B Fine. Now, I assume if I'm ordering 100 units (8) **on** a regular basis, I can buy them **at** a discount?

A Certainly. Now let's see. The goods you'd be ordering are already (9) **in** stock. You'd cover insurance, we'd cover freight charges and it would be a regular monthly order. **Under** the circumstances, I think I can offer you our top discount rate. That's 4%.

B 4%? I'm afraid you'll have to do better than that.

Preposition + noun + preposition Complete the following extracts from business letters, faxes and e-mails using the nouns in the box. Pay particular attention to the prepositions on either side of each noun.

terms	case	behalf	view	effect
regard	touch	accordance	favour	
agreement	addition	pressure	account	

a I am writing with **regard** to your advertisement in *Marketing Week*.

b We are basically in **agreement** with the main points in your proposal.

c I've been in **touch** with our distributors in Poland concerning your enquiry.

d There are one or two points in **addition** to those we discussed which we now need to address.

e No one at the meeting was in **favour** of the idea.

f The goods have been insured in **case** of damage in transit.

g There will be a 3% price increase with **effect** from January 1st.

h Plan A has been rejected on **account** of the considerable costs involved.

i We decided, in **view** of the political difficulties, not to export to Iraq.

j We are again under **pressure** from head office to reduce overheads.

k Certainly, in **terms** of experience, she's the best candidate we've seen so far.

l We are investigating the complaints in **accordance** with our normal procedures.

m May I, on **behalf** of myself and the whole team, thank you for making our visit so enjoyable.

16 Solving problems

Conditionals (past reference)

You can use *if* to speculate about the likely effects of things being different in the past. You often use this type of conditional to talk about regrets and make accusations.

*If we **hadn't invested** so heavily in dotcoms, we'**d have saved** ourselves a fortune!* (1)
(but we invested heavily and we didn't save a fortune)

*You **could have got** an interview with that company if only you'**d taken** my advice.* (2)
(but you didn't get an interview because you didn't take my advice)

*If our lawyers **hadn't spotted** that mistake in the contract, we'**d be** in a real mess!* (3)
(but they spotted it and so we are not in a real mess)

*If you'**d told** me about it sooner, I **might have been able to** do something.* (4)
(but you didn't tell me sooner so I couldn't do anything)

*He **might** never **have been able to** start his own business if his father **hadn't helped** him.* (5)
(but he started his own business because his father helped him)

*If she'**d taken** her studies more seriously, she **wouldn't be flipping** burgers at McDonald's.* (6)
(but she didn't take her studies seriously and now she's working at McDonald's)

Practice 1 Study the information above and answer the questions.

a What grammatical tense is used in the *if*-clause of all the examples? past perfect

b What modal verbs are used in the main clause?
would, could, might

c What tenses follow the modal verbs in the examples? present perfect

d Which sentences directly refer to the effects of the past on the present? 3 6

e Which sentences directly refer to the effects of the past on the more recent past? 1 2 4 5

Practice 2 Complete the conversation using the pairs of words in the box.

would + could   hadn't + wouldn't
have + known   could + tried   done + have
promised + would

Two colleagues are having an argument.

A All I'm saying is, if you'd (1) done_____ something about it sooner, we could have_____ prevented this whole nightmare from happening.

B I know, I know. And I (2) would____ have if I could_____ have, but I couldn't.

A You (3) could____ have if you'd tried____, you mean.

B Maybe if I hadn't already (4) promised, I would____ be able to put them all off.

A Well, anyway, it's too late now. You know, I'd never (5) have_____ asked you to organise these visits if I'd known____ you weren't clear about it.

B Well, if you (6) hadn't____ said you wanted us to get involved in the local community more, I probably wouldn't have had the idea in the first place.

A I mean, what were you thinking of? You've organised factory tours for three infant schools, an old people's home and the Bulgarian Embassy all on the same morning!

Which example above does **not** contain the Past Perfect?   2

Lexis: People and products

How come, when I want a pair of hands, I get a human being as well?
Henry Ford, first mass market car manufacturer

People or products? Decide whether the adjectives below can be used to describe people (staff), products or both. Tick the correct boxes.

	staff	products		staff	products
best-selling	☐	✓	unique	☐	✓
efficient	✓	✓	luxury	☐	✓
high-quality	☐	✓	loyal	✓	☐
fully qualified	✓	☐	marketable	☐	✓
household	☐	✓	permanent	✓	☐
dedicated	✓	☐	part-time	✓	☐
			reliable	✓	✓

The workforce

1 List the verbs and verb phrases in the box with those below which have a similar meaning.

recruit	lay off	resign	motivate
instruct	quit	take industrial action	
transfer	teach	take on	relocate
inspire	dismiss	down tools	

hire	train	move	leave
recruit	instruct	transfer	resign
take on	teach	relocate	quit

fire	encourage	go on strike
lay off	motivate	take industrial action
dismiss	inspire	down tools

2 Complete the following sentences using appropriate words and phrases from 1.

a During the last recession we were unfortunately forced to **lay off** a lot of our workers.

b Knowledge of foreign languages is an advantage, as we sometimes **transfer** people overseas.

c A lot of staff **went on strike** in protest when we introduced Japanese production methods.

d Of course, we **train** all our people in the basic skills of the job.

e Two directors **resigned** over our decision to manufacture components for the arms industry.

3 The adjectives below can all be used to describe people in a company. Change each adjective into its opposite by adding *un-*, *in-*, *im-*, *ir-* or *dis-*.

a	**un** reliable		**k**	**in** articulate
b	**in** flexible		**l**	**dis** honest
c	**dis** organised		**m**	**ir** rational
d	**im** patient		**n**	**in** decisive
e	**ir** responsible		**o**	**un** supportive
f	**un** creative		**p**	**in** competent
g	**in** consistent		**q**	**un** assertive
h	**un** inspiring		**r**	**un** sociable
i	**un** committed		**s**	**in** considerate
j	**im** practical		**t**	**un** competitive

4 Complete the following staff appraisals using an appropriate positive or negative adjective from 3.

a Laura's a real ideas person. She's exceptionally **creative**.

b Brian can only do things his way. He's a bit **inflexible**.

c Max is always there to give people a hand when they need it. He's really very **supportive**.

d With Olaf it's just one mistake after another. He's completely **incompetent**.

e Greta tends to take no notice of other people's needs. She's rather **inconsiderate**.

f Richard's office looks like a bomb hit it – papers everywhere! He's totally **disorganised**.

g With Miyumi the job always comes first. She's totally **committed**.

h Sam can never make up his mind about anything. He's extremely **indecisive**.

i Callum really knows how to motivate his staff. He's incredibly **inspiring**.

j You can never depend on Leo to do what he's supposed to do. He's totally **unreliable**.

k Elena meets all her targets month after month. She's incredibly **consistent**.

l Jeanette too often allows her personal life to interfere with her work. She's rather **uncommitted**.

m Eric always has to be the best at everything. He's extremely **competitive**.

n Gareth tends to keep himself to himself. He's a bit **unsociable**.

The production line

1 Match the verbs and verb phrases in the box with those below which mean the opposite.

withdraw	go out of	reintroduce
scale down	halt	reduce

go into	←→	**go out of**
start	←→	**halt** production
step up	←→	**scale down**
launch	←→	**withdraw** a product
discontinue	←→	**reintroduce**
boost	←→	**reduce** productivity

2 Complete the following sentences using appropriate words and phrases from 1.

a We always **launch** new products in January at the annual Trade Fair.

b We'll need to **step up** production to keep up with demand.

c A staff incentive scheme helped us to **boost** productivity.

d We had to **halt** production completely until we'd found the fault.

e There were some complaints about the product, so we had to **withdraw** it to make the necessary modifications. We'll **reintroduce** it next month.

Grammar and Lexis links

18 Eating out

The passive

You form the passive with the appropriate tense of the verb *to be + past participle.*

- *The components for Ford cars* **are manufactured** *in fifteen different countries.*
- *In Spain dinner often* **isn't eaten** *until 10 or 11 in the evening.*
- *Steve Jobs* **was re-appointed** *head of Apple Computers in 1997.*
- *When* **was** *the Euro first* **introduced**?
- *As an exporter of computer software, the USA* **has been overtaken** *by the Republic of Ireland.*

You can also use the passive with modal verbs:

A *How soon* **will** *the project* **be completed**?
B *Well, it* **must be finished** *by the end of the year.*
A *Yes, but* **can** *it* **be speeded up**, *do you think?*
B *Well, we***'d have to be given** *a bigger budget.*
A *I think that* **could be arranged**.

You use the passive when it is unimportant or obvious who or what does something. It is, therefore, common to use the passive to talk about **processes** and **procedures**.

Practice 1 Look at these two examples:

Active: *These days, e-mail* **has** *largely* **superseded** *the fax machine.*
Passive: *These days, the fax machine* **has been** *largely* **superseded** *by e-mail.*

a What's the subject of the first sentence? <u>e-mail</u>
b What's the subject of the second sentence? <u>the fax machine</u>
c In the second sentence what word comes before the performer of the action? <u>by</u>
d Which of the sentences are you more likely to hear in a conversation about fax machines? <u>passive</u>

In both examples above our attention is focused on the subject of the sentence. You use the passive when you're more interested in the subject than the performer of the action.

Practice 2 The passive can sound more impersonal than the active. This can either be a good or a bad thing, depending on your intention. Look at these examples, then answer the questions.

Active: *We* **hold** *group meetings every other Friday.*
Passive: *A group meeting* **is held** *every other Friday.*
Active: *You* **told** *us there would be a bigger discount.*
Passive: *We* **were told** *there would be a bigger discount.*

a Which of the sentences about the meeting sounds friendlier? <u>active</u>
b Which of the sentences about a discount sounds less confrontational? <u>passive</u>
c Make this sentence more friendly: *You may be asked to a second interview.*
<u>We may ask you to a second interview.</u>
d Make this sentence less confrontational: *You promised us another month to finish the study.*
<u>We were promised another month to finish the study.</u>

Practice 3 Complete the article using the correct passive form of the verbs in brackets.

Lloyd's: Insuring the famous and the bizarre
Virtually anything (1) <u>can be insured</u> (can / insure) at Lloyd's. In fact, over the last hundred years London's most celebrated insurance company (2) <u>has been asked</u> (ask) to issue some of the most bizarre policies ever! Here are just a few.

Car insurance is big business these days. But the very first car (3) <u>to be insured</u> (insure) at Lloyd's (4) <u>was covered</u> (cover) by a marine policy. Cars were such a novelty in those days, motor policies (5) <u>were written</u> (write) on the basis that cars were just ships that sailed on the land!

Actors have always been paranoid. Hollywood film idol, Betty Grable, was so worried her famous legs (6) <u>might be injured</u> (might / injure) during filming, they (7) <u>were insured</u> (insure) by Lloyd's for a million dollars.

Multi-millionaire rock stars worry too. Bob Dylan, Eric Clapton, Michael Jackson, Elton John, Rod Stewart and the Rolling Stones have all insured their voices. Bruce Springsteen's (8) <u>is believed</u> (believe) to be worth £3.5 million.

Food critic and gourmet Egon Ronay runs a different risk. Obviously, his career (9) <u>would be destroyed</u> (would / destroy) if he was ever to lose his sense of taste. So a Lloyd's policy for £250,000 (10) <u>has been taken out</u> (take out) to protect him against waking up one day not knowing a haggis from a hamburger.

Photocopiable

Insuring works of art is nothing new, but the laughter (11) __could be heard__ (could / hear) all over the city when a grain of rice with a portrait of the Queen and the Duke of Edinburgh engraved on it (12) __was estimated__ (estimate) to be worth $20,000. The question is: worth $20,000 to whom?

A few years ago, a killer whale called Namu (13) __was captured__ (capture) off the Canadian coast and (14) __was dragged__ (drag) to Seattle for display in an aquarium. The captors insured themselves for $8,000 against Namu (15) __being rescued__ (rescue) by other whales! Unfortunately, he wasn't.

One rather confident comedy theatre group insured itself against the risk of a member of the audience dying laughing. So far, however, the insurance (16) __has not been claimed__ (not / claim) ...

Lexis: Food and drink

When I read about the evils of drinking, I gave up reading. *Henny Youngman, American comedian*

What's it like?

1   What do the following adjectives describe? Choose nouns from the box.

lunch	fish	salad	meat	dish
steak	vegetables			

1   heavy/light/late/3-course   __lunch__
2   fillet/rare/medium/well-done __steak__
3   green/side/Waldorf/fruit __salad__
4   fried/raw/smoked/freshly-caught __fish__
5   roast/tough/tender/juicy __meat__
6   fresh/frozen/seasonal/mixed __vegetables__
7   traditional/exotic/local/vegetarian __dish__

coffee	bread	food	cheese
beer	dessert	fruit	

8   rich/spicy/plain/fast __food__
9   dried/tropical/ripe/tinned __fruit__
10 crusty/stale/garlic/wholemeal __bread__
11 strong/mild/blue/cream __cheese__
12 fattening/refreshing/light/chocolatey __dessert__
13 draught/light/bottled/local __beer__
14 liqueur/milky/instant/black __coffee__

2   You can often turn a food noun into an adjective by adding -y.
•   containing lots of salt = *salty*
•   containing lots of sugar = *sugary*

a   Find five more food adjectives ending in -y in the lists above.

__juicy__   __spicy__   __crusty__ __chocolatey__ __milky__

b   How would you describe a dish with lots of

oil? __oily__   fruit? __fruity__   taste? __tasty__
fat? __fatty__   pepper? __peppery__   nuts? __nutty__

How to sound intelligent about wine!

1   Complete the description of a wine below using the words in the box.

from	of	with	with

It's a *crisp, dry white* wine __with__ a *delicate bouquet*.
It comes __from__ the *Napa valley* region __of__ *California* and goes very well __with__ *fish*.
1995 was *a reasonable* year.

2   Think of a wine you like and prepare a description of it using the words below. Try some of the other food and drink adjectives as well. Don't worry if you sound a bit strange – so do wine experts!

soft	classic	fruity	flowery	sparkling	red	France	pasta
rich ruby colour		peppery		powerful bouquet		smooth	seafood
light golden colour		vintage		a very good		cheese	an exceptional
Spain	young	robust	full bodied	sweet	steak	rosé	Rioja
Bordeaux		a disappointing					

Reporting

In business it is important to be able to report accurately what people said in meetings, on the phone and in private conversation. Occasionally we repeat the exact words someone used, but usually it is sufficient to report the basic message.

Original statement: *There's no way I'm going to accept cuts.*

Direct speech: *He said: 'There's no way I'm going to accept cuts.'* (1)

Reported speech: *He says there's no way he's going to accept cuts.* (2)

He said there was no way he was going to accept cuts. (3)

Reporting verb: *He refused to accept cuts.* (4)

Practice 1 Study the information above and answer the questions. Which expression would you use to:

a   quote exactly what the speaker said in a meeting? **1**

b   report exactly what the speaker said in a meeting? **3**

c   summarise the general idea? **4**

d   tell someone in the meeting what the speaker just said? **2**

NB When the reporting verb is in the past, you often put the reported speech in the past too:
I'm under a lot of pressure.
Reported speech: *He said he was under a lot of pressure.*

Practice 2 Change the statements below into reported speech.

a   **Fritz**: I'm ready.
Fritz said he was ready.

b   **Akio**: I'm going to wait and see.
Akio said he was going to wait and see.

c   **Claire**: I've had enough.
Claire said she had had enough.

d   **Philippe**: I must be going.
Philippe said he had to be going.

e   **Maria**: I'll be in touch.
Maria said she would be in touch.

f   **Sergio**: I just can't face it.
Sergio said he just couldn't face it.

Reporting the general idea of what someone said (eg. offering, inviting, complaining, thanking, suggesting) is often more useful than reporting their exact words. To do this, you can use the verbs *say, tell* and *ask*, as well as many other verbs. It is important to learn which prepositions, objects and verb forms follow these reporting verbs.

Practice 3 Decide how the following sentences (1–10) were later reported (a–j). Write your answers in the boxes.

1   Don't forget to do it. **e**
2   Have you done it? **i**
3   Could you do it, please? **g**
4   It was you who did it! **h**
5   Why don't you do it? **a**
6   Would you like me to do it? **j**
7   I'm not doing it! **f**
8   Sorry, I did it. **c**
9   I'm sorry I did it. **b**
10 I didn't do it. **d**

a   She suggested I do it.
b   He regretted doing it.
c   She apologised for doing it.
d   He denied doing it.
e   She reminded me to do it.
f   He refused to do it.
g   She asked me to do it.
h   He accused me of doing it.
i   She asked me if I'd done it.
j   He offered to do it.

Practice 4 The human resources department of a medium-sized company is deciding how much money to allocate to training. Read the following short extract from their meeting.

Gerry: OK, now, about our training budget for next year. What does everybody think?

Anna: Well, I think we really must spend more on advanced IT skills training.

Ingmar: Hm, I'm not so sure that's what's needed. In fact, it's basic computer skills that most of our people still lack.

Gerry: Yes, I think so too. But isn't this really a recruitment problem? I think we should require all new recruits to be computer literate before we employ them.

Anna: Now, just a minute. We're forgetting that these are our entry-level staff we're talking about.

Ingmar: And?

Anna: Well, if you look at the salaries we're paying new recruits, you'll see that we simply don't pay them enough to expect computer skills. IT training is our responsibility.

Gerry: Well, if we don't change our recruitment policy, we'll have to spend a fortune on training.

Anna: Actually, the current cost of training is negligible, Gerry. That's why I say we should be spending more.

Now complete a report of the meeting using the verbs in the box.

> **a – e** pointed out   insisted   invited
> raised   doubted
>
> **f – j** reminded   suggested   came in
> wondered   agreed
>
> **k – o** recommended   added   assured
> explained   warned

Report

Gerry (a) _raised_ the issue of the training budget and (b) _invited_ comments from the group. Anna (c) _insisted_ that we spend more on advanced IT skills, but Ingmar (d) _doubted_ that was what was needed. He (e) _pointed out_ that it was basic computer skills that most of our personnel lack. Gerry (f) _agreed_ and (g) _wondered_ if it wasn't a recruitment problem. He (h) _suggested_ we make computer literacy a requirement for employment. Anna (i) _came in_ at this point and (j) _reminded_ everyone that we were talking about entry-level staff. She (k) _explained_ that we didn't pay sufficient to expect computer skills and (l) _added_ that IT training was the company's responsibility. Gerry (m) _warned_ us that if we didn't change our recruitment policy, we'd have to spend a fortune on training, but Anna (n) _assured_ him the current cost of training was negligible and (o) _recommended_ we spend more.

Practice 5 Do you have a favourite line from a movie? Read the following collection of quotes from some of the 20th century's most famous films. Report each one using a combination of reporting verbs and reported speech. Use the words in brackets to help you. There are different possibilities.

a *Bond, James Bond.* Sean Connery, Dr No (1962)
(say/name) _He said his name was James Bond._

b *Play it Sam.* Humphrey Bogart, Casablanca (1942)
(ask/Sam) _He asked Sam to play it._

c *Mrs Robinson, I can't do this. It's all terribly wrong.* Dustin Hoffman, The Graduate (1967)
(say/because) _He said he couldn't do it because it was terribly wrong._

d *Are you talking to me?* Robert De Niro, Taxi Driver (1976)
(ask/me) _He asked me if I was talking to him._

e *Frankly, my dear, I don't give a damn.* Clark Gable, Gone with the Wind (1939)
(inform/her) _He informed her that he didn't give a damn._

f *Come up and see me sometime.* Mae West, Goin' to Town (1935)
(invite/me) _She invited me to go up and see her sometime._

g *Hang on, lads. I've got a great idea.* Michael Caine, The Italian Job (1969)
(tell/us) _He told us to hang on because he'd got/he had a great idea._

h *What have the Romans ever done for us?* John Cleese, The Life of Brian (1979)
(want/know) _He wanted to know what the Romans had ever done for us._

i *Go ahead. Make my day.* Clint Eastwood, Dirty Harry (1971)
(invite) _He invited him to make his day._

j *You're going to need a bigger boat.* Roy Scheider, Jaws (1975)
(advise) _He advised him that he was going to need a bigger boat._

k *I've had people walk out on me before, but not when I was being so charming.* Harrison Ford, Blade Runner (1982)
(admit) _He admitted that he had had people walk out on him before._

l *I'll be back.* Arnold Schwarzenegger, Terminator (1984)
(threaten/return) _He threatened to return._

Grammar of diplomacy

In business, the grammatical and lexical choices you make can have a powerful effect on the outcome of a meeting or negotiation. Compare the following:

1   *We reject your offer.*
2   *I'm afraid at this point we would be unable to accept your offer.*

In 2 the use of softeners (*I'm afraid*), restrictive phrases (*at this point*), modal verbs (*would*) and rephrased negatives (*unable to accept*) make the rejection itself more acceptable.

Look at the following ways of making what you say in a negotiation more diplomatic:

1   **Modals:** *would, could, may, might*
   - *This is a problem.* > *This **would** be a problem.*
   - *Of course, there's a disadvantage to this.* > *Of course, there **could** be a disadvantage to this.*

   In both examples above the speaker sounds less direct, but in the first example the basic message doesn't change. *This would be a problem* still means it is a problem! But it sounds better.

2   **Qualifiers:** *slight, a bit, rather, a few,* etc.
   - *There may be a delay.* > *There may be a **slight** delay.*
   - *We're disappointed with the discount you're offering.* > *We're **rather** disappointed with the discount you're offering.*

   Qualifiers soften the impact of bad news, but don't actually change it.

3   **Rephrased negatives 1:** *not very, totally, completely* + positive adjective
   - *We're unhappy with this arrangement.* > *We're **not very happy** with this arrangement.*
   - *I'm unconvinced.* > *I'm **not totally convinced**.*

   Using positive adjectives makes you sound more positive – even when you use them in the negative!

4   **Rephrased negatives 2:** *unable, not able, not in a position to*
   - *We can't go any higher than 7%.* > *We're **unable to** go any higher than 7%.*
   - *We won't accept anything less.* > *We're **not in a position to** accept anything less.*

   Try to avoid using *can't* and *won't*. They make you sound powerless and obstructive.

5   **Negative question forms:** *shouldn't we ...?, wouldn't you ...?* etc.
   - *We should be working together on this.* > ***Shouldn't we** be working together on this?*

   - *You'd be taking an enormous risk.* > ***Wouldn't you** be taking an enormous risk?*

   Negative question forms are incredibly powerful in negotiations. Questions sound more tentative than statements and are also more persuasive. Use them to make suggestions and give warnings.

6   **Comparatives:** *-er, more, less*
   - *We're looking for something cheap.* > *We're looking for something **cheaper**.*
   - *Would you be prepared to consider this?* > *Would you be **more prepared** to consider this?*

   The use of comparatives makes what you say sound more negotiable.

7   **Softeners:** *unfortunately, I'm afraid, to be honest, with respect,* etc.
   - *This doesn't meet our needs.* > ***Unfortunately**, this doesn't meet our needs.*
   - *You don't quite understand.* > ***With respect**, you don't quite understand.*

   Softeners at the beginning of a statement signal bad news. *With respect* is a particularly bad sign!

8   **Restrictive phrases:** *at the moment, at this stage, so far,* etc.
   - *That's our position.* > *That's our position **at the moment**.*
   - *I don't think we can go any further.* > *I don't think we can go any further **at this stage**.*

   Using a restrictive phrase does not exclude the possibility of future movement.

9   **The passive:** *it was understood, it was assumed,* etc.
   - *You said you were ready to sign.* > ***It was understood** you were ready to sign.*
   - *We thought you had accepted these terms.* > ***It was assumed** you had accepted these terms.*

   By avoiding the use of statements beginning *You said ...* and *We thought ...* and using passive forms instead, you depersonalise the situation and reduce the amount of personal responsibility or blame.

10 **The *-ing* form:** *were aiming, had been hoping*
   - *We aimed to reach agreement today.* > *We **were aiming** to reach agreement by today.*
   - *We had hoped to see some movement on price.* > *We **had been hoping** to see some movement on price.*

   Using the Past Continuous keeps your options open – you were aiming to reach agreement and still are. The Past Perfect Continuous closes the door a little more – you've stopped hoping, but could be persuaded to hope again.

Photocopiable

Practice Study the information opposite and make the direct remarks below more diplomatic using the words in brackets to help you.

a This is too expensive. (unfortunately / would)
Unfortunately, we would need something cheaper.

b We're not interested in your economy model.
(would / less) *We would be less interested in your economy model.*

c It will be difficult to sell the idea to my boss.
(unfortunately / may / very easy)
Unfortunately, it may not be very easy to sell the idea to my boss.

d We should be near a decision by now.
(shouldn't / a bit nearer?) *Shouldn't we be a bit nearer a decision by now?*

e We can't pay straight away. (afraid / might not / able) *I'm afraid we might not be able to pay straight away.*

f I won't make any promises. (not / position / this stage) *I'm not in a position to make any promises at this stage.*

g This is difficult for us to accept. (would / a little / the moment) *We would find this a little difficult to accept at the moment.*

h You said you wanted immediate delivery.
(understood) *I understood that you wanted immediate delivery.*

i We hoped you would provide after-sales service.
(honest / hoping) *To be honest, we were hoping you would provide after-sales service.*

j Our discussions have been unproductive.
(not very / so far) *Our discussions haven't been very productive so far.*

k A fixed interest rate would be a good idea.
(wouldn't / better?) *Wouldn't a fixed interest rate be better?*

l We had aimed to get further than this this morning.
(aiming / slightly) *We were aiming to get slightly further than this this morning.*

Lexis: Negotiations

When a man says he's going to put all his cards on the table, I always look up his sleeve.
Lord Hore-Belisha, British politician

Conducting negotiations Complete the collocations by writing the nouns and noun phrases in the right-hand boxes. They are all things you might do during a negotiation.

| terms | pressure | options | a breakthrough |
| a deadlock | time out | | |

reach break	*a deadlock*	negotiate agree	*terms*
look for make	*a breakthrough*	apply give in to	*pressure*
call take	*time out*	generate weigh up	*options*

Sales negotiations

1 The following things were said in a sales negotiation. Who do you think probably said them – the buyer, the seller or could it be either?

a What kind of a guarantee can you give us? *B*
b Would that be a regular order? *S*
c Is that your best price? *B*
d There are no hidden extras. *S*
e I'm afraid it's not really what we're looking for. *B*
f Would you like to have the product on a trial basis? *S*
g What sort of quantity were you thinking of? *S*
h How flexible can you be on delivery times? *B*
i I'd like to think it over. *E*
j I can't be any fairer than that. *E*
k What immediate benefits could we expect to see? *E*
l Supposing we were to offer you deferred payment? *S*
m We'll match any price you've been quoted. *S*
n What sort of discount could you offer us on that? *B*
o Could we rely on you to meet all our deadlines? *B*
p Now, we'll just need to sort out one or two details. *E*
q So, if you'd just like to sign here. *E*

2 The following collocations all appeared in the negotiation in 1. Try to find the other half of each one in under 90 seconds!

a regular *order*	quote a *price*
immediate benefits	*hidden* extras
offer *a discount*	deferred *payment*
give a guarantee	*sort out* the details
delivery *times*	match a *price*
meet deadlines	a *trial* basis

Additional material

4 Keeping track

Clarifying specific points

Speaker A

1   Read out the text below to your partner. When you read the information in **bold**, whisper so he/she can't understand! Your partner should ask you for clarification. If not, keep reading!

THE FAMOUS

BUDWEISER COMPANY

Budweiser is the world's bestselling brand of beer. In the USA it represents **22 per cent** of total beer sales. The American company that makes it is the biggest brewery in the world with 50 per cent greater **output** than its nearest competitor, the Dutch multinational, **Heineken**. Budweiser is the all-American beer. With its enormous **marketing budget**, it spent more than **32 million** dollars to be 'an official partner' in the soccer World Cup. Over the last 40 years, the company has had many **advertising slogans**. But by far the most successful is 'Budweiser: the King of **Beers**'.

---

2   Listen to your partner reading out a similar text. Ask him/her to clarify anything you don't hear or understand.

4 Keeping track

Pointing out discrepancies

Speaker A

1   Read out the following sentences to your partner. Each one contains a silly discrepancy. Can he/she spot it?
   a   I love Scotland, especially Dublin.
   b   I always drink German wine. Bordeaux's my favourite.
   c   I first met Ulrike yesterday. She's one of my closest friends.
   d   I've nearly given up smoking. I'm down to about 30 a day now.
   e   Let me introduce you to my wife. And then I'll introduce you to her husband.

2   Listen to your partner reading out some sentences. Can you spot the discrepancies? Query any you hear using some of the expressions on page 18.

6 Business travel

The nightmare journey

Speaker A

Work with a partner. In each of the situations below you are a business traveller. Your partner is the other speaker.

06.00
Business traveller: You didn't get your 5 o'clock alarm call at your hotel this morning, so you overslept! Now you've missed your taxi to the airport. Your plane leaves in 90 minutes and it's at least half an hour to the airport. Go and complain at the reception desk. Get them to book you another taxi and telephone Heathrow airport to say you are on your way. **You start:** *What happened to my alarm call?*

06.15
Business traveller: Your taxi has finally arrived. Explain that your plane leaves in an hour and a quarter and that you must be on it. If you miss the Zurich meeting at 11.00, your boss is going to kill you! You thought about taking the Underground, but you have a very heavy bag of product samples to carry.
You start: *Heathrow airport. Terminal 1. And please hurry!*

07.00
Business traveller: By some miracle, you have arrived at Heathrow! But your plane leaves in half an hour. You'll have to run! You didn't have time to change any money at the hotel, so you only have three £50 notes and your credit cards. Pay the taxi driver and go!

07.15
Business traveller: You are at check-in with your case of product samples for the Zurich meeting and your hand luggage. Fortunately, the hotel phoned the airport and they were expecting you. Thank god you're travelling business class!

07.30
Business traveller: After all the panic to get to the airport, your British Airways flight is going to be delayed for an hour and a half! You wanted to fly Crossair, but they only had economy class seats left. Now there's nothing to do but wait. Luckily, your meeting is three hours away, so you can still just make it.

09.15

Business traveller: You managed to get a seat in economy on the Crossair flight. You're scheduled to arrive in Zurich in an hour, which gives you another 45 minutes to get to your meeting. You might just do it! Suddenly, you hear the following announcement: *Good morning, ladies and gentlemen. This is your captain speaking. I'm afraid I've just been notified that, due to bad weather over Zurich, we've been diverted to Geneva. I am very sorry for the inconvenience this may cause, and will keep you informed of any further changes to our schedule.* You must call Zurich! Ask a flight attendant if it's OK to use your mobile. **You start:** *Er, excuse me!*

6 Business travel

The red-eye

Speaker A

It is 9.30pm. You are in the crowded arrivals area at Newark airport in New York. There has just been a terrible thunderstorm and it is still pouring with rain.

You are picking up a senior colleague who works in your Cologne office. Because of the weather, their flight is two hours late, but your boss told you to 'look after them well' – take them out to a top-class restaurant, maybe a nightclub or two. You have never met them before, so you are holding up a large piece of card with their name written on it.

Your car is just five minutes away in the car park. You have booked a table at *Guastavino's*, a fabulous restaurant in Manhattan and are looking forward to an enjoyable evening. According to your boss, 'money is no object'. If he can, he's going to join you both later for drinks.

You've been working very hard recently. Tonight you are going to relax and have fun!

7 Handling calls

Unexpected phone calls

Speaker A
Call 1 You make the call 1730 local time

You work in the marketing department of Shiseido Cosmetics, Tokyo. Phone the advertising department of *Cosmopolitan* magazine, Paris. You want to speak to either Monique Leblanc or Philippe Roussel about the cost of a full-page advertisement.

Call 2 You receive the call 1030 local time

You work for Barclays Global Mutual Funds in New York and deal with corporate investment. Your colleague, Neil Thomas, deals with company pension schemes, but you have no idea where he is. He went out to get a bagel an hour and a half ago and hasn't been seen since. You're very busy and have to keep putting Speaker B on hold to deal with different problems. Neil's mobile number is 181 650 777.

Call 3 You make the call 1500 local time

You are a sales representative for Fujitsu computers, UK. You're calling Speaker B at General Accident Insurance with a quote for 25 laptops, which they asked for by responding to one of your company's Internet advertisements. You have a range of discounted prices you can offer from $19,000 to $48,000 depending on the model. You could e-mail these, but prefer to phone because it gives you a chance to get an appointment.

Call 4 You receive the call 1045 local time

You work for Burson-Marsteller, the world's biggest public relations company, and are based in Boston, USA. In the course of your job, you get to go to a lot of conferences and meet a lot of people. You can't always remember them all, although it's an important part of your job to pretend to do so. You've just got a new boss, who you don't like very much, and are on your way to a meeting with her now.

8 Making decisions

The decision-making meeting

Plan B

⏺ **8.4** If you are unable to reach a decision on the new Bond, perhaps it is because the film series itself needs to be brought into the 21st century. Why not break with tradition altogether and make the Bond character a woman? You could reverse all the stereotypes and attract a completely new audience. You know the actress below is interested in the idea. Read her profile, then listen to an interview extract.

NAME AND AGE
Diane Fairchild   26

NATIONALITY
Anglo-French

MARITAL STATUS
single

HEIGHT AND BUILD
1.78m   slim, athletic

PHYSICAL PURSUITS
Swam for her university. Black belt Taekwondo.

EXPERIENCE
Did a law degree at Cambridge before going into acting. A rising star who has become 'hot property' in Hollywood after her huge success in the action thriller *Spider-Web*. Just completed a twelve-week run on Broadway. Though 'typically British', the Americans love her.

ACHIEVEMENTS
Won a Golden Palm at the Cannes Film Festival for her first Hollywood film.

USUAL FEE
Diane's 'bankability' has increased dramatically in the last two years. Now earns at least $2 million a film.

COMMENTS
Likes to combine serious theatre work with escapist films. Says she thinks a female Bond is just what the 007 series needs.

15 Snail mail

Could I see you a moment?

Speakers A and B

Situation 1

Speaker A, you are the boss. Your secretary, Speaker B, just gave you this letter to sign. Point out the mistakes in it and tell him/her how to rewrite it. There are 22 mistakes in all. Don't sign anything until he/she writes it properly!

Speaker B, defend yourself! You were in a rush when you wrote the letter and can probably correct a lot of it without your boss's help.

Speaker A starts: *Could I see you a moment ...?*

> ^c ^rd
> De̷ember 3RD̶
>
> ^ea ^Mr
> Da̶e̶r M̶i̶s̶t̶e̶r̶ Barghiel/,
> I am ^p   December 7th
> I'am writing to confirm our ap/ointment on Dec 7̶. Of/
>   ^d
> course, I have your ad/ress, but I a̶m̶ wonder if you
>
> could t̶o̶ send t̶o̶me instruction/on how to get to your
>   because   ^ing
> office f̶o̶r̶ t̶h̶a̶t̶ I will be com̶e̶ by m̶y̶ car.
> Many   ^am   ^ing
> A̶ l̶o̶t̶ o̶f̶ thanks. I /ery much a̶m̶ look/orward to meet ing
> you.
>
>   sincerely
> Yours f̶a̶i̶t̶h̶f̶u̶l̶l̶y̶,

Useful language

You don't need ...
That's spelled ...
That should be ..., not ...
With an 's' / without 's'
ff = double f
ABC = capital letters
abc = lower case letters
, = comma
' = apostrophe
Mr, Ms, Dr = abbreviation
? = question mark
. = full stop/period
( ) = brackets

Situation 2

Repeat the previous activity. This time, Speaker B is the boss and Speaker A is the secretary. There are 23 mistakes in the letter.

Speaker B starts: *Could I see you a moment ...?*

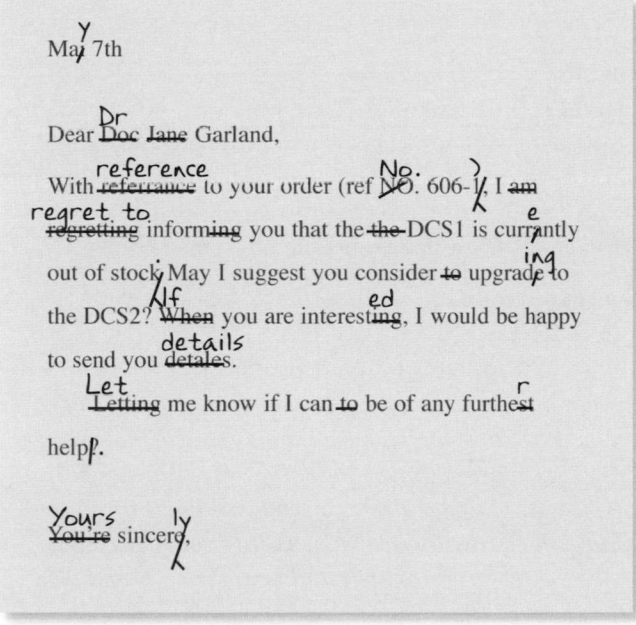

20 Negotiating

The transfer

Negotiating team 1: The player's agents

You represent the interests of _____ *(choose or invent a name)*, the 18-year-old superstar striker who plays for _____ *(choose or invent a club)*. Already a member of his national squad, your client clearly has a brilliant career ahead of him. His current team has set a transfer fee of £8 million, which is quite a lot for such a young player, but fair considering his enormous potential. The final transfer fee will be agreed between the two clubs and is nothing to do with you. Your job is to negotiate your client's financial package with the management of Manchester United.

You do not have to reach an agreement with Manchester. Barcelona, Juventus and Arsenal are also very interested in your client. But you do know he particularly wants to play for them, so you have approached them first.

It is in your interests to:
- get a higher than average wage for such a superb player of international status (more than £350,000)
- get a good annual fee (your agent's commission will be calculated on the basis of this!)
- go for the shortest contract you can get or one with a very low termination penalty (your client may not be as happy at Manchester as he hoped)
- secure a fair percentage of merchandising profits (maybe 15% – the fans are sure to want to buy products with your client's name on).

But you may need to be flexible on some of these points.

Your client has also asked you to try to get:
- a penthouse apartment in central Manchester (he wants to enjoy the nightlife)
- two left-hand drive sports cars (preferably Ferraris or Porsches) for himself and his new wife
- first-class air tickets for his immediate family (eight people) to come and visit him occasionally plus half a dozen trips home for himself every year.

At present your client has a £100,000 a year sponsorship deal with Nike, which he would like to keep.

The negotiation is scheduled to be held at Old Trafford. First, with your team, work out your opening, target and walk away positions for each of the following points. When the other team is ready, they will invite you into the boardroom. You may take two five-minute time-outs during the meeting, if you need them. Write down any terms you agree to.

	OP	TP	WAP
Basic wage			
Annual fee			
Length of contract			
Contract termination fee			
Percentage of merchandising profits			
Accommodation			
Car			
Flights home			

4 Keeping track

Clarifying specific points

Speaker B

1 Listen to your partner reading out a text. Ask him/her to clarify anything you don't hear or understand.

2 Read out the text below to your partner. When you read the information in **bold**, whisper so he/she can't understand! Your partner should ask you for clarification. If not, keep reading!

THE ORIGINAL

BUDWEISER COMPANY

Budweiser is one of the Czech Republic's oldest and most famous beers. In fact, the brewery which makes it is over **700** years old. It shares its name with the best-known US brand because in **1876** the Americans decided to name their product after the small Hungarian town of **Budweis**.

After a long **legal dispute**, the Czech company now markets its product under the Budweiser name in more than **40** different countries. Obviously, this has confused some **consumers**. So the Czechs, with far fewer resources than the Americans, have responded by advertising it simply as 'Budweiser: the beer of **Kings**'.

---

4 Keeping track

Pointing out discrepancies

Speaker B

1 Listen to your partner reading out some sentences. Can you spot the discrepancies? Query any you hear using some of the expressions on page 18.

2 Read out the following sentences to your partner. Each one contains a silly discrepancy. Can he/she spot it?

- **a** I've got three children – one of each.
- **b** We met the French negotiating team at their headquarters in Lisbon.
- **c** I'm worried about this trip to Denmark. For one thing, I don't speak a word of Dutch.
- **d** The managing director must be at least 70. But it's his grandfather who really runs the company.
- **e** I work for a firm called Network Software. We make washing machines, fridges, that kind of thing.

6 Business travel

The nightmare journey

Speaker B

Work with a partner. In each of the situations below your partner is a business traveller. You are the other speaker.

06.00

Hotel receptionist: You have just come on duty at the Novotel reception desk. Your colleague, who went home five minutes ago, says there has been a problem with the internal telephone system all night. Since you arrived it's been one complaint after another!

06.15

Taxi driver: You have just picked up someone at the Novotel who wants to go to Heathrow airport. On your way to the hotel you heard this on the radio: *Traffic news now, and there's been a major accident on the M25 this morning involving three lorries and eight cars. Police say to expect delays of up to an hour. If you're travelling to Heathrow this morning, you're advised to take the Underground to Paddington station and then the Heathrow Express ...*

07.00

Taxi driver: Fortunately, the traffic was not as bad as you expected. But your last two passengers paid you in £50 notes and took nearly all your change – you only have a £10 note and three pound coins. There is a cashpoint machine in the airport terminal if you need it, but another customer is waiting to get into your taxi. **You start:** *Well, we made it! That's £23, please.*

07.15

Check-in clerk: You are checking in a late business class passenger. Their hand luggage is OK, but their suitcase is well over the 25 kilo limit – 38 kilos! The flight is full and due to depart in 15 minutes. You cannot accept their luggage. You could book it onto a later flight if they pay excess baggage. **You start:** *I'm sorry but your case is too heavy.*

07.30

BA representative: You are at Gate 42, Heathrow airport. Flight BA922 to Zurich is delayed and you have a lot of unhappy passengers sitting in the departure lounge. A few have already asked for seats on the 8.30 Crossair flight. You have just received this message on your mobile: *The plane has serious mechanical problems and cannot leave London today. Another plane is flying out from Zurich, but there will now be a delay of approximately four hours.* **You start:** *British Airways regrets to announce ...*

09.15

Flight attendant: You are the chief steward on Crossair flight 711 from London Heathrow to Zurich. Unfortunately, your flight has just been diverted to Geneva because of bad weather. A lot of passengers are getting angry and insisting they make phone calls. The use of mobile phones is strictly prohibited on aircraft and in-flight phones are only available in business class.

6 Business travel

The red-eye

Speaker B

It is 9.30pm. You are in the crowded arrivals area at Newark airport in New York. There has just been a terrible thunderstorm and it is still pouring with rain. You have just arrived two hours late after a nightmare flight from Cologne. Normally, you are a good flier, but there was so much turbulence you were almost sick on the plane. You don't know who is meeting you, so you are looking for a sign with your name on it.

To be honest, you don't feel like talking much and would just like to go straight to your hotel, have a shower and go to bed. But maybe you should eat something light first – it's a long day of meetings tomorrow and you want to be on good form.

This is your first time in New York. It's a pity you feel so ill.

7 Handling calls

Unexpected phone calls

Speaker B
Call 1 You receive the call 0930 local time

You are a student of journalism in Paris working for *Cosmopolitan* magazine during your summer vacation. There was no one in the office when the phone rang, so you picked it up. You've never spoken English on the phone before and misunderstand everything Speaker A tells you. After a minute or so, end the call by offering to get someone who speaks better English.

Call 2 You make the call 1630 local time

You work in the finance department at Daimler-Chrysler in Stuttgart and are responsible for the management of the company pension scheme. You want to query something with the fund manager at Barclay's Global Mutual Funds in New York, Neil Thomas. It's rather urgent. You finish work at six.

Call 3 You receive the call 1500 local time

You work in the sales department of General Accident Insurance, UK. You are holding a meeting in your office to discuss the training programme for your new intake of 25 sales personnel. At first, you have no idea who

Speaker A is when he/she calls – probably a sales rep from one of the computer companies you contacted on the Internet the other day. Be civil, but get him/her off the phone.

Call 4 You make the call 1045 local time

You work for a small public relations company in Bath, UK. 18 months ago you met Speaker A at an international conference in Chicago. He/She works for Burson-Marsteller, the world's biggest PR firm. You got on very well and stayed up till three in the morning. You mentioned you'd love to work for a bigger company and he/she offered to introduce you to his/her boss if you ever came to Boston. You're in Boston, at the Logan Airport Hotel. Your mobile number is 751 533 200.

20 Negotiating

The transfer

Negotiating team 2: Manchester United

You represent the management of Manchester United Football Club and are interested in buying an 18-year-old superstar striker _____ (ask Team 1 for his name) who plays for _____ (ask Team 1 for the name of his club). His current team is asking for a transfer fee of £8 million, which is quite a lot for such a young player, but fair considering his enormous potential. However, you are not negotiating the transfer fee today. Your job is to negotiate the financial package on offer.

You do not have to sign this player. There is no shortage of young internationals wanting to play for the world's most famous football club. But he is something special. With the right training, he could become one of the world's top players within the next five years.

It's in your interests to:
- pay no more than the standard wage (already high at £300,000)
- keep the annual fee as low as possible (it could always be raised on renewal of contract if your new player lives up to his potential)
- go for a five-year contract with a heavy penalty for early termination (you don't want to invest in the development of a player who disappears to another club after just a few seasons)
- pay as low a percentage of merchandising profits as possible (perhaps 5% – you don't know how popular the new player will be with supporters).

But you may need to be flexible on some of these points.

You can also offer:

- the use of a £950,000 house with six bedrooms and swimming pool, in a quiet suburb twelve miles outside Manchester
- a brand-new, top-of-the-range 4-wheel-drive Jeep for driving to and from matches and training sessions
- three first-class flights home with British Airways.

You understand the player currently has a sponsorship deal with Nike, which would have to be cancelled. Nike sponsor your main rivals in the Premier League, Arsenal.

The negotiation is scheduled to be held at Old Trafford. First, with your team, work out your opening, target and walk away positions for each of the following points. When you are ready, welcome the player's agents into your boardroom. You may take two five-minute time-outs during the meeting, if you need them. Write down any terms you agree to.

	OP	TP	WAP
Basic wage			
Annual fee			
Length of contract			
Contract termination fee			
Percentage of merchandising profits			
Accommodation			
Car			
Flights home			

4 Keeping track

Quiz answers (p19)

1 a billion

2 Michael Eisner of Disney

3 the VW Beetle

4 KLM

5 The Yomiuri Shimbun

6 Microsoft

7 Barbie

8 the electric light

9 Ireland

8 Making decisions

Questionnaire analysis (p32)

Whether you wrote *yes* or *no* is unimportant.

If you wrote *it depends* to five or more questions you are a **reflective decision-maker**. You like to take your time thinking things through before coming to a final decision. In some jobs this is a good strategy. But we live in a world of rapid change – be careful you don't take too long to make up your mind!

If you wrote *it depends* to two or fewer questions, you are a **reflexive decision-maker**. You'd rather think fast and make the wrong decision occasionally than take so long to decide you miss an opportunity. This can be a vital skill for a manager. Just make sure you're right more often than you're wrong!

If you wrote *it depends* to three or four questions, you are a **balanced decision-maker**. You don't waste time agonising over simple decisions, but you don't rush decisions that have serious implications either. You seem to be in control of both your head and your heart. But are you so in control you never take a risk?

10 Small talk

Comments on questionnaire (p40)

a Business people from Latin and Arab countries tend to have a more flexible, 'polychronic' attitude to time than their 'monochronic' North American and North European counterparts, for whom time really is money. Their 'high-context' culture also places greater emphasis on personal relationships than 'low-context' Northerners do. The message? Try not to be too busy for Brazilians or Italians and don't mess up Americans' tight schedules.

b A good sense of humour is an admired quality in many cultures – notably British, American and most Latin countries – though the type of humour may vary from wordplay to sharp sarcasm to innuendo and even the surreal. In other cultures, however – particularly Germanic ones – humour is not usually considered appropriate in a business context. The message? You don't have to be a comedian with the British, but always smile at their attempts at humour. With Germans or Swiss, leave the jokes for the bar after the meeting.

c The amount of socialising you do prior to and during a negotiation will depend both on your own and the opposing team's negotiating styles and where the negotiation is being held. In Japan, for example, the negotiation process is long and relationship-building plays an important part. The same is true of the Middle East. In the USA things move faster and their negotiating style tends to be both more informal and adversarial. In Germany there may be little time for small talk. The message? Follow your opponents' lead, but do all you can to create rapport.

d Mixing with colleagues out of work-hours is an integral part of business in America where many companies are run like sports teams with the boss as both captain and coach. Elsewhere, there may be a strong dividing line between work and home. The message? In social situations simply be yourself. Neither do anything that offends you nor that you think may offend your hosts.

e Different people have different ideas about where is an appropriate place to do business. For some, talking about golf all morning at the office, and business all afternoon on the golf course is quite normal. Others do more business in bars than boardrooms. But these days people are more culturally aware and don't usually expect foreigners to observe their own business customs. The message? A polite refusal to go to a Finnish sauna or a Spanish bullfight will not usually offend.

11 E-mail

Answers (p44, ex4)

According to the Institute of Directors, the majority of business people receive around **30** e-mails a day. As it takes about **5** minutes to read and reply to (or ignore) each, that means **2 and a half** hours' work or **a quarter** of the working day.

According to Ferros Research, the average executive spends **326** hours a year dealing with e-mail, and this actually increases productivity by **15–20%**. Unfortunately, another **115** hours are wasted deleting 'spam' (unwanted publicity material) from their inboxes.

According to a recent Internet survey, nearly **three quarters** of business people have sent an e-mail and then regretted it. Hastily written messages can easily sound too direct or even rude, and upsetting a colleague with an angry e-mail (or 'flame') can seriously damage your professional relationship.

According to the Society for Human Resource Management, roughly **a third** of employers look at their employees' e-mail, and over **70%** believe they have a right to read virtually anything written on the company's electronic communications system.

14 Being heard

Comments on questionnaire (p57)

The questionnaire shows what type of 'animal' you are in meetings. First add up your total number of points.

a Agree = 0 points   Disagree = 1 point

b Agree = 1 point   Disagree = 0 points

c Agree = 1 point   Disagree = 0 points

d Agree = 0 points   Disagree = 1 point

e Agree = 0 points   Disagree = 1 point

f Agree = 1 point   Disagree = 0 points

g Agree = 1 point   Disagree = 0 points

h Agree = 1 point   Disagree = 0 points

If you scored:

0–2 points
You're a mouse at meetings – shy, quiet, you don't like to be the centre of attention. You make a very good listener, but need to say what you really think more often.

3–4 points
You're a fox at meetings – sly, patient and sudden in your attacks on other people's points of view. You don't say much, preferring to let others give you all the information you need to destroy their arguments.

5–6 points
You're a horse at meetings – enthusiastic and full of energy, it takes a strong person to keep you under control. You work very hard to get your ideas across, but will sometimes do as you're told just to keep the peace.

7–8 points
You're a bulldog at meetings – loud, proud and fond of the sound of your own voice. People know you always mean what you say, but you need to listen to what they're saying a bit more often.

Worksheet & author	Timing	Aim	Task
1 **Lifelines** Mark Powell	30 minutes	To share personal experiences and practise various tenses and structures	To move around a board by speaking about one's experiences at different ages
2a **Networking** Nicholas Sheard	30–40 minutes	To practise initiating and maintaining a conversation, and showing interest	To prepare for and take part in a mingling activity about an imaginary job
2b **Fugitives** Simon Clarke	40–45 minutes	To practise vocabulary for describing people	To categorise vocabulary for describing people and use it in a roleplay
3 **The right connections** Jon Hird	40 minutes	To practise and consolidate telephone expressions	To rephrase a telephone conversation and voice mail message using appropriate language and register
4 **Yank's or Chez Antoine?** Paul Dummett	30 minutes	To practise the language of comparison	To assess the pros and cons of two business opportunities, make a choice between the two and justify it
5 **The story of the stones** Nicholas Sheard	40 minutes	To practise reading for detail	To read a story about time management and discuss the ideas in it
6a **Destination desktop** Jon Hird	30 minutes	To practise reading for detail	To read an article, identify referents of collocations and discuss the pros and cons of videoconferencing
6b **Valerie's trip** Colin Benn	40 minutes	To recycle and practise the language of travel arrangements	To exchange information and finalise an itinerary
7 **Calculated guess** Mark Powell	30 minutes	To practise collocations	To play a team game assigning verbs to the nouns they collocate with
8a **Devil's advocate** Gina Cuciniello	30 minutes	To practise language for agreeing, disagreeing and clarifying	To discuss controversial statements
8b **Making decisions** Paul Dummett	30–40 minutes	To practise idiomatic expressions relating to decision-making	To complete sentences with idiomatic expressions relating to decision-making and use them to talk about one's own experiences
9 **What the CEO said** Paul Dummett	35 minutes	To promote discussion on aspects of running a business	To give one's views on aspects of running a business and evaluate quotations from experienced business people
10 **Small talk** Jon Hird	30 minutes	To practise expressions used in making small talk	To categorise expressions used in making small talk and use them in a roleplay
11a **A business trip** Paul Emmerson	40 minutes	To practise writing e-mails	To plan a (real or imaginary) business trip by e-mail and perform a roleplay based on this situation
11b **Spam** Simon Clarke	40 minutes	To practise reading for detail and giving opinions	To complete a cloze text about spam and then discuss spamming and other ways of marketing a product

Worksheet & author	Timing	Aim	Task
12a **Employees' centre** Colin Benn	40 minutes–1 hour	To practise using presentation techniques for impact and persuasion	To brainstorm, prepare and deliver a presentation
12b **I am a DVD** Mark Powell	30–45 minutes	To practise listening for specific information	To listen for collocational phrases containing the verbs *give*, *take*, *make* and *do*
13 **Bioethics** Paul Dummett	40 minutes–1 hour	To promote discussion on ethical questions relating to biotechnology	To assess and formulate responses to bioethical dilemmas
14a **The good consultant** Nicholas Sheard	35–45 minutes	To promote discussion on the role of business consultants and to practise using modal verbs	To read a story and discuss the role of business consultants
14b **Business behaviour** Jon Hird	30 minutes	To promote discussion on cultural differences in the business world	To assess the importance of specific behaviour and explain cultural characteristics in the business world
15 **Selling the company** Gina Cuciniello	45 minutes	To raise awareness of appropriate language for a formal letter	To select appropriate expressions and use them to write a formal letter
16a **Dragon boat racing** Nicholas Sheard	40 minutes	To practise reading for detail and to practise conditionals (past reference)	To read a story, put it in order and discuss the problem-solving technique used in the story
16b **Consultancy team** Gina Cuciniello	1 hour	To practise the language of suggestions and opinions	To solve the problem of inappropriate behaviour in meetings
17 **Cultural differences** Paul Emmerson	45 minutes	To practise the language and skills of discussion	To categorise cultural traits in a business context
18a **Piracy** Simon Clarke	45–50 minutes	To practise reading for detail and to practise passives	To read statistics and a text on piracy, then reconstruct passive sentences from the text
18b **A memorable meal** Mark Powell	25 minutes	To practise describing food and drink and to foster anecdote-telling skills	To listen to an anecdote and supply the missing information
19a **Boss or Big Brother?** Simon Clarke	30–40 minutes	To practise the language of agreement, disagreement and neutrality	To complete a cloze text and discuss the ideas in it
19b **A quality problem** Paul Emmerson	45–50 minutes	To address a business problem and to practise writing e-mails	To put a text in order and to write e-mails about a particular problem from different perspectives
20a **Peasants 1000 AD** Paul Emmerson	45 minutes–1 hour	To practise the language and skills of negotiating	To negotiate the best deal
20b **Mini-negotiations** Paul Dummett	45–50 minutes	To practise the language and skills of negotiating	To take part in a negotiation

1 Lifelines

Overview

This board game gives both teacher and students the opportunity to share personal experiences. As well as serving as an ice-breaker, it gives the teacher a diagnostic tool to assess the students' language.

Preparation

One copy of the *Lifelines* board, enlarged to A3, and one copy of the question cards, cut up, for each group of three students. Make sure the cards are kept in separate piles of As, Bs, Cs, etc. Each group will need a die and each student a counter.

Procedure

1   Divide the students into groups of three and give each group the *Lifelines* board and questions.
2   Explain that *Lifelines* is not a competitive game or a race but an opportunity to share experiences. On the throw of a die, students take it in turns to move around the board.
    • If they land on an age group, they tell their group about a memory, plan, hope or ambition relating to that age.
    • If they land on a letter (A–G), they pick a question relating to that letter and tell the group the answer.
3   Encourage the students to use the sentence starters (*I can't remember exactly …*, etc.) on the right of the board.

2a Networking

Overview

Students prepare for and take part in a mingling activity about an imaginary job. They practise initiating and maintaining a conversation and showing interest in what someone is saying.

Preparation

One copy of the worksheet for each student.

Procedure

1   Students read the list of jobs and choose three they'd like to do and three they wouldn't. Monitor as they discuss the personal qualities and training required for these jobs, helping with vocabulary and pronunciation.
2   Students choose one of the jobs in Exercise 1 and imagine it's their real job. Ask them to write three facts about the job: one neutral, one negative and one positive.
3   Give students a few minutes to complete and memorise the key phrases in Exercise 3 before the mingling activity.
4   In the mingling activity, students practise starting and maintaining a conversation, and showing interest. Encourage them to use the expressions in the box. Monitor the activity.

2b Fugitives

Overview

Students categorise vocabulary for describing criminals, write a description of someone and then roleplay describing a suspected fugitive to an FBI agent.

Preparation

One copy of the worksheet for each student.

Procedure

1   Students read the introduction about the FBI's Ten Most Wanted Fugitives.
2   For each category in Exercise 1, students decide on the appropriate verb to use when describing someone. Check the answers.
3   Students assign the characteristics in Exercise 2 to a category by writing a category number in the boxes. Check the answers.
4   If students have access to the Internet, they go to the FBI website and choose a criminal to describe in Exercise 3. If not, they can describe a secretly chosen member of the class in these same terms, and their classmates decide who it is they are describing.
5   Students do the roleplay in Exercise 4. Monitor the activity.

Answers

Exercise 2   black: 6, 9   olive: 8, 9   white: 9   stocky: 4
tattoo on upper arm: 11   security guard: 5   medium: 3, 4
green: 7   salt and pepper: 6   bald: 6   mole below left eye: 11
American: 10   blue: 7   scar on chest: 11   dark/medium: 8
light: 8   male: 12   1.7 to 1.8 m: 2   Whitey: 1
approximately 73 kg: 3   is known to frequent libraries and
historic sites: 12   white/silver: 6   thin: 4   El Comandante: 1
large: 4   uses disguises to alter his appearance: 12

3 The right connections

Overview

Students rephrase a telephone conversation and voice mail message using appropriate language to practise and consolidate telephone expressions.

Preparation

One copy of the worksheet for each student.

Procedure

1   Individually or in pairs, students rewrite the dialogue in Exercise 1 using more appropriate language. There are several possible alternatives.
2   Students compare what they have written with others before sharing their ideas with the rest of the class.
3   Students act out their reformulated dialogues.
4   They repeat the task with the voice mail message in Exercise 2. Ask students to discuss the possible scenario and the likely roles of Barry and Silvia.

Sample answers

1   A: Hello. CCC.
    B: Is that Crystal Communications Consultants?
    A: Yes, it is. How can I help you?
    B: Could I speak to Silvia Garcia please?
    A: Certainly. Hold the line. I'll see if she's available.
    B: OK, thank you.
    A: I'm afraid she's in a meeting at the moment.
    B: OK. Do you know when she'll be available?

A: I'm afraid I couldn't say. Could you phone back this afternoon?
B: That will be difficult for me. Could I leave a message?
A: Of course.
B: Could you ask her to phone me, please?
A: Certainly. Can I have your name?
B: Barry Clough.
A: Sorry, could you repeat that, please?
B: Yes, it's Barry Clough.
A: And could you spell that?
B: B-A-R-R-Y, C-L-O-U-G-H.
A: OK, Mr Clough, I'll make sure she gets that.
B: Thank you.
A: Goodbye.

2 Hello. This is a message for Silvia from Barry Clough. I'm in Zurich. I'm rather concerned that you didn't return my call. Please could you ring me as soon as you can. The publicity material for the Zurich Expo hasn't arrived. The courier firm doesn't seem to know about it. Have you any idea what's happened, Silvia? Look, the Expo starts tomorrow – please would you organise a new courier. It's really very worrying.

4 Yank's or Chez Antoine?

Overview

Students choose which of two restaurants in a tourist town would make the better investment and justify their choice using the language of comparison.

Preparation

One copy of the worksheet for each student.

Procedure

1 Ask students if they have ever wanted to own or run a restaurant. Ask them what factors would be the most critical to its success. Check/Pre-teach: *turnover, rates.*

2 Elicit the language of comparison by asking the students if they had to choose between two hotels to buy in a seaside resort which they would choose, e.g. *The one with more rooms. The one nearer the beach. The one in better condition. The cheaper one,* etc.

3 Hand out copies of the worksheet and ask students to read the text at the top. Explain that they are buying a licensed business and its goodwill, not a piece of real estate. Focus their attention on the map, the restaurant fronts and the key facts and give them five minutes to study the information.

4 In pairs, students discuss and decide which restaurant they would prefer to buy.

5 Have a class feedback session where students explain their choices.

5 The story of the stones

Overview

Students read about and discuss time management, both personal and professional.

Preparation

One copy of the worksheet for each student.

Procedure

1 Individually, students complete two pie charts in Exercise 1 – one for a typical day and one for an ideal day – and compare their results with a partner.

2 Have a class feedback session to discuss any differences between the two pie charts.

3 Students read the text in Exercise 2. They then complete the sentences in Exercise 3 and discuss their ideas with a partner.

4 Students report to the class anything interesting from their discussions.

6a Destination desktop

Overview

Students read an article and discuss the advantages and disadvantages of electronic business communication, as opposed to conventional business travel.

Preparation

One copy of the worksheet for each student.

Procedure

1 In Exercise 1 students, in pairs or small groups, look at the title of the article and predict what the article is about. Then students read the article and check their predictions. Elicit from them the main points of the article.

2 Individually or in pairs, students find the words in the text and explain what nouns or noun phrases they refer to in Exercise 2. Check understanding as they do this.

3 Ask students what else in the business world each of the items in Exercise 2 could be used to describe e.g. *increasingly powerful: mobile phones, IT companies, top footballers,* etc.

4 Students discuss the questions in Exercise 3, and report to the class anything interesting from their discussions.

Answers

b) business communication   c) the desire for conventional business travel   d) the cost of electronic conferencing e) the Internet, desktop computers   f) e-mail, instant messaging and other applications   g) the assumption that corporate travel and in-person meetings is the only real way to do business

6b Valerie's trip

Overview

Students work in pairs exchanging information to update a business trip itinerary. This activity recycles and practises the language of travel arrangements, dates, times and spellings.

Preparation

One copy of the worksheet for each pair of students. Cut the worksheet into two.

Procedure

1 Depending on the class, you may want to start by revising prepositions of time and place (*in, on, at,* etc.), the alphabet and question forms.

2 Students work in pairs to discuss Valerie's itinerary, asking and answering questions but not showing each other their sheets. Monitor the activity and help with question forms, if necessary. At the end of the allotted time, students should have negotiated an itinerary between them, which they should note down.

3 Ask them to look at the form (beginnings and endings) and language of Student A's e-mail and to pick out any useful phrases which they could use in their own e-mail messages.

7 Calculated guess

Overview

This fast-paced, competitive team game receptively exposes students to 96 common verb-noun collocations and increases students' lexical spontaneity.

Preparation

One copy of the worksheet for each student. Distribute copies **after** the game. To play, photocopy the word boxes onto an OHP transparency or write them on the board.

Procedure

1 Ask students to work in teams and explain that they are going to compete in a vocabulary contest.
2 Explain that there are three rounds. In Round 1 the context is 'In the office'. Set the scene by asking students to think of things they have in their office, e.g. PCs, phone, fax machines, reports, etc.
3 Write up the nouns for Round 1 on the board or display them on an OHP. Explain that you are going to read out sets of verbs (see items 1–8 on the worksheet). There are four verbs in each set and every verb in the set will combine with just one of the nouns they can see. They must guess which noun it is as quickly as possible.
4 Read out each item slowly. The first team to guess correctly wins a point, but they must be careful! Some of the verbs will collocate with more than one of the nouns (but only one noun with all four verbs). Give the score at the end of Round 1.
5 For Round 2 'On the road', set the scene by asking your students to think about business trips they've been on. Then display the second set of nouns. Conduct the activity at a brisker pace this time and keep track of the score.
6 Repeat for Round 3 'In a meeting'. Ask students to think about what they discuss in meetings and then play the guessing game. Give out the final scores.
7 Now distribute the worksheets. Students write in the nouns next to the verb lists. This could be done collaboratively after the previous competitive stage.

Answers

Round 1: 1 a phone call 2 your computer 3 a report
4 a letter 5 a form 6 a computer file 7 a message
8 your e-mail

Round 2: 1 your hotel 2 a presentation 3 an agreement
4 your flight 5 an appointment 6 lunch
7 a meeting 8 your office

Round 3: 1 problems 2 ideas 3 proposals 4 figures
5 decisions 6 your colleagues 7 views 8 excuses

8a Devil's advocate

Overview

Students practise using language for agreeing and disagreeing, and asking for clarification in a group discussion activity. (NB Explain the expression *devil's advocate* **at the end of the activity** during the class feedback session.)

Preparation

One copy of the worksheet for each group. Cut the worksheet into three. (There should be a minimum of six students in the class for this activity.)

Procedure

1 Divide students into groups of three or four. Give a student in each group a card: A, B or C. It's a good idea to allocate C cards to more extrovert students if possible. It does not matter if one or two students do not have cards. Tell students not to show each other their cards.
2 Explain that the students with cards are going to lead a discussion on a controversial topic and get the group to reach a consensus. Give students a few moments to read their cards. During this time go round checking that Students C understand that they are to take an extreme, opposing view to provoke an argument (i.e. to play devil's advocate).
3 Give Students A five minutes for their discussion. Then the groups complete the manifesto statement before starting Student B's discussion.
4 Have a class feedback session to listen to the different groups' opinion on their chosen topics.
5 Ask a Student C to explain why they were difficult and show the picture on their card. Explain the expression *devil's advocate* (a person who disagrees in order to provoke a debate or test the strength of the opposing arguments).

8b Making decisions

Overview

Students learn some idiomatic expressions relating to decisions, apply these to situations they have experienced and suggest good principles for decision-making.

Preparation

One copy of the worksheet for each student. Cut the worksheet into two.

Procedure

1 Explain that students are going to look at some idiomatic phrases to do with making and changing decisions. Hand out copies of the top part of the worksheet and ask them, in pairs or small groups, to complete the phrases in Exercise 1. When they have finished, check the answers and the meaning of each phrase.
2 Hand out the bottom part of the worksheet and give the students five minutes to look at Exercise 2 and think of situations from their own experience. They do not need to think of situations for all the idioms. Students describe the situations to their partner. Monitor the activity, helping with vocabulary as necessary.
3 In pairs, students discuss the principles in Exercise 3 and suggest others. Ask pairs to share their thoughts and contribute to a definitive list drawn up by consensus of the class.

Answers

a) mind b) thought c) say d) thought/consideration
e) decision f) consideration g) mind h) issue i) mind
j) decision

9 What the CEO said

Overview

Students read the advice of well-known CEOs on various aspects of running a business. Before reading the quotations, they give their own views on these aspects.

Preparation

One copy of the worksheet for each student. Cut the worksheet into two.

Procedure

1 Hand out copies of the top half of the worksheet and ask the students to do Exercise 1 individually. Students then discuss the questions in Exercise 2 in pairs. Spend a little more than a third of class time on this stage. Go round helping with vocabulary as necessary.

2 Check/Pre-teach: *but = except, steamroller, nimble, trembling.* Then hand out the bottom half of the worksheet and get the students, one at a time, to read out each quotation, making sure they understand them. As you go, find out what their views were on each question and whether they agree with what the CEO said.

3 Ask if anyone has a favourite business quotation or memorable piece of advice given by a manager or CEO. If nothing is immediately forthcoming, ask students to bring one to the next lesson.

10 Small talk

Overview

Students categorise and practise useful language for small talk: opening, directing and closing a conversation, and showing interest.

Preparation

One copy of the worksheet for each student.

Procedure

1 In pairs, students categorise the phrases and expressions by completing the table in Exercise 1.

2 Check the answers with the class. Ask some of the students to improvise sentences to illustrate and check meaning and use.

3 Ask students to imagine they are at a conference reception and to mingle around the classroom having brief conversations with each other. Encourage them to use the phrases and expressions in Exercise 1. Monitor the activity.

Answers

Opening a conversation: b, f, h, l, n, p, r, v.
Directing a conversation: c, o, q, t, u, w.
Showing interest: d, g, j, s.
Closing a conversation: a, e, i, k, m.

11a A business trip

Overview

Students write e-mails and perform a roleplay based on a real or imaginary business trip.

Preparation

One copy of the worksheet for each student.

Procedure

1 Ask the students about their experiences of business trips and how they prepare in advance to maximise their time.

2 Students then work individually to plan the details for a real or imaginary business trip in Exercise 1.

3 Students write e-mail 1 in Exercise 2. E-mail 2 is optional, but it gives extra writing practice and a chance to prepare more ideas for the roleplay.

4 Divide the class into pairs with as similar a business background as possible. Ask students to exchange their e-mails, discuss the situation, and discuss what sort of reply they expect in Exercise 3. Monitor the activity.

5 Students work individually to write their reply e-mail in Exercise 4.

6 Students act out the roleplay in Exercise 5. Stress that the host is told to have a short business discussion, not a full negotiation. The pairs then change roles and repeat the roleplay.

7 Hold a short feedback session to give students a chance to mention any problems they encountered.

11b Spam

Overview

Students complete a cloze text about spam. They then discuss spamming and other ways of marketing a product.

Preparation

One copy of the worksheet for each student.

Procedure

1 Introduce the idea of *spam* to students, i.e. unsolicited e-mail messages. (Spam is the trade name of a poor-quality meat product sold in tins.) Check/Pre-teach: *junk, cold calling, hoax, chain.*

2 Students read the text and fill in the gaps in Exercise 1. Ask them to answer and discuss the follow-up questions in pairs or small groups.

3 Students discuss the promotion ideas in pairs in Exercise 2.

4 Have a class feedback session. You can award points to pairs for each new idea introduced into the discussion and for using the phrases.

Answers

1 unlikely   2 guess   3 carried   4 spend   5 hoax
6 colleagues   7 harmless   8 headache   9 adopt
10 set   11 receive   12 dealing   13 work   14 wage

12a Employees' centre

Overview

In groups, students plan and present their ideas for a new employees' centre at work. They practise the language of presentations and use delivery techniques to be persuasive.

Preparation

One copy of the worksheet for each student.

Procedure

1 In groups of three, students read about the competition in Exercise 1 and decide what sort of employees' centre they wish to propose.

2 In Exercise 2, students draw a floor plan and transfer it onto an OHT or flipchart, if appropriate.

3 Students each prepare one stage of the presentation in Exercise 3, bearing in mind the points on the checklist. Monitor the activity.

4 Invite each group to present their idea and hold a feedback session for each. Ask the class which project should be chosen, and why.

12b I am a DVD

Overview

Generative verbs such as *give, take, make* and *do* form the basis of many English expressions useful to a presenter. Students listen to a presentation given by their teacher ('the DVD player') and identify 24 such expressions.

Preparation

One copy of the worksheet for each student. Cut the worksheets into two. Distribute the soundtrack **after** the task.

Procedure

1 As a warmer, elicit a few examples of business expressions using the verbs *give, take, make* and *do*, e.g. *give an overview, give an example, make progress, make a point*, etc.

2 Explain that students are going to 'watch' a film of a business presentation which contains 24 examples of business expressions with *give, take, make* and *do*. However, as you don't have a DVD player with you, you are going to be the DVD and they are going to operate you by remote control!

3 Hand out the top part of the worksheet. Students fill in the functions of the buttons on a DVD player: *rewind, play, fast forward, stop* and *pause*.

4 Explain that you will give the presentation and that every time your students hear an expression using one of the four verbs, they should pause you and write down the whole expression in their notebooks. They can rewind and fast forward you as they need to. Students will have to listen very carefully, as the verbs do not always precede the expressions they belong to.

5 Students compare their answers in pairs.

6 Distribute the soundtrack. Students highlight the key expressions and check them against the ones they wrote down. Explain any unfamiliar vocabulary from the soundtrack to the class.

To make the task easier, read the whole presentation and simply ask students to raise their hand when they hear a key expression but to write nothing at this stage. Or, reduce the number of verbs the students are listening for or give different groups different verbs to listen for.

Answers

give: *It gives me great pleasure to; to give you a brief overview; given the extra resources; give you a chance to; giving a short talk on; To give you just one example; give you almost complete access to*

take: *I'd like to take this opportunity to; you'll be taken on a preliminary tour; we can take the lead; take as much time as you need; take notes; take a few minutes to*

make: *make the most of; made the final breakthrough; making such a discovery; have made considerable progress; to make headway; the point I want to make is*

do: *hope to be doing business with; do everything we can to; the work we're currently doing; the tests we've done; they'll do their best to*

13 Bioethics

Overview

Students discuss difficult ethical questions surrounding genetic engineering and cloning.

Preparation

One copy of the worksheet for each pair of students. Cut the worksheet into three.

Procedure

1 Ask the students what 'cloning' means and what its benefits and drawbacks are. Check/Pre-teach: *genes/genetic, science fiction, disease, cure, tissue, organs, embryo, foetus, abort, kidney/heart failure, cells, transplant.*

2 Ask students to work in pairs. Hand out the top part of the worksheet. Students read the introductory text. To check comprehension, ask students what cloning is and is not, according to the writer.

3 Hand out the definitions of embryonic stem cells and therapeutic cloning to alternate students and ask them to read and summarise their texts to one another.

4 Individually, students consider questions 1–5, then exchange their views in pairs. Monitor the activity.

5 Ask if anyone's opinion on these questions has changed from the beginning of the lesson and why.

14a The good consultant

Overview

Students read a text to stimulate a discussion on the role of business consultants.

Preparation

One copy of the worksheet for each student.

Procedure

1 Ask students to work in pairs or small groups and brainstorm reasons why companies use consultants.

2 Hand out the worksheets and ask students to match the sentence halves in Exercise 1.

3 Check the answers with the class. Then ask students to brainstorm any disadvantages associated with using consultants.

4 Explain that students are going to read a story which contains a consultant, a shepherd, sheep and a sheepdog. Check/Pre-teach: *flock (of sheep), log on to (a website), scrutinise (an area).*

5   Give students five minutes to read the text in Exercise 2.
6   In pairs students complete the sentences in Exercise 3 using their choice of modals. Monitor the activity.
7   Invite individual students to read their sentences to the class.

Answers

a 3   b 5   c 1   d 7   e 2   f 4   g 6

14b Business behaviour

Overview

Students assess the importance of specific behaviour in the business world and explain their culture's characteristics.

Preparation

One copy of the worksheet for each student.

Procedure

1   Students read the characteristics and grade them according to importance by placing a cross at the appropriate place on each line.
2   In groups, students share their views by comparing their completed worksheets. Encourage them to elaborate on each point, giving examples from their own experience where appropriate.

NB For mono-cultural classes, you could shift the emphasis onto differences between workplaces/companies. For multi-cultural classes, the emphasis can be on differences between cultures/countries.

15 Selling the company

Overview

Students choose the most appropriate extracts to use in a letter introducing their company to a new client. They then use some of these extracts to create their own letters.

Preparation

One copy of the worksheet for each student.

Procedure

1   In pairs, students decide in Exercise 1 which extracts from letters are appropriate to use in a letter introducing their company to a new client.
2   Reconvene as a group and discuss the extracts students selected. Ask them why the other extracts were not appropriate, e.g. too informal/too formal, unnecessarily long, too rude or abrupt.
3   In Exercise 2 students use at least eight of their selected extracts to make a complete letter, using their imagination to flesh out the details. Monitor the activity.
4   Ask individual students to read their letters out to the class.

Suggested answers

b, e, h, i, n, o, p, t, v, w, x, y.

16a Dragon boat racing

Overview

Students do a jigsaw reading about a management solution to a particular problem. They give their reactions to the solution using conditionals (past reference).

Preparation

One copy of the worksheet for each student. Cut the text into strips if you feel this will be helpful to students.

Procedure

1   Students read and discuss the questions in Exercise 1 in pairs or small groups. Have a short class feedback session.
2   In pairs, students put the story in Exercise 2 in order. Monitor, helping with vocabulary if necessary.
3   Check answers with the whole class.
4   Students discuss the question in Exercise 3 in pairs or small groups. Encourage students to use the past conditional.
5   Ask students to give real examples of how problems are solved in their company and to talk about their roles in the decision-making process.

Answers

1 A   2 F   3 I   4 C   5 H   6 E   7 B   8 G   9 D   10 J

16b Consultancy team

Overview

Students work as teams of management consultants to solve problems of inappropriate behaviour in meetings.

Preparation

One copy of the worksheet per two groups of students. Cut the worksheet into two.

Procedure

1   Divide students into an even number of groups of two or more students: A and B. Give Groups A worksheet A, and Groups B worksheet B.
2   Ask students to read the instructions. Make sure students understand that they are going to take on the role of both management consultants and directors.
3   Ask students to discuss the problem they have been given as management consultants and to think of suggestions to give the directors to remedy the situation. Monitor the activity, helping with vocabulary if necessary.

17 Cultural differences

Overview

Students match geographical groups to cultural descriptions and then discuss questions on cultural differences.

Preparation

One copy of the worksheet for each student.

Procedure

1   Write Cultural differences and the four box headings on the board, e.g. company values, etc. Elicit a few ideas for cultural differences under each heading. Then explain that students are going to read some ideas for each heading and then have a discussion.
2   Hand out copies of the worksheet and ask students to read the introduction and four boxes individually. Give students an opportunity to ask about any new vocabulary before they do the matching task.
3   Individually, students complete the matching exercise in Exercise 1.
4   Hold a feedback session and allow students to discuss their answers and the questions in Exercise 2.

Answers

Company values: a 3 b 2 c 1
Business relationships: a 1 b 3 c 2
Meetings: a 3 b 1 c 2
Presentations: a 2 b 3 c 1

18a Piracy

Overview

Students read statistics and a text on piracy. They then reconstruct sentences containing passives.

Preparation

One copy of the worksheet for each student.

Procedure

1   Introduce the idea of piracy and types of commercial piracy. Have students ever come across this sort of thing? Is their company affected in any way by the problem? What parts of the world do they think are most affected by this problem? For what reasons?
2   Hand out the worksheet and go over Exercise 1. Have a feedback session after students have discussed the questions in pairs.
3   Ask students to read the text to find the answers to the questions in Exercise 1. Explain any unfamiliar vocabulary.
4   Write the following on the board: 1) estimate + $12.2 billion   2) 108,000 + lose   3) 91% + sell   4) burn + $1   5) carry out + corporate level   6) issue + address   7) revenue rates + link   8) legitimate software market + affect
    Explain that students, in pairs, are going to reconstruct sentences from the text using the prompts. Do the first one together (*Losses due to piracy each year are estimated to be $12.2 billion*) and highlight the use of the passive.
5   Have a class feedback session to check the sentences.
6   Students discuss the questions in Exercise 3 in pairs.
7   Students match the sentence halves and decide if they agree with each statement in Exercise 4. Students report their ideas to the class.

Answers

Procedure 4: 2) Up to 108,000 jobs a year are lost due to software piracy. 3) 91% of software (which is) sold on Internet Auction sites is pirated. 4) Many copies of software are burned for $1 a CD. 5) A lot of piracy is carried out at corporate level. 6) In the US and Western Europe, the issue is addressed very seriously. 7) Revenue rates are not directly linked to piracy rates. 8) The growth of the legitimate software market is affected as developers face the possibility of pirate copies outnumbering legal ones.

Exercise 4: a 5 b 3 c 4 d 1 e 2

18b A memorable meal

Overview

Students help the teacher tell an anecdote by supplying information the teacher has 'forgotten'. This activity recycles food and drink vocabulary and fosters anecdote-telling skills, the language of paraphrase and approximation and the skill of supplying other speakers with the vocabulary they need.

Preparation

One copy of the worksheet for each student. Distribute the worksheet **after** the task.

Procedure

1   Tell students that you are going to try to tell them about a meal you had at a restaurant recently but you may need their help to describe some of the food.
2   Read out the script on the worksheet to them, supplying your own information in the gaps and struggling to recall the words marked in **bold**. Students should intervene to help you find the right words when you struggle. Here are a few tips on how to do this:
    • Read the script, but don't be too word-perfect. *Um* and *er* a bit.
    • Embellish the story a little. Add extra details to set the scene without digressing too much.
    • When you get to the words in bold, hesitate, use fillers, say what you don't mean and ask for help.
    • Don't reject any suggestions from your class out of hand. Encourage them to speculate as to what you might mean.
    • If no-one can guess exactly what you're trying to say, accept the nearest synonym and then supply the word you wanted as well.
    • If no-one has a clue what word you're looking for, suddenly remember it.
3   Hand out copies of the worksheet for students to keep as a reference.
4   Ask students to prepare the story of a meal they had to read out to the others in the same way. You may want to set this for homework. Refer to the vocabulary in Unit 18 of the Student's Book and the Lexis link on page 113 to help them prepare.

19a Boss or Big Brother ?

Overview

Students complete a cloze text on employers screening employees' e-mail. They then discuss the ideas in the text using the language of agreeing and disagreeing.

Preparation

One copy of the worksheet for each student.

Procedure

1   Introduce the subject of employers screening employees' e-mail. Ask students about their companies' policy on e-mail use. Check/Pre-teach: *survey, liable, halt, snoop, perk, scan*.
2   In pairs, students do Exercise 1. Then check the answers with the class.
3   Go over the expressions in Exercise 2 and encourage students to use them in their discussion. One possibility is to make the activity into a game by awarding points: one point for an argument, two points for a counter argument and a bonus point for every time they use one of the phrases correctly.

Answers

a) offensive + language   b) scanning + managers
c) systems + snooping   d) customers + worried
e) liable + e-mails   f) want + money   g) case + pay
h) says + issue   i) conducted + behalf   j) sexism + pathetic
k) thinks + halt   l) e-mails + words   m) take + telephone
n) e-mail + tool   o) perk + hot

.19b A quality problem

Overview

Students practise writing e-mails about a particular problem from a variety of perspectives, wording their e-mails appropriately.

Preparation

One copy of the worksheet for each student.

Procedure

1   As a warmer, write *A quality problem* on the board and ask students what kinds of problem in business are referred to as quality problems. (NB *quality* can refer to customer service as well as production, and to the service sector as well as manufacturing.)

2   Hand out the worksheets. Students do Exercise 1 individually or in pairs. Check the answers with the class.

3   Students begin by writing the first e-mail only in Exercise 2. Before they write, remind them of particular language or style points that they looked at in Units 19 (or 11) in the Student's Book. Monitor and make notes on good/bad language use.

4   Ask students to work in pairs to correct the language and improve the style of each other's e-mails.

5   Repeat steps 3 and 4 for e-mails 2 and 3. Build up a collective class version on the board using ideas from all the e-mails. Before e-mail 3 you may want to elicit some diplomatic language, e.g. *It seems to me that …, It might be a good idea to …, I think we need to consider …* (*+ing*).

6   Individually students prepare a real-life situation in Exercise 3 and then write an e-mail.

7   In Exercise 4, students take on the role of the receiver of their own e-mail and write a reply to it. In this case this is more appropriate than exchanging with a partner as students are likely to know about their own individual problems and find it interesting to see things from another point of view. Monitor, helping with vocabulary as before.

Answers

1 b   2 c   3 a   4 f   5 d   6 e

20a Peasants 1000 AD

Overview

In pairs, students practise the language and skills of negotiating in the role of a medieval peasant.

Preparation

One copy of the worksheet for each pair. Cut the worksheet into two.

Procedure

1   Write *peasant* on the board and elicit the meaning (a person, especially in the past, who works on a small piece of land growing food and keeping animals to feed the family). Tell students that they are going to be medieval peasants, and that they are going to practise negotiating.

2   Ask students how their own real-life negotiations usually begin, and elicit the importance of relationship building. Elicit, e.g. greeting, offering a drink, small talk about the journey to the meeting, weather, etc.

3   Ask students what relationship building will be like between the peasants.

4   Divide the class into two groups: A and B. Give out the correct half of the worksheet to each student. Give students time to read the instructions and to check any unfamiliar vocabulary.

5   Groups spend a few minutes preparing ideas together.

6   Ask each student from Group A to work with a student from Group B, to form pairs of neighbours. Start the activity, circulate and make a note of good/inappropriate language use to go over at the end.

7   Ask students, in their pairs, to discuss how effective they were at negotiating. Have a short class feedback session to discuss any points that arise.

20b Mini-negotiations

Overview

Students participate in two mini-negotiations using the language of negotiation presented in Unit 20 of the Student's Book.

Preparation

One copy of the worksheet for each student. Cut the worksheet into two.

Procedure

1   Introduce the subject of working time by asking students about working hours in their country (for managers and workers). Check/Pre-teach: *to do overtime, basic salary, concession.*

2   Hand out copies of the first half of the worksheet and ask students to read the text and make notes on the position of each side in the negotiation in the spaces provided in the table.

3   Divide the class into two groups: managers and union representatives. Give groups a few minutes to decide at least two concessions they will allow, and write notes on negotiation strategy, bargaining points, etc. in the second section of the table.

4   Put students into pairs of one manager and one union representative and give them time to negotiate. As they negotiate they fill in the final boxes – the terms of the productivity deal.

5   Have a feedback session to find out how the negotiating ended up.

6   For the Businessworks negotiation, follow the same steps as before, but open the subject of sales by asking students about targets that they have been set for this year. Check/Pre-teach: *to set a target, to achieve a target, a budget.*

7   Students plan in two groups: sales directors and area sales managers. Give them a few minutes to prepare. Tell them that they can be creative in developing concessions to achieve an agreement.

8   Put students into pairs and allow time for negotiations before having a final feedback session to discuss the outcome.

1 Lifelines

Mark Powell

Throw a die to move round the board. If you land on an age group, tell the group about a memory, plan, hope or ambition for that age. If you land on a letter, pick a question and tell the group the answer. Use the sentence starters on the right.

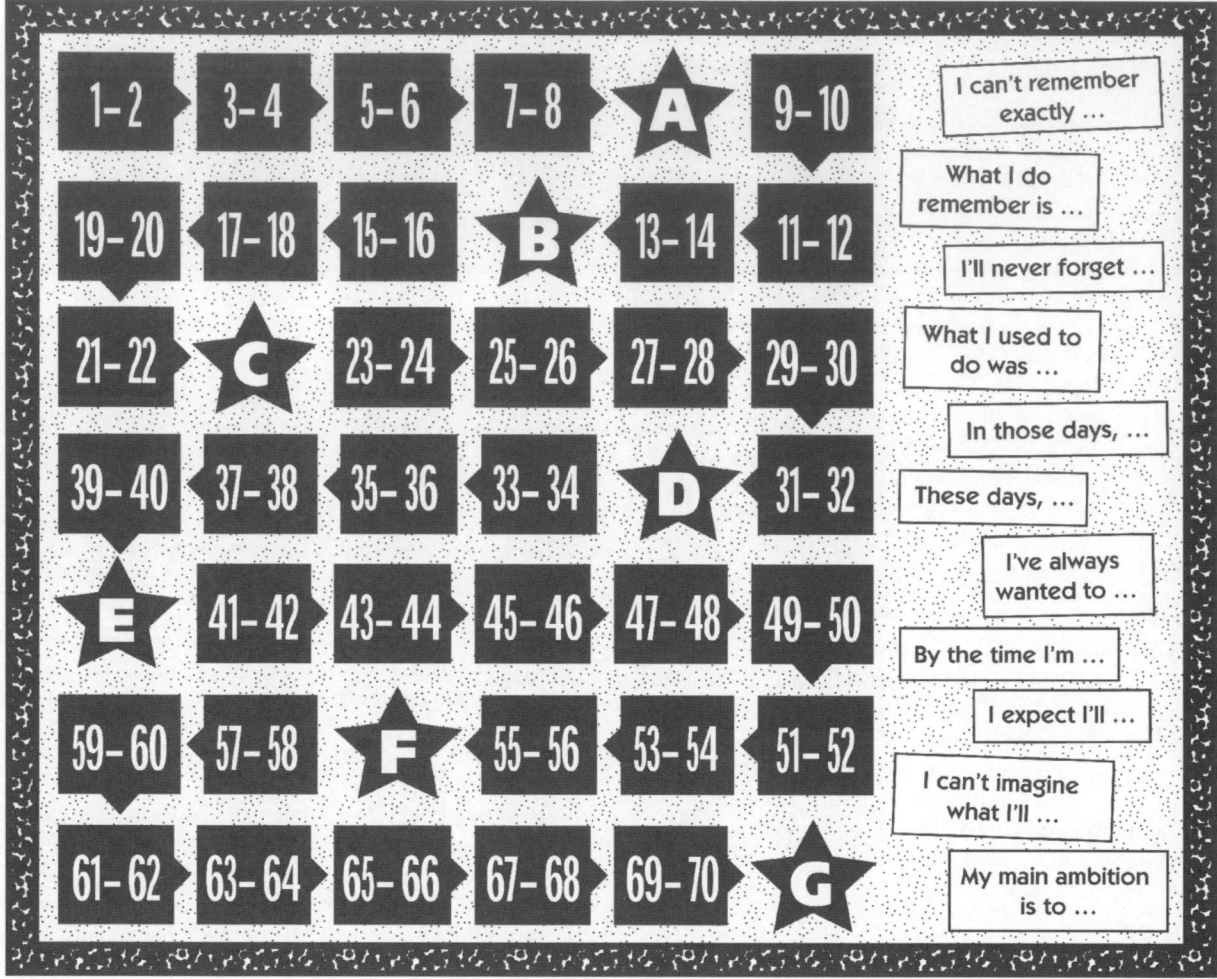

A When you were a kid, what did you want to be when you grew up?	A Did you have a best friend when you were a child?	A They say your schooldays are the happiest of your life. Were yours?
B Can you remember your first proper romance?	B What kind of music were you into in your teens?	B Were you a rebel as a teenager?
C Did you go to college or university? How hard did you work?	C What was your first job? What was your first boss like?	C When did you first buy a place of your own?
D Do you agree that if you haven't made it by 30, you never will?	D Do you think marriage is an outdated institution?	D John Paul Getty said 'To become rich, change jobs 12 times between 21 and 35.'
E They say life begins at 40. Do you agree?	E Is 45 too late to start a family?	E 'Love's better the second time around.' Is that true for you?
F The only good thing about getting old is that it's better than the alternative.	F How do you plan to spend your retirement?	F Someone once said life can only be lived forwards and understood backwards.
G Do you plan to grow old gracefully or disgracefully?	G They say we'll soon all be able to live to 120. Would you like to?	G What would you like to be remembered for?

2a Networking

Nicholas Sheard

1 Look at the list of jobs in the box. Choose three that you would like to do, and three that you wouldn't like to do. Compare with a partner, discussing the personal qualities and training required for the three jobs you have chosen.

astronaut	refuse collector	studio sound recorder	nurse	physiotherapist

make-up artist   farmer   stockbroker   news reporter   accountant

long-distance lorry driver   child psychologist   undertaker   taxi driver   circus acrobat

policewoman   private detective   model   nanny   management consultant

personal assistant   zoo keeper   film director   conductor   librarian   pilot

2 Choose one of the jobs in 1 and imagine that it's your real job. Prepare to talk about who you are and what you do. Write down three facts about your job: one neutral, one negative and one positive thing.

e.g. *I'm a nanny. I live with a family and look after their children. Sometimes I get very frustrated working with young children. However, I supervise their play and development, and it is lovely to see them grow.*

_____

_____

_____

_____

3 Complete the following comments that someone might make about the job you chose in 2. Suggest more suitable comments, if necessary.

That must be a very _____ *(difficult/interesting/boring/unusual/fulfilling/well-paid)* job.

I suppose you _____ *(travel a lot / work very long hours).*

I imagine your job affects your _____ *(private life / family / health).*

Tell me more about your _____ *(clients / patients / customers / typical day).*

4 Use what you have written above as the basis of a conversation with others about your and their chosen job. Use the expressions in the box to show interest and to react to what people say.

Really?   That's right.   I agree.   I didn't know that!   No!   How wonderful!   I know.

What?   Umm, no, not really.   I'm not sure, actually.   That's good.   Me too.

Oh dear!   Poor you!

- Mingle with other students in the class.

- Introduce yourself and ask them questions about their job.

- Comment with interest on their replies.

- Offer three facts about your own job.

2b Fugitives

Simon Clarke

Ten Most Wanted Fugitives

The FBI's Ten Most Wanted Fugitives programme is designed to publicise information about particularly dangerous criminals. Of the 468 fugitives who have been on the list since March 14 1950, 440 have been captured, 142 of them as a direct result of citizen cooperation. Originally this information appeared in posters and newspapers, but nowadays it is posted on the FBI's website at www.fbi.gov/mostwant/topten/fugitives/fugitives.htm

The descriptions of the fugitives include the following categories:

1	aliases	**7**	eyes
2	height	**8**	complexion
3	weight	**9**	race
4	build	**10**	nationality
5	occupation(s)	**11**	scars and marks
6	hair	**12**	remarks

---

1 Which is the appropriate verb to use when you are describing someone for each of the categories 1–12? Choose from the following:

> be   have   wear   look   use   work as   call yourself

For example:

aliases   He *calls himself* 'The Tiger'.
              He *uses* the name 'The Tiger'.

2 Match the words and phrases below to the categories 1–12.
(Some may be used in more than one category.)

black ☐   olive ☐   white ☐   stocky ☐   tattoo on upper arm ☐   security guard ☐

medium ☐   green ☐   salt and pepper ☐   bald ☐   mole below left eye ☐   American ☐

blue ☐   scar on chest ☐   dark/medium ☐   light ☐   male ☐   1.7 to 1.8 m ☐

Whitey ☐   approximately 73 kg ☐   is known to frequent libraries and historic sites ☐

white/silver ☐   thin ☐   El Comandante ☐   large ☐   uses disguises to alter his appearance ☐

3 If you have access to the Internet, go to the FBI website. Choose one of the fugitives on the list and write a description of the person based on the information provided.

4 Perform the following roleplay with a partner.

At the bottom of each poster in the FBI website it says 'If you have any information concerning this person, please contact your local FBI office or the nearest US embassy or consulate. There is usually a reward offered for information.'

Student A

You are an FBI agent on duty in the consulate in [your country]. You are passed a call from someone who claims to have seen one of the Ten Most Wanted Fugitives. Deal with the call.

Student B

You are attending a business conference. The other day you saw the FBI web page on the Internet and looked carefully at the information about wanted criminals. You are convinced one of the other delegates at the conference is one of these fugitives because they match the description perfectly. You have phoned the local US consulate, and your call has been passed to an FBI agent. Use the information from 2 to describe the man and explain why you think the person you have seen is a fugitive.

3 The right connections

Jon Hird

1 Rephrase the telephone dialogue using more appropriate language.

A Yes?	**A** _____
B Crystal Communications Consultants?	**B** _____
A Yes. What do you want?	**A** _____
B I want to speak to Silvia Garcia.	**B** _____
A Wait. Maybe she's here.	**A** _____
B Be quick.	**B** _____
A She's in a meeting.	**A** _____
B When can I speak to her then?	**B** _____
A Who knows? Phone back later.	**A** _____
B I don't want to. I want to leave a message.	**B** _____
A What is it?	**A** _____
B Tell her to phone me.	**B** _____
A Who are you?	**A** _____
B Barry Clough.	**B** _____
A What?	**A** _____
B I said Barry Clough.	**B** _____
A Spell your name.	**A** _____
B B–A–R–R–Y, C–L–O–U–G–H.	**B** _____
A OK, Barry. I'll tell her if I see her.	**A** _____
B You'd better.	**B** _____
A See you.	**A** _____

2 Silvia Garcia does not return Barry's call and, two days later, he telephones again and leaves a voice mail message. Rephrase his message using more appropriate language.

> *Where is everyone? Am I the only person doing any work? Look, I'm in Zurich. Oh, it's Barry by the way, Barry Clough. Silvia, I asked you to call me back. Why didn't you? Make sure you ring me back this time! Immediately! This is what it's about – the publicity material for the Zurich Expo, where on earth is it? The courier firm has never heard of you. What's going on, Silvia? You didn't make the arrangements, did you? The Expo starts tomorrow. Organise a new courier. Everything's going wrong and I don't think I can cope any more.*

4 Yank's or Chez Antoine?

Paul Dummett

Two businesses, both restaurants, have come up for sale in a historic town in England.
The town attracts a wide range of tourists, but is particularly popular with older
visitors interested in sightseeing and history. About 60% of visitors come only for a day trip.
The remaining 40% stay for two to three days. Using all the information below, decide which
you think is a better investment.

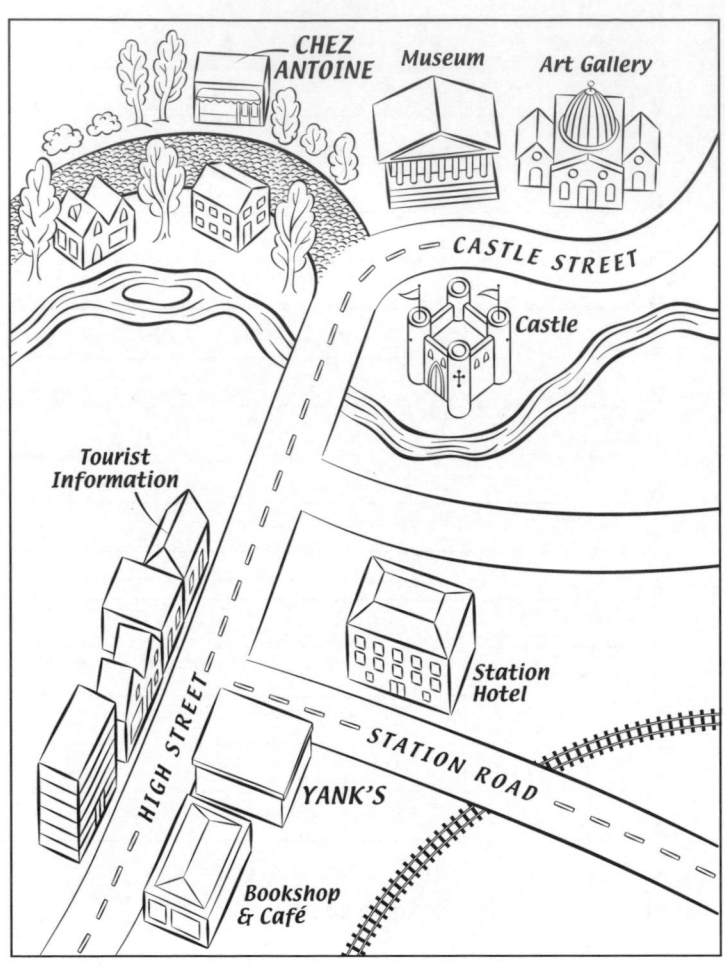

Restaurant type	zza, pasta and salads – American-style	nch, quite up-market
Location	n High Street in town centre	m from city centre in residential and tel area
Seating capacity		
Customers per day		
Current turnover	60,000 per year	48,000 per year
Amount spent per customer	.30	3.50
Potential for expansion	ne	nning permission to extend restaurant seat 24 more
Rent and rates	4,000 per year	4,000 per year
Salary bill last year	06,000	2,000
Cost	40,000	5,000

5 The story of the stones   Nicholas Sheard

1   What do you do with your time on a typical working day?
How, ideally, would you like to spend your time? Complete the pie charts using the list
of activities (a–j) or your own ideas. Then compare your pie charts with a partner.

a   at work
b   catching up with your family
c   with friends
d   sleeping
e   travelling
f   keeping fit
g   shopping
h   leisure activities / hobbies
i   household chores
j   eating and drinking

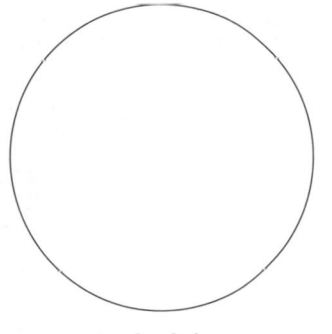

typical day   ideal day

2   Now read *The story of the stones*.

1   A business guru was asked to give a talk on time management to a group of fifteen executives from big companies. The guru slowly looked at each of the fifteen executives, and then put a big pot on the table
5   in front of him. Then he took out twelve big stones, about the size of tennis balls, and put them one by one into the big pot until it was impossible to add another stone.
     'Is the pot full?' he asked the executives.
     'Yes,' they all replied.
10   'Are you sure?' he said, taking out a bag of pebbles and pouring them over the big stones and into the pot.
     Once again he asked the executives, 'Is the pot full?'
     'Probably not,' one of them replied.
     'Good,' said the guru, this time taking a bag of sand
15   and pouring it over the pebbles and stones into the pot.
     'Is the pot full?' he asked once again.
     'No!' replied all the executives.
     'Quite right!' exclaimed the guru, taking a jug of water and filling the pot to the very top.

20   Having done this, the guru asked one final question: 'What great truth has this experience shown us?'
     One of the executives, knowing the subject of the talk was time management, answered: 'This shows us that when we think our diary is completely full, we can
25   always fit in more appointments, do more.'
     'No,' replied the guru. 'The great truth this has shown us is that if you don't put the big stones in the pot first, you can never put all the things in together.'
     There was a profound silence in the room. 'So, what
30   are the big stones in your life?' the guru continued. 'Your health? Your family? Your work? Your friends? Doing something you love? Learning? Defending a cause? Relaxing? Or something altogether different? Remember to always ask yourself, "What are the big stones in my
35   life?" and then prioritise them. If you give priority to little things, like pebbles or sand, you could be wasting precious time for the truly important things – the big stones in your life.'
     Slowly, and in silence, the business guru left the room.

3   Complete these sentences. Then discuss your ideas with a partner.

The big stones in my life today are _____

These days I seem to _____

The big stones when I was a student were _____

In those days _____

The big stones five years ago were _____

I used to _____

The big stones five years from now will probably be _____

I plan to _____

The big stones when I retire will be _____

By then I will have finished _____

6a Destination desktop

Jon Hird

1 Look at the title of the article. What do you think it is about? Read the article and find out.

Business travellers turn to their desktops

Just doing a bit of sight seeing before my next meeting

1 Business travel of the future is as likely to lead to the desktop as it is to the airport. Travel-reducing technology such as videoconferencing, web-meetings and other forms of electronic long-distance business communication are
5 increasingly being investigated by businesses worldwide.
    'The main driving force is not the cost of travel but the time that is lost,' said William Wood, business communications expert and author of *Virtual Teamwork*. The desire for conventional business travel is steadily
10 decreasing and there is now much greater demand for this kind of remote technology. At the same time, the cost of electronic conferencing is dropping dramatically and both the Internet and desktop computers are becoming increasingly powerful.
15   This means that the user can establish a real-time visual link from desktop to desktop anywhere in the world simply by clicking the mouse. You can sit at your desk and have several remote meetings a day. You could hold a one-to-one meeting with a colleague in Tokyo, followed by a group
20 session with people in, say, London, New York and Zurich and after that you could join a conference in Sweden.

In these meetings, it's possible to have all the participants on the screen with the documents in the middle.
    The technology also allows the participants to use
25 e-mail, instant messaging and other applications readily available at the computer terminal. All this creates, according to Wood, a much more productive environment. Participants can interact faster and better than in a face-to-face setting and no-one is disadvantaged by travel
30 schedules.
    The long-held assumption that corporate travel and in-person meetings is the only real way to do business, is being seriously reassessed.

2 What does each of the following refer to in the article? The first one has been done for you.

   a travel-reducing   *technology*
   b long-distance   _____
   c steadily decreasing   _____
   d dropping dramatically _____
   e increasingly powerful _____
   f readily available   _____
   g long-held   _____

3 Work in pairs or small groups and discuss the questions.

   a Do you think the article gives a realistic account of the future of business travel?
   b What are the advantages and disadvantages of conventional business travel?
   c What are the advantages and disadvantages of Internet meetings and other forms of electronic long-distance business communication?
   d What do you envisage will be the long-term consequences, benefits and disadvantages of this technology?

6b Valerie's trip

Colin Benn

Student A

JOEL PETERS
You work for the Helger Group at its headquarters in Paris. Your boss, Valerie Joule, the European Commercial Director, is planning to visit Helger Zorn, the subsidiary in Hamburg, Germany. She has sent you the following e-mail about the final arrangements for her visit. Your contact at Helger-Zorn is Susan Weil. Call her to check the details for the visit and note any problems or changes. Then write an e-mail to Valerie to confirm the arrangements.

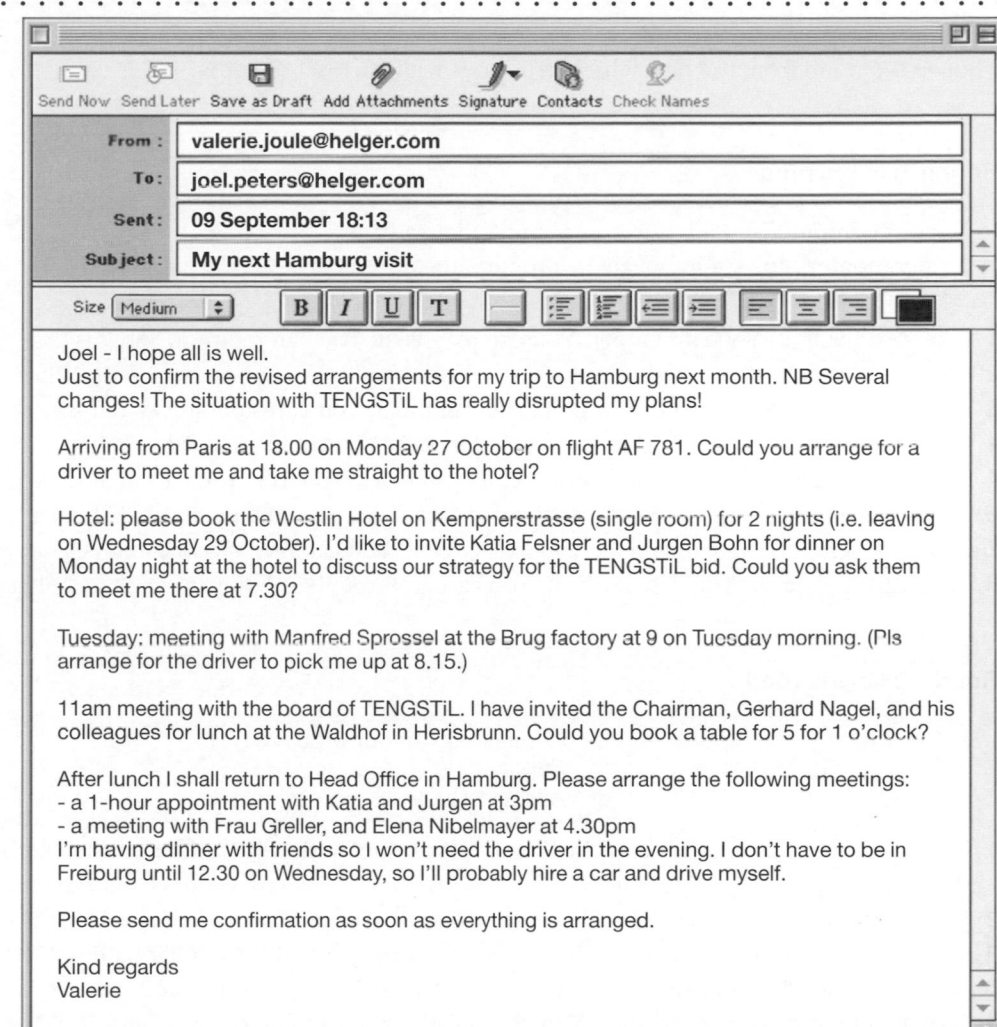

Send Now · Send Later · Save as Draft · Add Attachments · Signature · Contacts · Check Names

From: valerie.joule@helger.com
To: joel.peters@helger.com
Sent: 09 September 18:13
Subject: My next Hamburg visit

Size Medium · B I U T

Joel - I hope all is well.
Just to confirm the revised arrangements for my trip to Hamburg next month. NB Several changes! The situation with TENGSTiL has really disrupted my plans!

Arriving from Paris at 18.00 on Monday 27 October on flight AF 781. Could you arrange for a driver to meet me and take me straight to the hotel?

Hotel: please book the Westlin Hotel on Kempnerstrasse (single room) for 2 nights (i.e. leaving on Wednesday 29 October). I'd like to invite Katia Felsner and Jurgen Bohn for dinner on Monday night at the hotel to discuss our strategy for the TENGSTiL bid. Could you ask them to meet me there at 7.30?

Tuesday: meeting with Manfred Sprossel at the Brug factory at 9 on Tuesday morning. (Pls arrange for the driver to pick me up at 8.15.)

11am meeting with the board of TENGSTiL. I have invited the Chairman, Gerhard Nagel, and his colleagues for lunch at the Waldhof in Herisbrunn. Could you book a table for 5 for 1 o'clock?

After lunch I shall return to Head Office in Hamburg. Please arrange the following meetings:
- a 1-hour appointment with Katia and Jurgen at 3pm
- a meeting with Frau Greller, and Elena Nibelmayer at 4.30pm
I'm having dinner with friends so I won't need the driver in the evening. I don't have to be in Freiburg until 12.30 on Wednesday, so I'll probably hire a car and drive myself.

Please send me confirmation as soon as everything is arranged.

Kind regards
Valerie

Student B

SUSAN WEIL
You work for Helger-Zorn, in Hamburg. Helger-Zorn is the German subsidiary of the Helger Group whose headquarters are in Paris. Valerie Joule, the European Commercial Director, is planning to visit your company. Joel Peters at Group Headquarters in Paris will call you about the visit. You have prepared an itinerary for the visit. When he calls, check the arrangements and note any problems or changes. Then send an e-mail to all those concerned, attaching the new itinerary and explaining the details.

HELGER-ZORN
Visit of Valerie Joule, European Sales Director, 27–28 October

Monday 27	11.00	Driver pick-up from airport
	11.30	Arrival at Helger-Zorn. Reception with staff and senior management, lunch
	15.00	Visit to Rett store
	16.00	Check in to Hotel Westlin
	19.30	Dinner & theatre (Katia Felsner will accompany VJ)
Tuesday 28	8.30	Meeting with Manfred Sprossel, General Manager, Brug factory (driver to pick up from hotel at 7.45) NB Katia Felsner is in Berlin all day
	10.00	TENGSTiL board meeting
	12.30	Lunch with Jurgen Bohn
	14.00	Working from the Hamburg office
	17.40	Departure by train to Freiburg – book ticket?
Wednesday 29 – Friday 31		Conference in Freiburg

7 Calculated guess

Mark Powell

Choose the noun from the box which collocates with each set of verbs (1–8).

Round 1: In the office

your computer	a letter	a phone call	a form
a computer file	a message	a report	your e-mail

1 You can make it. You can take it. You can receive it. You can return it. What is it?
2 You can crash it. You can shut it down. You can play on it. You can reboot it. What is it?
3 You can complete it. You can draft it. You can file it. You can submit it. What is it?
4 You can get it. You can send it. You can address it. You can mail it. What is it?
4 You can sign it. You can make a copy of it. You can send it off. You can fill it in. What is it?
6 You can open it. You can delete it. You can create it. You can back it up. What is it?
7 You can send it. You can take it. You can leave it. You can listen to it. What is it?
8 You can reply to it. You can check it. You can go through it. You can delete it. What is it?

Round 2: On the road

your flight	an appointment	a meeting	your office
a presentation	an agreement	lunch	your hotel

1 You can go back to it. You can check into it. You can be dropped off at it. You can be picked up at it. What is it?
2 You can miss it. You can give it. You can attend it. You can take notes at it. What is it?
3 You can come to it. You can reach it. You can work it out. You can negotiate it. What is it?
4 You can enjoy it. You can change it. You can miss it. You can be booked on to it. What is it?
5 You can fix it. You can cancel it. You can keep it. You can fail to turn up for it. What is it?
6 You can skip it. You can grab it. You can go for it. You can pick up the bill for it. What is it?
7 You can organise it. You can hold it. You can speak at it. You can lead it. What is it?
8 You can phone it. You can e-mail it. You can check with it. You can keep in touch with it. What is it?

Round 3: In a meeting

decisions	problems	ideas	figures
excuses	views	proposals	your colleagues

1 You can address them. You can deal with them. You can foresee them. You can solve them. What are they?
2 You can develop them. You can share them. You can come up with them. You can brainstorm them. What are they?
3 You can make them. You can consider them. You can put them forward. You can withdraw them. What are they?
4 You can look at them. You can go through them. You can quote them. You can round them up. What are they?
5 You can make them. You can question them. You can reach them. You can put them off. What are they?
6 You can support them. You can attack them. You can back them up. You can chat with them. What are they?
7 You can air them. You can share them. You can express them. You can exchange them. What are they?
8 You can make them. You can look for them. You can invent them. You can refuse to accept them. What are they?

8a Devil's advocate

Gina Cuciniello

Student A

You are going to lead a discussion where you try to get everyone in your group to reach an agreement.

- Choose one of the following topics to discuss. The group can either agree or disagree with the statements.
- Summarise your conclusions in your manifesto statement.

> **a** Everyone should carry identity cards at all times.
> **b** The number of working hours should be reduced to 30 per week for everyone.
> **c** We should boycott goods made by companies who use child labour.

Manifesto statement: We believe that _____

provided that / unless / so long as _____

Student B

You are going to lead a discussion where you try to get everyone in your group to reach an agreement.

- Choose one of the following topics to discuss. The group can either agree or disagree with the statements.
- Summarise your conclusions in your manifesto statement.

> **a** Giving money to beggars does not help them in the long run.
> **b** Always start a presentation with a joke or funny story.
> **c** Companies should charge employees who use the Internet for personal use.

Manifesto statement: We believe that _____

provided that / unless / so long as _____

Student C

You are going to lead a discussion where you try to get everyone in your group to reach an agreement.

- Choose one of the following topics to discuss. The group can either agree or disagree with the statements.
- Summarise your conclusions in your manifesto statement.

> **a** Public transport should be subsidised by the state.
> **b** Mobile phones should carry a health warning.
> **c** Salary should depend on length of service in a company.

Manifesto statement: We believe that _____

provided that / unless / so long as _____

> **SECRET only for Student C:** Listen to the others' views first, then disagree strongly with them.

8b Making decisions

Paul Dummett

1   Use the following words to complete each expression.

> issue   say   mind   thought   decision   consideration

a   Originally, he agreed to work with us, but now he has **changed his** _____.

b   She said she would come, but now she's **having second** _____s.

c   The boss always **has the final** _____ in purchases over £500.

d   I've **given** the matter **a lot of** _____.

e   Everyone in the department **backed the** _____ to abandon the project.

f   There are several factors to **take into** _____.

g   There are several things that we should **bear in** _____.

h   They haven't addressed the problem at all: they've completely **dodged the** _____.

i   I**'m in two** _____s about whether to accept their proposal or not.

j   Time was short. We had to **make a snap** _____.

- -

2   Describe a situation in which you …

- were in two minds about accepting an offer.

- changed your mind about something you had previously agreed to.

- felt unable to back your boss's decision.

- dodged an issue.

- had to make a snap decision.

- gave something a lot of thought before making a decision.

- had second thoughts about something which seemed at first to be a good idea.

- had a lot of different people's interests to bear in mind.

- had the final say in an important decision.

- had to take many factors into consideration.

3   Which of the following principles do you follow when taking an important decision?

- Consider the best way to transmit your decision, e.g. channel of communication.

- Consider who will be affected by the decision and what the likely effect will be on them.

- Anticipate obstacles and objections.

- Think of all the possible outcomes in the longer term.

- Formulate a Plan B.

- If in doubt, postpone making a decision.

Suggest any other good principles which people could follow.

9 What the CEO said

Paul Dummett

1 Complete these sentences with your own opinions.

a Change is always _____ because _____

b Shareholders should not be allowed to _____

c Large companies tend to _____

d Acquiring a company usually _____

e The best way to save company expenditure is to _____

f The most important business ethic is _____

2 Keeping in mind your own beliefs expressed in 1, discuss the following questions in pairs. Try to find a joint opinion. Then summarise this opinion in one sentence.

1 What are the aims of your business? What should the aims of a large multinational company be?

2 In what order of importance to your company would you put these three groups: shareholders, customers, employees?

3 What should be the attitude of a modern company to change?

4 When the company needs to save money, which areas of a company's expenditure should you consider cutting first? What are dangerous areas to cut costs in?

5 What advantages do small companies have over large companies?

6 How can a company be sure it makes good acquisitions?

----

3 Read the quotes of these CEOs and see whether they agree in any way with your analysis in 2.

1
'A business that makes nothing but money is a poor kind of business.'
Henry Ford (Ford Motor Company)

4
'When you cut costs you have to be sure you don't damage your product. You can make a pizza so cheap nobody wants to eat it.'
Gordon Bethune (Continental Airlines)

2
'The traditional priorities of company boards are shareholders first, then customers, and last employees. But if you put the employees first, and look after them, then customer satisfaction will follow. And satisfied customers mean more profits for shareholders.'
Richard Branson (Virgin)

5
'People say smaller competitors have an advantage in being more nimble. That works so long as the guys who are big aren't nimble. Because big and nimble can overwhelm small and nimble.'
Mr Lee Raymond (Exxon Mobil)

3
'Change has become like a steamroller. If you're not on the steamroller, you're destined to become part of the road.'
R. Steve Letbetter (Reliant Energy)

6
'Acquisitions are very risky. Most do not deliver; most do not work. Any intelligent CEO approaches acquisitions with fear and trembling.'
Ralph Larsen (Johnson and Johnson)

10 Small talk

Jon Hird

1 Categorise the phrases and expressions a–w according to the following functions.
Three have already been done for you.

Opening a conversation	Directing a conversation	Showing interest	Closing a conversation
b	c		a

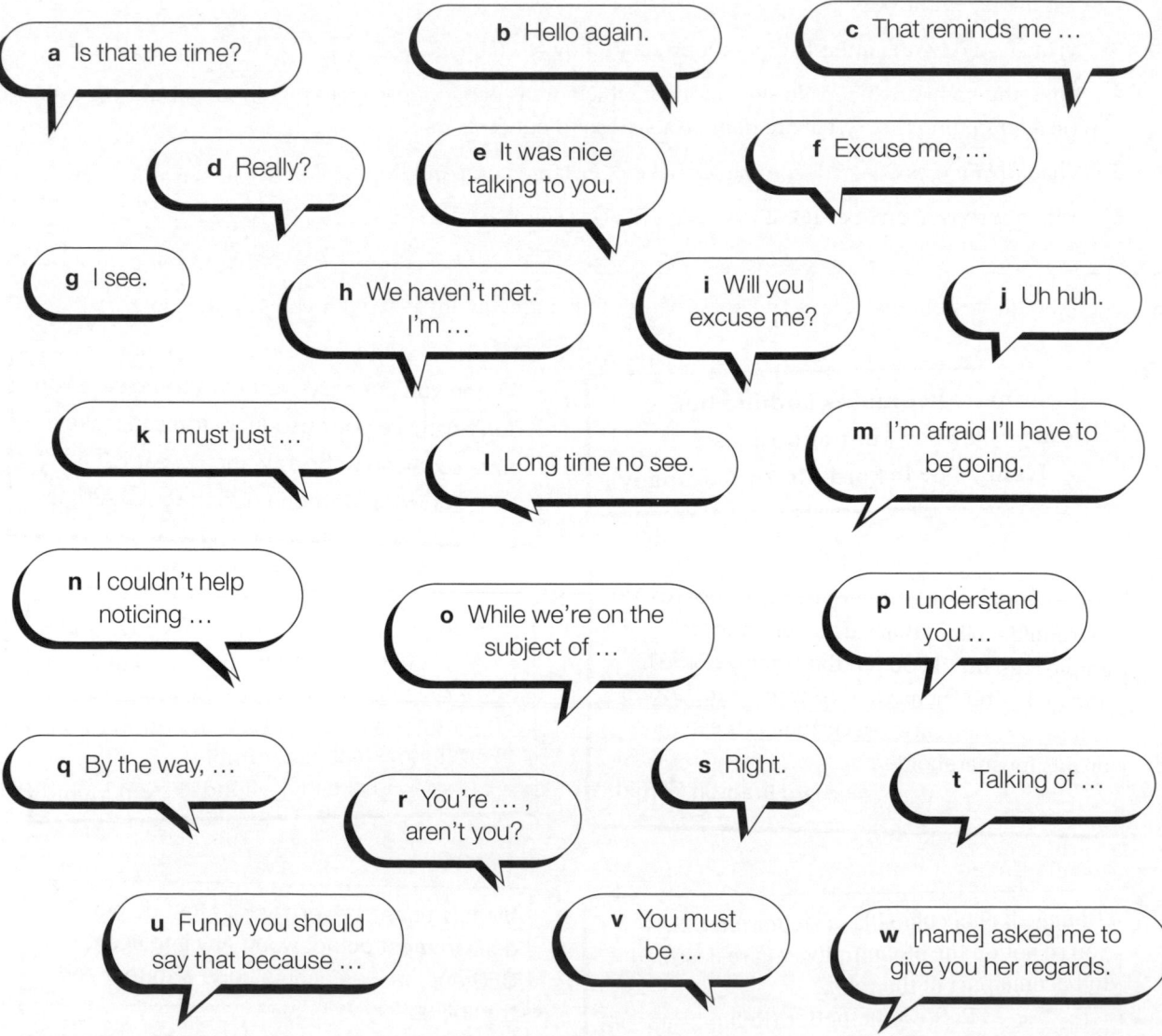

a Is that the time?

b Hello again.

c That reminds me …

d Really?

e It was nice talking to you.

f Excuse me, …

g I see.

h We haven't met. I'm …

i Will you excuse me?

j Uh huh.

k I must just …

l Long time no see.

m I'm afraid I'll have to be going.

n I couldn't help noticing …

o While we're on the subject of …

p I understand you …

q By the way, …

r You're … , aren't you?

s Right.

t Talking of …

u Funny you should say that because …

v You must be …

w [name] asked me to give you her regards.

2 Imagine you are at a conference reception. Walk round the classroom and improvise a brief conversation with as many people as you can. Use the phrases and expressions in 1.

11a A business trip

Paul Emmerson

1   You are planning to go on a business trip. Write the details below.
The situation can be imaginary, or you can make it similar to your real-life job.

Where are you going? _____

How long are you going to stay? _____

Why are you going? _____

_____

What is your itinerary (the places you will visit)? _____

_____

Who will you meet? _____

How well do you know them? Have you written / spoken to / met them before? _____

_____

_____

2   Write two e-mails, on separate sheets of paper, using the situation you created in 1. If possible, use real
people's names and a realistic content. The maximum length for each e-mail is 100 words.

e-mail 1: Write to the person you are going to meet. What do you need to tell them? Perhaps you
need to let them know what you want to discuss. Do you want them to arrange anything for you?

e-mail 2: Write an e-mail to all your colleagues. Tell them about your plans and ask them if they
want you to take / do / find out / bring back anything.

3   Work with a partner. Exchange e-mail 1, and read each other's situations from 1. Ask and answer questions
about your two situations. In particular, talk about the kind of reply your partner expects. You will need this
information in the next activity.

4   Work individually. Imagine that you are the person your partner is going to meet. Write a reply to your
partner's e-mail. The maximum length for the e-mail is 100 words.

5   Exchange and read the e-mails. When you are ready, act out two roleplays using the situations
that you and your partner created. In the first roleplay, Student A is the visitor and Student B is the host. Then
swap roles for the second roleplay.

Visitor

You are the visitor (who created the situation).
You arrived at your destination a few hours ago,
you have checked in to your hotel, and now you
have arrived at your host's office by taxi. The
receptionist has shown you to the office. Knock
on the door.

Host

You are the host, ready to receive the visitor.
Welcome your visitor, offer them a drink and
make some small talk (the journey? the hotel?
the news in their country? the state of the
market?). Have a short business discussion. End
in a friendly way and offer to take your visitor to
dinner this evening.

11b Spam

Simon Clarke

1 Complete the text below with the following words. Then answer the questions.

headache	work	adopt	receive	carried	unlikely	guess	spend	wage	harmless
colleagues	hoax	dealing	set						

Looking back over the e-mails I have received in the last couple of weeks, I can see there is at least one message a day from someone I don't know, offering some service or product I am (1) _____ to want. In some cases I can (2) _____ where they got my e-mail address from, but in others I have no idea. For me, this unsolicited junk e-mail is not a problem, I can just erase it from my computer. However, in a recent survey, (3) _____ out for the company Novell Inc. in the UK, 75% of those who were questioned claimed to receive as many as five junk e-mails a day, and 15% calculated that they (4) _____ at least an hour a day dealing with unsolicited spam.

Apart from spam which tries to sell products or services, there is also the problem of (5) _____ virus warnings, chain letters (where terrible things will happen to you if you don't pass on the message to fifteen other people) and jokes from friends and (6) _____. Although sometimes the content involved can be offensive and contain racist or sexist language, most of it is relatively (7) _____. On the other hand, in terms of wasting employees' time, it's a real (8) _____ for many businesses.

There are various strategies you can (9) _____ with spam. The easiest remedy is just to delete any messages which come from an unknown sender or look suspicious. To deal with nuisance mail which comes from a regular source, one solution is to (10) _____ up your e-mail program to ignore mail from that particular address. More legitimate spammers often give you the option to 'unsubscribe' so you don't (11) _____ any more of their messages, although in my experience this often doesn't seem to make any difference. Even so, while you are (12) _____ with spam you are not doing the work you were hired to do. If the data analysed in the survey is correct, 1.4% of the national (13) _____ force is unproductive for this reason at any time during a working day. With a national UK (14) _____ bill of £368bn a year, this means that for UK businesses spam represents an annual cost of around £5bn.

a What are the different types of spam?
b Why does it cost companies money?
c How much spam do you receive? What do you do about it? Is it a big problem for your company?

2 You work in the marketing department of a fast-food chain. You and your partner are working on a project to promote a new line of pizzas which people can order by phone or over the Internet. You are considering various methods of promotion. Discuss the advantages and disadvantages of these ideas:

- cold calling to selected telephone numbers
- flyers delivered by hand to people's homes
- direct mailing by post
- spamming to e-mail addresses on a database you have obtained

For each method consider the efficiency, cost and effect on your company's image. As you discuss your ideas, try to use the following phrases:

I (really don't) think that we should …	In my opinion …	I'm not so sure about …
I (don't) agree with your point …	That's an interesting idea, …	I suppose we should …
The advantage of …	The problem with …	You have to remember that …

12a Employees' centre

Colin Benn

1 Work in a group. Read about the competition and decide:
- what project would best suit the building.
- what employees need and how your idea would benefit them.
- what is required to make your project succeed, e.g. staff, finance, building work, facilities and equipment.

The company you work for has decided to create a new centre for its employees. (It could be a centre for sport, learning and personal development, health, relaxation, etc.) They are inviting people to submit projects and a committee will choose the winner. The company is offering a grant of 1.5m euros for the project and the centre will be located in the building where you are now.

> ## Have you got the winning idea?
> We want to hear your suggestions for a new employees' centre. Projects to be presented at a special meeting to be held at 2.30 p.m. next Friday.

2 Draw a simple floor plan of the employees' centre and label the rooms and areas.

3 Now prepare a short presentation to persuade the committee to adopt your project. Each member of the team should present one aspect of the project. Try to create maximum impact using pauses, repetition and rhetorical questions, and prepare visual aids to help you get your message across.

Checklist – don't forget these four key points

- [ ] Tailor the presentation to your audience: what do they know and what do they want to know?
- [ ] KISS (Keep it short and simple) and leave them wanting more ...
- [ ] Begin and end strongly because that's what people remember best.
- [ ] Use eye contact and body language to strengthen your argument.

12b I am a DVD

Mark Powell

1   Check you know the names of the controls on a DVD player. Write the words below the symbols.

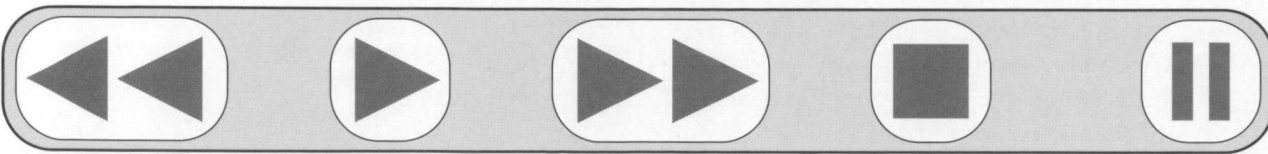

2   Your teacher is a DVD player and you have the remote control! Watch him/her play a film of a business presentation and listen carefully for expressions containing the verbs *give*, *take*, *make* or *do*. Pause the DVD each time you hear one and write down the complete expression in your notebook under the headings: *give*, *take*, *make* and *do*. Rewind if you need to listen again.

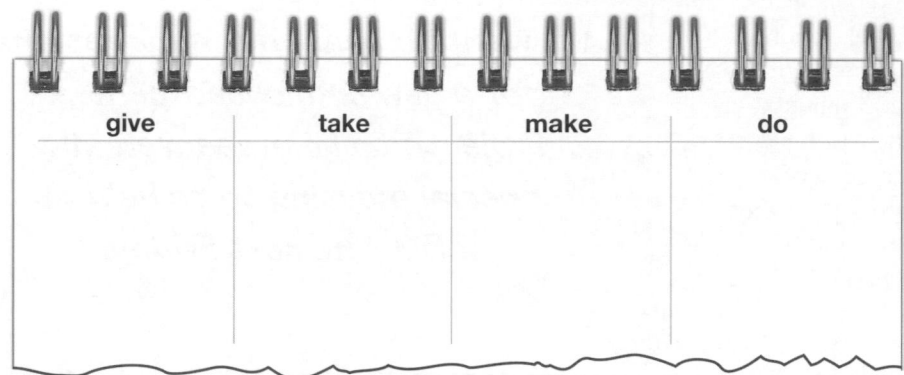

give	take	make	do

Soundtrack

1 Good morning, ladies and gentlemen. It gives me great pleasure to welcome you all to our research centre here in Vitry. I'd like to take this opportunity to thank Mr Oyama, in particular, for his hard
5 work in arranging this visit. As our two companies hope to be doing business with each other in the near future, we know there'll be a lot of things you want to see. We'll certainly do everything we can to help you make the most of your day with us.
10 So, just to give you a brief overview of the centre and the background to some of the work we're currently doing here, as you know, since 1997 our biotech facility has concentrated primarily on the development of a drug to combat bcl–2, the
15 gene that prevents cancer cells from dying. Now, we haven't yet made the final breakthrough, but, given the extra resources we hope your company can provide, we believe we are only a few years away from making such a discovery.
20 In a few moments, you'll be taken on a preliminary tour of the labs by our head of biotechnology, Dr Larousse. This will give you a chance to see for yourselves just how close we are to our objective. Dr Larousse will also be giving a
25 short talk this afternoon on the results of our latest research into other forms of gene therapy in the treatment of stroke, liver damage and heart disease, three areas in which, I think you'll agree, we have made considerable progress since our last meeting
30 in Cambridge.

I can report that we are continuing to make headway in all our areas of research. But it is the results we're getting from the tests we've done on our anti–bcl–2 drug which are particularly
35 exciting. To give you just one example, we have now been able to hold a cancer in remission, in a test subject, for three months without the need for radiology or chemotherapy. The point I want to make is that, with your collaboration, we are
40 confident we can take the lead in this important area of clinical medicine.

Please take as much time as you need to talk to our research scientists during the tour. I'm sure they'll do their best to answer any technical
45 questions you may have. The security passes you have been issued with give you almost complete access to our research facility. Feel free to take notes and compare data with our informatics department.
50 Now, if I could just take a few minutes to talk to you about the use of protective clothing …

13 Bioethics

Paul Dummett

Read the text about cloning and then look at some bioethical dilemmas (1–5). Before you consider the dilemmas, your teacher will give you a definition of an important term in this discussion. Read it and summarise it to your partner. Then consider dilemmas 1–5 for a few minutes before discussing them.

> The next technological revolution is likely to be in the field of genetic research and engineering. Cloning, the name popularly given to these technologies, is often associated with science fiction horror stories, because it suggests the creation of identical people. In reality, it is impossible to create two identical people. Personality, character and behaviour are not determined only by genetic factors. The real aims of cloning technology are to help in the development of tissue for transplantation, in genetic diagnosis and in biological research. But cloning technology raises some very difficult bioethical questions.

1 Scientists take stem cells from an aborted foetus for their research. Is this acceptable?

2 A two-year-old boy has a rare blood disease and needs a blood donor to save him. None of his brothers' or sisters' blood is an exact match. Through genetic diagnosis, scientists are able to tell the parents if the next foetus they conceive will be a match. The parents can then choose whether to keep or to abort the foetus. Is this acceptable?

3 Therapeutic cloning will give the possibility of extending human lifespan (to 100, 120, perhaps 140 years), but it will be expensive. Rich people will be able to regenerate their failing organs, just as they now pay for plastic surgery. Is this acceptable?

4 With genetic engineering, scientists will be able to eliminate some diseases and create healthier people. But once our genetic make-up has changed will we still be human or a different species?

5 Private health companies will patent procedures and fix their own prices for treatment. Is this acceptable?

Student A

> **Embryonic stem cells:** These are the first cells of life, found in a newly fertilised human egg. Each embryonic stem cell has the capacity, with the aid of chemical stimuli, to transform itself into any type of cell in the body: a skin cell, a blood cell, heart tissue, etc. Once the embryo is fully formed there are no more stem cells as all the organs and bodily functions have been determined. Scientists are very interested to learn how to programme these cells to regenerate old or worn out organs and tissue so that they can cure such illnesses as heart disease and kidney failure.

Student B

> **Therapeutic cloning:** This is a procedure in which cells, usually skin cells, are taken from a patient. The nucleus is extracted and inserted into a fertilised egg whose nucleus has been removed. The cell that is created is permitted to divide repeatedly. Scientists then extract stem cells from the ball of divided cells, and use those cells to grow tissue which is a perfect genetic match for the patient. The cells created by therapeutic cloning can potentially be transplanted into the patient to treat a disease from which the patient suffers.

14a The good consultant

Nicholas Sheard

1 Companies use consultants for many reasons. Match the sentence halves to discover a few of them.

a	Consultants are not involved	**1**	fresh ideas to the company.
b	Consultants have experience of	**2**	specialist knowledge.
c	Consultants bring	**3**	in internal company politics.
d	Consultants can be used	**4**	things realistically and objectively.
e	Consultants have	**5**	working with other companies.
f	Consultants see	**6**	quickly and efficiently.
g	Consultants work	**7**	by management to take the criticism for unpopular decisions.

2 Read the story of *The consultant, the shepherd and the sheep.*

1 Once upon a time there was a shepherd. He was standing by the side of the road, looking after his flock of sheep. Suddenly, a brand new Cherokee Jeep appeared and stopped near the shepherd. A young man wearing a Hugo Boss shirt, Yves St. Laurent trousers and Nike trainers got out and said to the shepherd: 'If I can guess how many sheep you have in your flock, will you give me one of them?'

5 The shepherd looked at the man, looked at his sheep – who were eating grass peacefully – and said: 'Yes, OK then.'

The young man parked his car and took out his laptop computer and a GSM phone. Then he logged on to a NASA website and scrutinised the local area with the help of a GPS (global positioning system). Next, he created a database and 60 Excel tables full of statistics. After that, using a hi-tech micro-printer, he printed

10 a 150-page report. Finally, he turned to the shepherd and said: 'You have 1,586 sheep in your flock.' The shepherd replied: 'You're absolutely right, I do have 1,586 sheep in my flock. Now you can take your sheep.'

The young man took a sheep and put it in the back of his Jeep. When he had done this, the shepherd said: 'If I can guess your profession, will you give me my sheep back?' 'Yes,' said the young man. 'You are a

15 business consultant,' said the shepherd. 'How did you guess?' asked the young man. 'Three things,' said the shepherd. 'Firstly, you came here when nobody asked you to. Secondly, you charged me a sheep to tell me what I already knew. And thirdly, you have no idea what I do, because you took my dog, not a sheep!'

3 Complete the sentences with a partner using the following modal verbs. Try to use a different one for each sentence. Use the Grammar link on pages 106–107 of the Student's Book to help you.

| must | mustn't | should | shouldn't | has | doesn't have to | can |

a A good consultant _____

b A good shepherd _____

c A consultant's report _____

d A company employing a consultant _____

e The recommendations in the report _____

14b Business behaviour

Jon Hird

1   How important are the following characteristics in your workplace or for business in your country?
Put a cross in the appropriate place on each line.

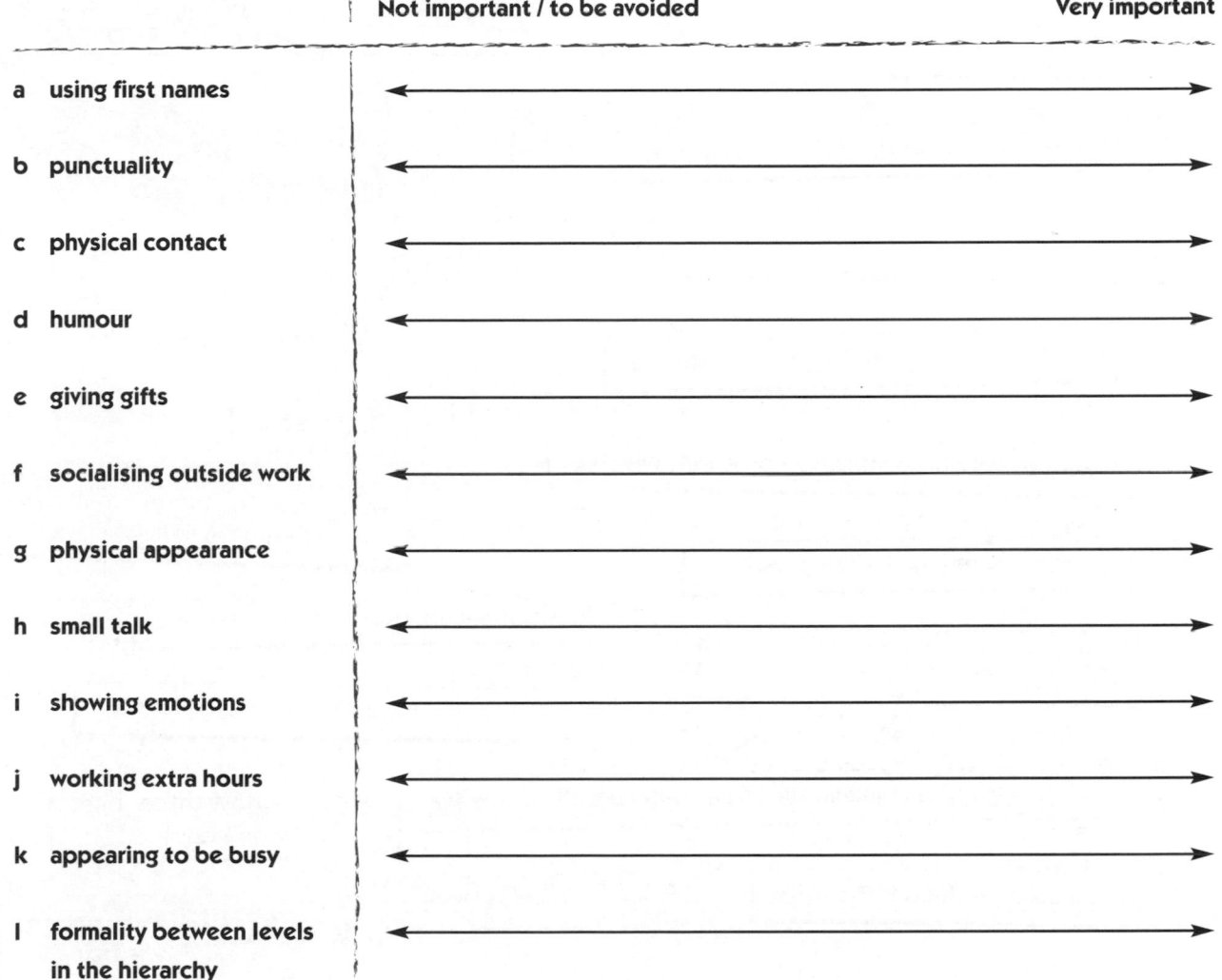

	Not important / to be avoided	Very important
a using first names		
b punctuality		
c physical contact		
d humour		
e giving gifts		
f socialising outside work		
g physical appearance		
h small talk		
i showing emotions		
j working extra hours		
k appearing to be busy		
l formality between levels in the hierarchy		

2   Work in groups and share your profiles with each other. Give examples from your own experiences to explain the characteristics of your culture or company's business behaviour. Use the following expressions:

It is always a good idea to ... because ...
One thing you should never do is ... because ...
People tend to / tend not to ... because ...
A lot of people ... but I don't because ...
It's usually appreciated if you avoid (-*ing*), because ...
On the whole, people don't ... because ...
It's just 'not done' to ... because ...

15 Selling the company

Gina Cuciniello

1 Read the following extracts from letters and tick those which you could use in a letter introducing your company to a new customer.

a ☐ Let me tell you about us.

b ☐ As I will be in your area next week, I would like to …

c ☐ I would like to introduce myself and my company.

d ☐ We want to present to you our company which …

f ☐ Best wishes

e ☐ I have attached our most recent brochure which …

g ☐ We can give you lots of products to choose from.

h ☐ We are a small company which specialises in …

i ☐ We have an international clientele.

j ☐ You are requested to inform us of a time as soon as possible.

k ☐ Can we come and show you our products?

l ☐ I saw your website and thought you could really do with our services.

m ☐ Just wanted to let you know …

n ☐ Our range of products is extensive.

o ☐ Yours sincerely

r ☐ It'd be great to hear your views.

p ☐ I will call you at the end of the week to find out when would be a convenient time.

q ☐ You won't find prices better than ours.

s ☐ All for now. Bye.

t ☐ In the meantime, if you would like further information, please do not hesitate to …

u ☐ People from all over the world buy from us.

v ☐ I look forward to meeting you very much.

w ☐ We have a great deal of experience in …

x ☐ Our prices are very competitive.

y ☐ We would be happy to arrange a meeting at your convenience.

2 Now write a complete letter to a new customer which your company would like to do business with, using at least eight of the extracts you have selected. Use your imagination to provide the details and expand where you feel it is necessary.

16a Dragon boat racing

Nicholas Sheard

1 Discuss the questions in pairs or small groups.

   a Have you ever worked as part of a team to solve a problem?

   b Was your team successful? Why / Why not?

   c What are the advantages of teamwork compared to working on your own?

2 Read the story of a boat race. Put the story in the correct order. A is the first sentence and J is the last.

A A company decided to buy a rowing boat and enter a team for a boat race.

B The management decided to implement the consultant's recommendations.

C The management called in an internal consultant to analyse the situation.

D With this new team, the company entered a new race. Again, they lost the race by a huge distance.

E Based on these preliminary findings, the consultant delivered her advice: to increase the number of rowers on the boat.

F The company put together a team of rowers and the team trained hard for two months.

G The new team was made up of one executive director, one deputy director, one manager, one supervisor, one coordinator, one drummer and four rowers.

H Her report stated that of the ten people on the boat, only two had actually been rowing. The other boats in the race had had at least eight rowers, with one drummer and one oarsman to steer the boat.

I Despite this, the company came last in its first race by more than 200 metres.

J This time, the management made a quick decision. They fired the four rowers and the drummer and sold the boat. They stopped all further investment straightaway. Then, with the money from the sale they gave the managers and supervisors a bonus, and raised the salaries of the directors in recognition for completing the project under budget.

Correct order

1	A	2		3		4		5		6		7		8		9		10	J

3 Would you have done anything differently if you had been part of the company management?

16b Consultancy team

Gina Cuciniello

Group A

1 You are a team of management consultants who have been asked by the directors of a company to provide advice on a problem they are experiencing with their management meetings.

The problem

The managers in the company are being difficult and uncooperative in the weekly management meetings which take place at 9.00 a.m. on Monday mornings.

- attendance is poor
- the managers frequently arrive late or leave early
- the managers are quiet and unresponsive
- there is a sense of a group secret or private joke going on

Discuss the problem and decide on your solutions to present to the directors of the company.

2 You are the directors of a company. You have asked a team of management consultants to provide advice on a problem you are experiencing with your management meetings.

The problem

The managers in the company are being difficult and uncooperative in the weekly management meetings which take place at 9.00 a.m. on Monday mornings.

- one or two of the managers are dominating the meeting
- the discussion frequently goes off the point and becomes irrelevant
- the managers are not listening to each other
- the managers have not prepared adequately for the meeting

Listen to the management consultants' solutions to your problem.

Group B

1 You are the directors of a company. You have asked a team of management consultants to provide advice on a problem you are experiencing with your management meetings.

The problem

The managers in the company are being difficult and uncooperative in the weekly management meetings which take place at 9.00 a.m. on Monday mornings.

- attendance is poor
- the managers frequently arrive late or leave early
- the managers are quiet and unresponsive
- there is a sense of a group secret or private joke going on

Listen to the management consultants' solutions to your problem.

2 You are a team of management consultants who have been asked by the directors of a company to provide advice on a problem they are experiencing with their management meetings.

The problem

The managers in the company are being difficult and uncooperative in the weekly management meetings which take place at 9.00 a.m. on Monday mornings.

- one or two of the managers are dominating the meeting
- the discussion frequently goes off the point and becomes irrelevant
- the managers are not listening to each other
- the managers have not prepared adequately for the meeting

Discuss the problem and decide on your solutions to present to the directors of the company.

17 Cultural differences

Paul Emmerson

1 Many books about multicultural management suggest that the world can be divided into three geographical groups:

1 North America
2 Europe, Latin America, Middle East
3 Japan, China, East Asia

Try to match the groups to the descriptions below. Write the number 1–3 in the box.

Company values

a ☐ Group harmony, long-term relationships, loyalty, company reputation.
b ☐ Trust between individuals, compromise, personal reputation. People work to live.
c ☐ Competition between individuals, achievement, action, risk-taking, directness, informality, innovation. People live to work.

Business relationships

a ☐ Friendly and informal, but a continuing personal relationship is not so important. Much business is done over the phone.
b ☐ Done on a group basis, although relationships based on mutual respect are important. Often there is an older authority figure who rarely appears but has ultimate power.
c ☐ Personal relationships are very important. Some time is needed to build trust before business can begin. Preference for doing business face to face.

Meetings

a ☐ Objective is to gather information. Communication style is often 'monologue – pause – monologue' rather than dialogue. Arguments are often indirect, and there are no sudden changes of viewpoint in meetings. Decisions are made by group consensus over a long time period.
b ☐ Objective is to make a deal or decision. Communication style is direct, factual, informal and at times confrontational. Decisions are based on facts, and are often made instantly in the meeting.
c ☐ Objective is to establish relationships, build understanding, clarify, and issue instructions. Communication style depends on national culture. Decisions are made by key individuals, outside the meeting.

Presentations

a ☐ Complicated language may be used to show education. Audience expects formality and a logical structure, but a touch of imagination is also appreciated. May want a more personal 'extra' talk afterwards where you tell them the 'truth'.
b ☐ Indirect, conservative language. Audience appreciates a quiet, formal presentation with visual aids and lots of opportunity to ask questions and check understanding. They expect separate handouts, prepared for different people, by job function.
c ☐ Direct, simple language. Audience expects jokes, modernity, logic, slogans, informality and a hard sell. Audience may ask questions or interrupt while someone is speaking, and will openly question inconsistent facts.

2 Discuss the questions in pairs or small groups.

a Did you get the same answers as other people? If you did, does it mean the differences are real?
b Does your own country match the description of its particular group? How is it different?
c How do individual countries in your geographical group differ from each other?
d In which ways is globalisation making business more similar, reducing cultural differences? Which cultural differences remain strong, resisting the effects of globalisation?
e Is globalisation just a polite way of saying Americanisation?

18a Piracy

Simon Clarke

1 Study the figures for software piracy in different regions of the world, then consider the questions.

Region	Piracy rate*	Loss**
Western Europe	34%	$3,629.4 million
Eastern Europe	70%	$505.2 million
North America	26%	$3,631.2 million
Latin America	72%	$1,127.6 million
Asia/Pacific	47%	$2,791.5 million
Middle East	63%	$284.4 million
Africa	56%	$193.7 million

* Percentage of total software installed
** Retail software revenue loss to piracy

a In Western Europe and North America, the piracy rates are lower, but the losses are higher. Why do you think this is so?

b How do you think piracy affects the growth of the legitimate software market?

c How easy do you think it is to prosecute for piracy?

arrr... I've sailed the seven CDs

2 Read the article below to find the answers to the questions in 1. Are they the same as your answers?

1 Losses due to software piracy are estimated at $12.2 billion a year just in business applications. The figures for the games industry are no less impressive. Up to 108,000 jobs, $4.5 billion in wages,
5 and $1 billion in tax revenues are also lost. According to Peter Beuk (vice-president for anti-piracy programs at the Software Industry Information Association – SIIA), most of the software being sold on Internet Auction sites (91%) is pirated. Many of
10 these copies are burned at home for about $1 a CD, and then sold as *warez for $25–500 plus shipping.
There is more to piracy than just disk swapping among friends. It has become an illegitimate business on its own, and is sometimes carried out on a
15 corporate level (enterprises which use multiple copies of a single licensed program to cut down on costs), or in ways unknown to the end user (dealers who install pirate copies on new computers). With huge sums of money involved, it is no surprise that organised crime
20 has taken an interest in it.

*warez = pirated software

Even in the United States and Western Europe, where the issue is addressed very seriously, the piracy rate averages 30–40% from country to country. Russia and Asia have the most active pirate markets,
25 with Vietnam and China leading the list with astounding 100% and 97% rates respectively. Revenue rates are not directly linked to piracy rates because in many countries with a high piracy rate, the software market is not very big, whilst regions
30 with relatively low piracy rates like North America suffer higher losses due to the large internal market.
Inevitably the growth of the legitimate software market is affected as developers face the real possibility of pirate copies outnumbering legal ones,
35 turning an otherwise successful product into a financial failure for the company. Prosecution can prove difficult or impossible, as copyright laws differ from country to country. Imagine convincing the Indian police to arrest a Chinese citizen because of a
40 court order emitted by a French tribunal on behalf of a US company!

3 Discuss the following questions with a partner.

a Have you ever made an illegal copy of software or music? Why?

b In what circumstances do you, or would you, use illegal software or buy a pirated album?

c What is your company's policy regarding software on its computers?

d In your opinion, what is the solution to the problem of piracy?

4 Match the two halves of the sentences. Then discuss the ideas with a partner.

a If software wasn't so expensive, …

b If the item isn't paid for, …

c Sony make equipment that is used to make pirate copies of CDs.

d Companies complain that piracy means lost jobs

e Computer companies should not complain;

1 but would more jobs be created if piracy didn't exist?

2 demand for hardware is created by pirated software.

3 it's stolen property.

4 However, they also hold copyright on music.

5 there wouldn't be any piracy.

In Company Intermediate Teacher's Book © Macmillan Publishers Limited 2002

18b A memorable meal

Mark Powell

Did I tell you I went to this *(type)* _____ restaurant the other day? Yeah, me and *(name of another person)* _____. *(Name of restaurant)* _____ , it's called.

I've been there before, actually. It's got a really nice **atmosphere**. The staff are very **friendly**. And I've had some absolutely **delicious** meals there in the past. They offer a good range of dishes, too – everything from simple **traditional** dishes like *(give examples)* _____ , to more **exotic** things like *(give examples)* _____ . But this time I have to say the meal we had was a bit **disappointing**.

Anyway, I ordered my usual steak, which I always have very, very **rare**. Because with a good steak you shouldn't have to cook it too much. It should still be **tender** and **juicy**. And I didn't want potatoes and vegetables so I just asked for a **side salad**.

Now, of course, with a steak you should really drink a good red wine. And the kind of red I usually go for is really **full-bodied**. But *(name of other person)* _____ prefers white. So we had white. Actually, I don't mind white as long as it's nice and **dry**. But *(name of other person)* _____ prefers it a bit **sweeter**, so we ended up with this really dreadful dessert wine, but, anyway, that wasn't the worst of it.

When the wine arrived it wasn't only sweet. It was also much too **warm**. I mean, white wine should always be **chilled**. It also had a peculiar taste. The salad didn't look very **fresh** to me either. And, as for the steak! It was so **tough** I could hardly get my teeth through it. It obviously wasn't rare – it was completely **well-done**!

Anyway, I called the waiter over and said, 'Excuse me, but this wine tastes a bit **funny**.' He said, 'We prefer to call it amusing, sir.' I said, 'No, I mean it tastes strange, it's **off**.' He said, 'I'll change it immediately. By the way, how's your steak?' 'Well-done,' I said. 'Thank you very much, sir,' he said. I said, 'No, I mean I ordered it rare and this one's been **overcooked**. It tastes like wood!' He offered to replace it, but I said I wasn't so hungry now, and could I just have something a bit **lighter**?

Anyway, after all that, we didn't even order a dessert because most of them looked too **fattening** and we hadn't really enjoyed our meal. I just asked for the **bill** and we left. It's the first time I've left a restaurant without leaving a **tip**!

19a Boss or Big Brother?

Simon Clarke

1 Read the extract from an article on e-mails. In each sentence there are two words missing.
Fill the gaps with the following word pairs.

liable + e-mails   case + pay   thinks + halt   e-mail + tool   e-mails + words   says + issue
systems + snooping   want + money   conducted + behalf   perk + hot   offensive + language
sexism + pathetic   take + telephone   scanning + managers   customers + worried

UK employers are keeping a close eye on

(a) _____ e-mails in an effort to trap

those using sexist or racist _____ .

Automatic (b) _____ equipment is being

used to seek out potentially offensive words that set

off an internal alarm, and _____ are

then alerted.

Philip Ryan, from IT company Peapod, says in

reality the (c) _____ he develops are

more about protecting companies than

_____ on employees. 'Our (d)

_____ are

very _____ . They don't want to

be (e) _____ for things written in

_____ . People do not

(f) _____ to end up in court and

lose _____ .' Mr Ryan points to the

(g) _____ of Norwich Union, an

insurance company, which had to _____

out £450,000 after its employees sent out e-mails

insulting a market rival.

Professor Helen Petric (h) _____ UK

employers may be overreacting to the e-mail

_____ . She recently

(i) _____ a survey of e-mail content

on _____ of MSN. There was a bit

of (j) _____ and some fairly

_____ jokes. The University of

Hertfordshire academic (k) _____

employers' time might be put to better uses than

trying to _____ their workers' personal

e-mails. Most (l) _____ are between

50 and 100 _____ . It doesn't

(m) _____ very long to read or type

them, especially compared to the time a person could

spend on the _____ . Ms Petric says

(n) _____ has proved an invaluable

_____ to workers. It should be regarded

as a small (o) _____ of the job, one

people should not get too _____ under

the collar about.

2 What is your opinion about employers scanning their employees' e-mail?
Discuss the ideas in the text using some of the following expressions:

I don't really think …	On the other hand …
I agree with what it says about …	I'm not really sure …
It's ridiculous to say …	It's not something that bothers me, but …
I don't agree with the idea that …	I don't have an opinion either way.
I see what people mean about …	

19b A quality problem

Paul Emmerson

1 Your company makes flat-screen TVs. There is a quality problem in the factory and the CEO is writing an e-mail to all the senior managers. The sentences a–f from his e-mail are not in the correct order. Decide which order is best and write the sentence letter in the numbered boxes.

a This is unacceptable – we are falling a long way behind our competitors in terms of quality.

b I am very concerned about quality levels in our plant over the last quarter.

c I've just been given the figures – defects are up 8% compared to the same period last year.

d When I have your initial thoughts by e-mail, I'll write a short report and call a meeting to discuss it in more detail.

e Please give this matter your urgent attention, and reply by no later than the end of next week.

f The situation cannot continue and I want to know your opinions about why quality is so poor.

Correct order

| 1 | | 2 | 3 | | 4 | | 5 | | 6 | |

2 Write one, two or three e-mails in reply using the information below. Use separate sheets of paper. Expand the ideas and feel free to change details or invent extra details. The maximum length for each e-mail is 100 words.

e-mail 1: You are the plant manager. You think the problem is due to poor industrial relations in the factory. The workers have no motivation. You think more money should be spent on health and safety, improved salaries and sports facilities for the workers and their families.

e-mail 2: You are the head of quality control. You think it is a waste of time trying to motivate the workers. The only solution is more automation using industrial robots, and at the same time reducing the number of workers. Automation is expensive, but in the long term the investment will be justified.

e-mail 3: You are the finance director. You think that the problem is due to the plant manager and head of quality control not doing their jobs properly. They should train the workers better, link pay rises and bonuses to improvements in quality, and investigate in detail why the level of defects is so high. Instead of this, they try to avoid any responsibility. Be careful how you make these points in your e-mail.

3 Think of a quality problem in your own company or organisation. Answer the following questions.

a What is the problem?

_____

b Why do you think it has happened?

_____

c Who do you need to e-mail about this problem?

_____

d Now write an e-mail to the person you named in c. The maximum length for your e-mail is 100 words.

4 Imagine that you are the person who receives the e-mail written in 3. How would you answer it? Write the reply.

20a Peasants 1000 AD

Paul Emmerson

Peasant A

You are a medieval peasant. You and your family live a simple, honest life.
You grow food and keep animals on a small piece of land. You are friendly with your neighbour.

1 Study the table. The second column shows items that you have now, and the third column shows what you need (in total, not in addition). Note that there are some items where you have more than you need, but other items that you will have to get from your neighbour. You

	What you have in your farm now	What you need for your family	What you have after the negotiation
Potatoes	40 kg	10 kg	
Cabbages	20 kg	50 kg	
Beans	None	20 kg	
Chickens	30	15	
Pigs	None	2	
Cows	8	6	
Milk	20 litres	20 litres	
Eggs	40	25	
Wine	40 bottles	70 bottles	
Firewood	20 bundles	40 bundles	

are going to negotiate and exchange items. You may not get a good deal for them. What are your priorities?
Your cows won a prize, so insist on a very good deal for them.

2 Prepare your ideas, then meet your neighbour. There are no rules for how much anything is worth – it is up to you to get the best deal you can through discussion and negotiation. Before you begin negotiating, talk a little about the weather, life in the village, the quality of your products, etc.

Peasant B

You are a medieval peasant. You and your family live a simple, honest life.
You grow food and keep animals on a small piece of land. You are friendly with your neighbour.

1 Study the table. The second column shows items that you have now, and the third column shows what you need (in total, not in addition). Note that there are some items where you have more than you need, but other items that you will have to get from your neighbour. You are going to negotiate

	What you have in your farm now	What you need for your family	What you have after the negotiation
Potatoes	10 kg	20 kg	
Cabbages	40 kg	40 kg	
Beans	30 kg	10 kg	
Chickens	10	15	
Pigs	6	2	
Cows	1	4	
Milk	None	20 litres	
Eggs	None	30	
Wine	80 bottles	70 bottles	
Firewood	60 bundles	50 bundles	

and exchange items. You may not get a good deal for them. What are your priorities?
Your pigs won a prize, so insist on a very good deal for them.

2 Prepare your ideas, then meet your neighbour. There are no rules for how much anything is worth – it is up to you to get the best deal you can through discussion and negotiation. Before you begin negotiating, talk a little about the weather, life in the village, the quality of your products, etc.

20b Mini-negotiations

Paul Dummett

Jason Electrics: Negotiating a reduction in working time

1 Read the text and complete the first section of the table with notes.

2 You are going to roleplay a negotiation with another student.

a First decide which of you is going to be the Manager and which is going to be the Union Representative.
Think of two concessions you would make in the negotiation and write notes in the second section of the table.

b As you negotiate, complete the third section of the table.

You work for Jason Electrics, a company that manufactures electrical cable. It employs 95 people and is based in an industrial park near Swindon, England. The regular working week for production staff is 39 hours, compared with a maximum of 37 hours in other, similar companies on the estate. The union would like to negotiate a reduction in working hours to 37, without any reduction in basic salary. They realise that in return for this they will probably have to increase productivity. The management is happy to consider a reduction in hours if it can win greater productivity and flexibility in working time. (It often needs to ask staff to do overtime for special orders.)

	Management	Unions
What they want		
What they can offer		
Concessions	1	1
	2	2
Productivity deal		

Businessworks: Negotiating the allocation of extra resources

1 Read the text and complete the first section of the table with notes.

2 You are going to roleplay a negotiation with another student.

a First decide which of you is going to be the Sales Director and which is going to be the Area Sales Manager.
Think of two concessions you would make in the negotiation and write notes in the second section of the table.

b As you negotiate, complete the third section of the table.

You work for the sales department of a company which makes accounting software. There are four export sales managers, each responsible for a different area in Europe. The manager responsible for Scandinavia feels that he is overworked and that without extra staff he cannot achieve the targets he has been set. He thinks that with extra sales staff and a bigger budget he can increase the sales potential. The sales director would like proof that sales can be increased before providing extra staff and resources. She is prepared to risk employing extra staff for the area if the manager will share some of the risk also.

	Sales Director	Area Sales Manager
What they want		
What they can offer		
Concessions	1	1
	2	2
Risk-sharing deal		

Macmillan Education
Between Towns Road, Oxford OX4 3PP
A division of Macmillan Publishers Limited
Companies and representatives throughout the world

ISBN: 978 0 333 95733 2

Note to teachers

Text by Helena Gomm

Resource materials by Colin Benn; Simon Clarke; Gina Cuciniello;
Paul Dummett; Paul Emmerson; Jon Hird; Mark Powell; Nicholas
Sheard

Designed by eMC Design
Illustrated by Mike Stones, icons; Mark Duffin pp T153, T157;
Julian Mosedale pp T139, T142, T145, T156, T160, T161;
Stephen Dew pp T140.
Original cover concept by Jackie Hill at 320 Design
Cover illustration by Mike Stones

The authors and publishers wish to thank the following who have
kindly granted permission to use copyright material: Extract in *18a
Piracy* used with kind permission of GameSpy Industries
http://www.gamespy.com; Extract in *18a Piracy* used with kind
permission of International Planning & Research Corporation;
Quotations in *9 What the CEO said*: Henry Ford (Ford Motor
Company), R. Steve Letbetter (Reliant Energy), Gordon Bethune
(Continental Airlines), Mr Lee Raymond (Exxon Mobil) & Ralph
Larsen (Johnson and Johnson)

Student's Book acknowledgements

Text © Mark Powell

Design and illustration © Macmillan Publishers Limited 2002
Designed by Jackie Hill at 320 Design
Illustrated by Mike Stones icons; Julian Mosedale pp10, 20, 46, 65;
Liam O'Farrell pp16, 67; Flatliner p31; Kim Williams p52

The publishers would like to thank Bob Ratto, Byron, Rome; Angela
Wright, British Council, Rome; Norman Cain, IH Rome; Fiona
Campbell, Teach-In, Rome; Sue Garton, Lois Clegg and Irene
Frederick, University of Parma; Simon Hopson and Gordon Doyle,
Intensive Business English, Milan; Dennis Marino, Bocconi
University, Milan; Mike Cruikshank, Advanced Language Services,
Milan; Christine Zambon, Person to Person, Milan; Fiona O'Connor,
In-Company English, Milan; Peter Panton, Panton School, Milan;
Colin Irving Bell, Novara; Marta Rodriguez Casal, Goal Rush Institute,
Buenos Aires; Elizabeth Mangi and Silvia Ventura, NET New English
Training, Buenos Aires; Graciela Yohma and Veronica Cenini, CABSI,
Buenos Aires; Viviana Pisani, Asociación Ex Alumnos, Buenos Aires;
Claudia Siciliano, LEA Institute, Buenos Aires; Cuca Martocq, AACI,
Buenos Aires; Laura Lewin, ABS International, Buenos Aires; Charlie
Lopez, Instituto Big Ben, Buenos Aires; Alice Elvira Machado; Patricia
Blower; Valeria Siniscalchi; Carla Chaves; Virginia Garcia; Cultura
Inglesa, Rio de Janeiro; Susan Dianne Mace, Britannia, Rio de Janeiro;
John Paraskou, Diamond School, Sèvres; Dorothy Polley and Nadia
Fairbrother, Executive Language Services, Paris; Claire MacMurray,
Formalangues, Paris; Claire Oldmeadow, Franco British Chamber of
Commerce, Paris; Ingrid Foussat and Anne James, IFG Langues, Paris;
Karl Willems, Quai d'Orsay Language Centre, Paris; Louis Brazier,
Clare Davis, Jacqueline Deubel, Siobhan Mlacak and Redge,
Télélangue, Paris; John Morrison Milne, Ian Stride, Gareth East and
Richard Marrison, IH Madrid; Gina Cuciniello; Helena Gomm;
Paulette McKean. Special thanks to the photo researcher, Sally Neal.

The authors and publishers would like to thank the following for
permission to reproduce their material: Cambridge University Press
for 'The World's Top Ten Languages' from *The Cambridge
Encyclopedia of Language* edited by David Crystal (Cambridge
University Press, 1987), reprinted by permission of the publisher; The
Penguin Group (UK) for an extract from *Getting Things Done* by
Roger Black (Michael Joseph, 1987), copyright © Duncan Petersen
Publishing Ltd and Roger Black 1987; Newsweek Inc for an extract
from 'The NY-LON Life' by Stryker McGuire and Michelle Chan from
Newsweek Magazine 13.11.00, copyright © Newsweek Inc 2000. All
rights reserved; Extract from *When Cultures Collide* by Richard D
Lewis (Nicholas Brealey Publishing, 1996), reprinted by permission of
the publisher; Oval Projects Ltd for an extract from *The Bluffer's
Guide® to the Internet* (Oval Books, London, 1999), copyright © Oval
Projects Ltd. www.bluffers.com 1999; The British Library for an
extract from Track 12 '1930 G.B. Shaw and Albert Einstein' Speaker,
George Bernard Shaw, from *The Century in Sound* (The British
Library); Source *firstdirect.com* - First Direct is a division of HSBC
Bank plc which is a member of the HSBC Group, reproduced by
permission of First Direct. First Direct banking facilities are available
to UK residents only; Extract from *The Dilbert Principle* by Scott
Adams (Boxtree, 1996); Extract from *Riding the Waves of Culture* by
Fons Trompenaars and Charles Hampden-Turner (Nicholas Brealey
Publishing, 1998), copyright © 1997, reprinted by permission of the
publisher; Fast Company for an extract from 'This Organization is
Dis-Organization' from *Fast Company* Magazine, Issue No: 3, June
1996. All rights reserved. To subscribe, please call 800-542-6029 or
visit www.fastcompany.com; Pearson Educational Limited for an
extract from *Tricky Business Letters* by Gordon Wainwright (Institute
of Management, 1993); Extract from *The Cluetrain Manifesto* by Rick
Levine, Christopher Locke, Doc Searls and David Weinberger (ft.com,
2000); The Random House Group Limited for an extract from *Getting
Past No* by William Ury (Century Business, 1992); Extract from
Complete Idiot's Guide to Winning Through Negotiation, 2/e by John
Ilich (Alpha Publishing, 1999), copyright © Alpha Publishing 1999,
reprinted by permission of the publisher, as represented by Pearson
Computer Publishing, a division of Pearson Education; Short
quotation from 'It's an Internet Jumble Out There' by Lucy Kellaway
from *Financial Times* 5.6.00, reprinted by permission of the
publisher; Short quotation by Paul Theroux.

The authors and publishers would like to thank the following for
permission to reproduce their photographs: AllSport p87; Anthony
Blake Photo Library p19; D.C. Comics courtesy Vin Mag p32;
Disneyland® Resort Paris p6(3); Foodpix p75; Getty Images pp6(2),
8; Robert Harding/C.Andreaso p47; Hulton Archive pp35, 49(b), 58,
63, 115; Image Bank pp15(1), 60, 79(1), 84; ImageState pp5(c), 5(f),
30, 36(br), 42, 56, 70, 79(3), 79(4), 83, 120; Impact Photos/J.
Wishnetsky p5(e), M. Henley p18, R.Roberts p74; Jumeirah
International Picture Library p6(1); Mark Henley Photos p72; MTV
p73; Photodisc pp9, 28(t), 30(t), 97; Photonica/J.Bartholomew
pp25(t), 85; Powerstock Zefa pp5(a), 5(b), 5(d), 11(bl), 14(tl), 15(3),
17, 24(t), 24(b), 36(tr), 36(bl), 37(t), 43, 55, 71(l), 71(r), 77, 79(2),
79(5); Science Photo Library/Jesse p14(br), D.Gifford p28, C.Butler
p38, Laguna Design p45, US Library of Congress p50, P.Menzel p54,
Tek Image p64; Stone pp11(tr), 20, 21, 22, 26(m), 26(l), 27, 61, 67, 95;
Telegraph Colour Library pp15(2), 23, 25(bl), 36(tl), 37(b), 39, 49(t),
52, 68.

Printed and bound in China